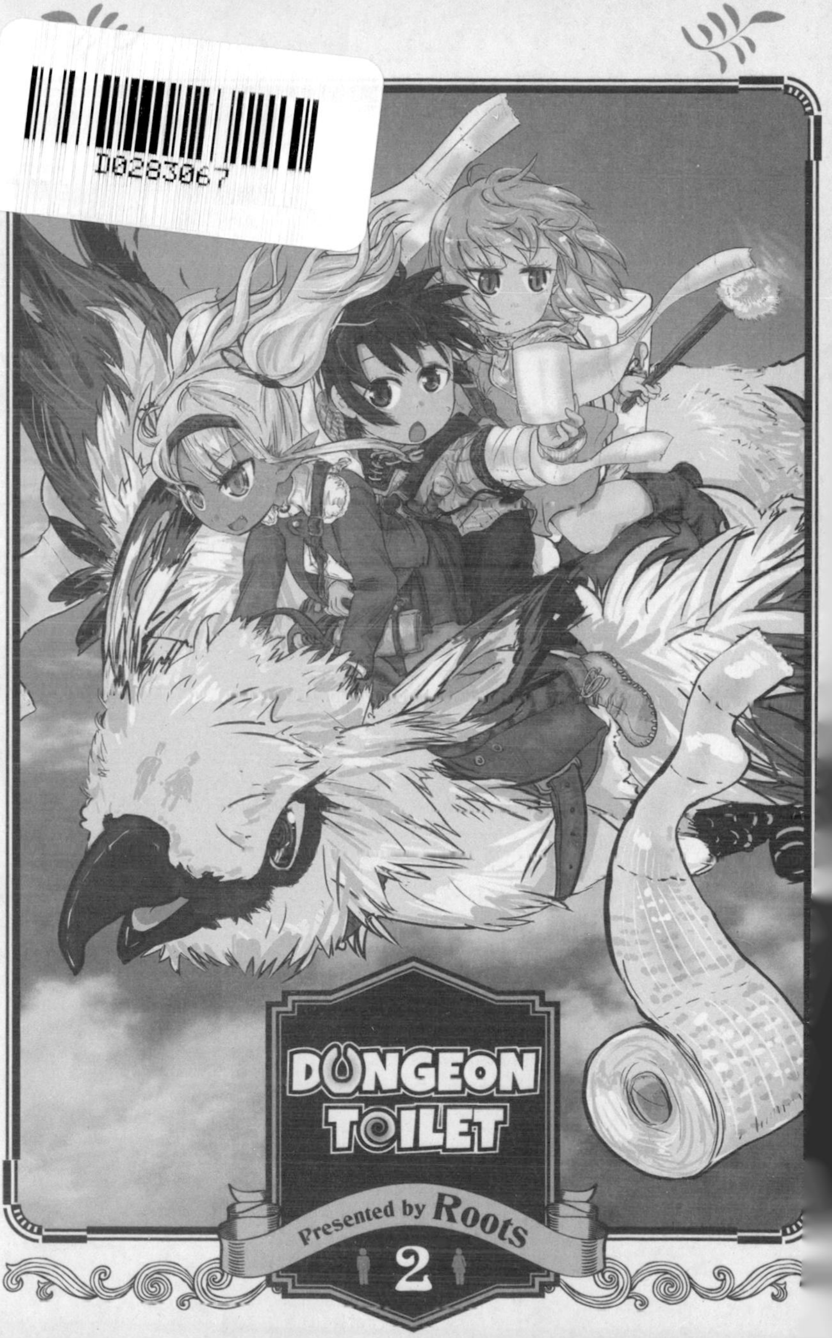
DUNGEON TOILET
Presented by Roots
2

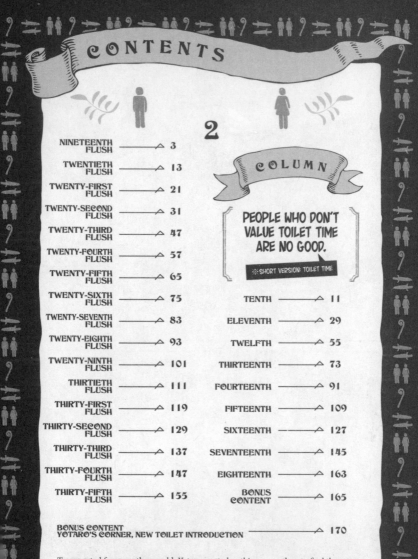

CONTENTS

2

NINETEENTH FLUSH	3
TWENTIETH FLUSH	13
TWENTY-FIRST FLUSH	21
TWENTY-SECOND FLUSH	31
TWENTY-THIRD FLUSH	47
TWENTY-FOURTH FLUSH	57
TWENTY-FIFTH FLUSH	65
TWENTY-SIXTH FLUSH	75
TWENTY-SEVENTH FLUSH	83
TWENTY-EIGHTH FLUSH	93
TWENTY-NINTH FLUSH	101
THIRTIETH FLUSH	111
THIRTY-FIRST FLUSH	119
THIRTY-SECOND FLUSH	129
THIRTY-THIRD FLUSH	137
THIRTY-FOURTH FLUSH	147
THIRTY-FIFTH FLUSH	155

COLUMN

> PEOPLE WHO DON'T VALUE TOILET TIME ARE NO GOOD.
>
> ☀ SHORT VERSION: TOILET TIME

TENTH	11
ELEVENTH	29
TWELFTH	55
THIRTEENTH	73
FOURTEENTH	91
FIFTEENTH	109
SIXTEENTH	127
SEVENTEENTH	145
EIGHTEENTH	163
BONUS CONTENT	165

BONUS CONTENT
YOTARO'S CORNER, NEW TOILET INTRODUCTION ⸺ 170

Transported from another world, Yotaro wanted nothing more than to find the most comfortable toilet. Despite being completely useless as an adventurer, he somehow convinced Gigi and Nurael to travel with him. When the desert kingdom of Abaf was attacked by an army of demons, Yotaro and his friends rushed to defend it. But in the middle of the battle, Yotaro returned to the real world!

THE BATTLE SURE GOT HEATED. EVERYONE OKAY?

HERO SHIZUYA AND HIS FRIEND!!!

NINETEENTH FLUS

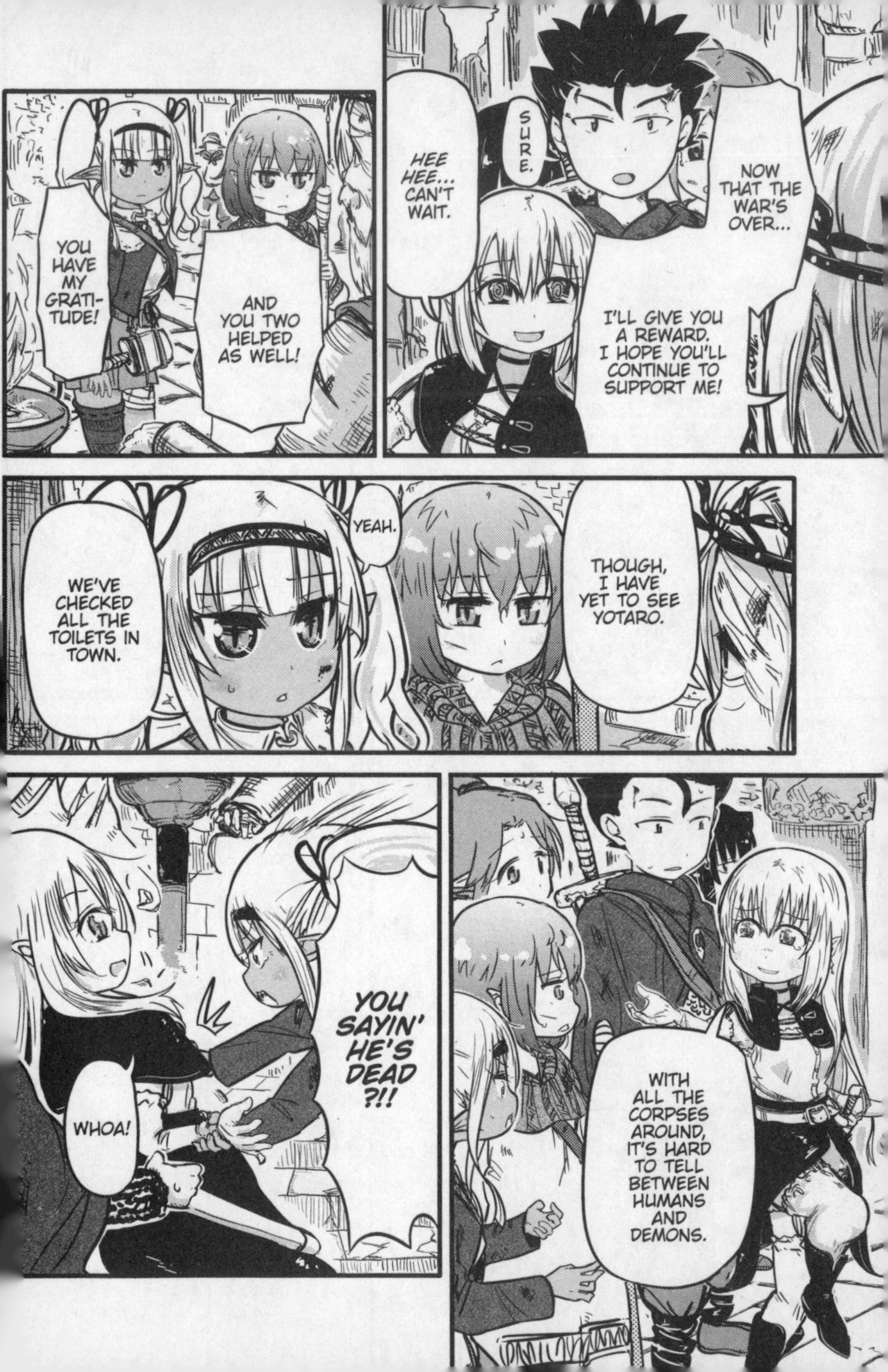
NOW THAT THE WAR'S OVER...
I'LL GIVE YOU A REWARD. I HOPE YOU'LL CONTINUE TO SUPPORT ME!
SURE.
HEE HEE... CAN'T WAIT.
AND YOU TWO HELPED AS WELL!
YOU HAVE MY GRATITUDE!
THOUGH, I HAVE YET TO SEE YOTARO.
YEAH.
WE'VE CHECKED ALL THE TOILETS IN TOWN.
WITH ALL THE CORPSES AROUND, IT'S HARD TO TELL BETWEEN HUMANS AND DEMONS.
YOU SAYIN' HE'S DEAD?!!
WHOA!

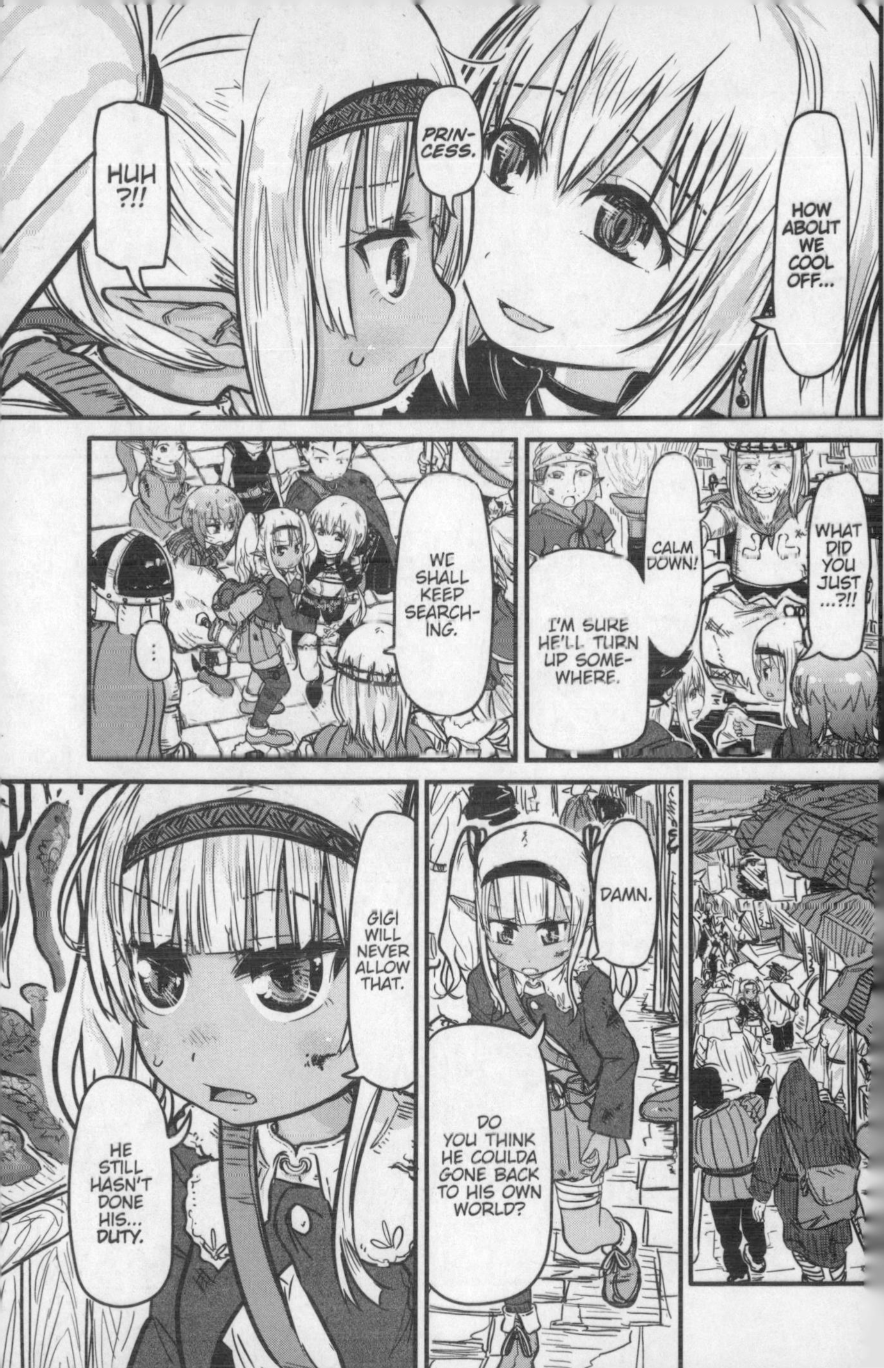
HOW ABOUT WE COOL OFF...
PRIN-CESS.
HUH?!!
WHAT DID YOU JUST ...?!!
CALM DOWN!
I'M SURE HE'LL TURN UP SOME-WHERE.
WE SHALL KEEP SEARCH-ING.
...
DAMN.
DO YOU THINK HE COULDA GONE BACK TO HIS OWN WORLD?
GIGI WILL NEVER ALLOW THAT.
HE STILL HASN'T DONE HIS... DUTY.

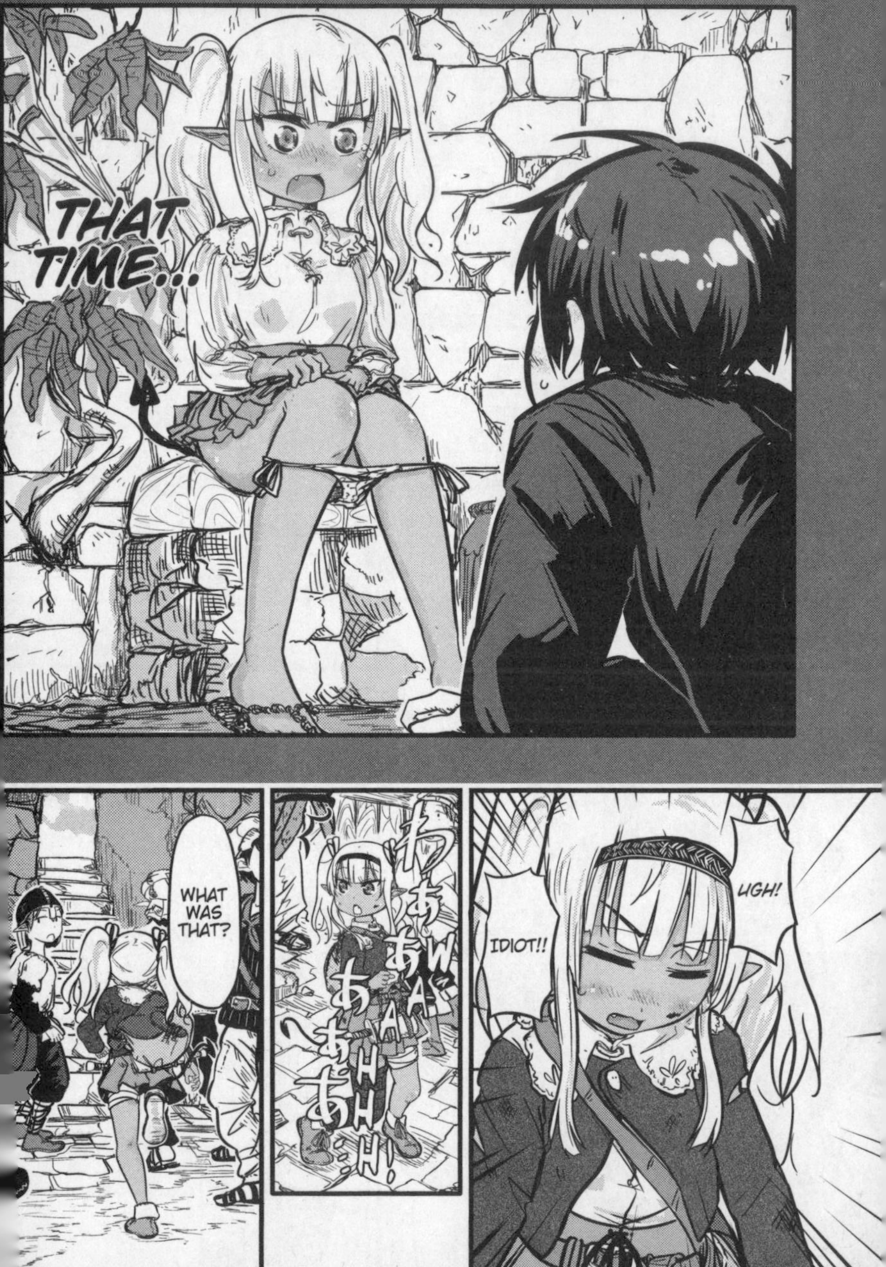

THAT TIME...
UGH!
IDIOT!!
わあああああ…!
WAAAHHHH!
WHAT WAS THAT?

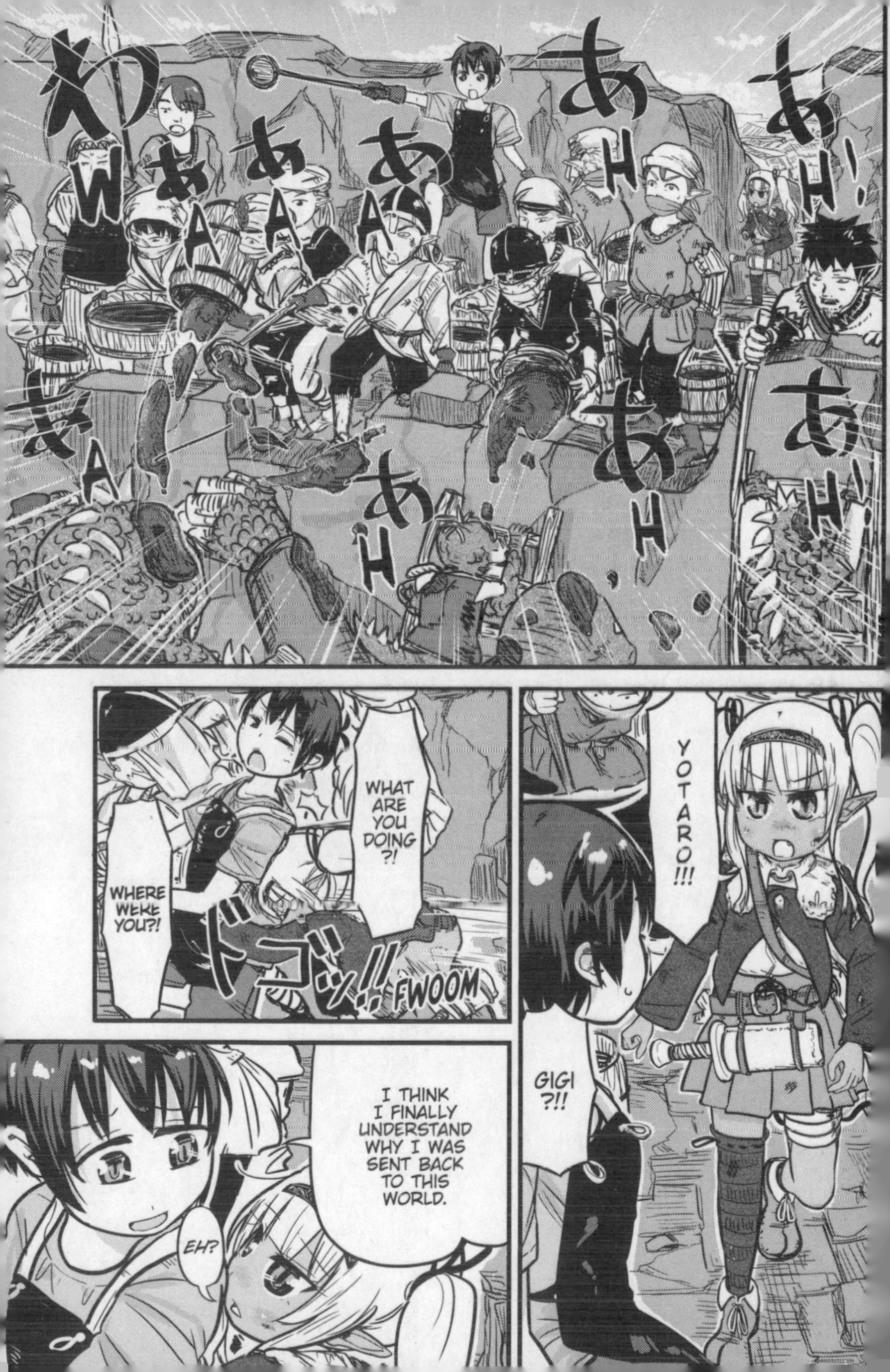

WAAAAHHHH!!
YOTARO!!!
GIGI?!!
WHAT ARE YOU DOING?!
WHERE WERE YOU?!
FWOOM
I THINK I FINALLY UNDERSTAND WHY I WAS SENT BACK TO THIS WORLD.
EH?

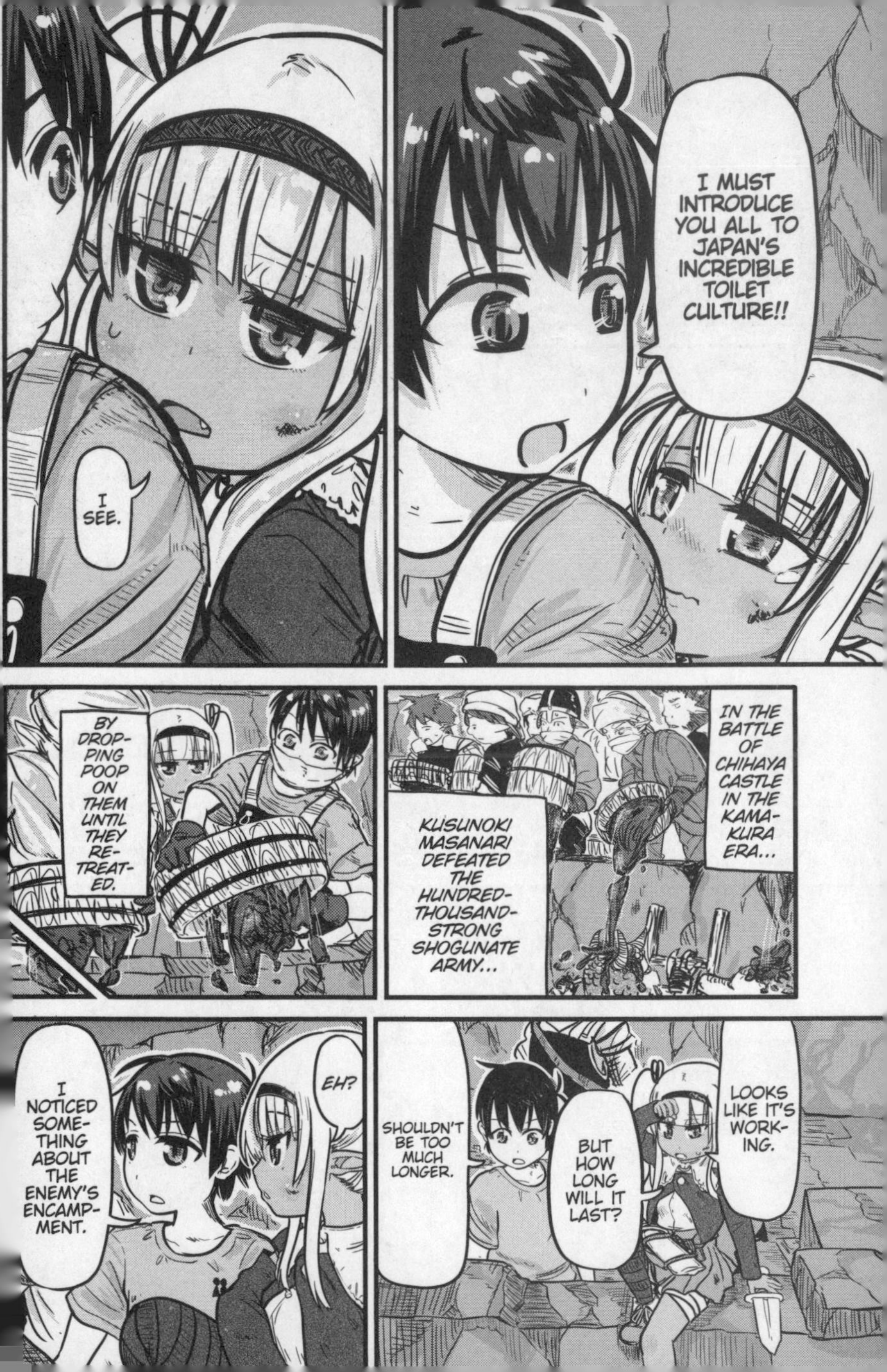
I MUST INTRODUCE YOU ALL TO JAPAN'S INCREDIBLE TOILET CULTURE!!
I SEE.
IN THE BATTLE OF CHIHAYA CASTLE IN THE KAMAKURA ERA...
KUSUNOKI MASANARI DEFEATED THE HUNDRED-THOUSAND-STRONG SHOGUNATE ARMY...
BY DROPPING POOP ON THEM UNTIL THEY RETREATED.
LOOKS LIKE IT'S WORKING.
BUT HOW LONG WILL IT LAST?
SHOULDN'T BE TOO MUCH LONGER.
EH?
I NOTICED SOMETHING ABOUT THE ENEMY'S ENCAMPMENT.

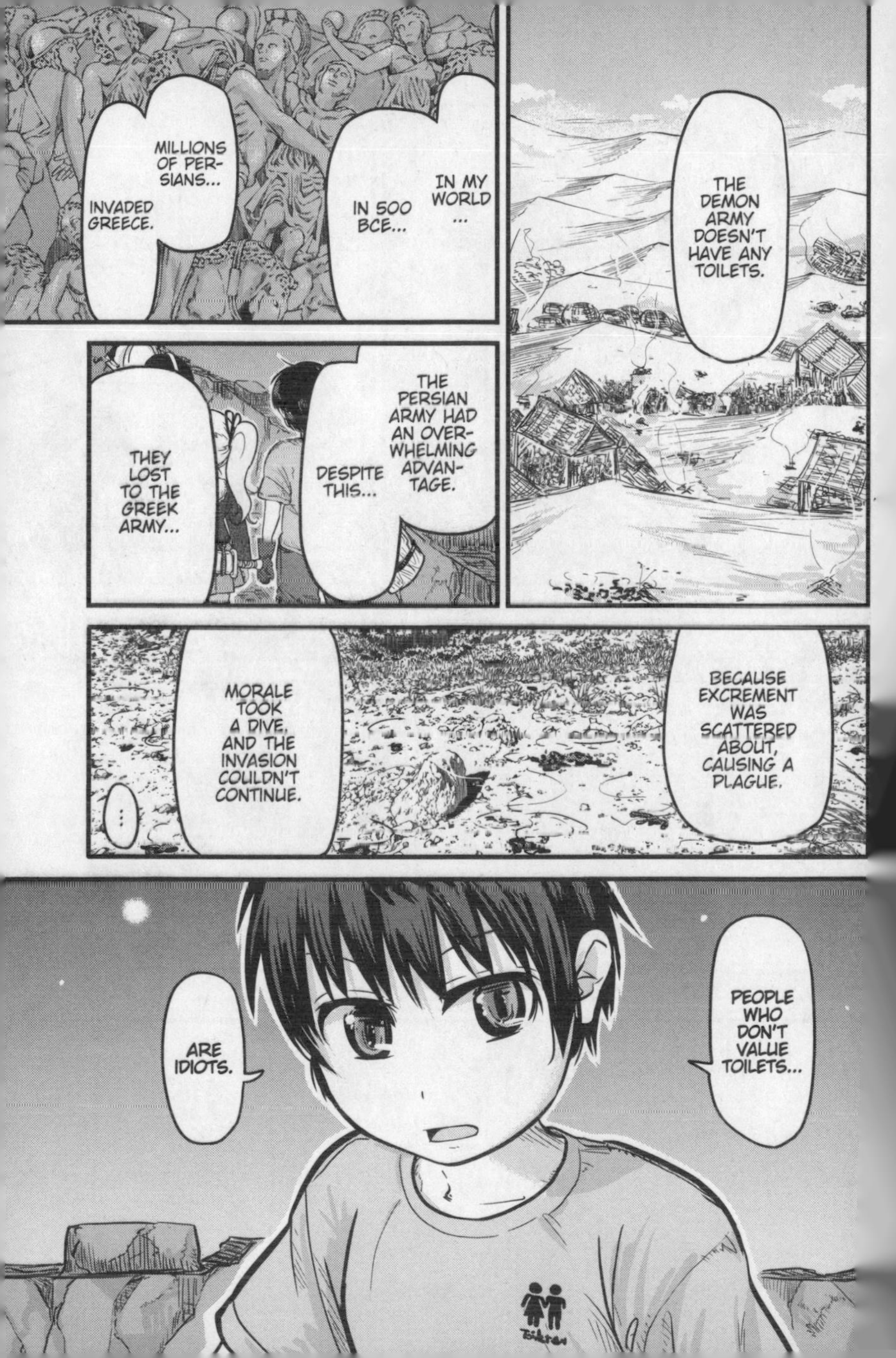
THE DEMON ARMY DOESN'T HAVE ANY TOILETS.
IN MY WORLD ...
IN 500 BCE...
MILLIONS OF PERSIANS...
INVADED GREECE.
THE PERSIAN ARMY HAD AN OVERWHELMING ADVANTAGE.
DESPITE THIS...
THEY LOST TO THE GREEK ARMY...
BECAUSE EXCREMENT WAS SCATTERED ABOUT, CAUSING A PLAGUE.
MORALE TOOK A DIVE, AND THE INVASION COULDN'T CONTINUE.
...
PEOPLE WHO DON'T VALUE TOILETS...
ARE IDIOTS.

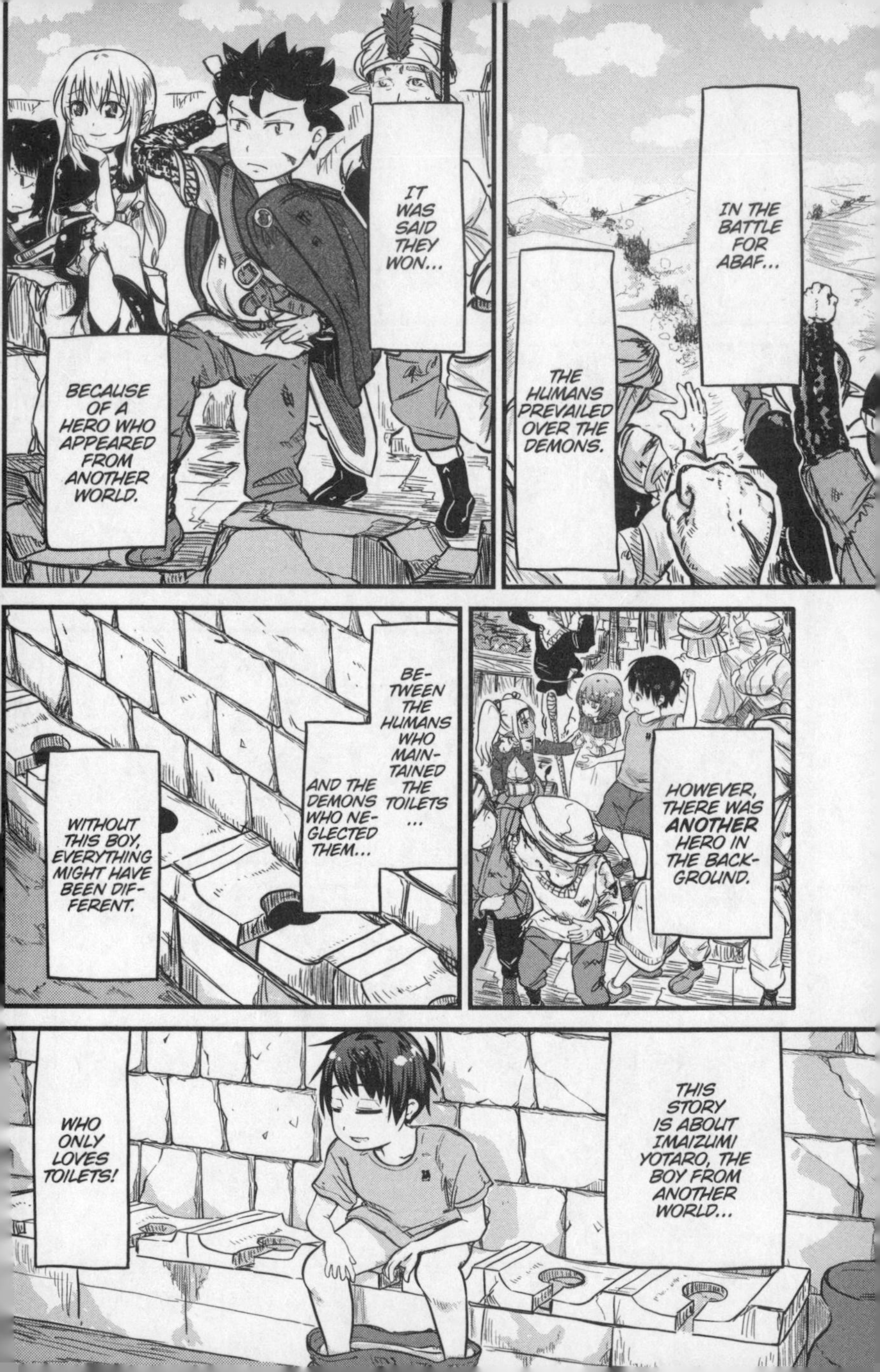
IN THE BATTLE FOR ABAF...
THE HUMANS PREVAILED OVER THE DEMONS.
IT WAS SAID THEY WON...
BECAUSE OF A HERO WHO APPEARED FROM ANOTHER WORLD.
HOWEVER, THERE WAS ANOTHER HERO IN THE BACKGROUND.
BETWEEN THE HUMANS WHO MAINTAINED THE TOILETS...
AND THE DEMONS WHO NEGLECTED THEM...
WITHOUT THIS BOY, EVERYTHING MIGHT HAVE BEEN DIFFERENT.
THIS STORY IS ABOUT IMAIZUMI YOTARO, THE BOY FROM ANOTHER WORLD...
WHO ONLY LOVES TOILETS!

ROOTS

PEOPLE WHO DON'T VALUE TOILET TIME ARE NO GOOD.

TENTH TOILET TIME

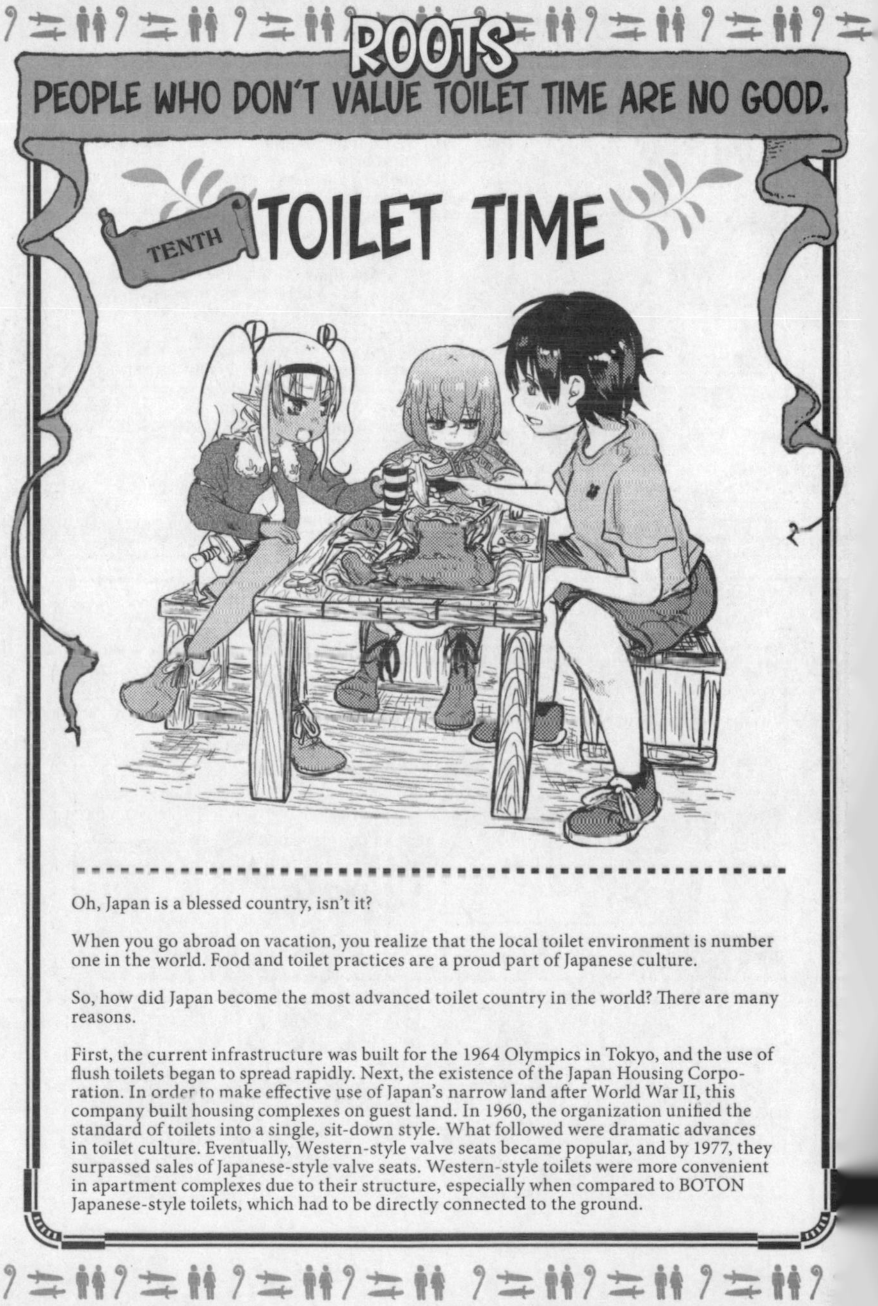

TOILET TIME

Oh, Japan is a blessed country, isn't it?

When you go abroad on vacation, you realize that the local toilet environment is number one in the world. Food and toilet practices are a proud part of Japanese culture.

So, how did Japan become the most advanced toilet country in the world? There are many reasons.

First, the current infrastructure was built for the 1964 Olympics in Tokyo, and the use of flush toilets began to spread rapidly. Next, the existence of the Japan Housing Corporation. In order to make effective use of Japan's narrow land after World War II, this company built housing complexes on guest land. In 1960, the organization unified the standard of toilets into a single, sit-down style. What followed were dramatic advances in toilet culture. Eventually, Western-style valve seats became popular, and by 1977, they surpassed sales of Japanese-style valve seats. Western-style toilets were more convenient in apartment complexes due to their structure, especially when compared to BOTON Japanese-style toilets, which had to be directly connected to the ground.

Then came two illustrious companies that must be mentioned when talking about modern Japanese toilets: TOTO and INAX (now LIXIL Group).

Although these two companies were originally part of the same corporate group (the Morimura Group) they played an important role in the development of toilets in Japan through their friendly rivalry.

In 1980, the Washlet was born. With its famous catchphrase, "Our butt wants to be washed, too," and the bubble economy, Washlet became a big hit, and now the growth rate of hot-water toilet seats is almost 80%.

In summary, 1) the spread of water and sewage systems, 2) the spread of Western-style toilet bowls, 3) competition between TOTO and LIXIL, and 4) the appearance of the Washlet. These are the main factors that led to the trend and development of modern toilets in Japan.

In ancient times, throwing feces and corpses at the enemy in warfare was used all over the world. It's said that the battle of Chihaya Castle was the first time this tactic was used in Japan. I would like to end this article by introducing some trivia that has nothing to do with the above story.

IN OTHER WORDS

THIS MAXIM

"OUR BUTT WANTS TO BE WASHED, TOO."

(TOTO WASHLET COMMERCIAL, 1982)

IS THIS FROM YOUR WORLD?
YEAH.
THEY SENT ME HERE WITH ONLY THE CLOTHES ON MY BACK.
...
TUG
ぐいっ
TAKE IT OFF.
HUH?!!
I WANT A CLOSER LOOK.

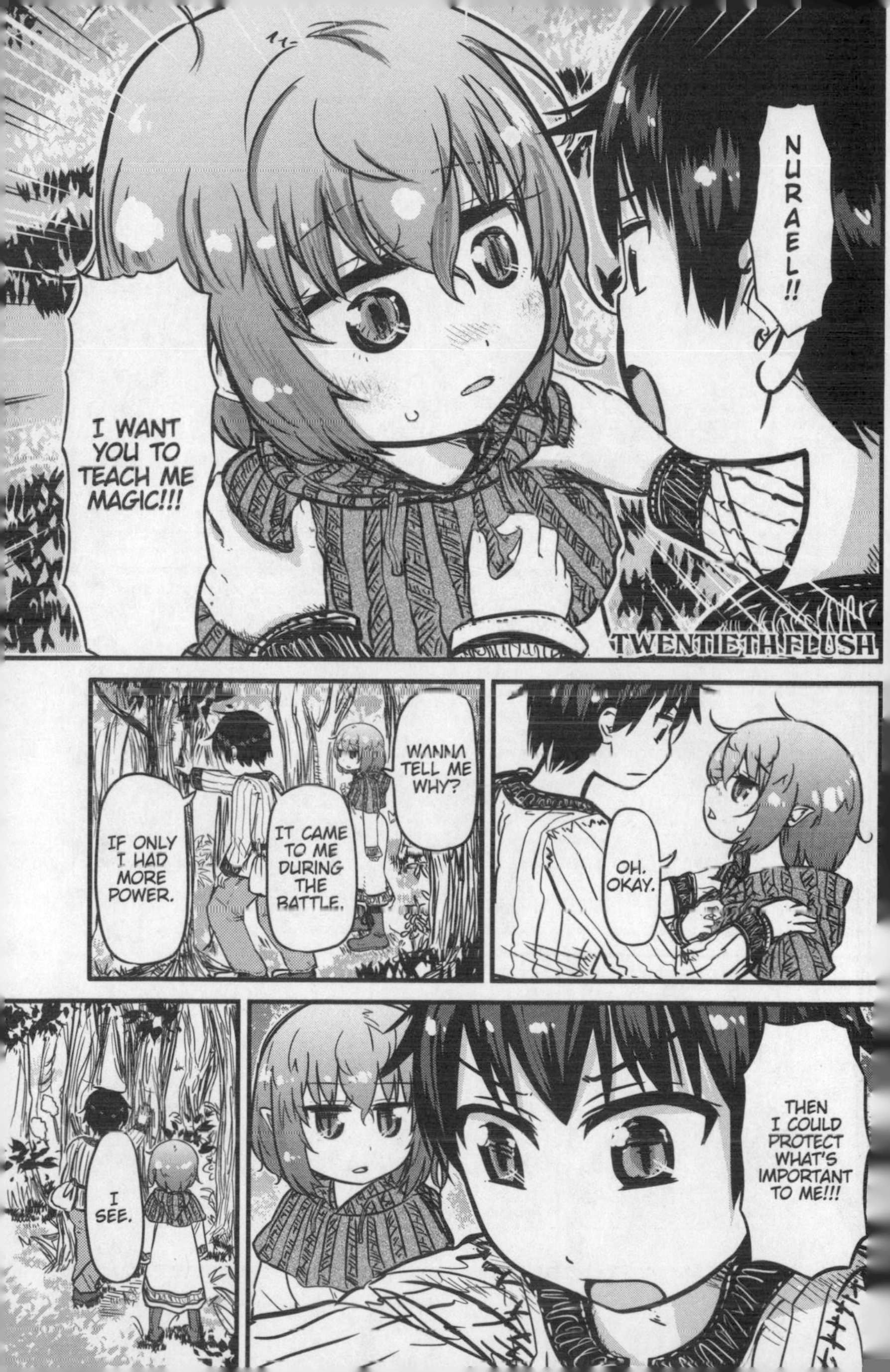
NURAEL!!
I WANT YOU TO TEACH ME MAGIC!!!
TWENTIETH FLUSH
OH. OKAY.
WANNA TELL ME WHY?
IT CAME TO ME DURING THE BATTLE.
IF ONLY I HAD MORE POWER.
THEN I COULD PROTECT WHAT'S IMPORTANT TO ME!!!
I SEE.

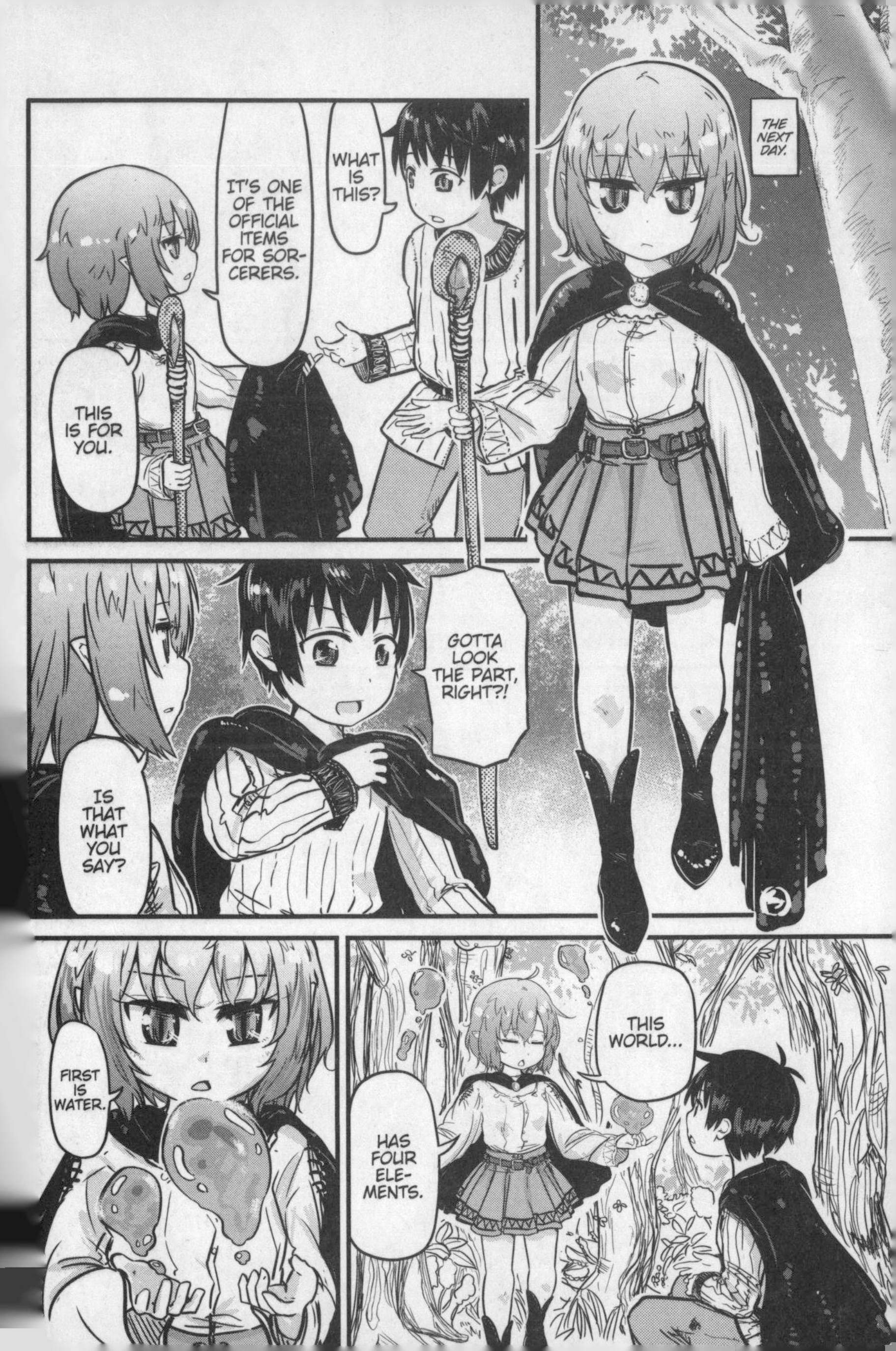
THE NEXT DAY.
WHAT IS THIS?
IT'S ONE OF THE OFFICIAL ITEMS FOR SOR-CERERS.
THIS IS FOR YOU.
GOTTA LOOK THE PART, RIGHT?!
IS THAT WHAT YOU SAY?
THIS WORLD...
HAS FOUR ELE-MENTS.
FIRST IS WATER.

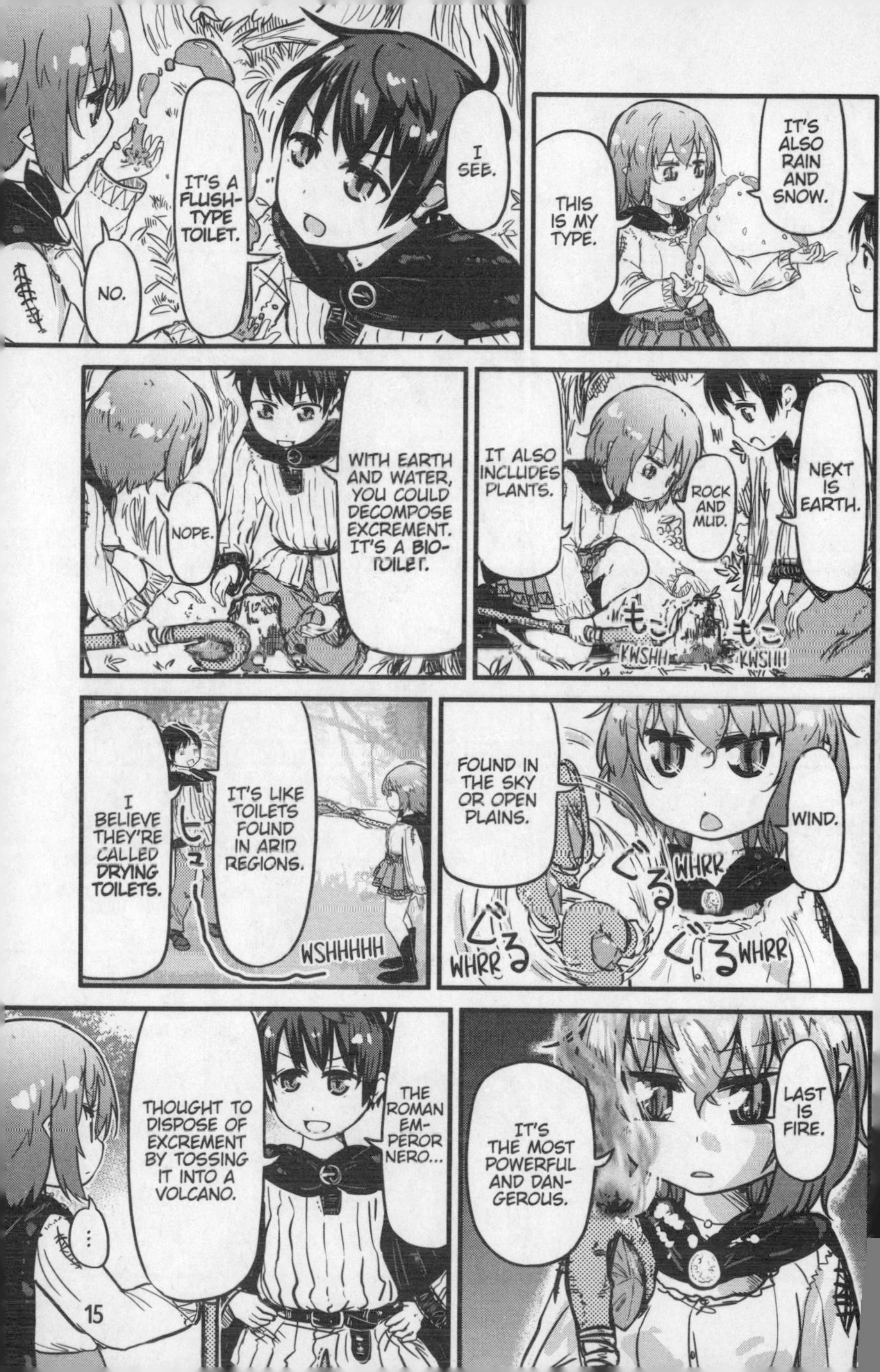
IT'S ALSO RAIN AND SNOW.
THIS IS MY TYPE.
I SEE.
IT'S A FLUSH-TYPE TOILET.
NO.
NEXT IS EARTH.
ROCK AND MUD.
IT ALSO INCLUDES PLANTS.
もこ KWSHH
もこ KWSHH
WITH EARTH AND WATER, YOU COULD DECOMPOSE EXCREMENT. IT'S A BIO-TOILET.
NOPE.
WIND.
FOUND IN THE SKY OR OPEN PLAINS.
ぐる WHRR
ぐる WHRR
ぐる WHRR
IT'S LIKE TOILETS FOUND IN ARID REGIONS.
I BELIEVE THEY'RE CALLED DRYING TOILETS.
ヒュ
WSHHHHH
LAST IS FIRE.
IT'S THE MOST POWERFUL AND DANGEROUS.
THE ROMAN EMPEROR NERO...
THOUGHT TO DISPOSE OF EXCREMENT BY TOSSING IT INTO A VOLCANO.
...

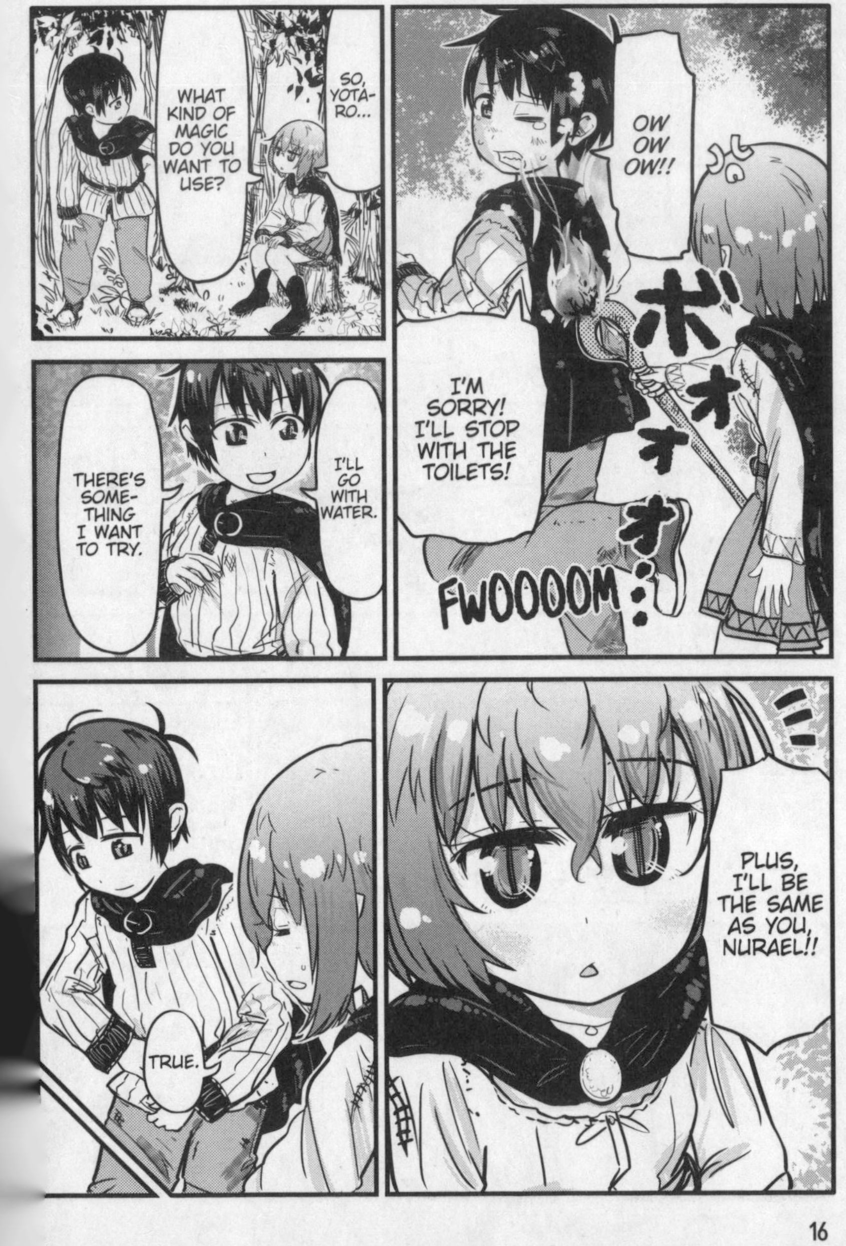
OW OW OW!!
ボォォォ…
I'M SORRY! I'LL STOP WITH THE TOILETS!
FWOOOOM
SO, YOTA-RO...
WHAT KIND OF MAGIC DO YOU WANT TO USE?
I'LL GO WITH WATER.
THERE'S SOME-THING I WANT TO TRY.
PLUS, I'LL BE THE SAME AS YOU, NURAEL!!
TRUE.

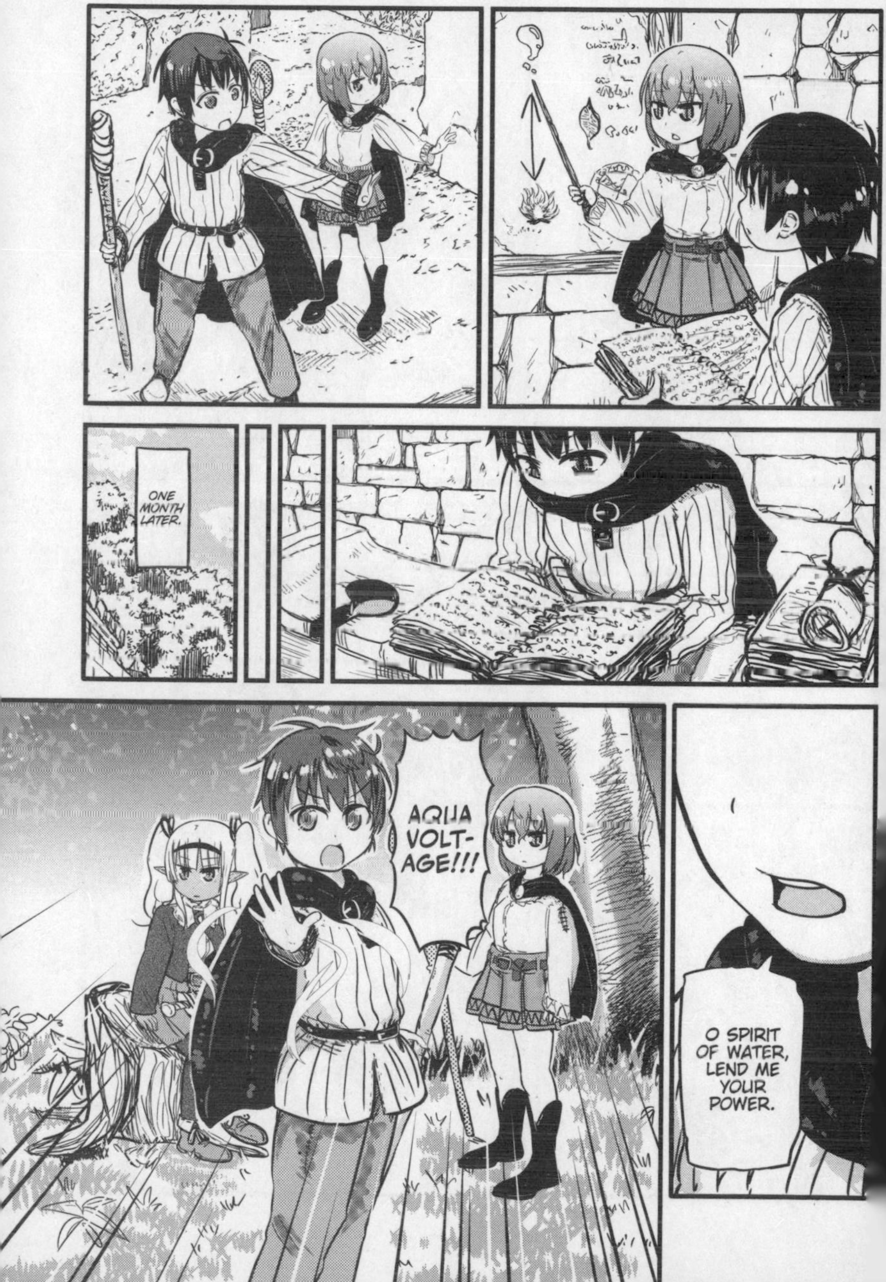
ONE MONTH LATER.
O SPIRIT OF WATER, LEND ME YOUR POWER.
AQUA VOLT-AGE!!!

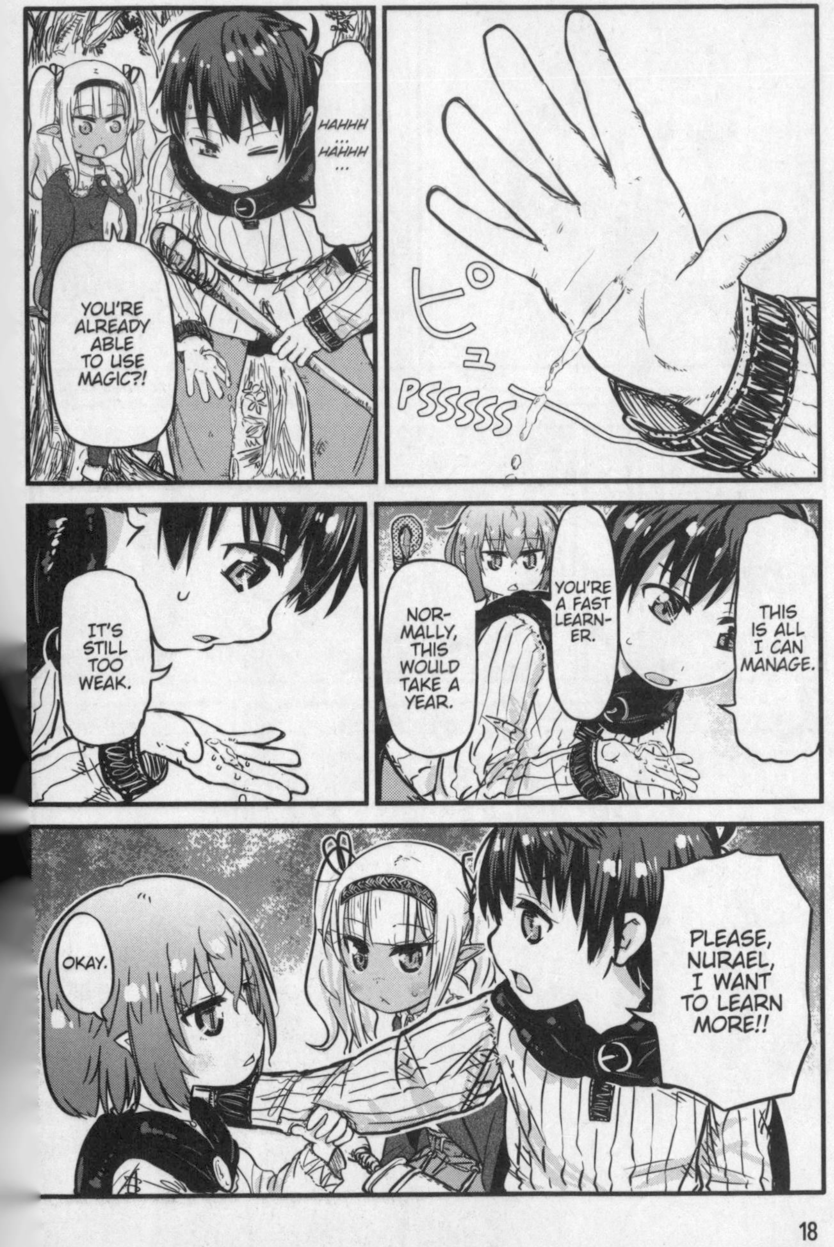
ピュ
PSSSSS
HAHHH ... HAHHH ...
YOU'RE ALREADY ABLE TO USE MAGIC?!
THIS IS ALL I CAN MANAGE.
YOU'RE A FAST LEARNER.
NOR-MALLY, THIS WOULD TAKE A YEAR.
IT'S STILL TOO WEAK.
PLEASE, NURAEL, I WANT TO LEARN MORE!!
OKAY.

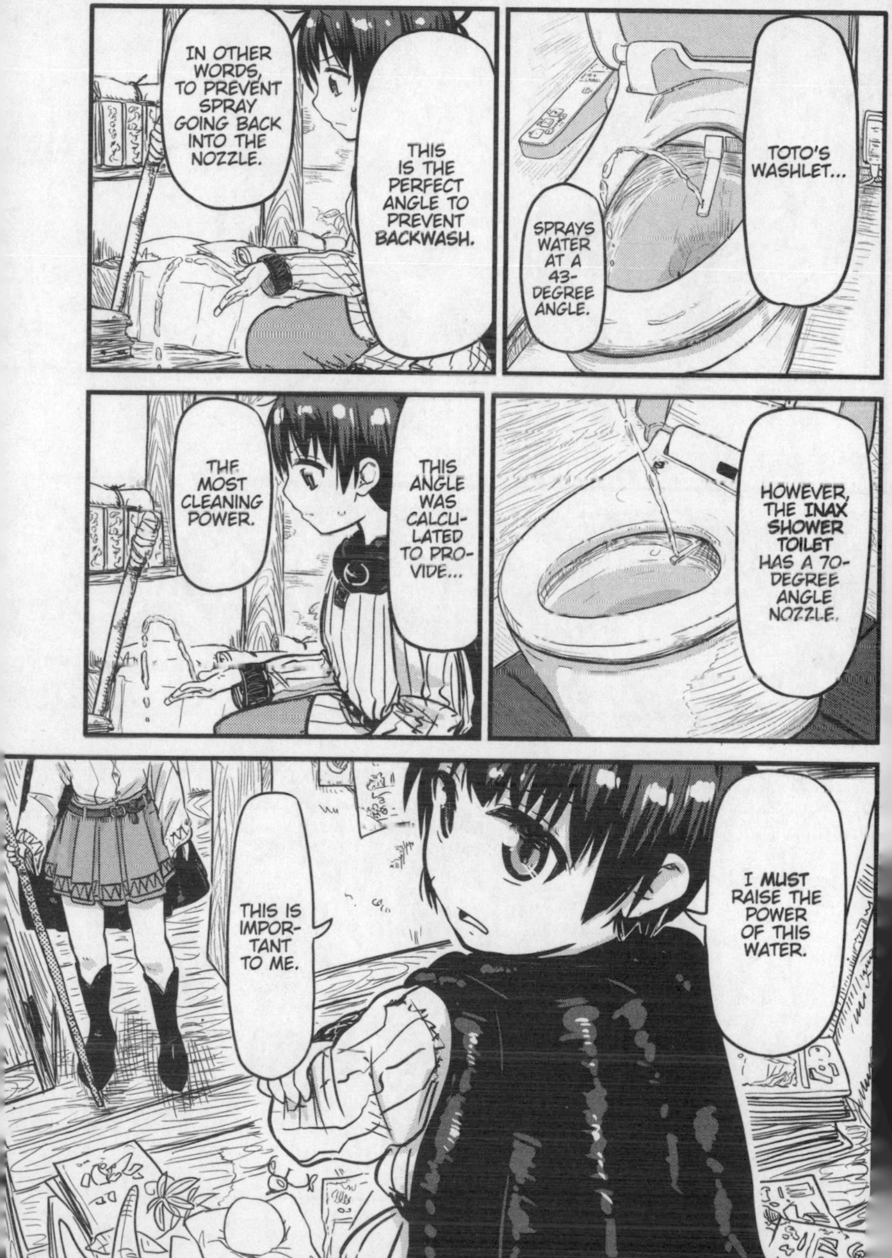
TOTO'S WASHLET...
SPRAYS WATER AT A 43-DEGREE ANGLE.
THIS IS THE PERFECT ANGLE TO PREVENT BACKWASH.
IN OTHER WORDS, TO PREVENT SPRAY GOING BACK INTO THE NOZZLE.
HOWEVER, THE INAX SHOWER TOILET HAS A 70-DEGREE ANGLE NOZZLE.
THIS ANGLE WAS CALCU-LATED TO PRO-VIDE...
THE MOST CLEANING POWER.
I MUST RAISE THE POWER OF THIS WATER.
THIS IS IMPOR-TANT TO ME.

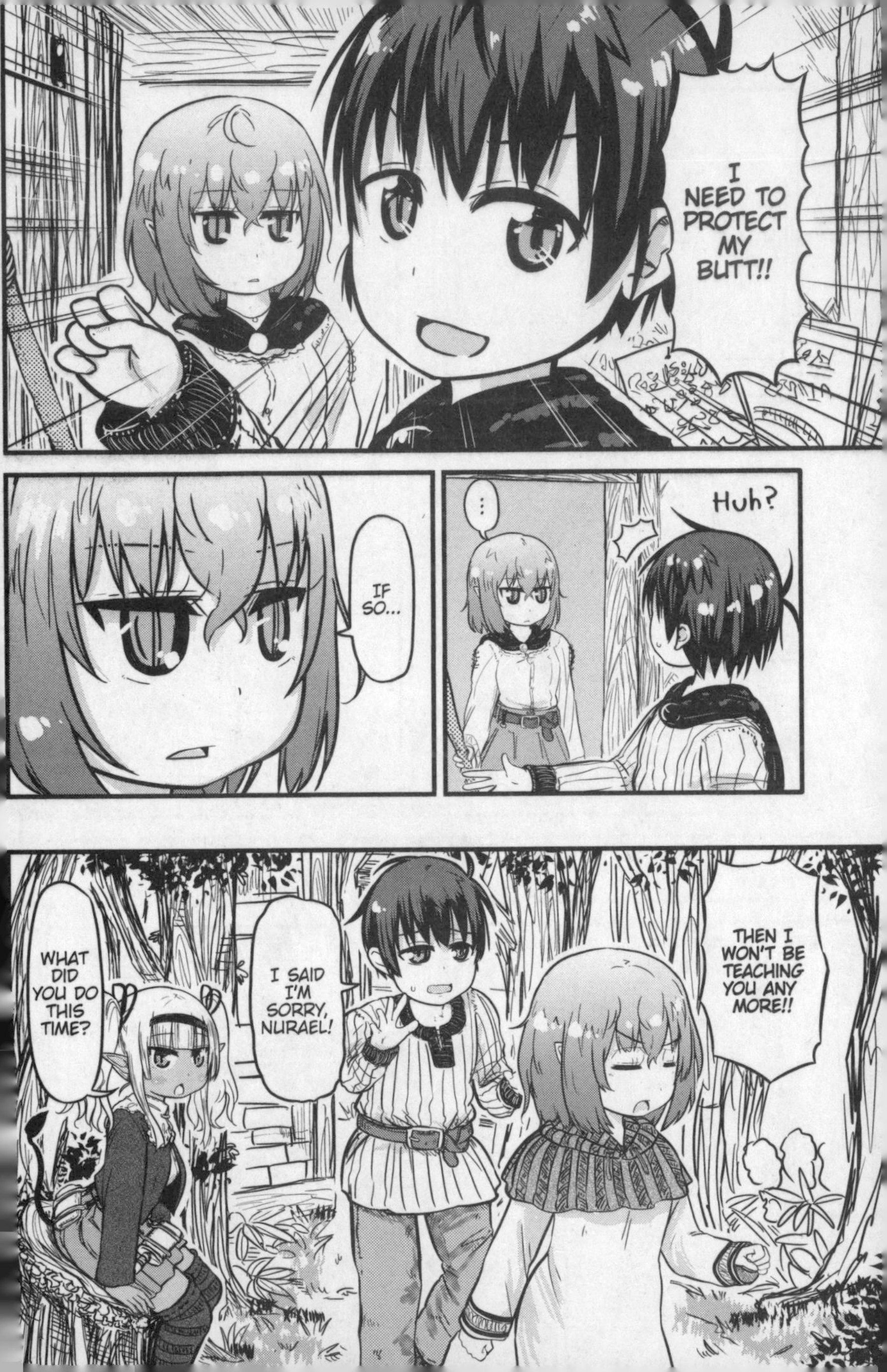

I NEED TO PROTECT MY BUTT!!
Huh?
...
IF SO...
THEN I WON'T BE TEACHING YOU ANY MORE!!
I SAID I'M SORRY, NURAEL!
WHAT DID YOU DO THIS TIME?

TWENTY-FIRST FLUSH

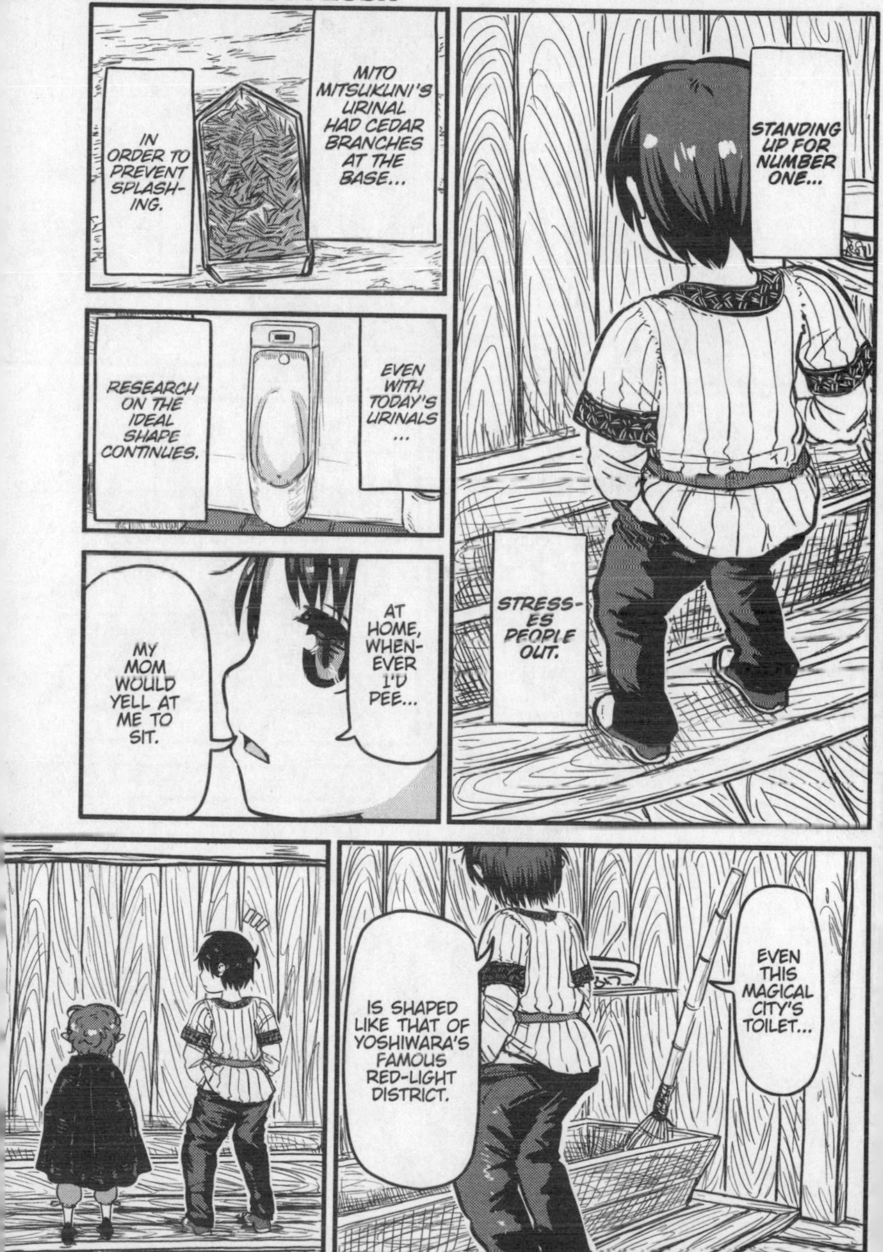
STANDING UP FOR NUMBER ONE...
STRESSES PEOPLE OUT.
MITO MITSUKUNI'S URINAL HAD CEDAR BRANCHES AT THE BASE...
IN ORDER TO PREVENT SPLASHING.
EVEN WITH TODAY'S URINALS...
RESEARCH ON THE IDEAL SHAPE CONTINUES.
AT HOME, WHENEVER I'D PEE...
MY MOM WOULD YELL AT ME TO SIT.
EVEN THIS MAGICAL CITY'S TOILET...
IS SHAPED LIKE THAT OF YOSHIWARA'S FAMOUS RED-LIGHT DISTRICT.

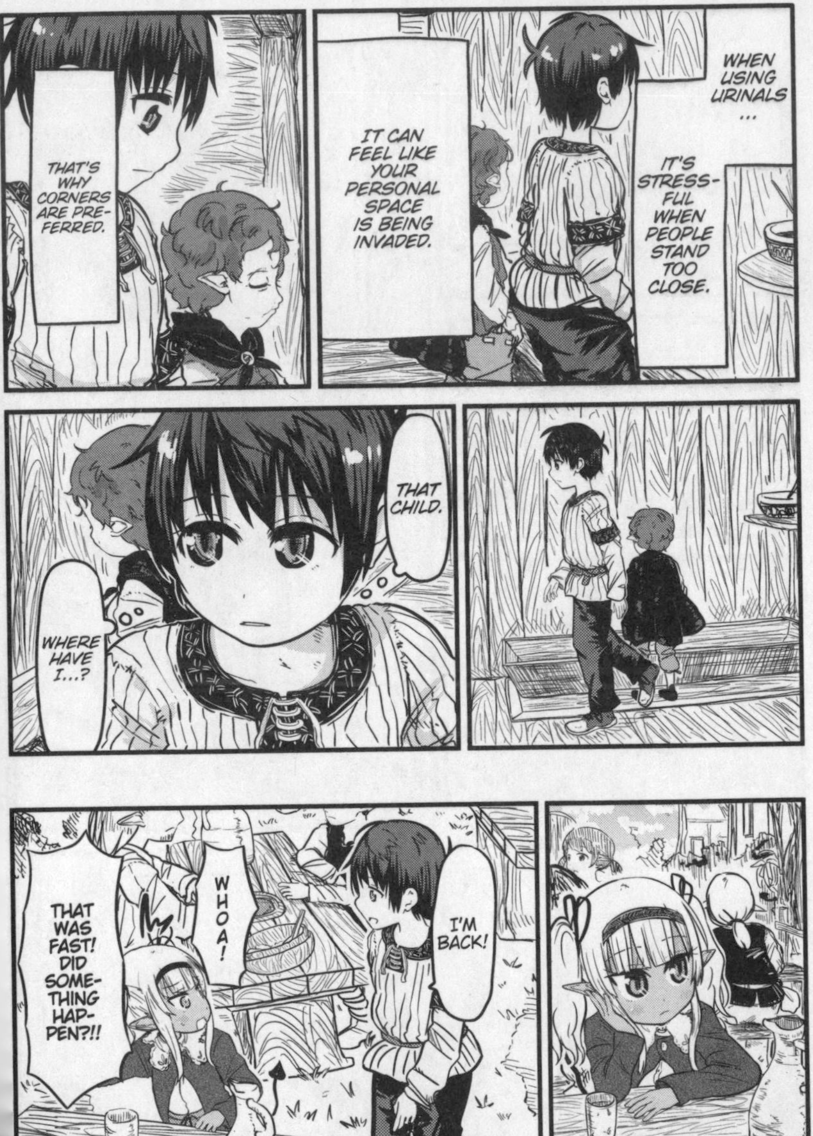
WHEN USING URINALS ...
IT'S STRESS-FUL WHEN PEOPLE STAND TOO CLOSE.
IT CAN FEEL LIKE YOUR PERSONAL SPACE IS BEING INVADED.
THAT'S WHY CORNERS ARE PRE-FERRED.
THAT CHILD.
WHERE HAVE I...?
I'M BACK!
WHOA!
THAT WAS FAST! DID SOME-THING HAP-PEN?!!

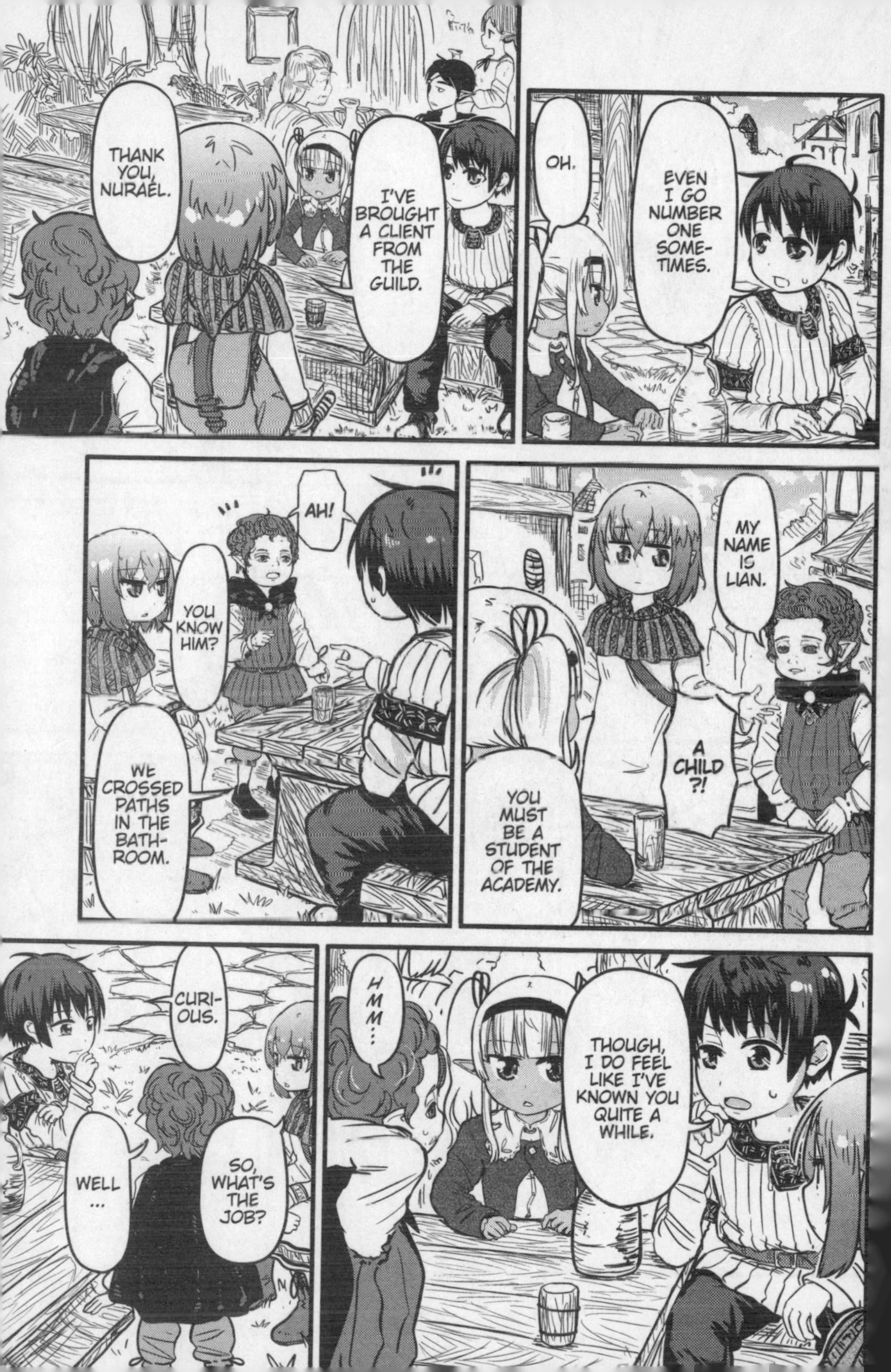
EVEN I GO NUMBER ONE SOME-TIMES.
OH.
I'VE BROUGHT A CLIENT FROM THE GUILD.
THANK YOU, NURAEL.
MY NAME IS LIAN.
A CHILD ?!
YOU MUST BE A STUDENT OF THE ACADEMY.
AH!
YOU KNOW HIM?
WE CROSSED PATHS IN THE BATH-ROOM.
THOUGH, I DO FEEL LIKE I'VE KNOWN YOU QUITE A WHILE.
HMM...
CURI-OUS.
SO, WHAT'S THE JOB?
WELL ...

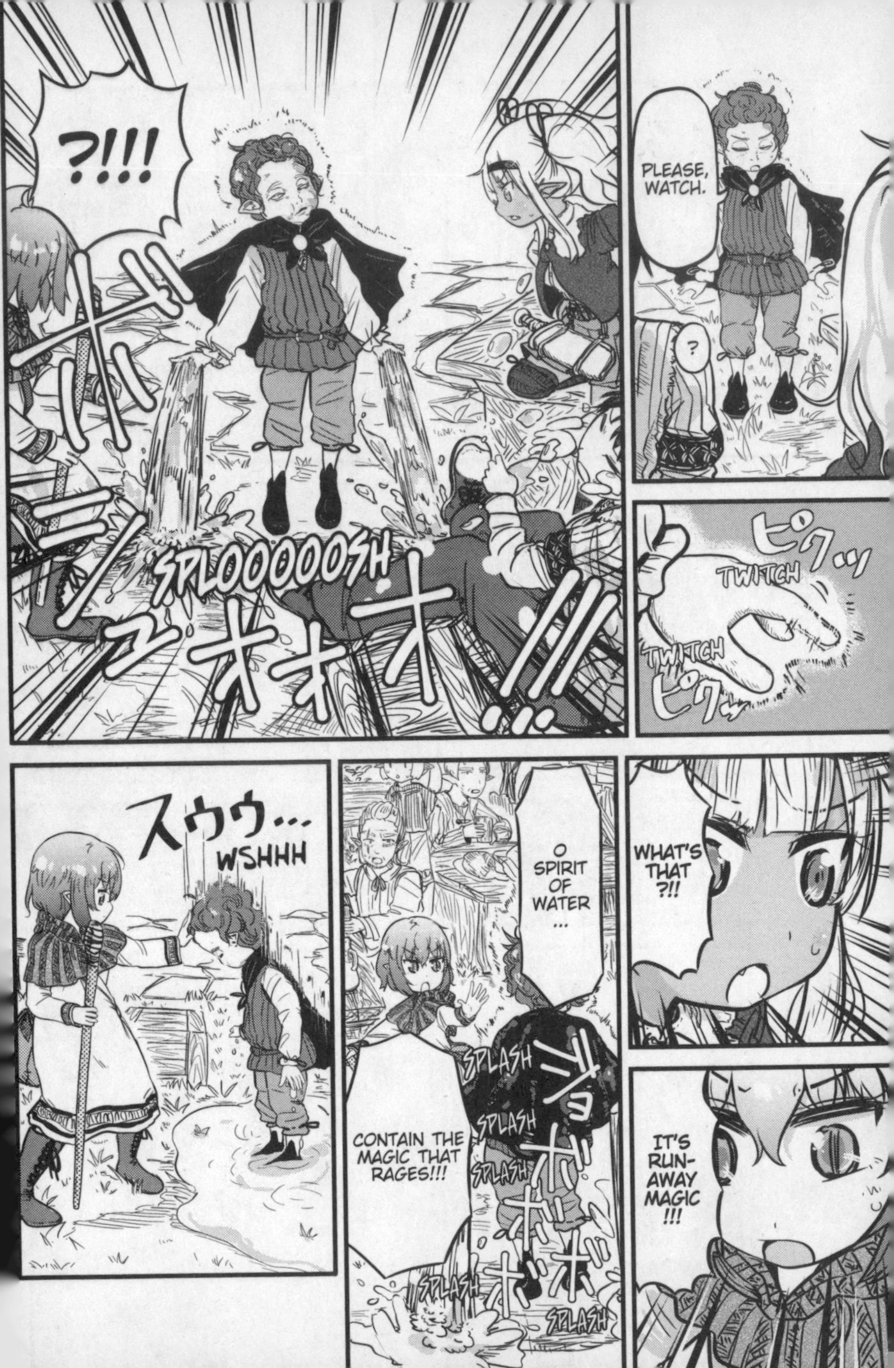

PLEASE, WATCH.
?
ピクッ
TWITCH
TWITCH
ピクッ
?!!!
SPLOOOOOSH
WHAT'S THAT?!!
IT'S RUN-AWAY MAGIC!!!
O SPIRIT OF WATER...
CONTAIN THE MAGIC THAT RAGES!!!
SPLASH
SPLASH
SPLASH
SPLASH
SPLASH
スウウ...
WSHHH

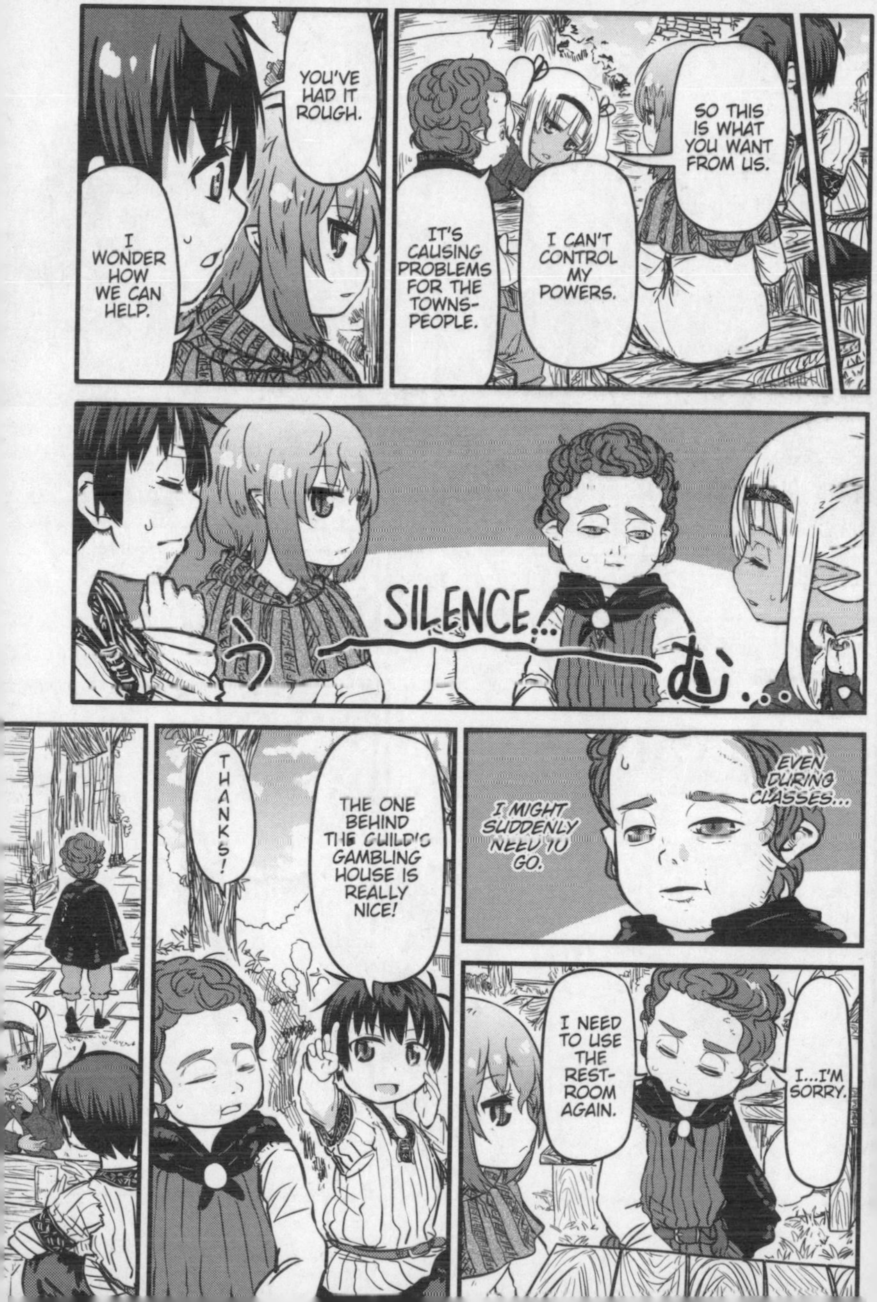
SO THIS IS WHAT YOU WANT FROM US.
I CAN'T CONTROL MY POWERS.
IT'S CAUSING PROBLEMS FOR THE TOWNS-PEOPLE.
YOU'VE HAD IT ROUGH.
I WONDER HOW WE CAN HELP.
SILENCE...
う———む...
EVEN DURING CLASSES...
I MIGHT SUDDENLY NEED TO GO.
I...I'M SORRY.
I NEED TO USE THE REST-ROOM AGAIN.
THE ONE BEHIND THE GUILD'S GAMBLING HOUSE IS REALLY NICE!
THANKS!

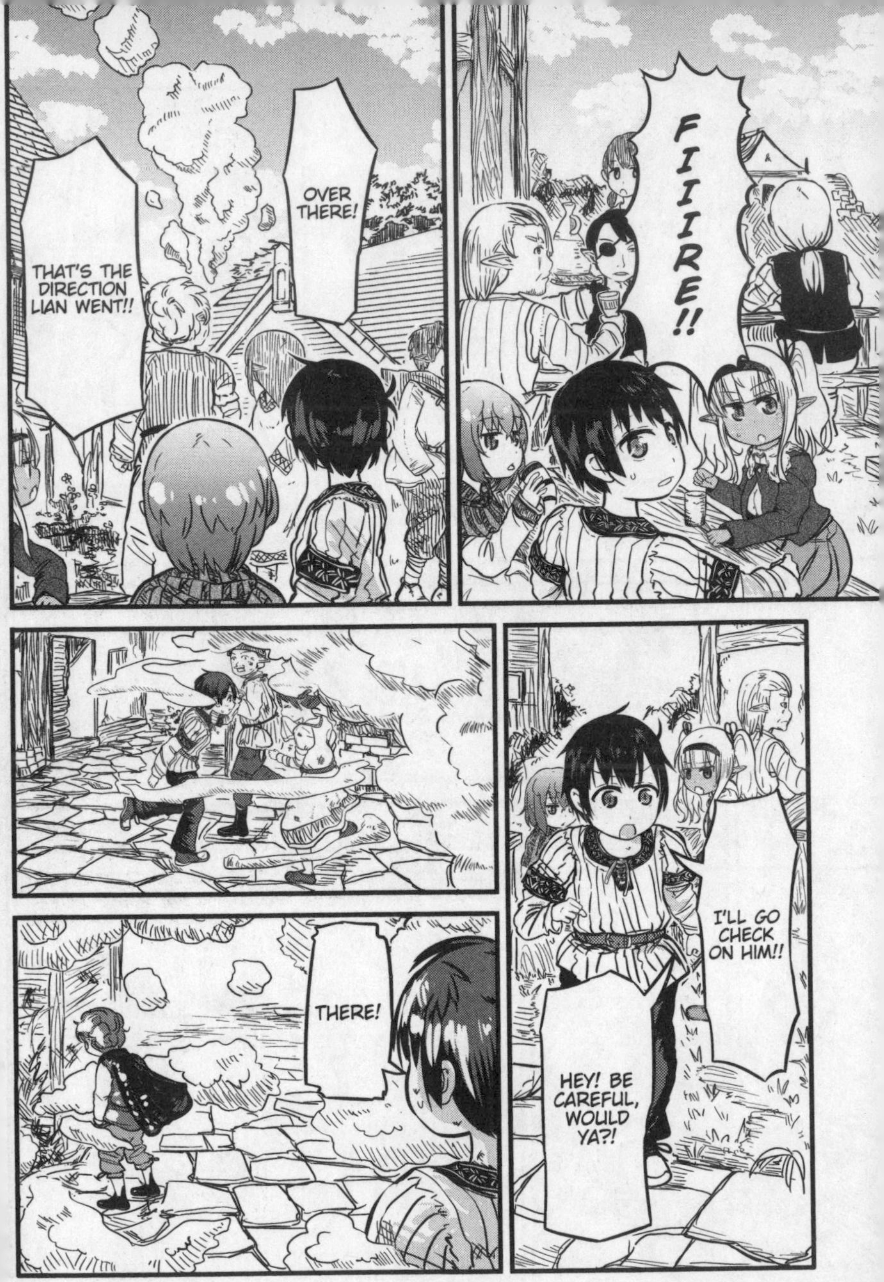
FIIIRE!!
OVER THERE!
THAT'S THE DIRECTION LIAN WENT!!
I'LL GO CHECK ON HIM!!
HEY! BE CAREFUL, WOULD YA?!
THERE!

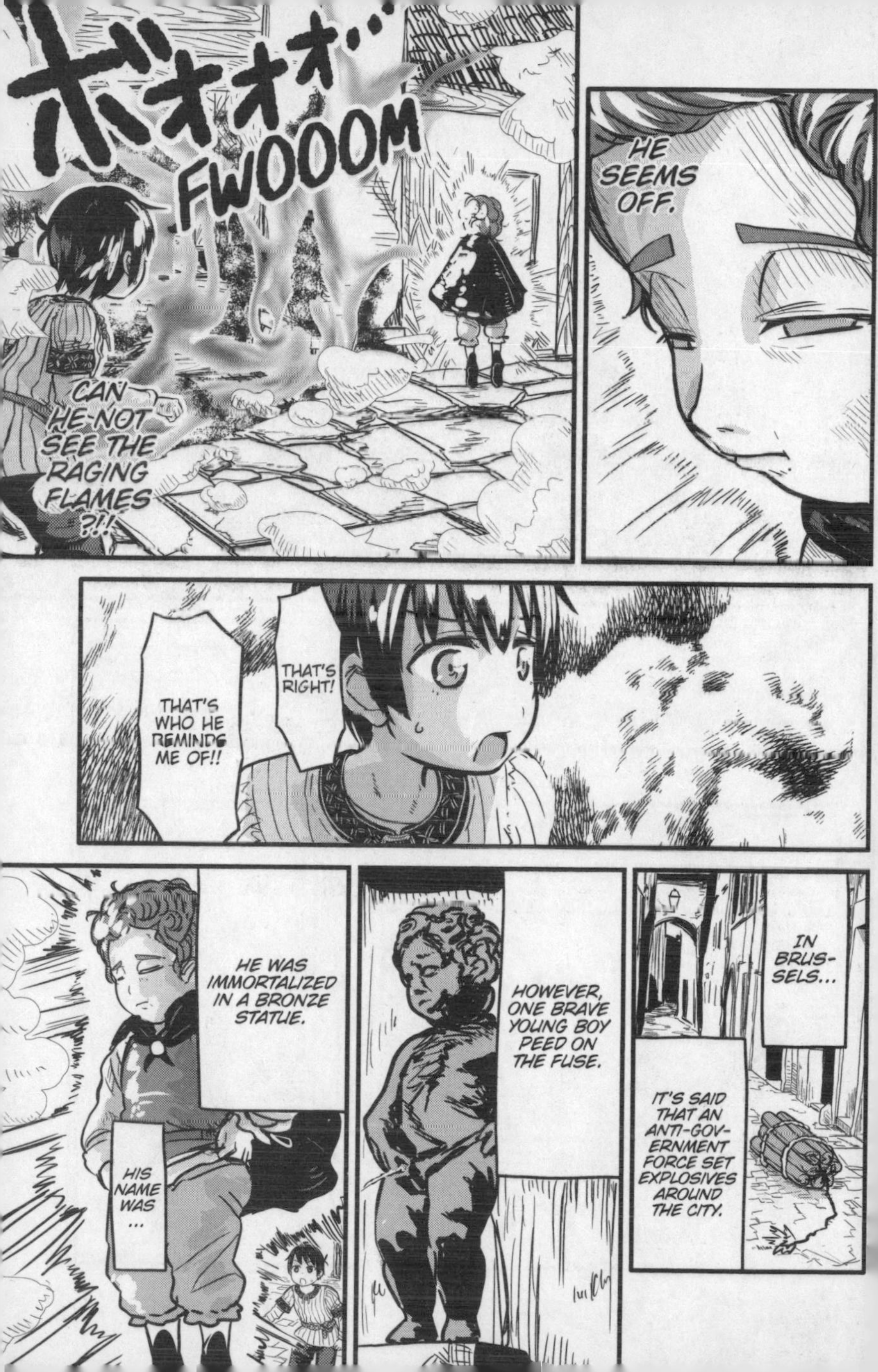

HE SEEMS OFF.
ボオオオ…
FWOOOM
CAN HE NOT SEE THE RAGING FLAMES?!!
THAT'S RIGHT!
THAT'S WHO HE REMINDS ME OF!!
IN BRUSSELS...
IT'S SAID THAT AN ANTI-GOVERNMENT FORCE SET EXPLOSIVES AROUND THE CITY.
HOWEVER, ONE BRAVE YOUNG BOY PEED ON THE FUSE.
HE WAS IMMORTALIZED IN A BRONZE STATUE.
HIS NAME WAS ...

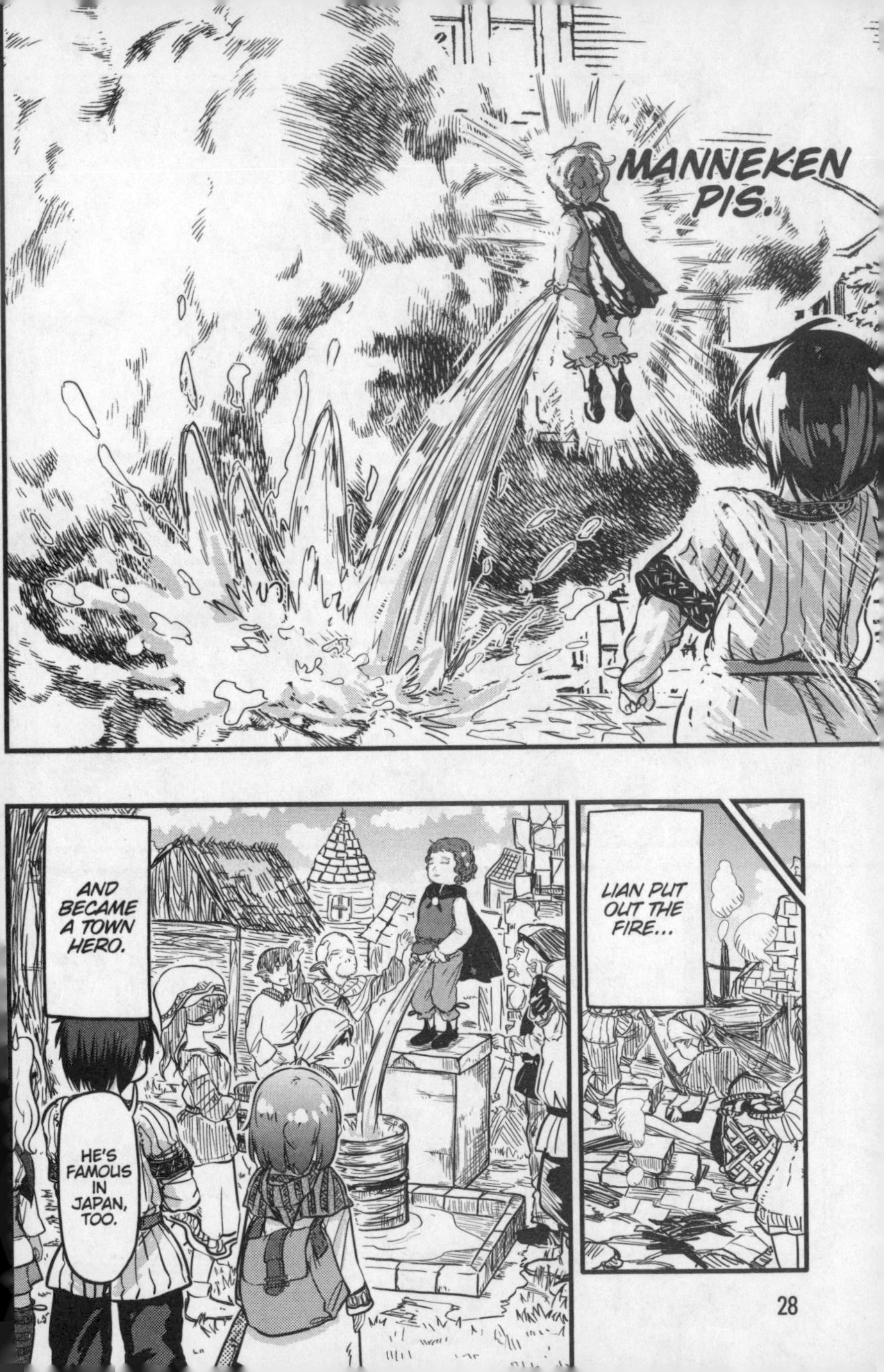
MANNEKEN PIS.
LIAN PUT OUT THE FIRE...
AND BECAME A TOWN HERO.
HE'S FAMOUS IN JAPAN, TOO.

ROOTS

PEOPLE WHO DON'T VALUE TOILET TIME ARE NO GOOD.

ELEVENTH TOILET TIME

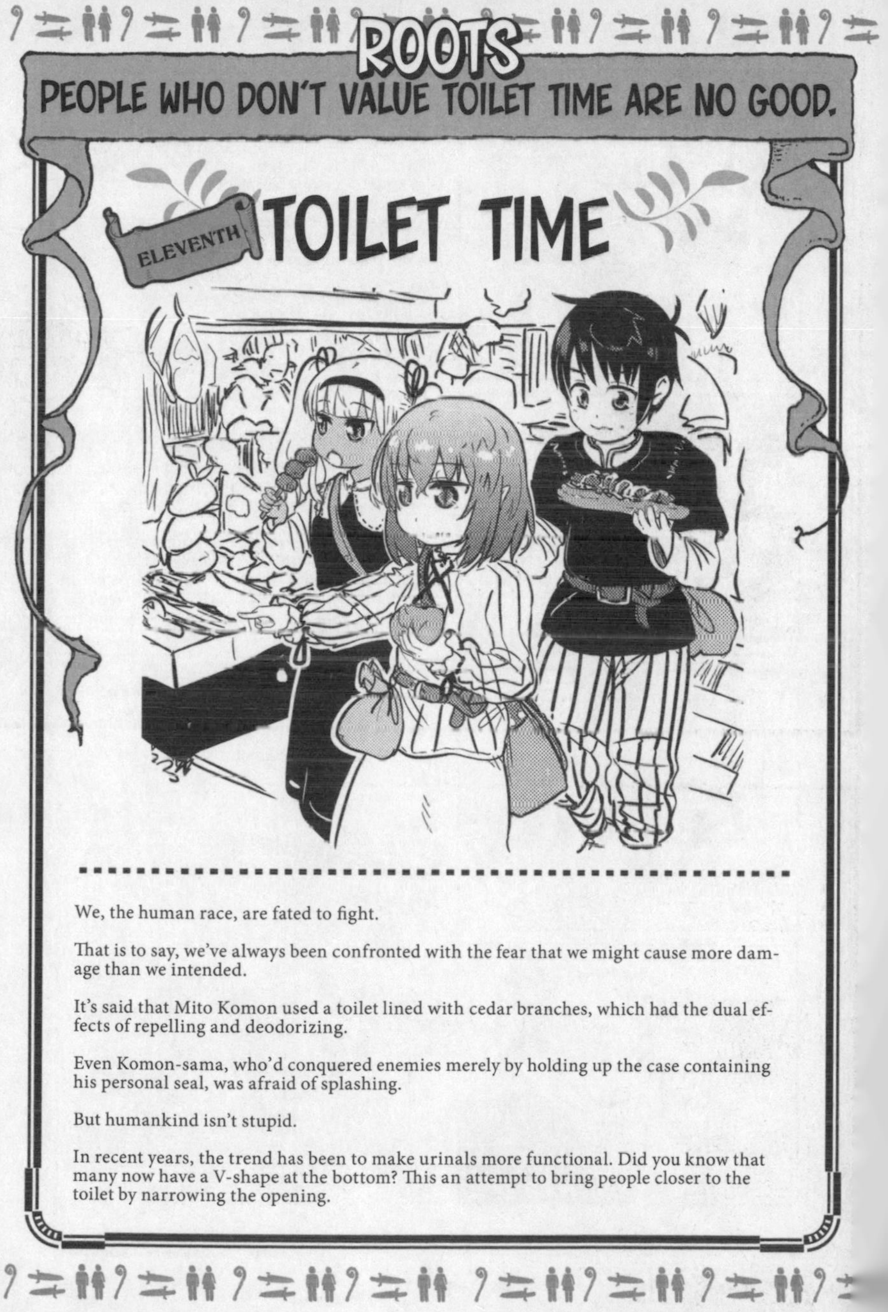

We, the human race, are fated to fight.

That is to say, we've always been confronted with the fear that we might cause more damage than we intended.

It's said that Mito Komon used a toilet lined with cedar branches, which had the dual effects of repelling and deodorizing.

Even Komon-sama, who'd conquered enemies merely by holding up the case containing his personal seal, was afraid of splashing.

But humankind isn't stupid.

In recent years, the trend has been to make urinals more functional. Did you know that many now have a V-shape at the bottom? This an attempt to bring people closer to the toilet by narrowing the opening.

There are also urinals with targets on them, to make it easier to aim.

There are even toilets that have playful functions like a game, measuring the strength and speed of your stream.

Beyond the toilet bowl, the part where it stands (the staining stone) has also become more advanced. It plays an important role in catching the urine when you miss your target. Granite, a building material that's resistant to water and stains, is often used.

And the innovation doesn't stop there. In recent years, a patent has been filed for a design in which the stained stone is slightly indented so that the user feels a sense of discomfort in their heels and naturally takes a step forward.

Urinals will continue to evolve. We humans are just beginning to turn fear into joy. When you take a piss, thrust your chest out. Let's thank our ancestors and piss with pride.

As an aside, the most popular public restroom is the one in the front, followed by the one next to it, and then the one in the back.

IN OTHER WORDS

THIS MAXIM

"AT HOME, WE SIT AND GO."

DO YOU HAVE ANY INTEREST IN MAGIC...
BESIDES WATER?
EH?
I SUPPOSE, IF PRESSED ...
WHOOOSH
MAYBE WIND?
GOOD CHOICE.
WATER AND WIND GO WELL TOGETHER.

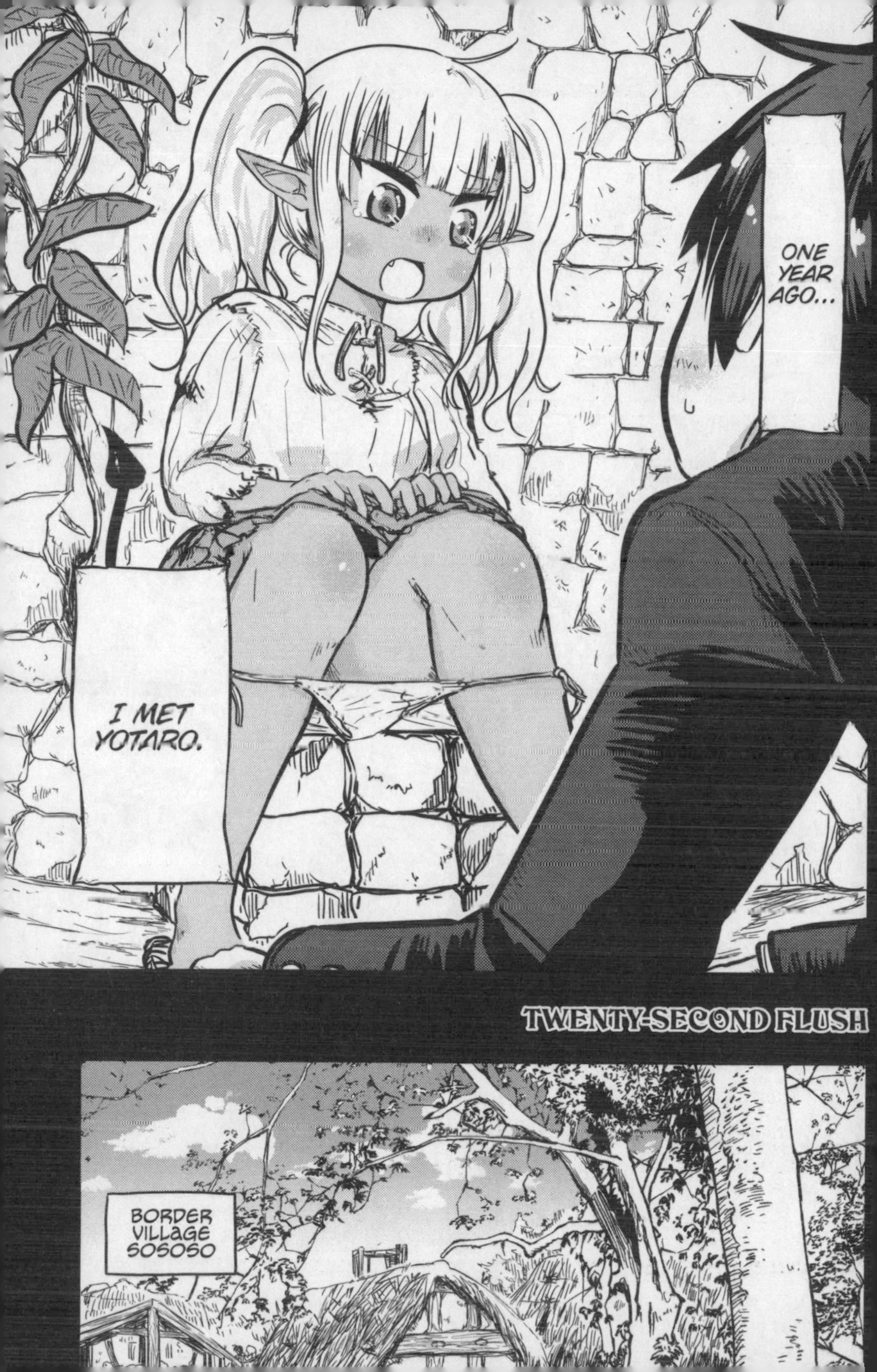
ONE YEAR AGO...
I MET YOTARO.
TWENTY-SECOND FLUSH
BORDER VILLAGE SOSOSO

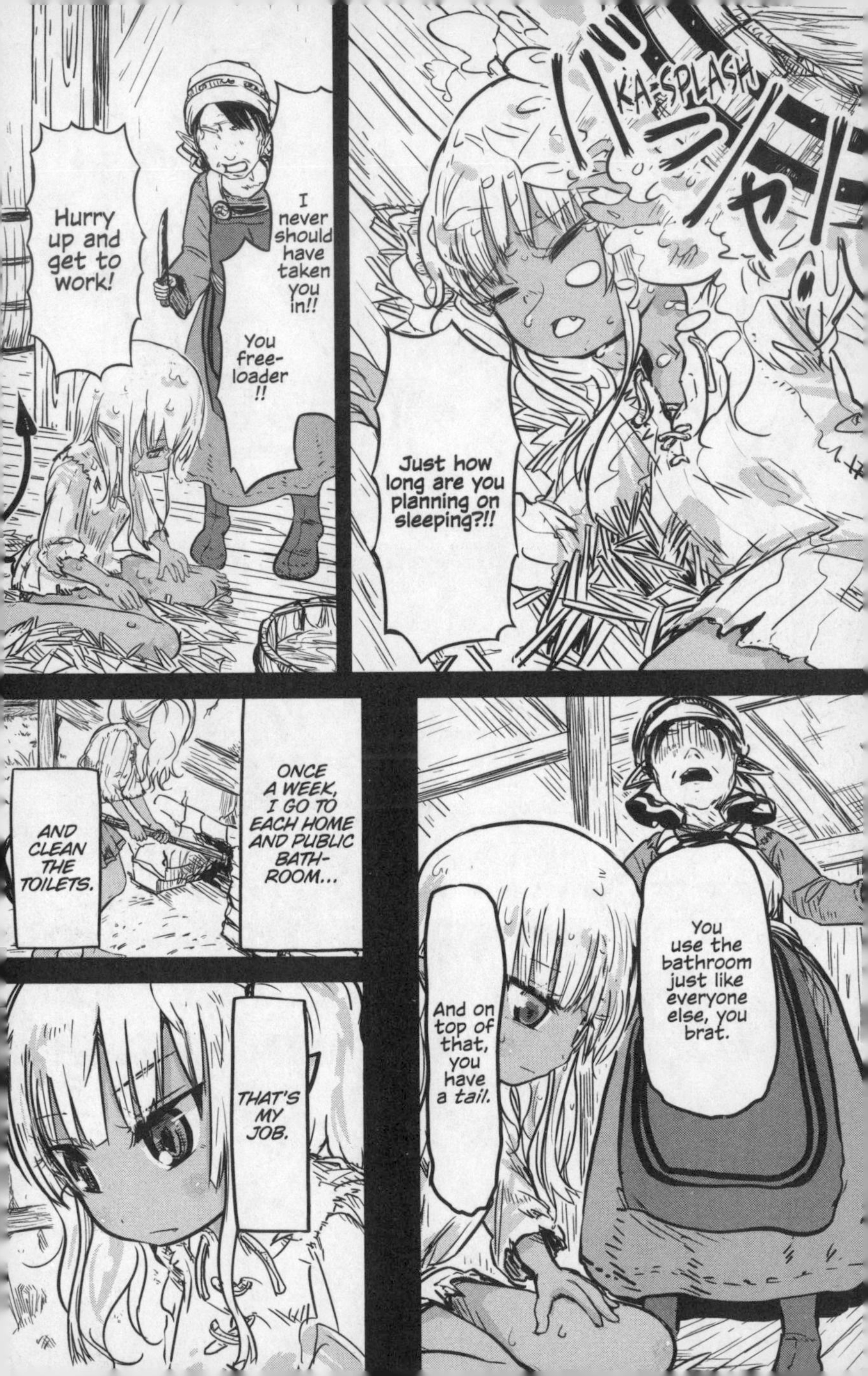
KA-SPLASH
Just how long are you planning on sleeping?!!
I never should have taken you in!!
You free-loader !!
Hurry up and get to work!
You use the bathroom just like everyone else, you brat.
And on top of that, you have a *tail*.
ONCE A WEEK, I GO TO EACH HOME AND PUBLIC BATH-ROOM...
AND CLEAN THE TOILETS.
THAT'S MY JOB.

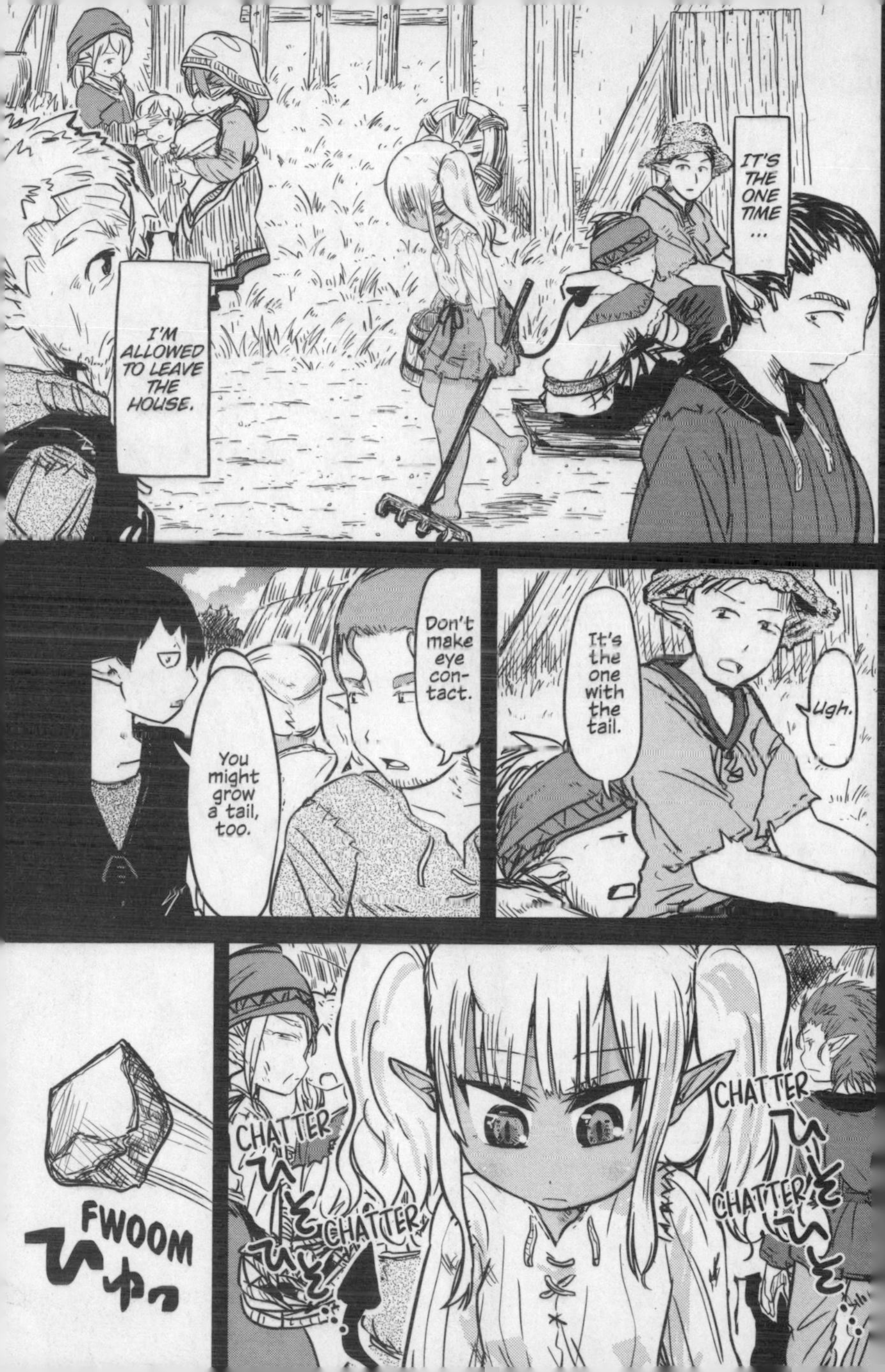
IT'S THE ONE TIME...
I'M ALLOWED TO LEAVE THE HOUSE.
It's the one with the tail.
Ugh.
Don't make eye contact.
You might grow a tail, too.
CHATTER
CHATTER
CHATTER
CHATTER
FWOOM
ひゅっ

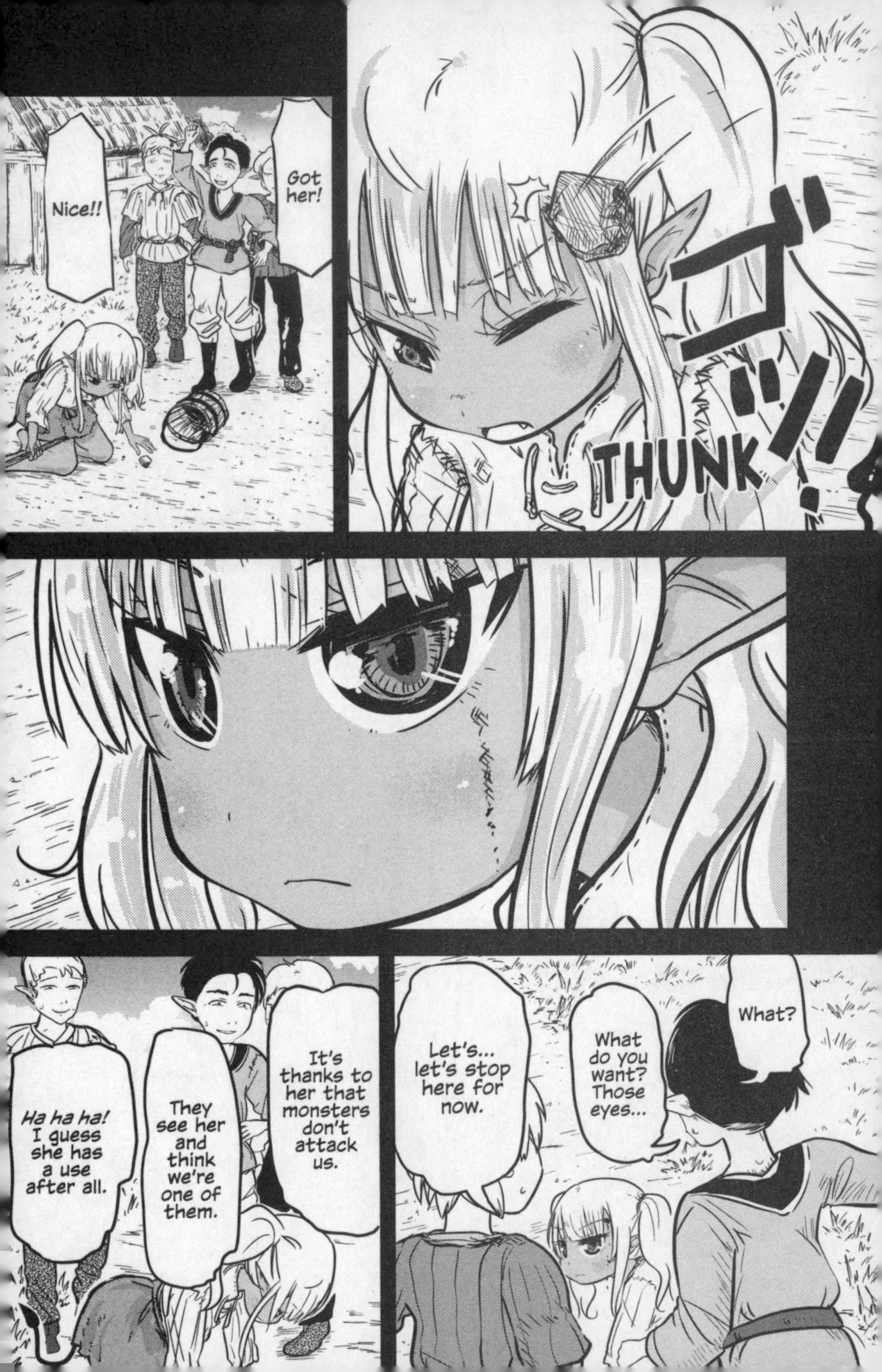
ゴッ!!
THUNK!
Got her!
Nice!!
What?
What do you want? Those eyes...
Let's... let's stop here for now.
It's thanks to her that monsters don't attack us.
They see her and think we're one of them.
Ha ha ha! I guess she has a use after all.

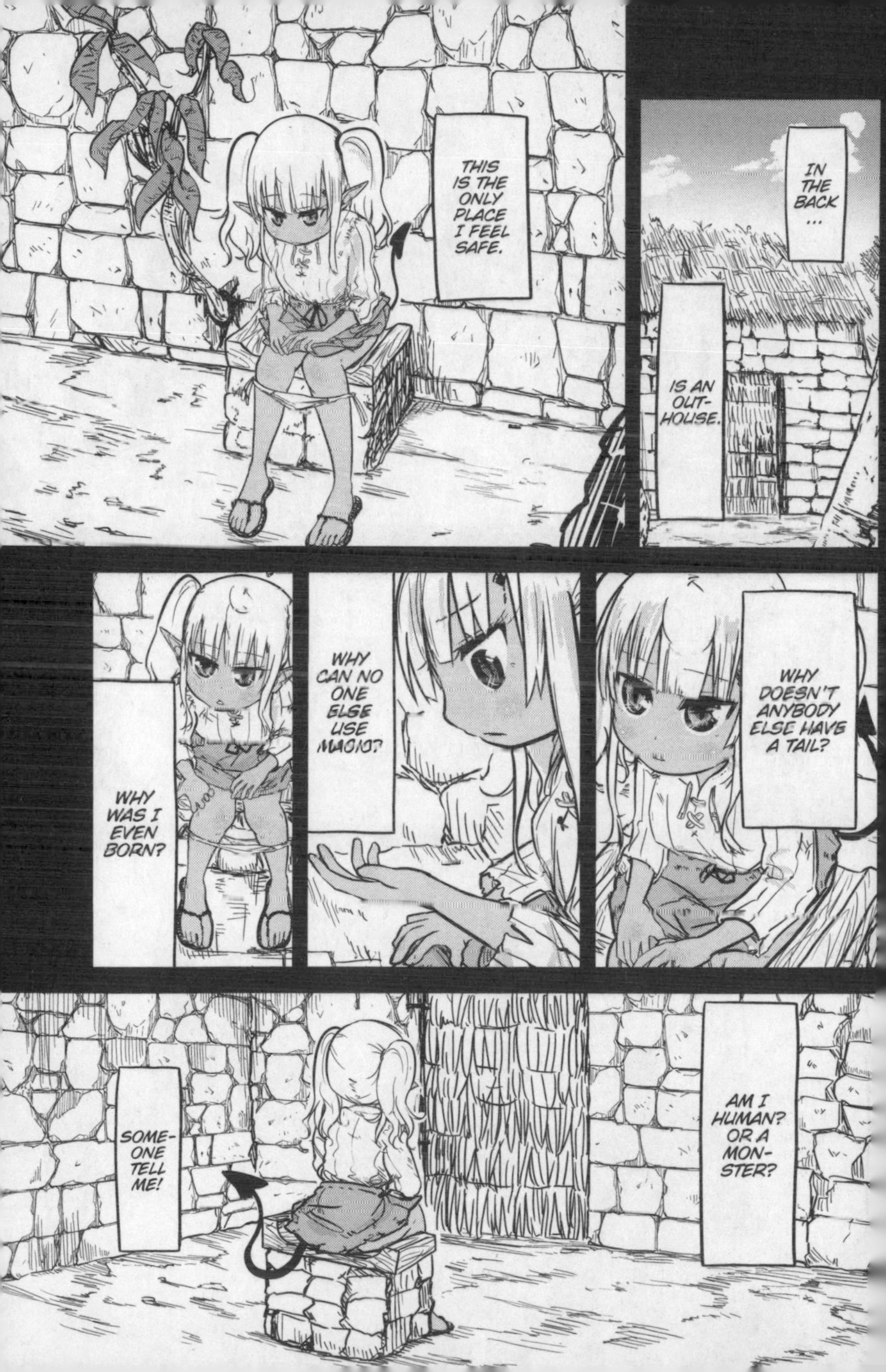
IN THE BACK ...
IS AN OUT-HOUSE.
THIS IS THE ONLY PLACE I FEEL SAFE.
WHY DOESN'T ANYBODY ELSE HAVE A TAIL?
WHY CAN NO ONE ELSE USE MAGIC?
WHY WAS I EVEN BORN?
AM I HUMAN? OR A MONSTER?
SOME-ONE TELL ME!

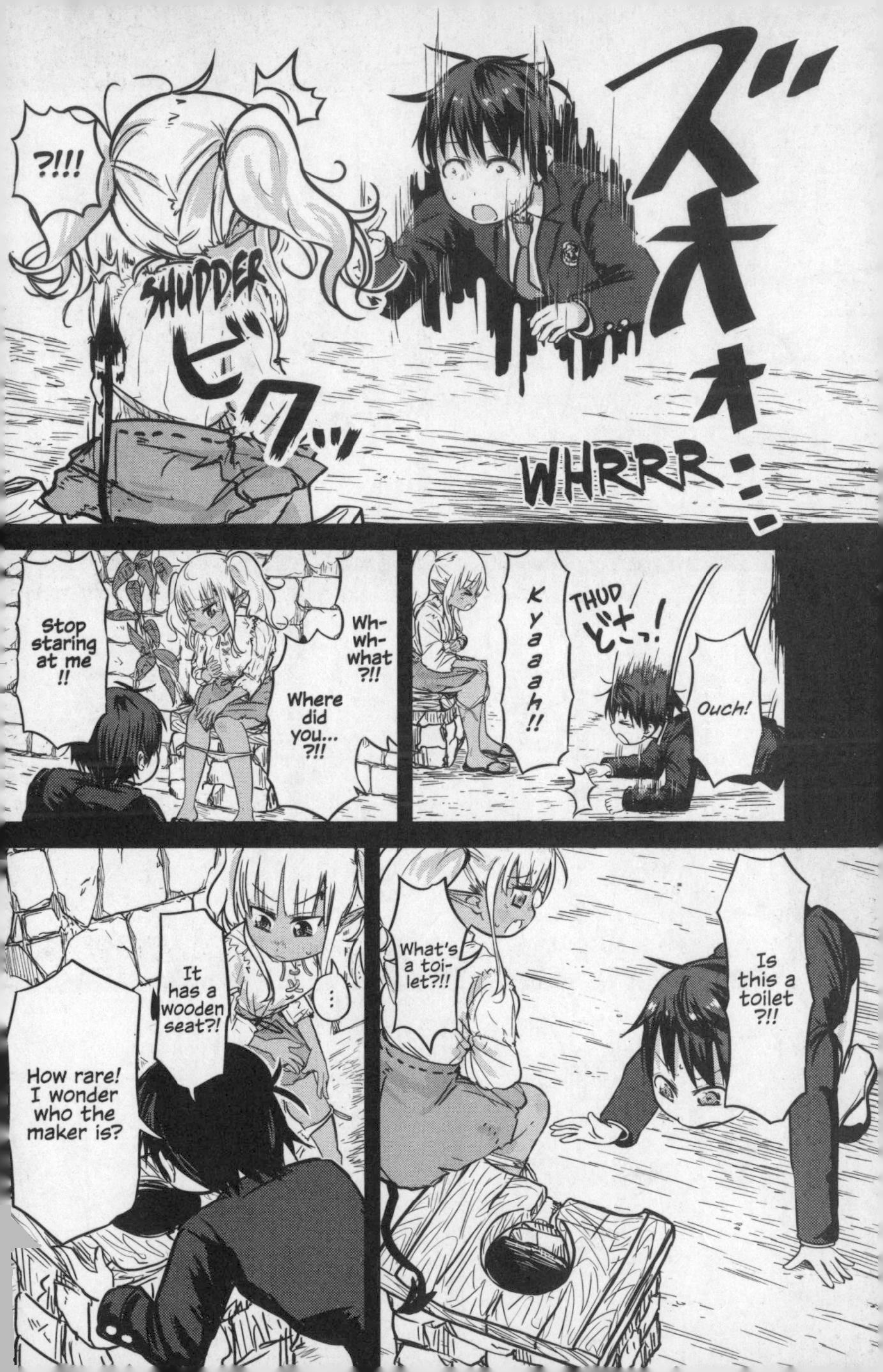

ズオォ…
WHRRR
?!!!
SHUDDER
ビクッ
THUD
どさっ!
Kyaaah!!
Ouch!
Wh-wh-what?!!
Where did you...?!!
Stop staring at me!!
Is this a toilet?!!
What's a toilet?!!
...
It has a wooden seat?!
How rare! I wonder who the maker is?

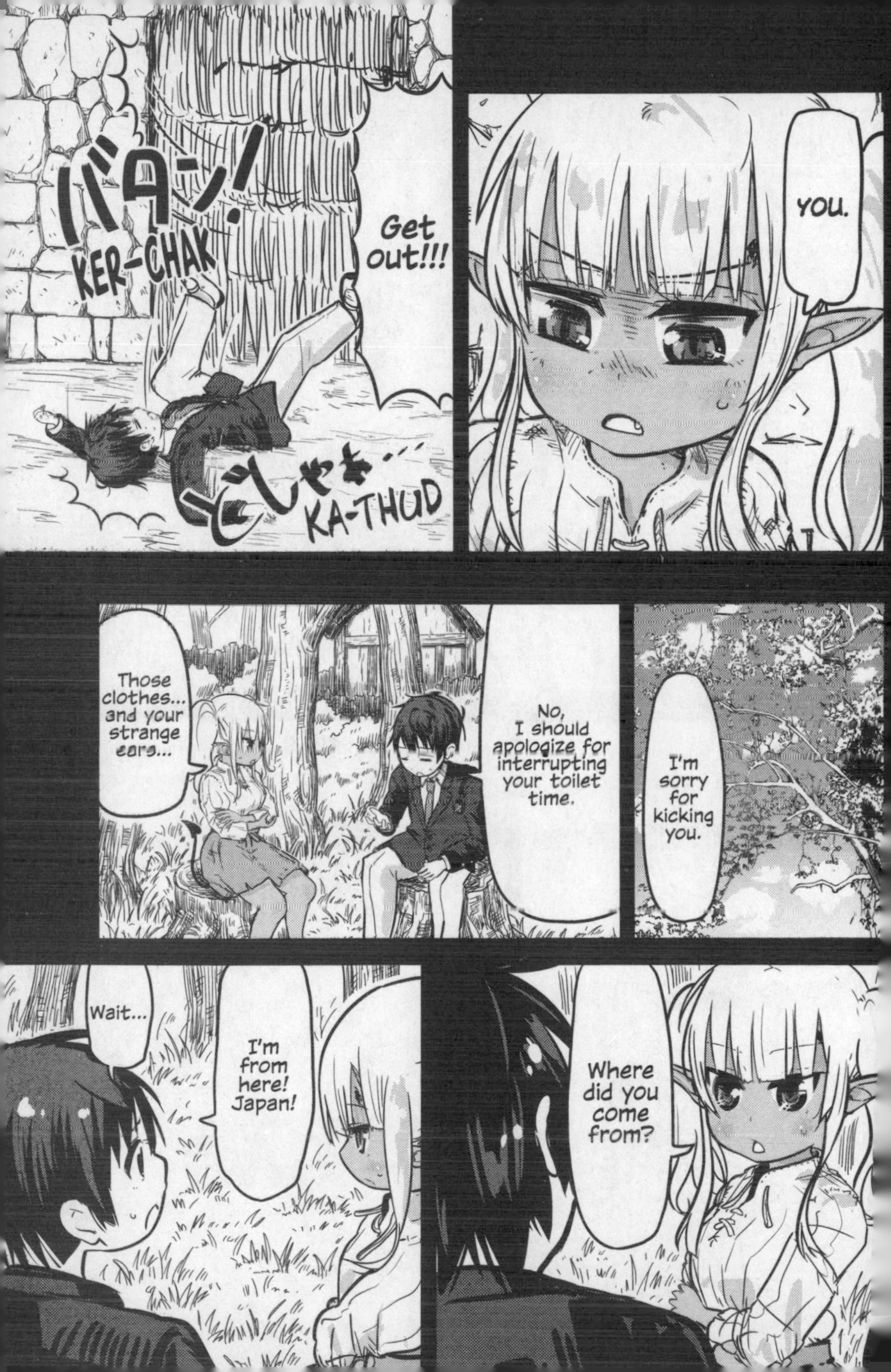
You.
Get out!!!
バターン!
KER-CHAK
KA-THUD
I'm sorry for kicking you.
No, I should apologize for interrupting your toilet time.
Those clothes... and your strange ears...
Where did you come from?
I'm from here! Japan!
Wait...

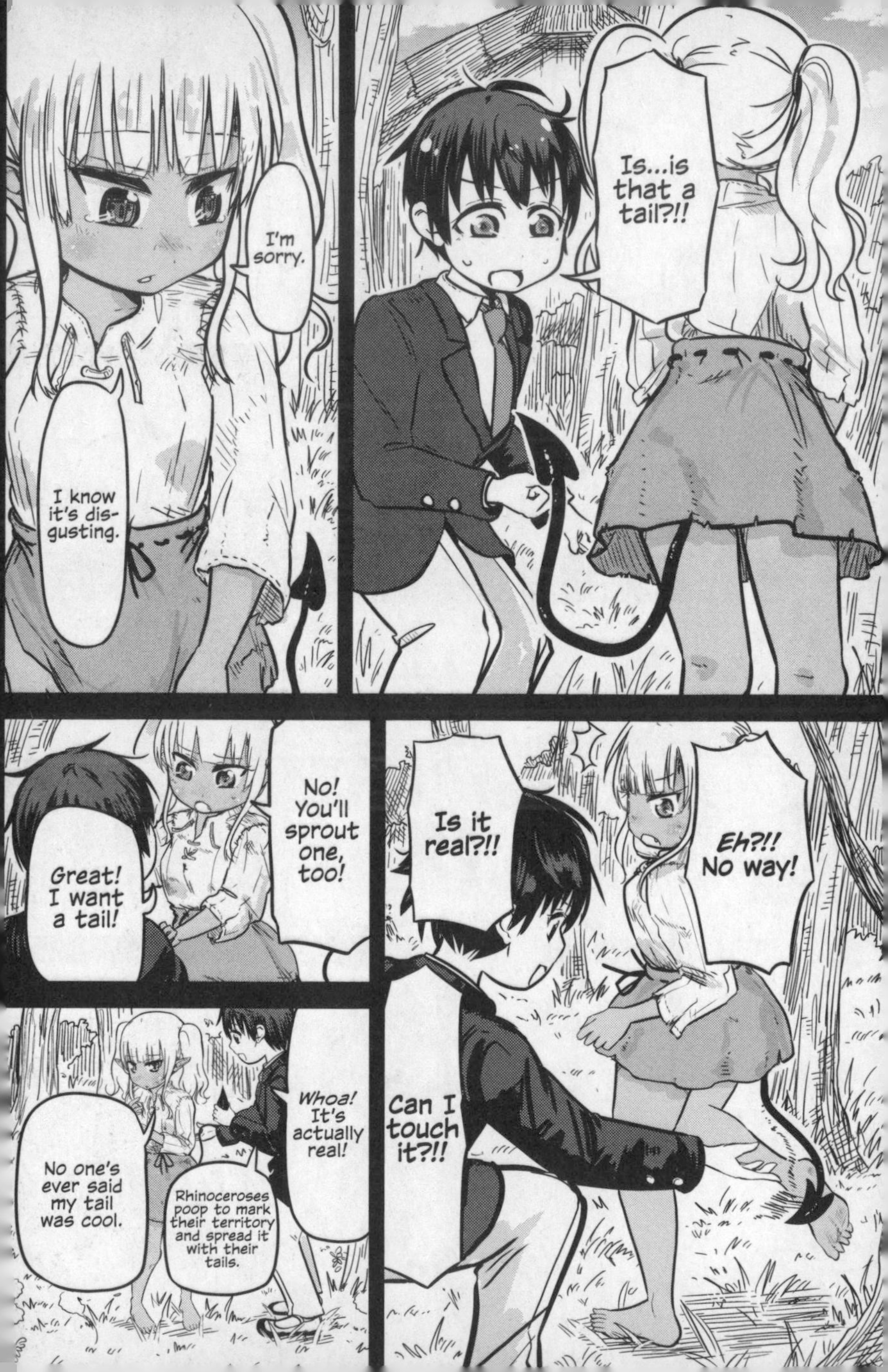
Is...is that a tail?!!
I'm sorry.
I know it's disgusting.
Eh?!! No way!
Is it real?!!
Can I touch it?!!
No! You'll sprout one, too!
Great! I want a tail!
Whoa! It's actually real!
Rhinoceroses poop to mark their territory and spread it with their tails.
No one's ever said my tail was cool.

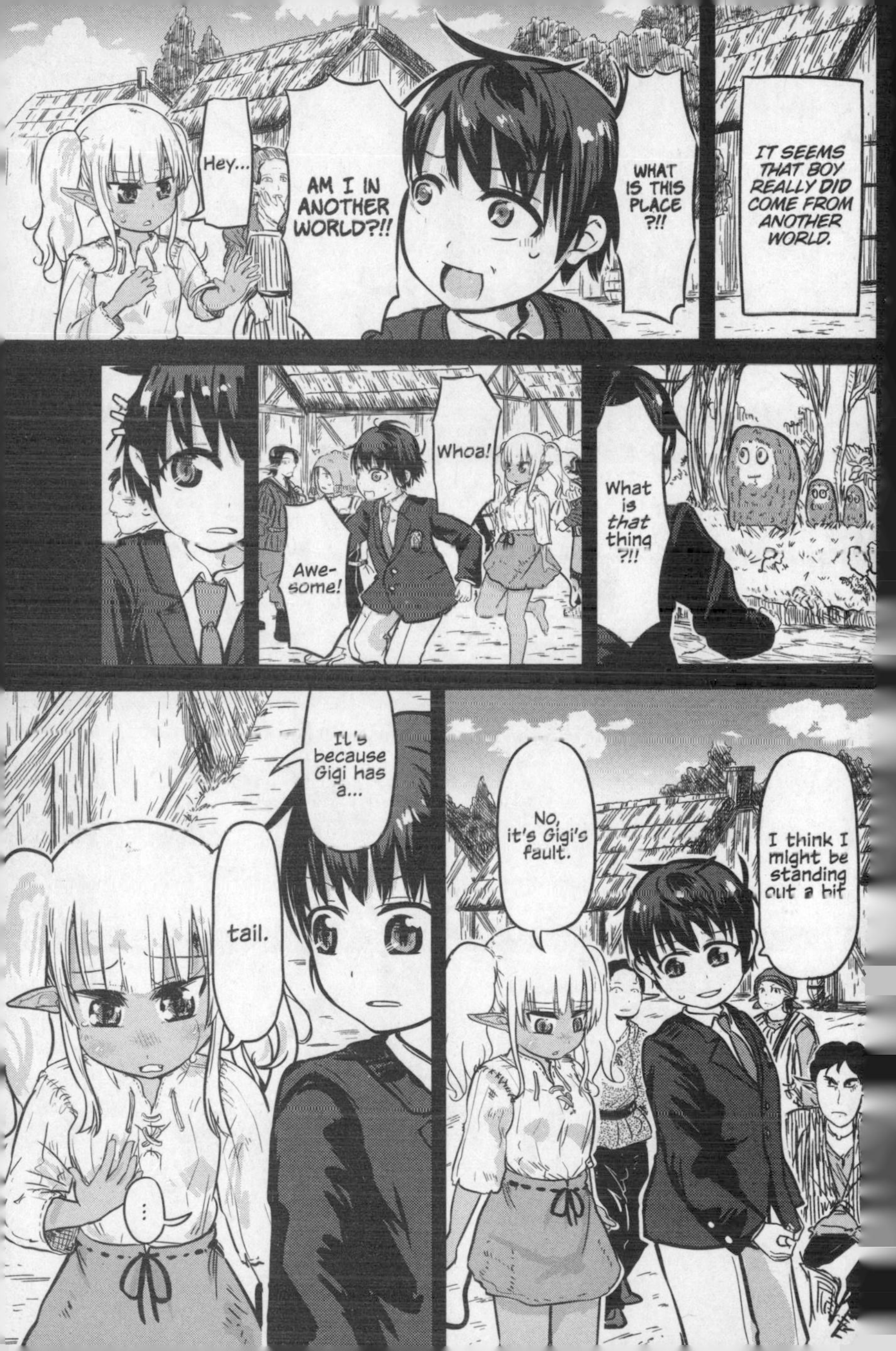
IT SEEMS THAT BOY REALLY DID COME FROM ANOTHER WORLD.
WHAT IS THIS PLACE?!!
AM I IN ANOTHER WORLD?!!
Hey...
What is *that* thing?!!
Whoa!
Awesome!
I think I might be standing out a bit
No, it's Gigi's fault.
It's because Gigi has a...
tail.
...

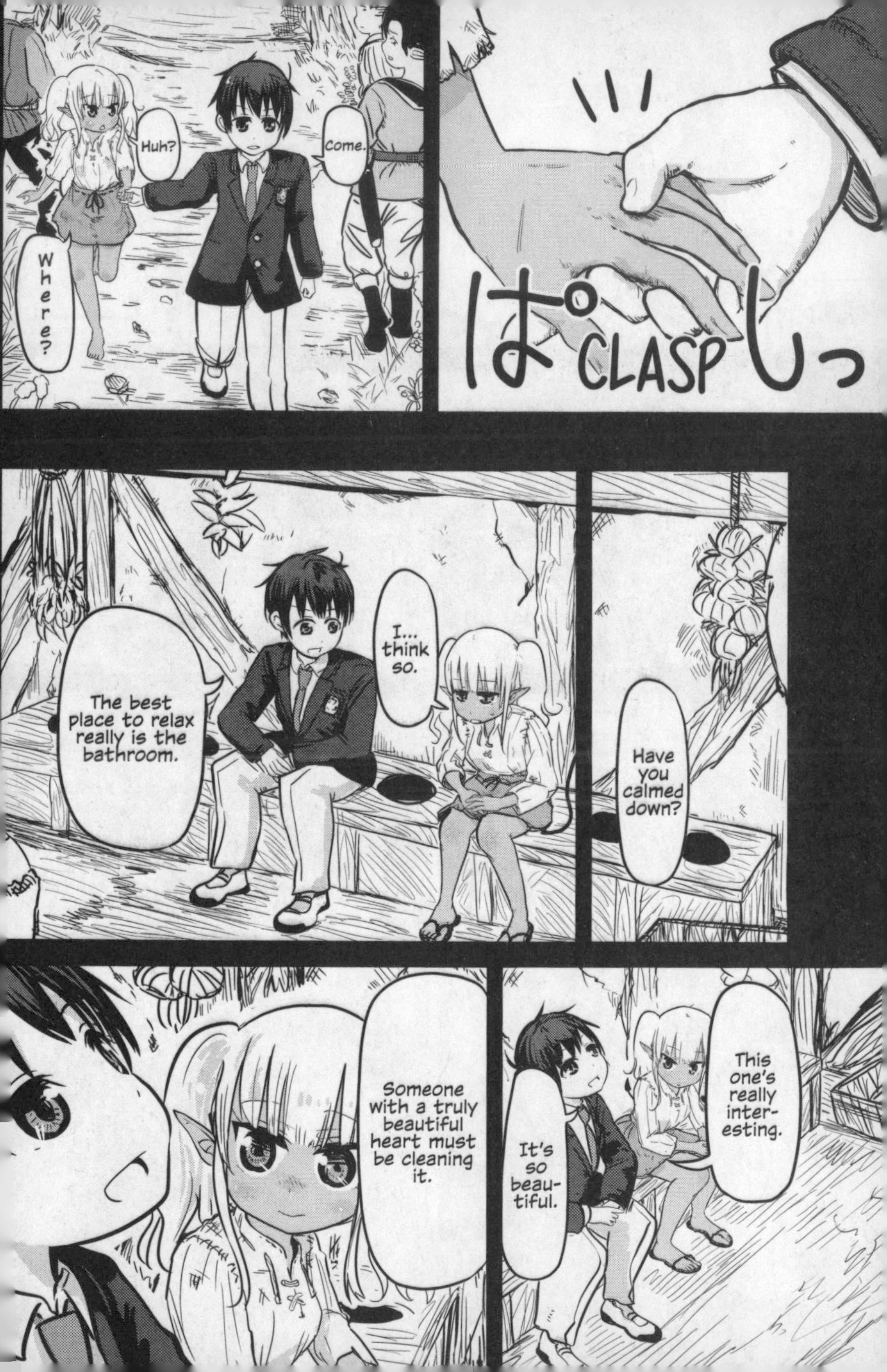
ぱしっ
CLASP
Come.
Huh?
Where?
Have you calmed down?
I... think so.
The best place to relax really is the bathroom.
This one's really interesting.
It's so beautiful.
Someone with a truly beautiful heart must be cleaning it.

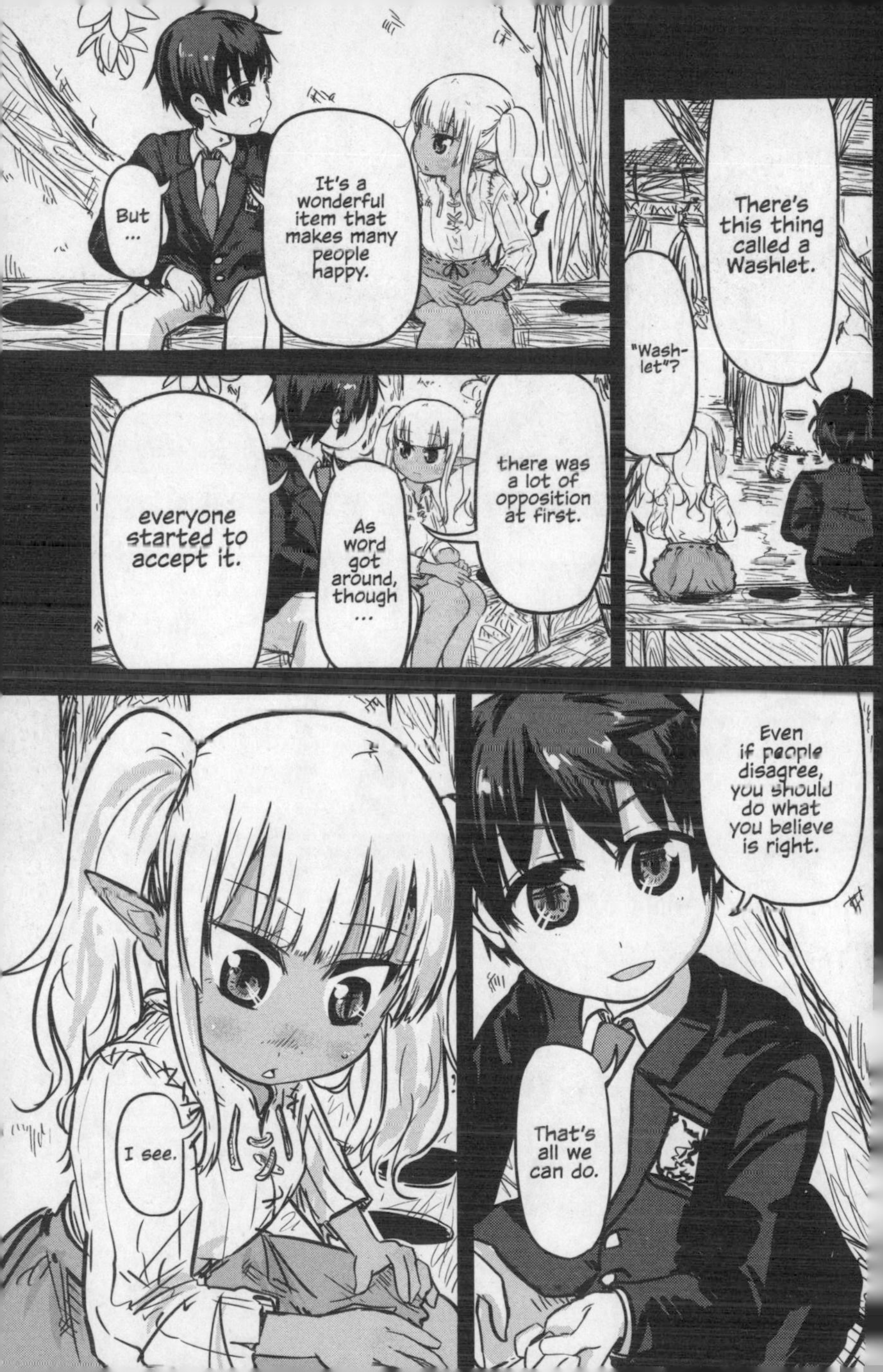
There's this thing called a Washlet.
"Wash-let"?
It's a wonderful item that makes many people happy.
But ...
there was a lot of opposition at first.
As word got around, though ...
everyone started to accept it.
Even if people disagree, you should do what you believe is right.
That's all we can do.
I see.

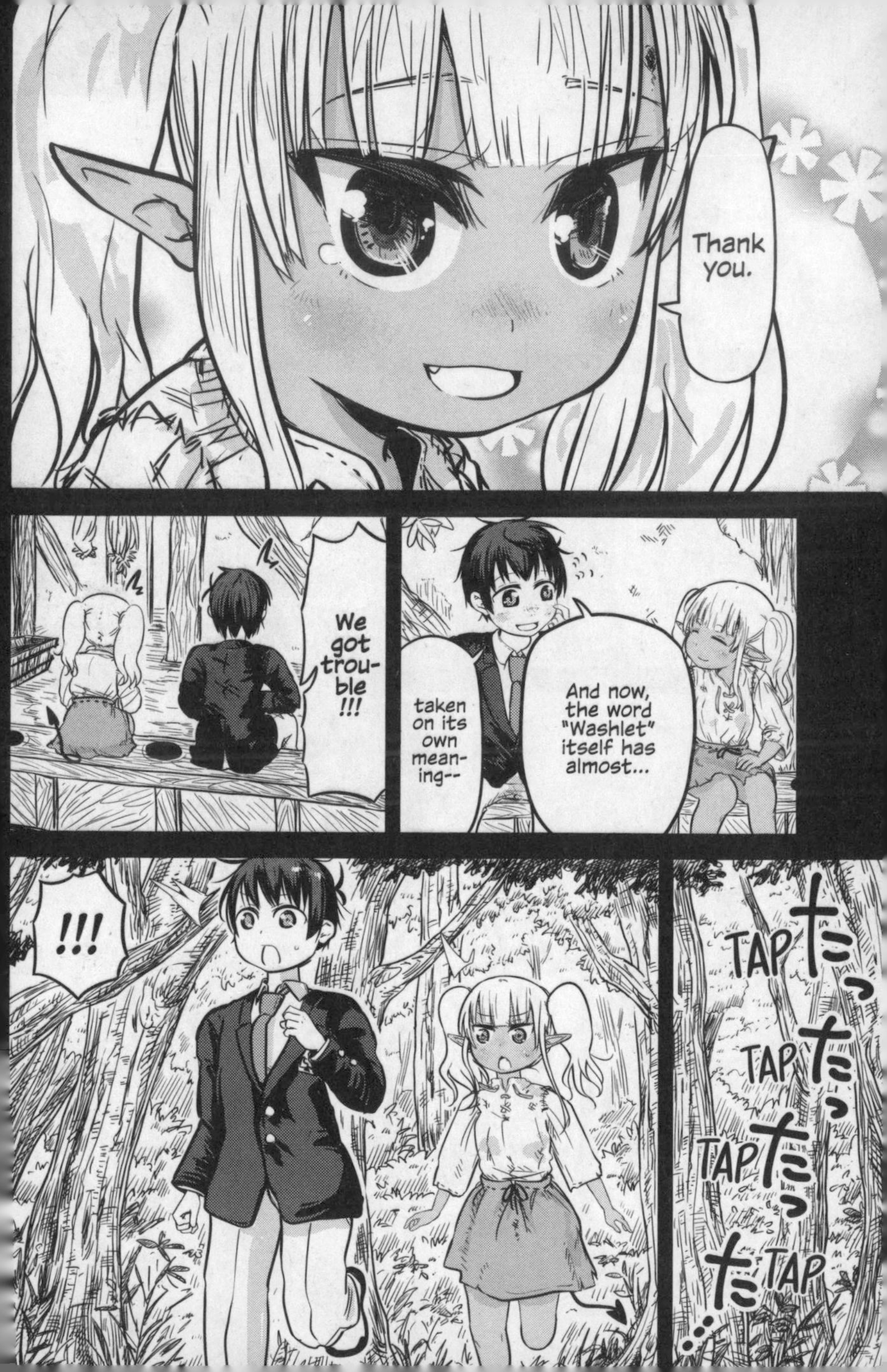
Thank you.
And now, the word "Washlet" itself has almost...
taken on its own meaning--
We got trouble!!!
TAP
TAP
TAP
TAP
!!!

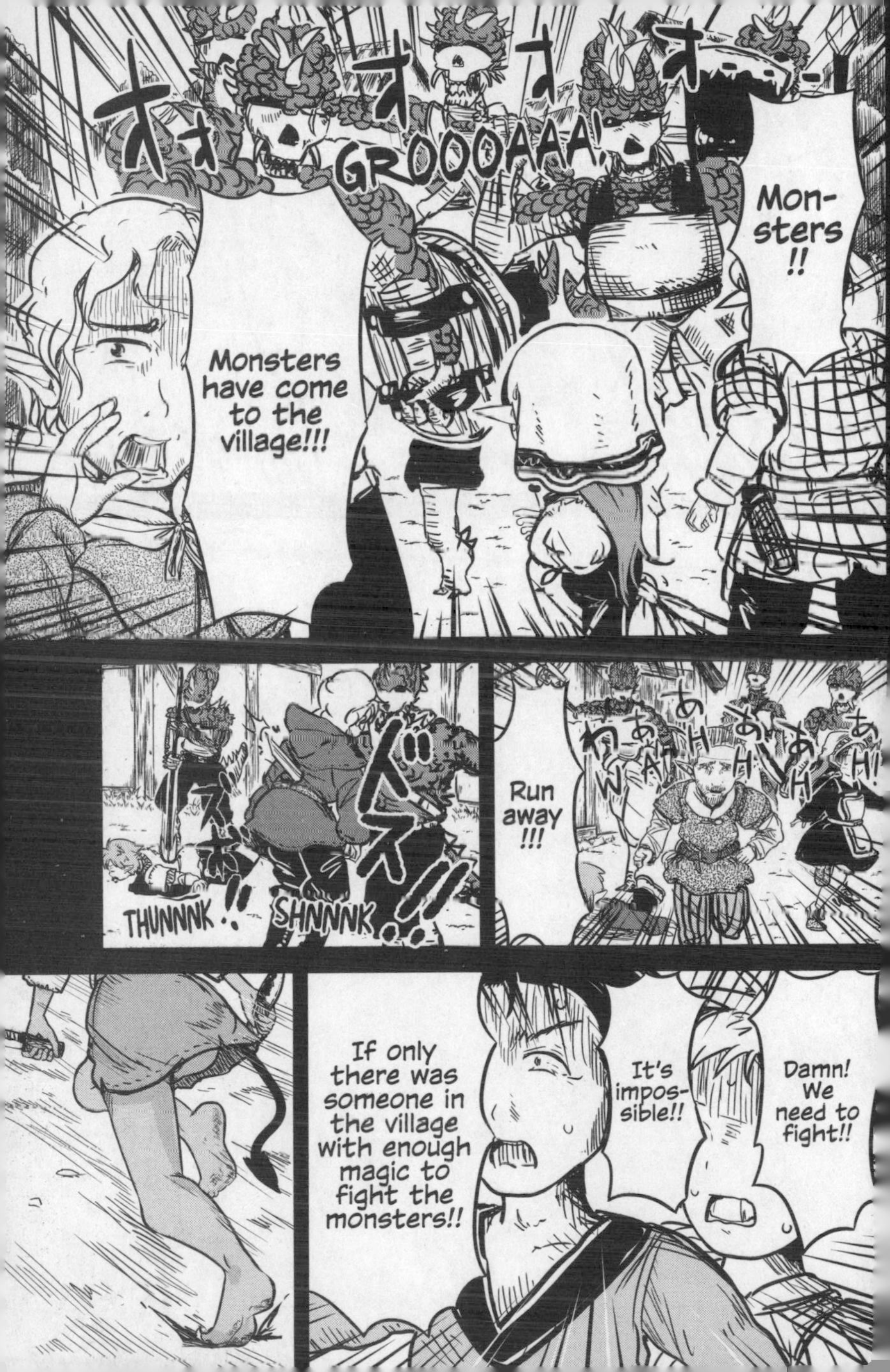
GROOOAAA!
Monsters!!
Monsters have come to the village!!!
Run away!!!
THUNNNK!!
SHNNNK!!
Damn! We need to fight!!
It's impossible!!
If only there was someone in the village with enough magic to fight the monsters!!

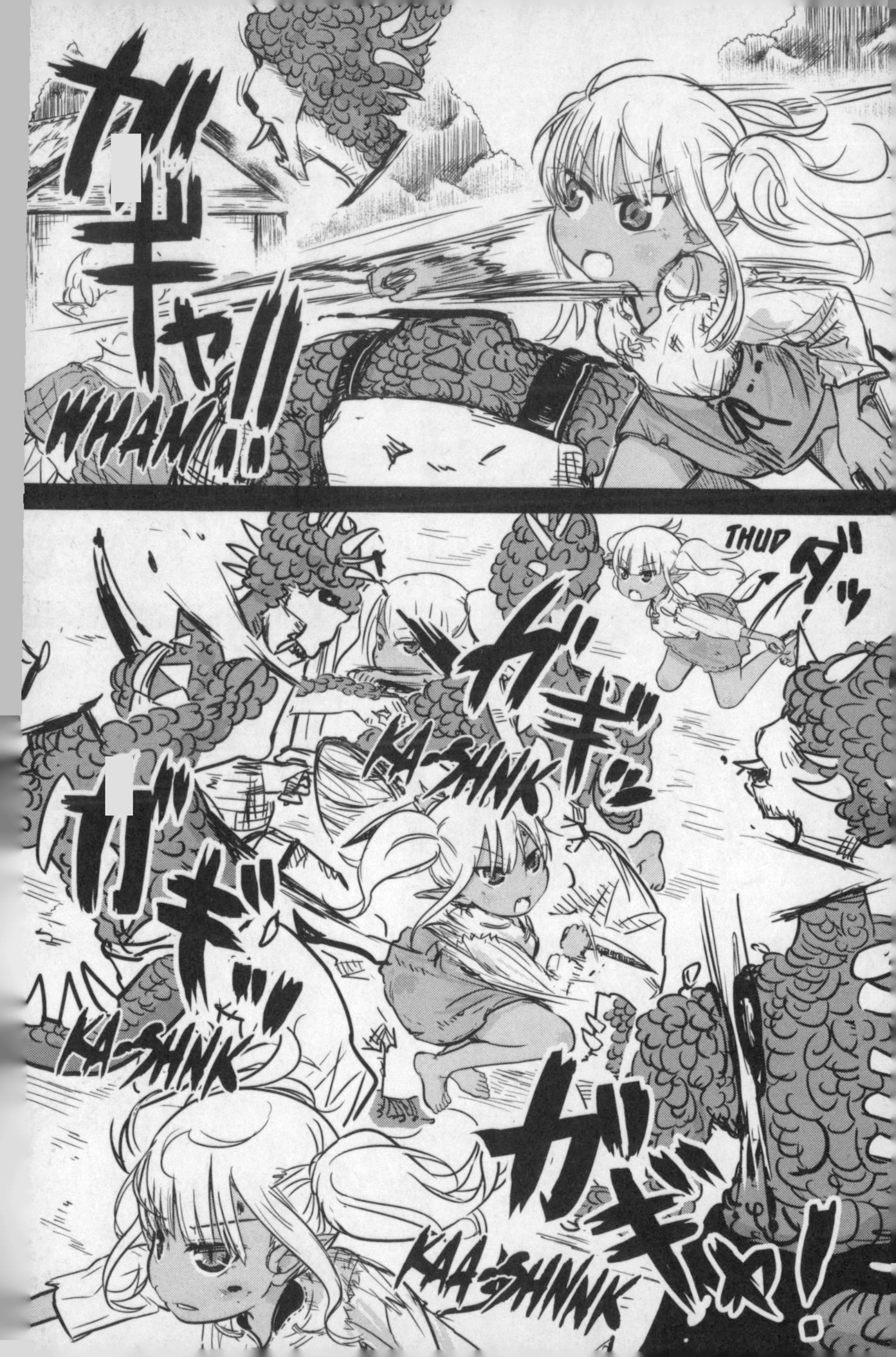
WHAM!!
THUD
ダッ
KA-SHINK
KA-SHINK
KAA-SHINNK

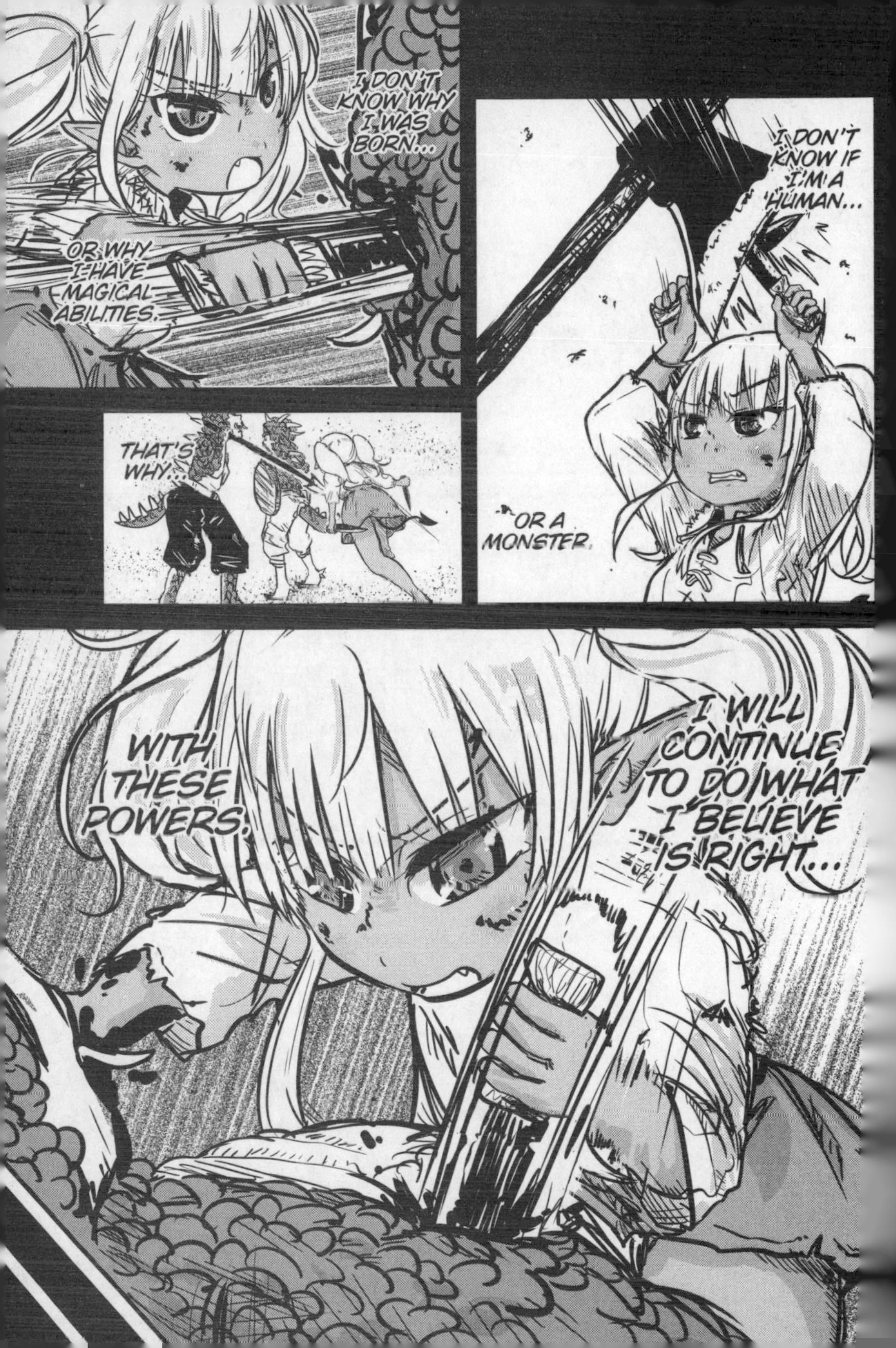
I DON'T KNOW IF I'M A HUMAN...
...OR A MONSTER.
I DON'T KNOW WHY I WAS BORN...
OR WHY I HAVE MAGICAL ABILITIES.
THAT'S WHY...
I WILL CONTINUE TO DO WHAT I BELIEVE IS RIGHT...
WITH THESE POWERS.

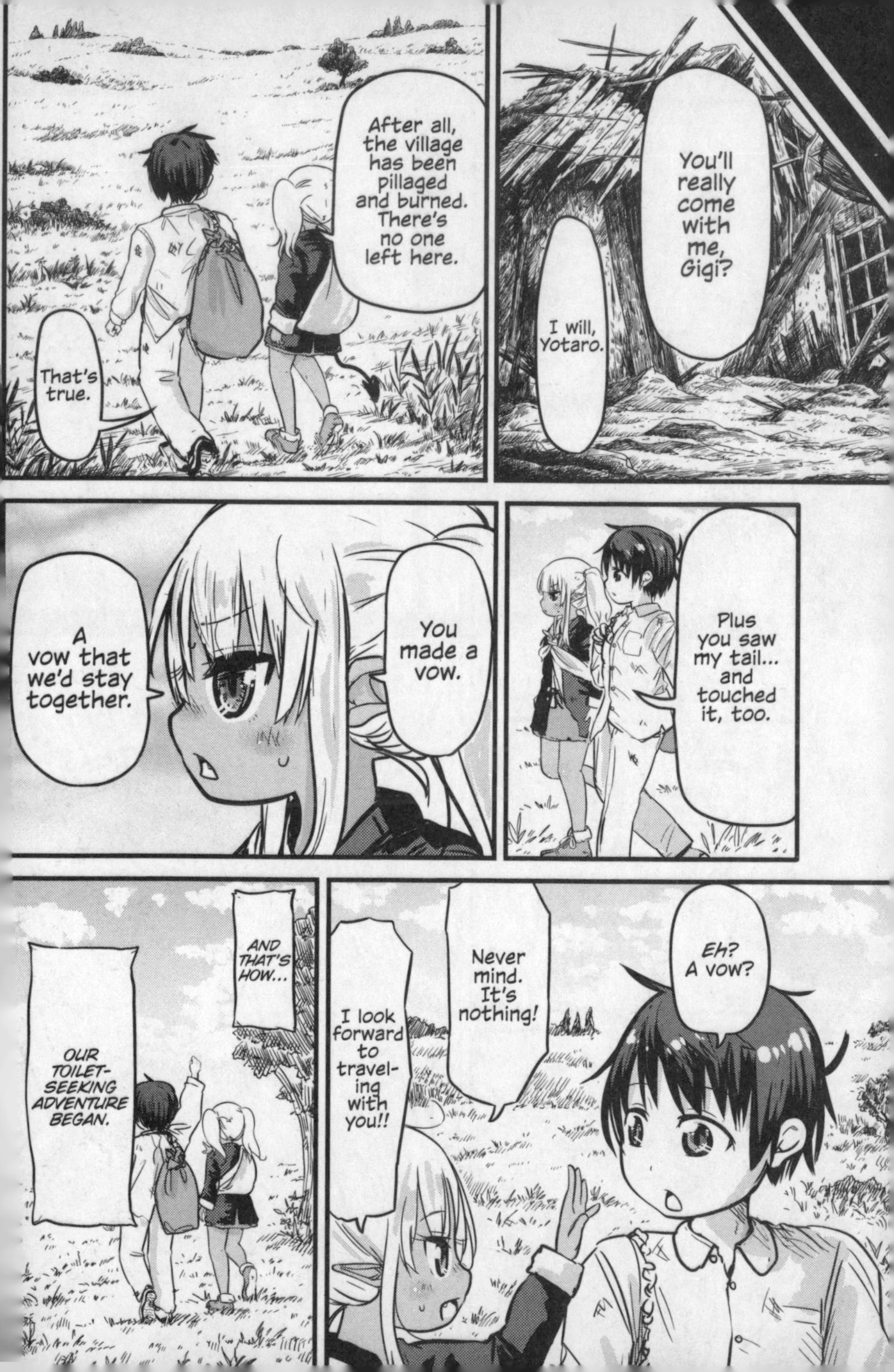
You'll really come with me, Gigi?
I will, Yotaro.
After all, the village has been pillaged and burned. There's no one left here.
That's true.
Plus you saw my tail... and touched it, too.
You made a vow.
A vow that we'd stay together.
Eh? A vow?
Never mind. It's nothing!
I look forward to travel-ing with you!!
AND THAT'S HOW...
OUR TOILET-SEEKING ADVENTURE BEGAN.

TWENTY-THIRD FLUSH

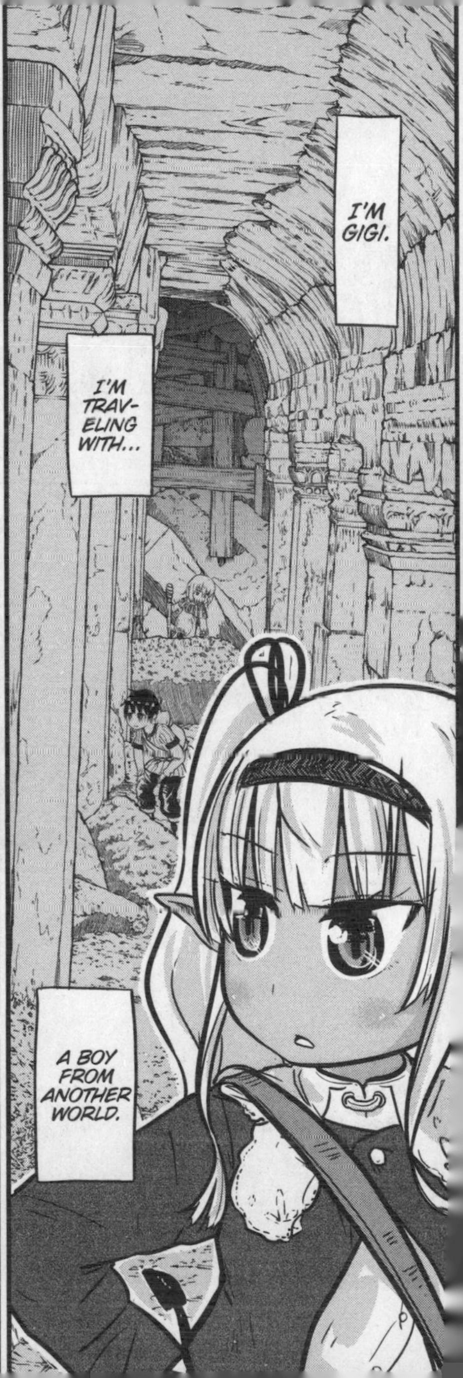
I'M GIGI.
I'M TRAVELING WITH...
A BOY FROM ANOTHER WORLD.

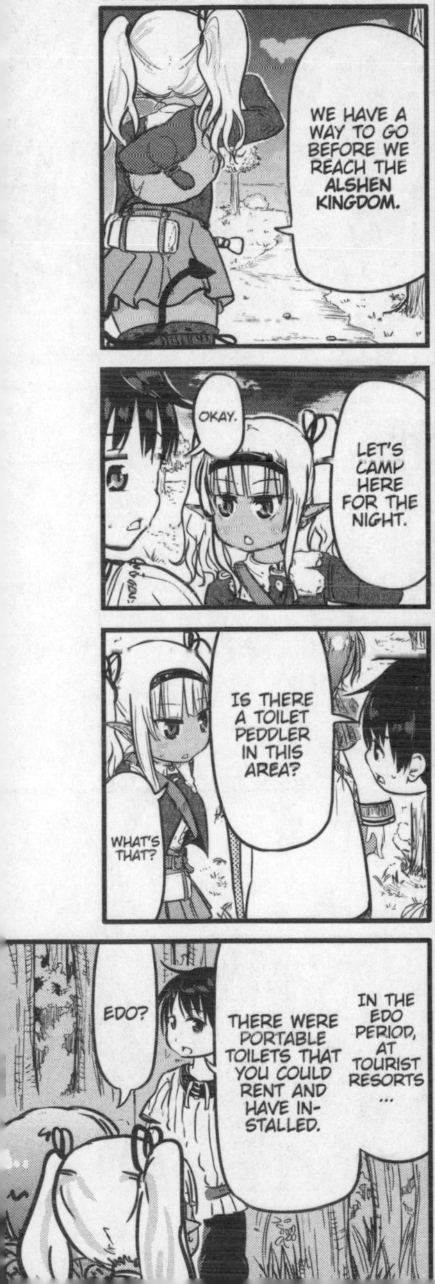
WE HAVE A WAY TO GO BEFORE WE REACH THE ALSHEN KINGDOM.
LET'S CAMP HERE FOR THE NIGHT.
OKAY.
IS THERE A TOILET PEDDLER IN THIS AREA?
WHAT'S THAT?
IN THE EDO PERIOD, AT TOURIST RESORTS...
THERE WERE PORTABLE TOILETS THAT YOU COULD RENT AND HAVE INSTALLED.
EDO?

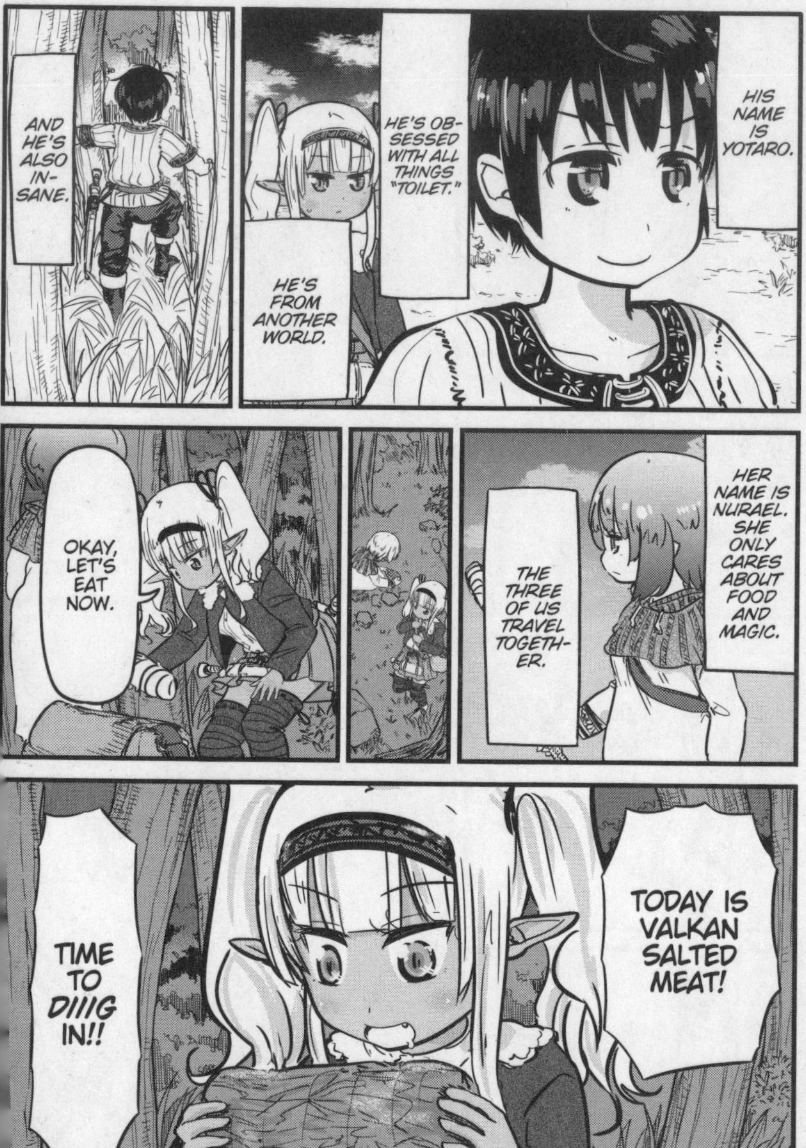

HIS NAME IS YOTARO.
HE'S OBSESSED WITH ALL THINGS "TOILET."
HE'S FROM ANOTHER WORLD.
AND HE'S ALSO INSANE.
HER NAME IS NURAEL. SHE ONLY CARES ABOUT FOOD AND MAGIC.
THE THREE OF US TRAVEL TOGETHER.
OKAY, LET'S EAT NOW.
TODAY IS VALKAN SALTED MEAT!
TIME TO *DIIIG* IN!!

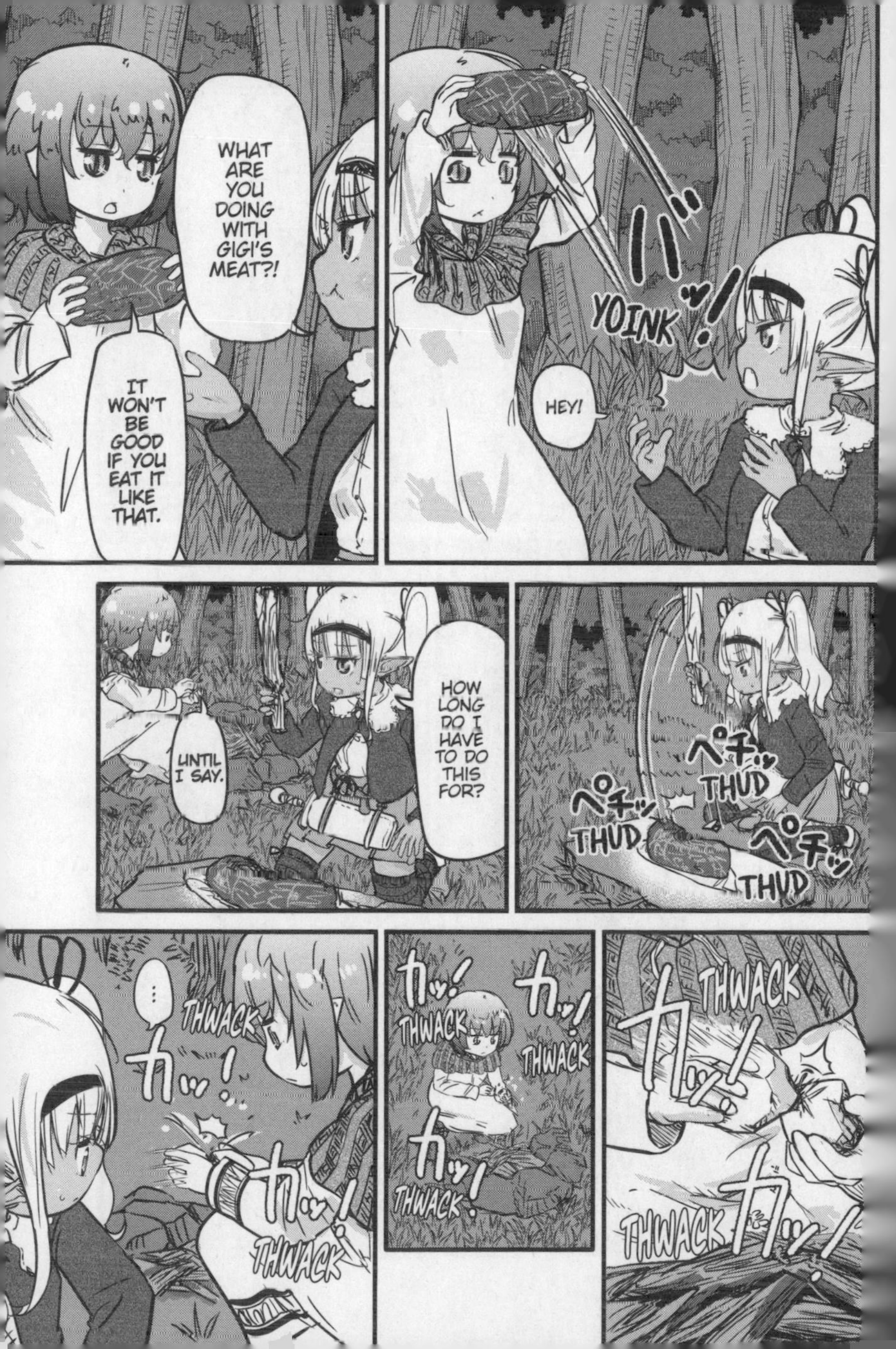
バッ
YOINK
HEY!
WHAT ARE YOU DOING WITH GIGI'S MEAT?!
IT WON'T BE GOOD IF YOU EAT IT LIKE THAT.
ペチッ
THUD
ペチッ
THUD
ペチッ
THUD
HOW LONG DO I HAVE TO DO THIS FOR?
UNTIL I SAY.
THWACK
カッ!
THWACK
カッ!
カッ!
THWACK
THWACK
THWACK
カッ!
THWACK
…
THWACK
カッ!
カッ!
THWACK

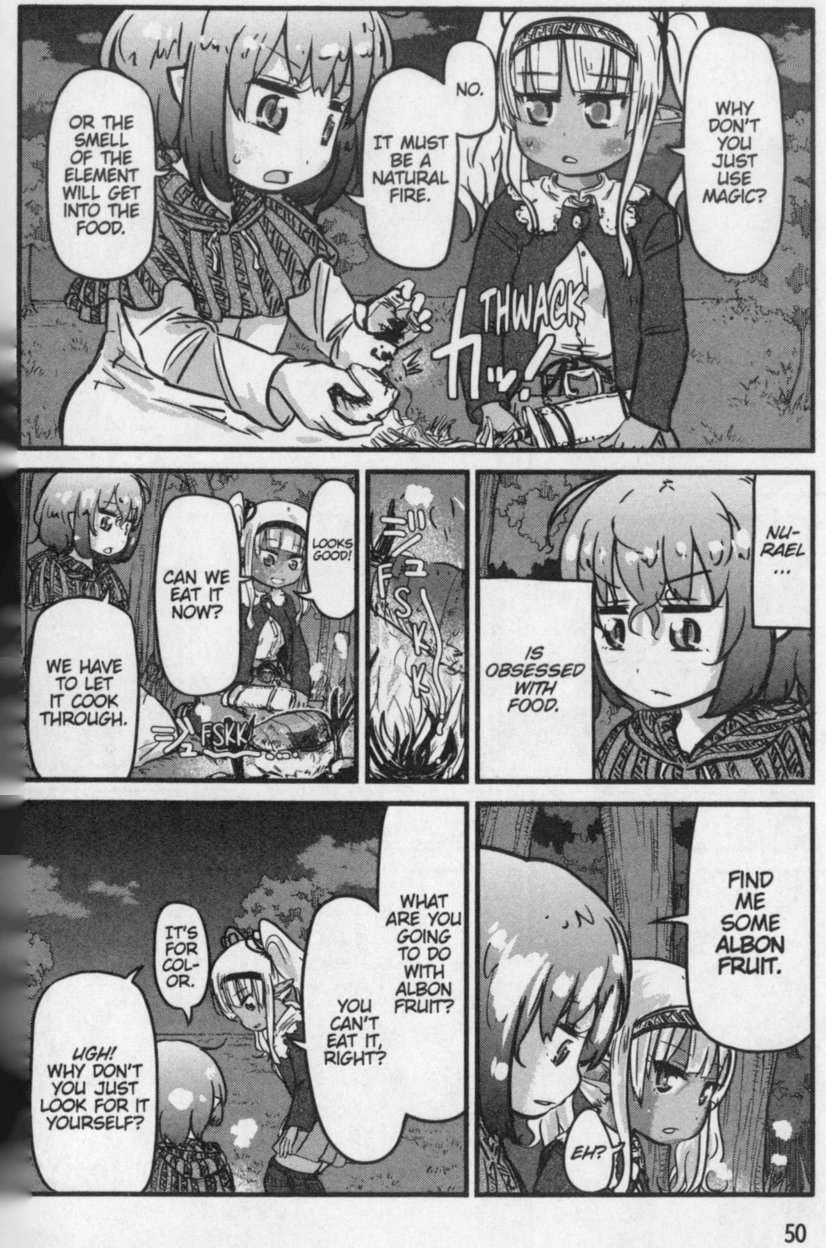
WHY DON'T YOU JUST USE MAGIC?
NO.
IT MUST BE A NATURAL FIRE.
OR THE SMELL OF THE ELEMENT WILL GET INTO THE FOOD.
THWACK
NU-RAEL...
IS OBSESSED WITH FOOD.
FSKK
LOOKS GOOD!
CAN WE EAT IT NOW?
WE HAVE TO LET IT COOK THROUGH.
FSKK
FIND ME SOME ALBON FRUIT.
EH?
WHAT ARE YOU GOING TO DO WITH ALBON FRUIT?
YOU CAN'T EAT IT, RIGHT?
IT'S FOR COL-OR.
UGH! WHY DON'T YOU JUST LOOK FOR IT YOURSELF?

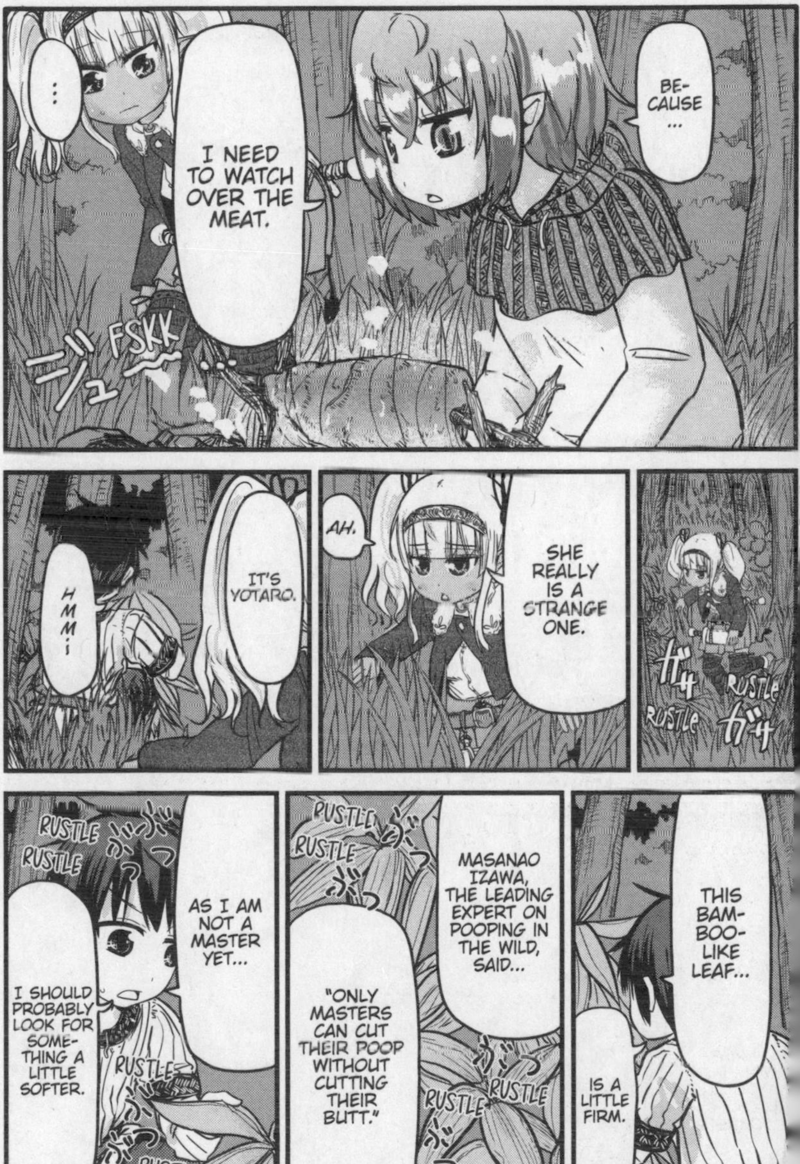
BE-CAUSE ...
I NEED TO WATCH OVER THE MEAT.
...
FSKK
RUSTLE
RUSTLE
AH.
SHE REALLY IS A STRANGE ONE.
IT'S YOTARO.
HMM!
THIS BAMBOO-LIKE LEAF...
IS A LITTLE FIRM.
RUSTLE
RUSTLE
MASANAO IZAWA, THE LEADING EXPERT ON POOPING IN THE WILD, SAID...
"ONLY MASTERS CAN CUT THEIR POOP WITHOUT CUTTING THEIR BUTT."
RUSTLE
RUSTLE
RUSTLE
RUSTLE
AS I AM NOT A MASTER YET...
I SHOULD PROBABLY LOOK FOR SOMETHING A LITTLE SOFTER.
RUSTLE
RUSTLE

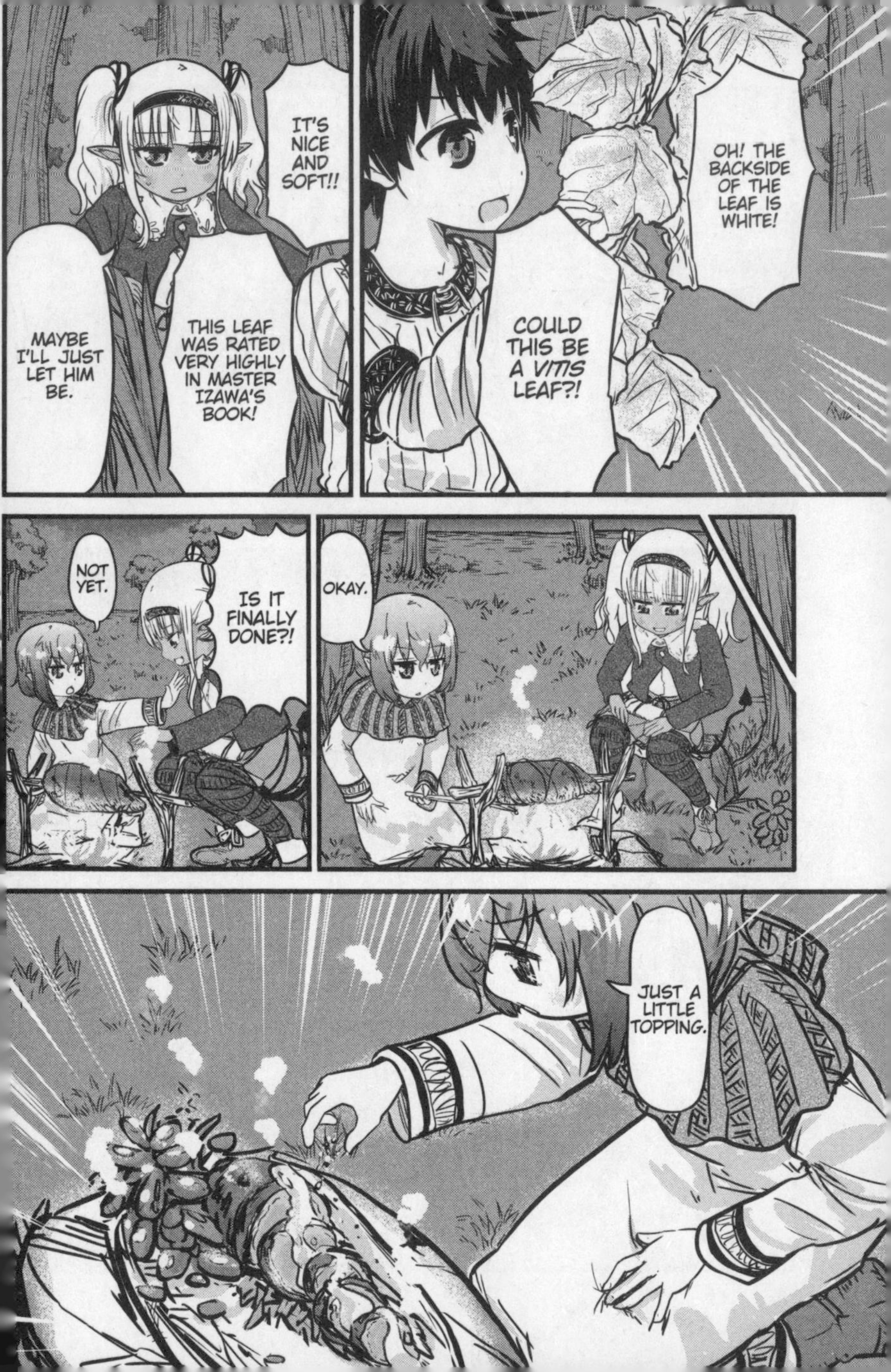
OH! THE BACKSIDE OF THE LEAF IS WHITE!
COULD THIS BE A *VITIS* LEAF?!
IT'S NICE AND SOFT!!
THIS LEAF WAS RATED VERY HIGHLY IN MASTER IZAWA'S BOOK!
MAYBE I'LL JUST LET HIM BE.
OKAY.
IS IT FINALLY DONE?!
NOT YET.
JUST A LITTLE TOPPING.

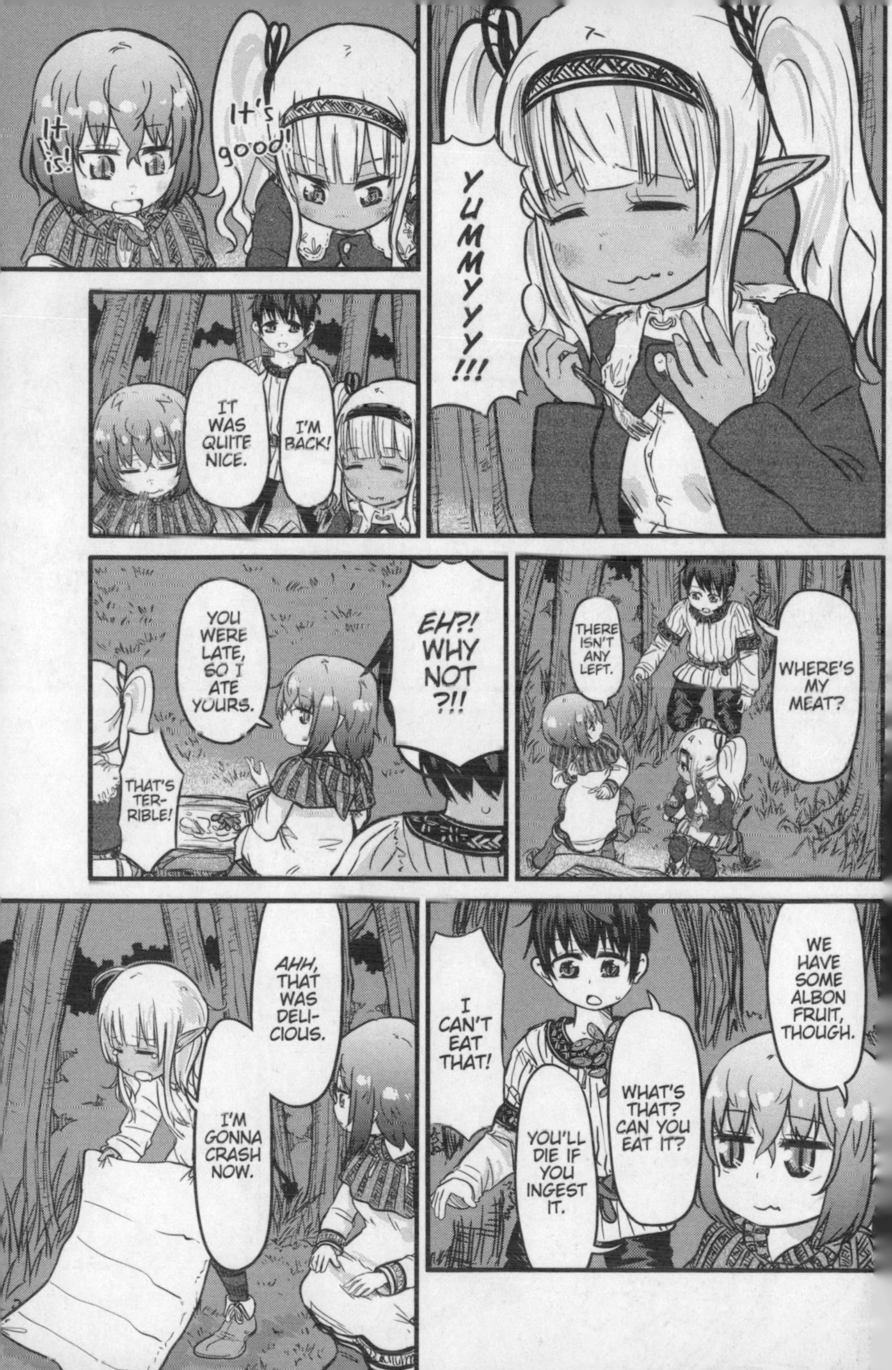
YUMMYYY!!!
It's good!
It is!
I'M BACK!
IT WAS QUITE NICE.
WHERE'S MY MEAT?
THERE ISN'T ANY LEFT.
EH?! WHY NOT?!!
YOU WERE LATE, SO I ATE YOURS.
THAT'S TER-RIBLE!
WE HAVE SOME ALBON FRUIT, THOUGH.
WHAT'S THAT? CAN YOU EAT IT?
YOU'LL DIE IF YOU INGEST IT.
I CAN'T EAT THAT!
AHH, THAT WAS DELI-CIOUS.
I'M GONNA CRASH NOW.

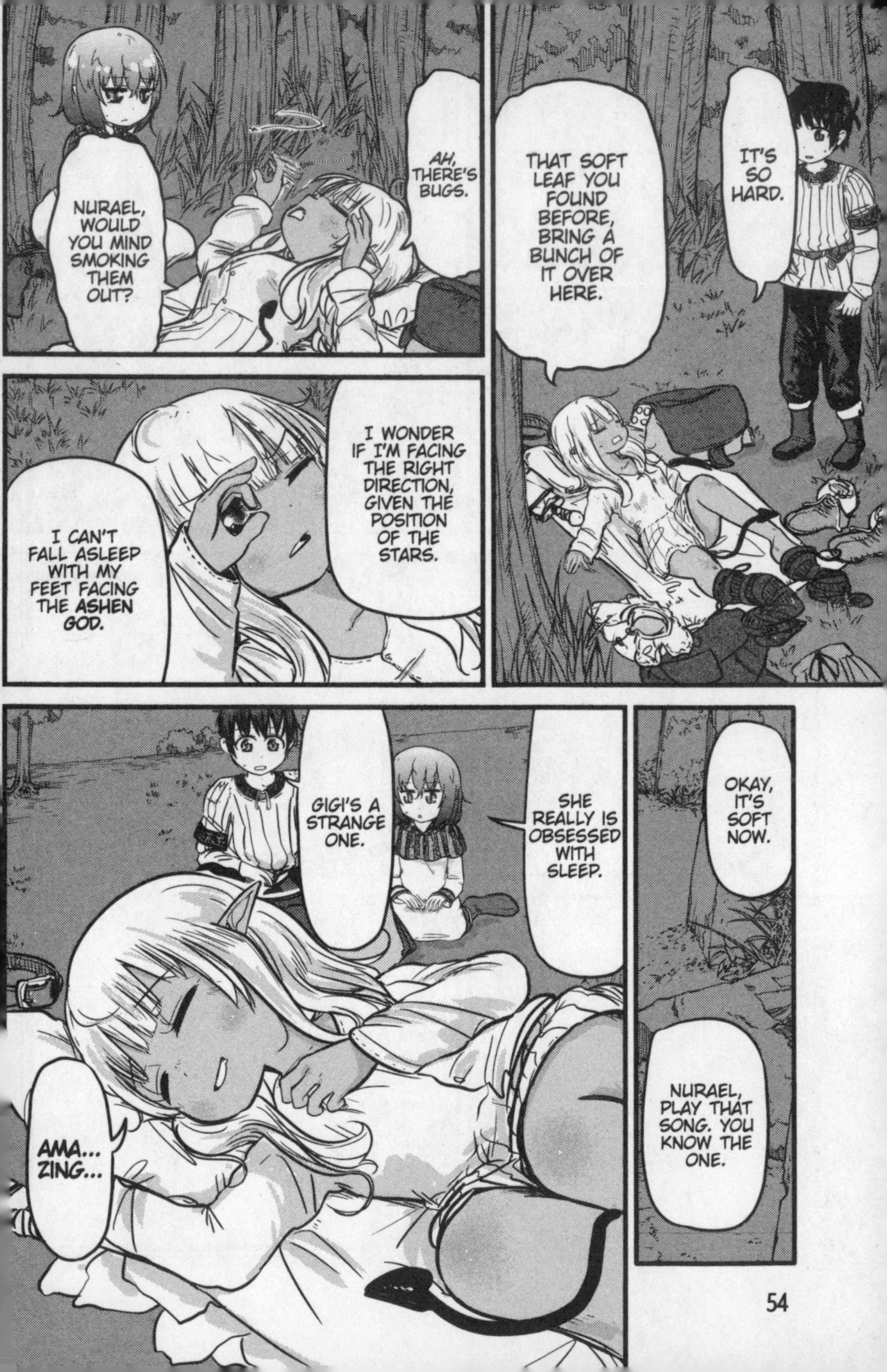
IT'S SO HARD.
THAT SOFT LEAF YOU FOUND BEFORE, BRING A BUNCH OF IT OVER HERE.
AH, THERE'S BUGS.
NURAEL, WOULD YOU MIND SMOKING THEM OUT?
I WONDER IF I'M FACING THE RIGHT DIRECTION, GIVEN THE POSITION OF THE STARS.
I CAN'T FALL ASLEEP WITH MY FEET FACING THE ASHEN GOD.
OKAY, IT'S SOFT NOW.
NURAEL, PLAY THAT SONG. YOU KNOW THE ONE.
SHE REALLY IS OBSESSED WITH SLEEP.
GIGI'S A STRANGE ONE.
AMA... ZING...

ROOTS

PEOPLE WHO DON'T VALUE TOILET TIME ARE NO GOOD.

TWELFTH TOILET TIME

In this column, I'd like to introduce various ways to make your bathroom more comfortable.

First, I'll talk about how different cultures wipe their butts in an article titled, "The End-all of Butts in the East and West." How did we arrive at the Washlet we know today? It may have been a longer journey than you think.

No. 1: Paper
Paper is probably the most familiar tool for wiping your bottom. The first record of humans wiping with paper can be found in the sixth century Chinese book *Yanshi Jiaxun*. I'd like to give the Nobel Prize to the first person who used paper, but the details remain a mystery.
By the way, the current roll-type toilet paper was born in the U.S. around 1880.

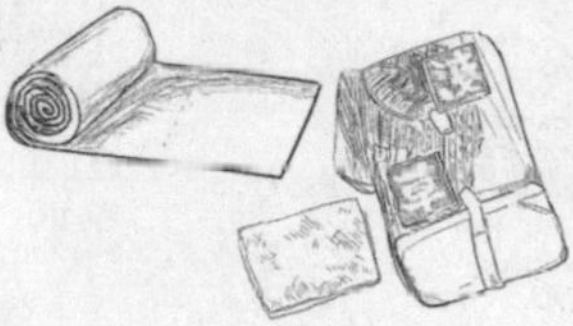

No. 2: Sand and Stone
In some desert areas, such as Saudi Arabia, people used to wipe their butts with sand. The fine grains are gentle on the buttocks. Once you wipe, the rest comes right off, and your bottom is clean. In other areas, such as Egypt, people used pebbles to wipe their bottoms. There are endless stones available, so you can just throw them away after using them. Please note that freshly chosen stones can be hot, so let them cool down first.

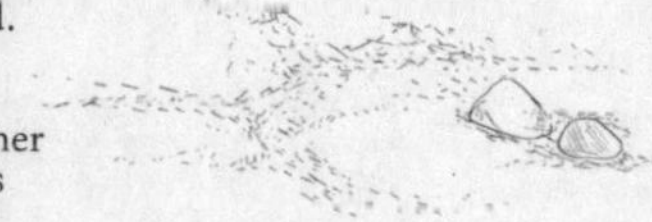

No. 3: Water and Finger
This is a revolutionary method that is still used in India. First, you must drip water around the tailbone, which will naturally flow between your cheeks. Then, after wiping with your fingers, use the remaining water to clean yourself. However, you must use your left hand to wipe. You might think, "Disgusting!" But it's actually much cleaner and less likely to cause hemorrhoids than wiping with paper.

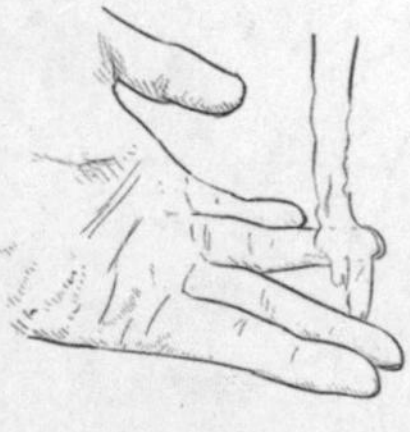

No. 4: Plants
Wiping with the leaves and stems of various plants has always been a favorite of humankind around the world. In particular, wiping with the leaves of Japanese butterbur is said to be quite comfortable. In the U.S., it was common to wipe with a corn cob. I call this "hipcorn."

Summary
Don't say, "Why don't you just leave my butt alone?" Humankind has developed many ways to wipe our butts, and we should continue to develop new and better methods. Due to page limitations, we can't introduce them all in this article, but there are many other methods out there! May you all have a wonderful toilet life this year!

IN OTHER WORDS

THIS MAXIM

"ONLY MASTERS CAN CUT THEIR POOP WITHOUT CUTTING THEIR BUTT."
-MASANAO IZAWA, *POOPING IN THE WILD*

THE RHINOCEROS IS KNOWN...
FOR ITS POOP SPRAY.
IT USES ITS POO TO MARK ITS TERRITORY.
THEN SPREADS IT AROUND WITH ITS TAIL.
IT ALSO MAKES ITS NEWBORNS EAT POOP.
THIS TRANSFERS HELPFUL BACTERIA TO THE BABY'S SYSTEM.
YOU SEE? TAILS ARE A GOOD THING!
REALLY?

TWENTY-FOURTH FLUSH

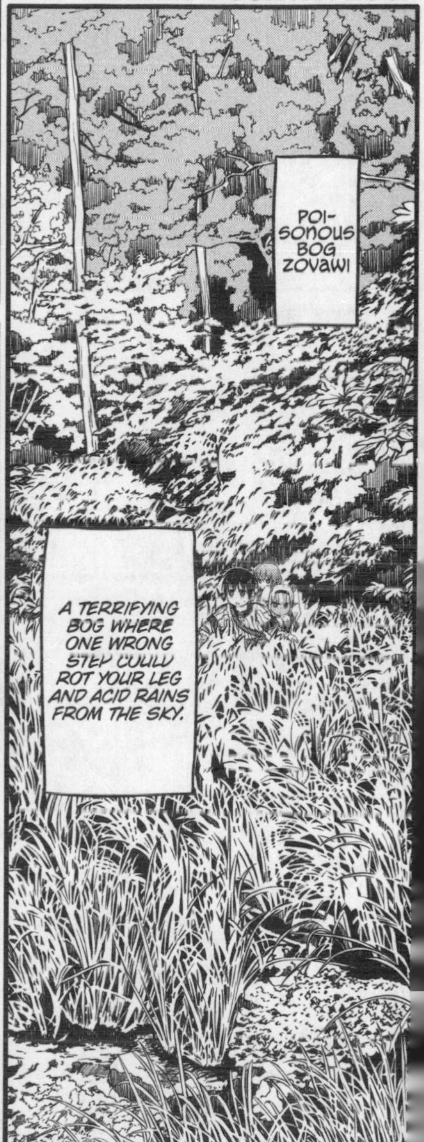
POI-SONOUS BOG ZOVAWI
A TERRIFYING BOG WHERE ONE WRONG STEP COULD ROT YOUR LEG AND ACID RAINS FROM THE SKY.

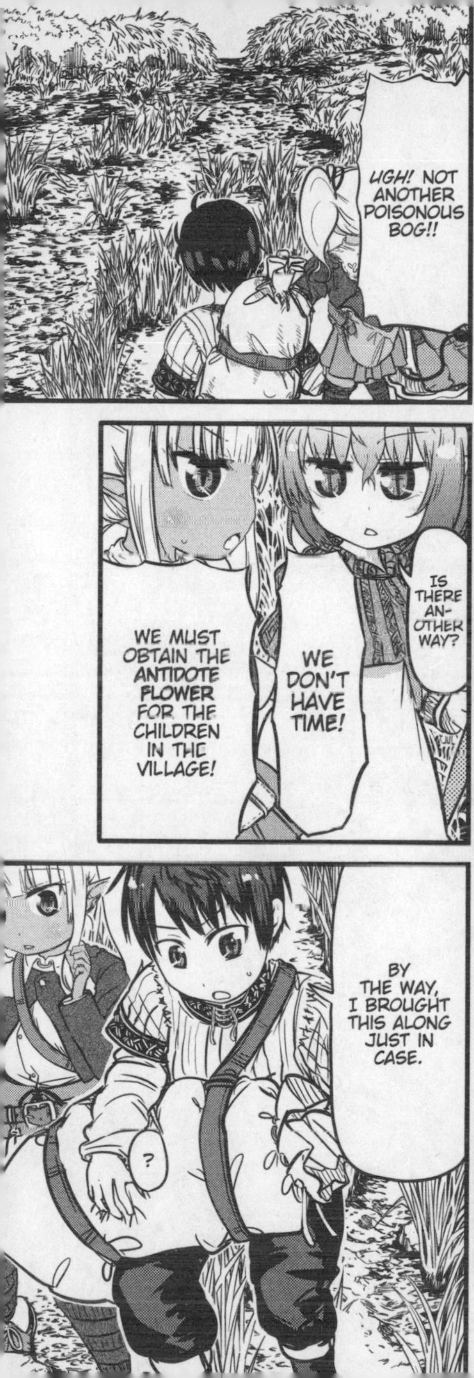
UGH! NOT ANOTHER POISONOUS BOG!!
IS THERE AN-OTHER WAY?
WE DON'T HAVE TIME!
WE MUST OBTAIN THE ANTIDOTE FLOWER FOR THE CHILDREN IN THE VILLAGE!
BY THE WAY, I BROUGHT THIS ALONG JUST IN CASE.
?

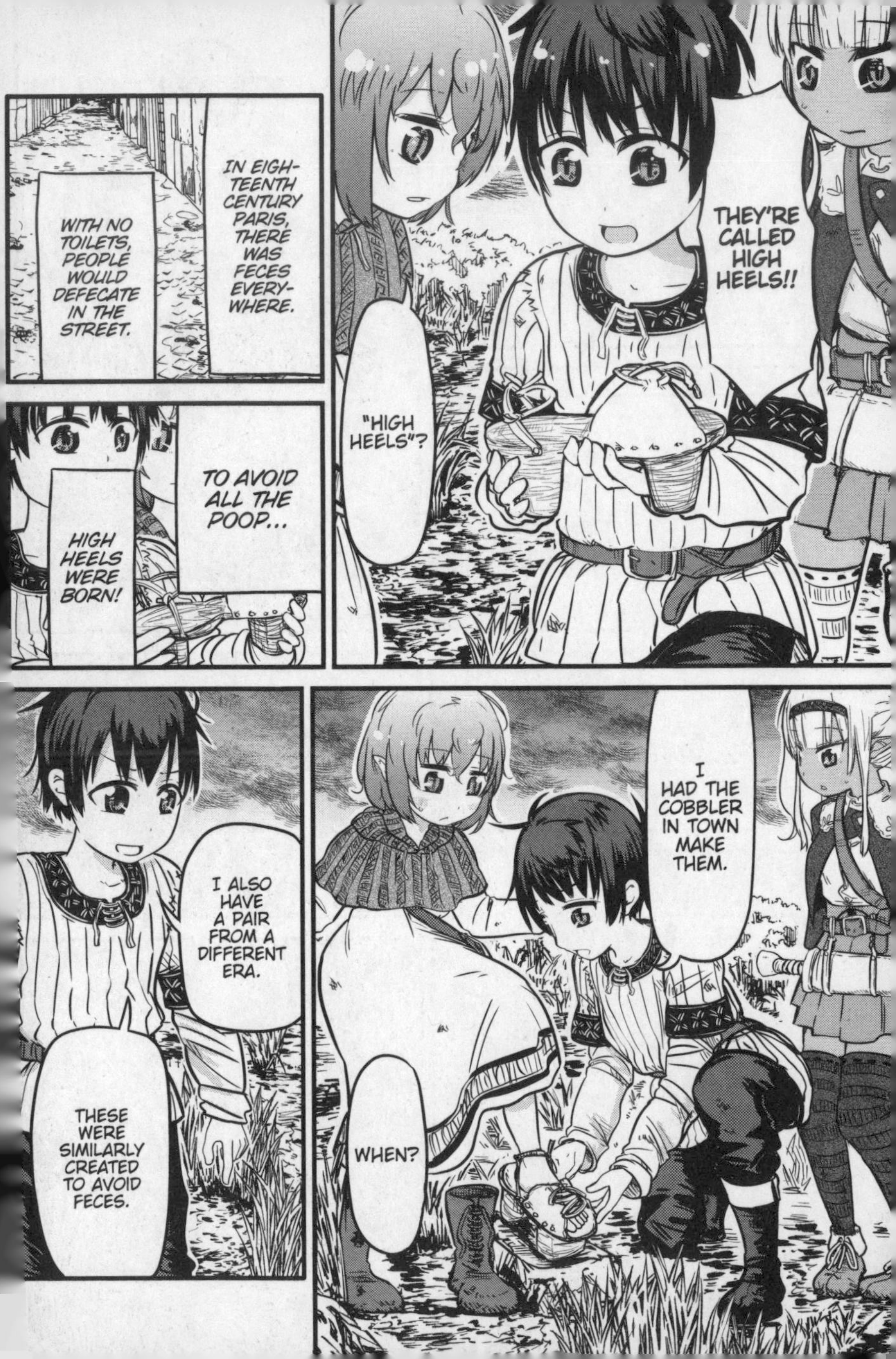
THEY'RE CALLED HIGH HEELS!!
"HIGH HEELS"?
IN EIGHTEENTH CENTURY PARIS, THERE WAS FECES EVERYWHERE.
WITH NO TOILETS, PEOPLE WOULD DEFECATE IN THE STREET.
TO AVOID ALL THE POOP...
HIGH HEELS WERE BORN!
I HAD THE COBBLER IN TOWN MAKE THEM.
WHEN?
I ALSO HAVE A PAIR FROM A DIFFERENT ERA.
THESE WERE SIMILARLY CREATED TO AVOID FECES.

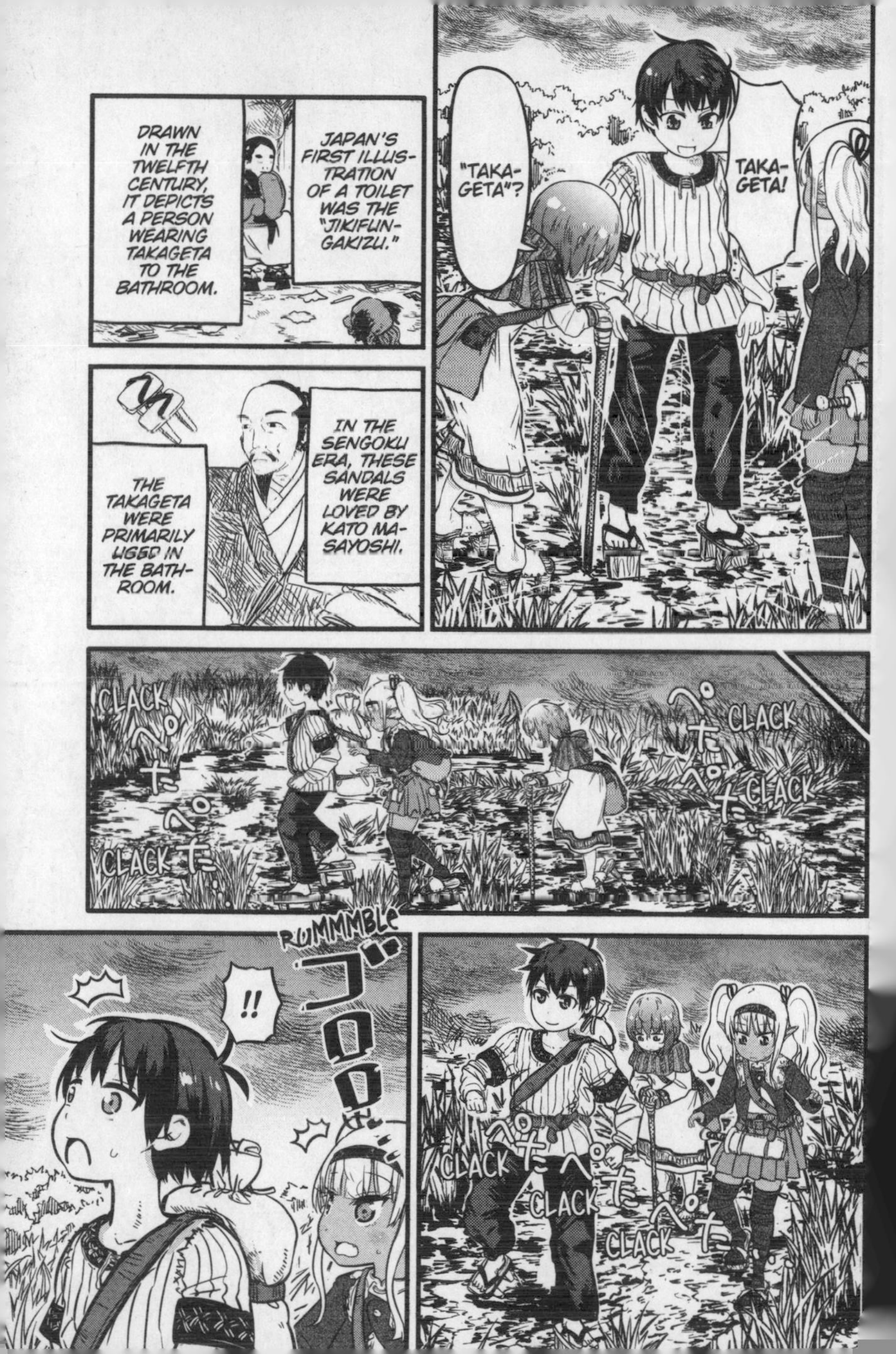
TAKA-GETA!
"TAKA-GETA"?
JAPAN'S FIRST ILLUSTRATION OF A TOILET WAS THE "JIKIFUN-GAKIZU."
DRAWN IN THE TWELFTH CENTURY, IT DEPICTS A PERSON WEARING TAKAGETA TO THE BATHROOM.
IN THE SENGOKU ERA, THESE SANDALS WERE LOVED BY KATO MASAYOSHI.
THE TAKAGETA WERE PRIMARILY USED IN THE BATHROOM.
ぺた CLACK
ぺた CLACK
CLACK ぺた
CLACK ぺた
CLACK ぺた
CLACK ぺた
CLACK ぺた
RUMMMBLE
ゴロロ
!!

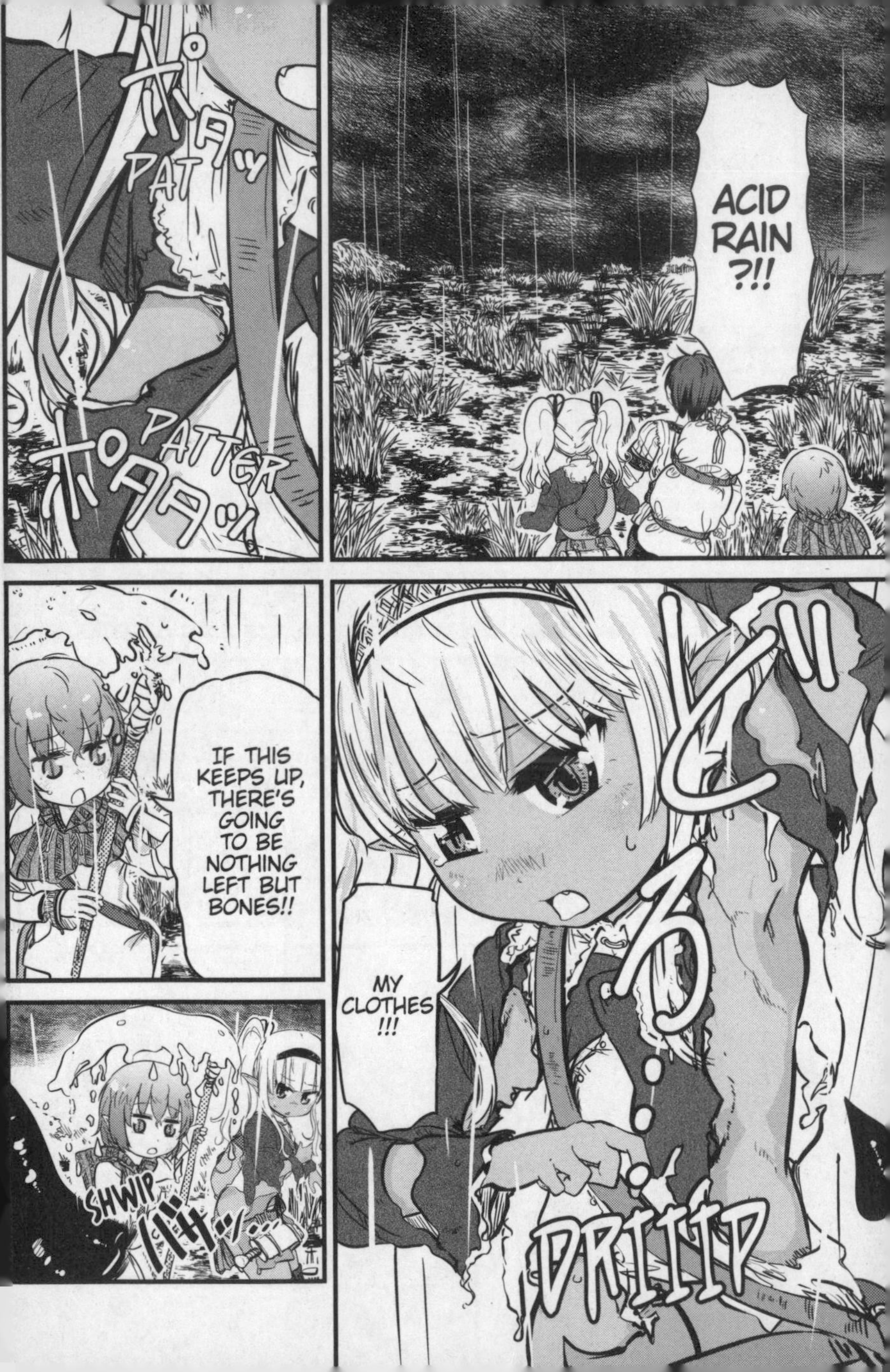
ACID RAIN ?!!
PAT
PATTER
MY CLOTHES !!!
DRIIIP
IF THIS KEEPS UP, THERE'S GOING TO BE NOTHING LEFT BUT BONES!!
SHWIP

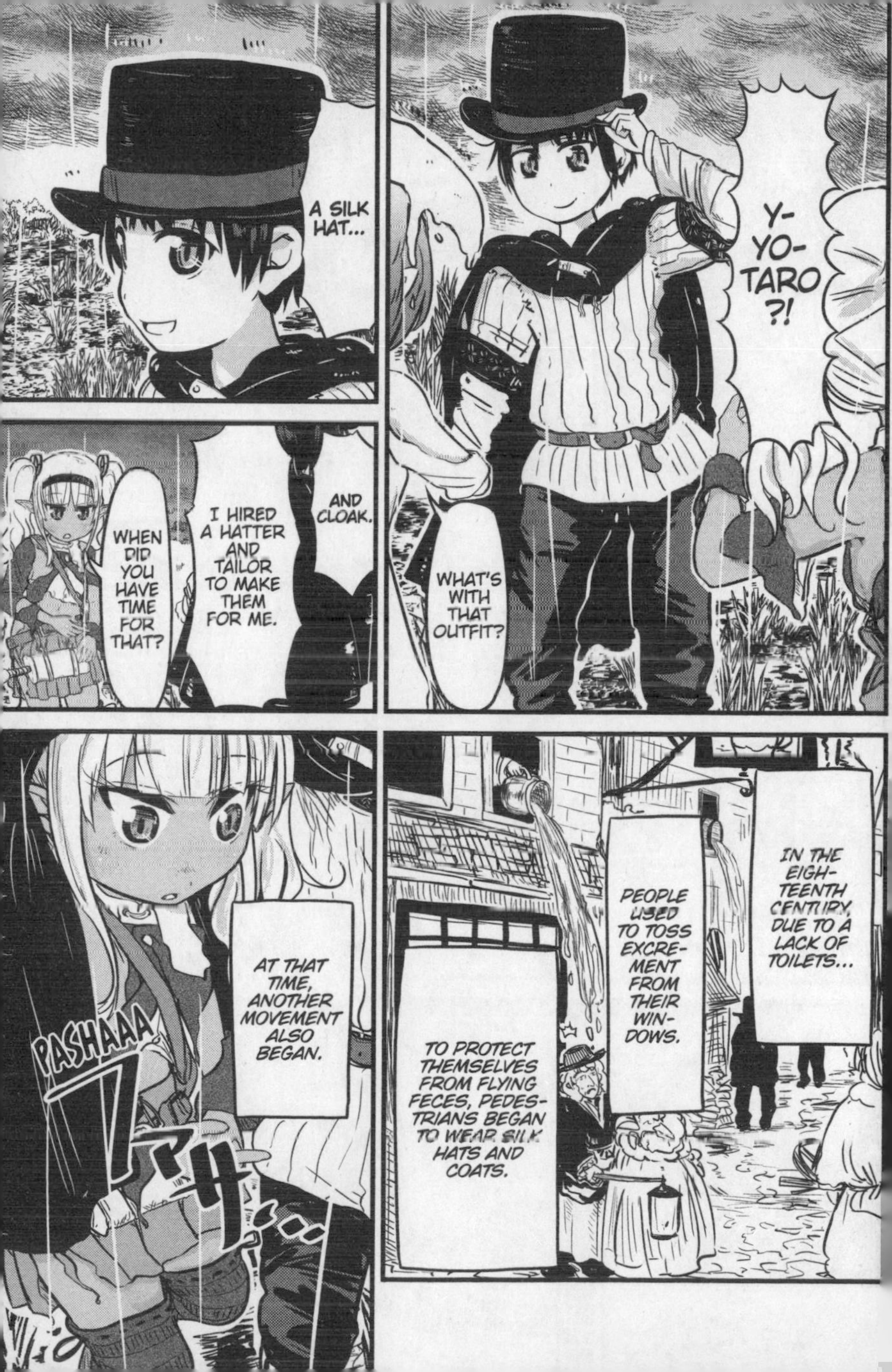

Y-YO-TARO?!
WHAT'S WITH THAT OUTFIT?
A SILK HAT...
AND CLOAK.
I HIRED A HATTER AND TAILOR TO MAKE THEM FOR ME.
WHEN DID YOU HAVE TIME FOR THAT?
IN THE EIGHTEENTH CENTURY, DUE TO A LACK OF TOILETS...
PEOPLE USED TO TOSS EXCREMENT FROM THEIR WINDOWS.
TO PROTECT THEMSELVES FROM FLYING FECES, PEDESTRIANS BEGAN TO WEAR SILK HATS AND COATS.
AT THAT TIME, ANOTHER MOVEMENT ALSO BEGAN.
PASHAAA

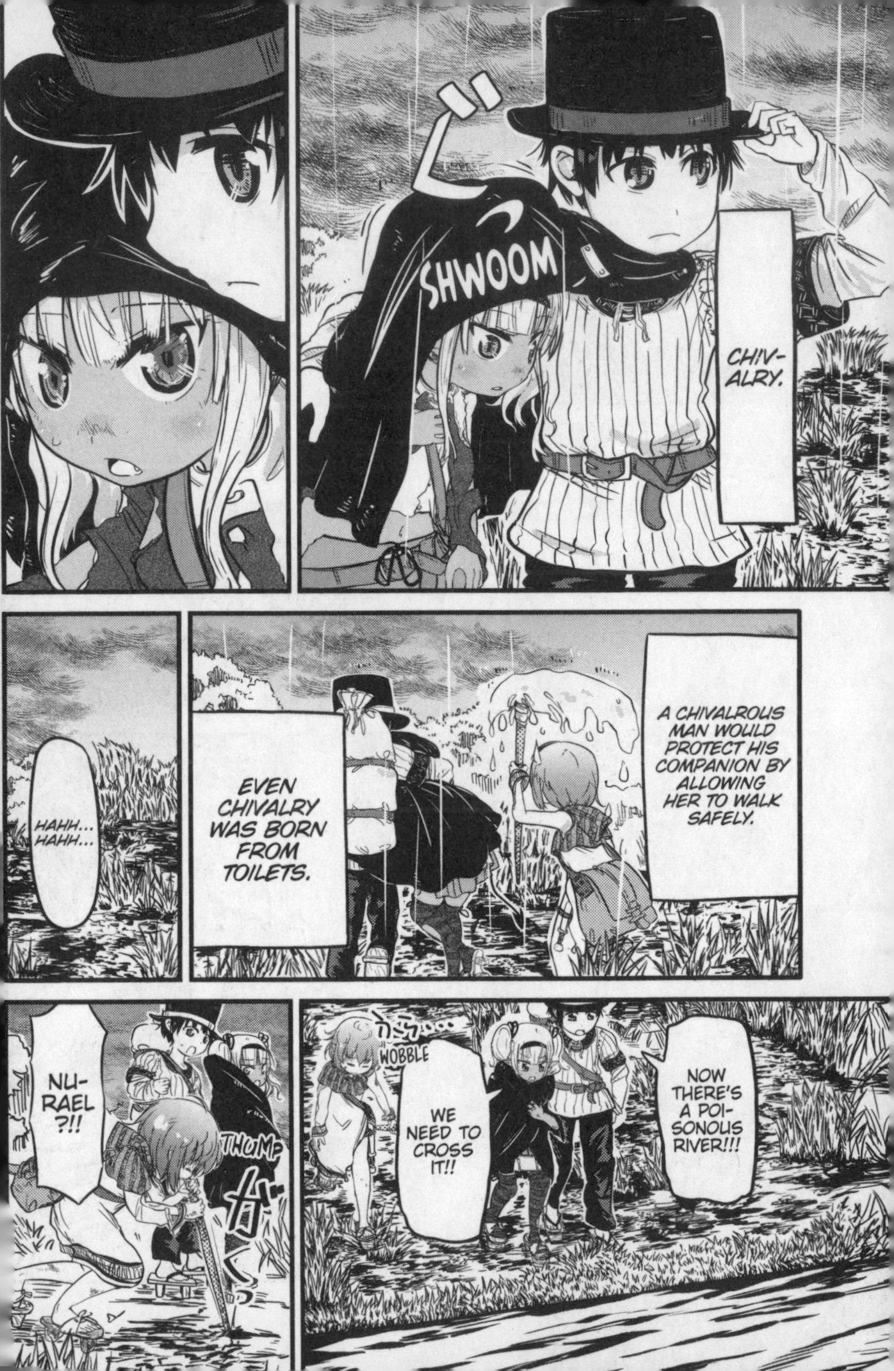
SHWOOM
CHIV-ALRY.
A CHIVALROUS MAN WOULD PROTECT HIS COMPANION BY ALLOWING HER TO WALK SAFELY.
EVEN CHIVALRY WAS BORN FROM TOILETS.
HAHH... HAHH...
NOW THERE'S A POI-SONOUS RIVER!!!
WOBBLE
WE NEED TO CROSS IT!!
NU-RAEL ?!!
THUMP

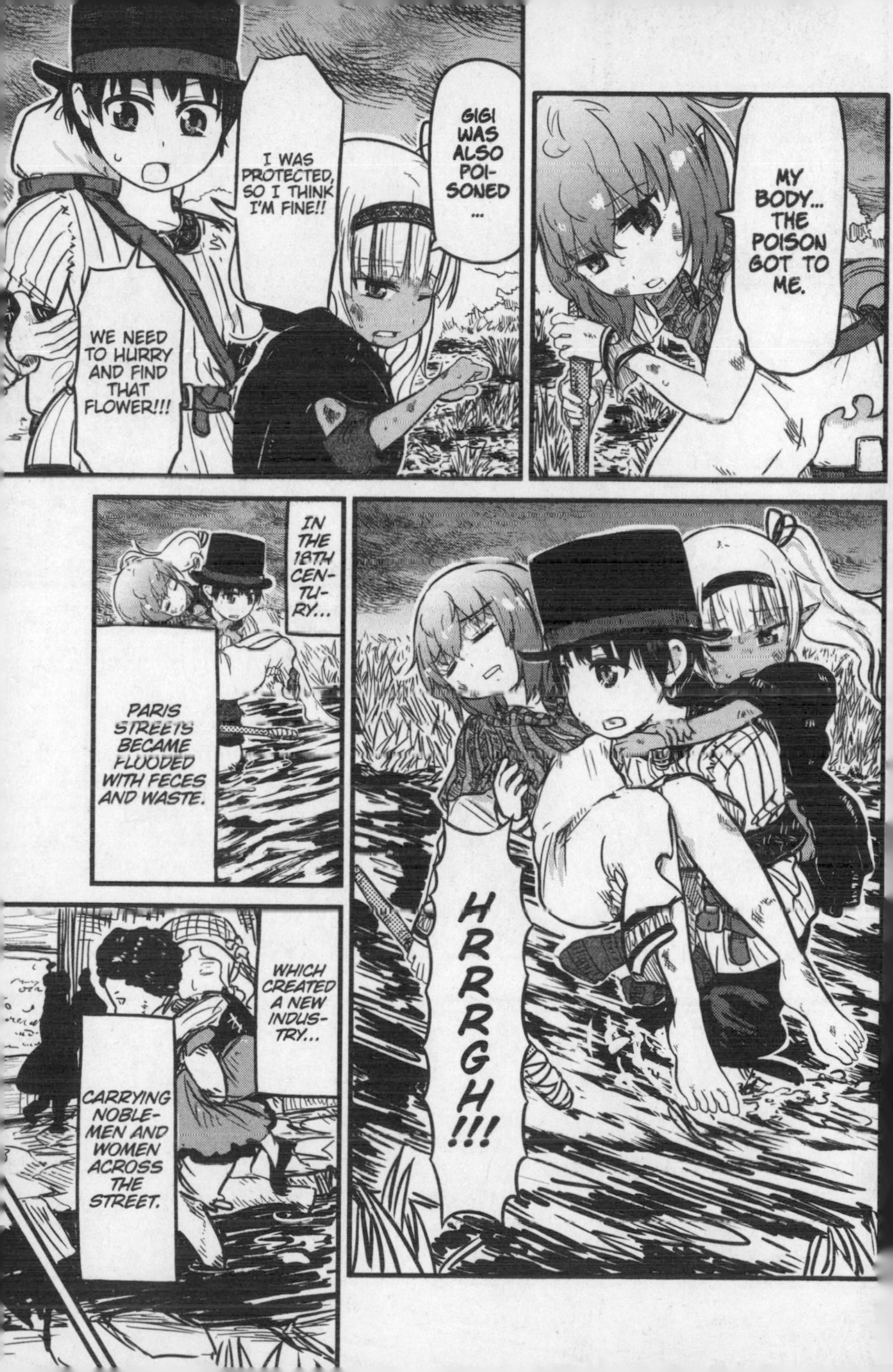
MY BODY... THE POISON GOT TO ME.
GIGI WAS ALSO POI-SONED ...
I WAS PROTECTED, SO I THINK I'M FINE!!
WE NEED TO HURRY AND FIND THAT FLOWER!!!
HRRRGH!!!
IN THE 18TH CEN-TU-RY...
PARIS STREETS BECAME FLOODED WITH FECES AND WASTE.
WHICH CREATED A NEW INDUS-TRY...
CARRYING NOBLE-MEN AND WOMEN ACROSS THE STREET.

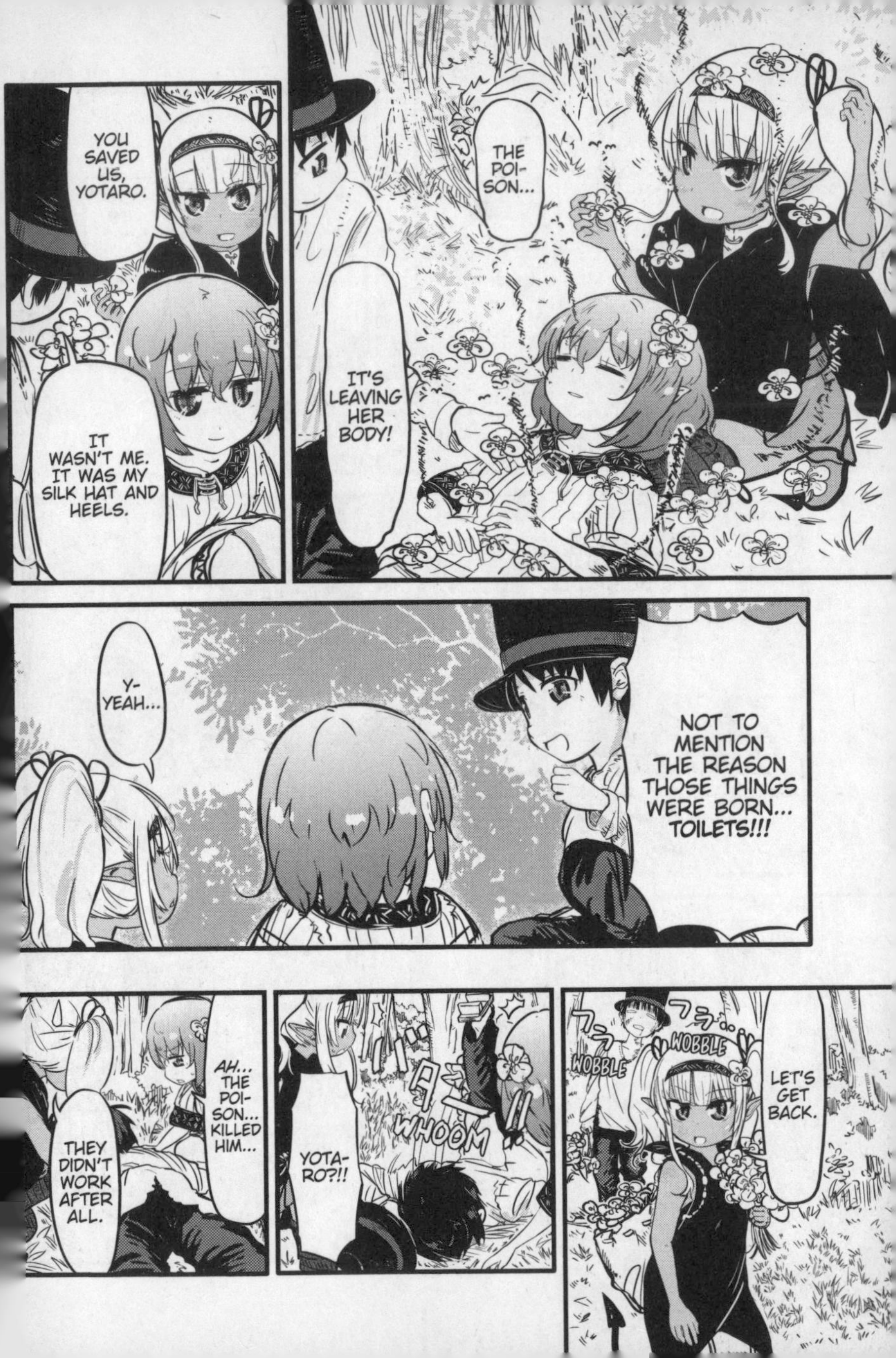
THE POI-SON...
IT'S LEAVING HER BODY!
YOU SAVED US, YOTARO.
IT WASN'T ME. IT WAS MY SILK HAT AND HEELS.
NOT TO MENTION THE REASON THOSE THINGS WERE BORN... TOILETS!!!
Y-YEAH...
WOBBLE
WOBBLE
LET'S GET BACK.
WHOOM
YOTA-RO?!!
AH... THE POI-SON... KILLED HIM...
THEY DIDN'T WORK AFTER ALL.

TWENTY-FIFTH FLUSH

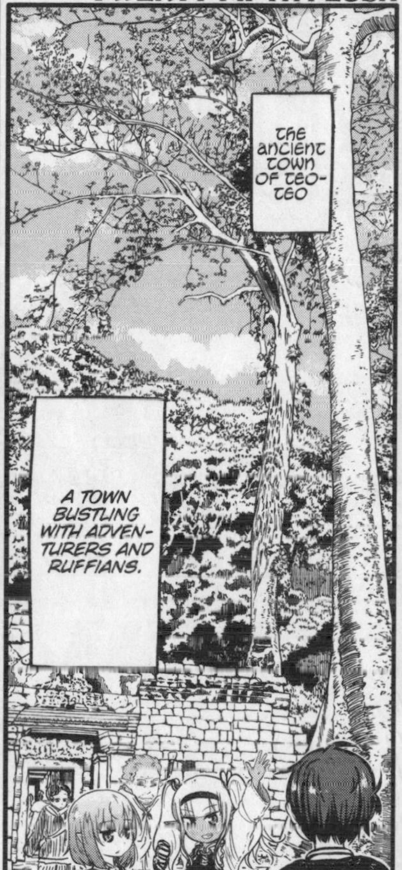
THE ANCIENT TOWN OF TEO-TEO
A TOWN BUSTLING WITH ADVENTURERS AND RUFFIANS.

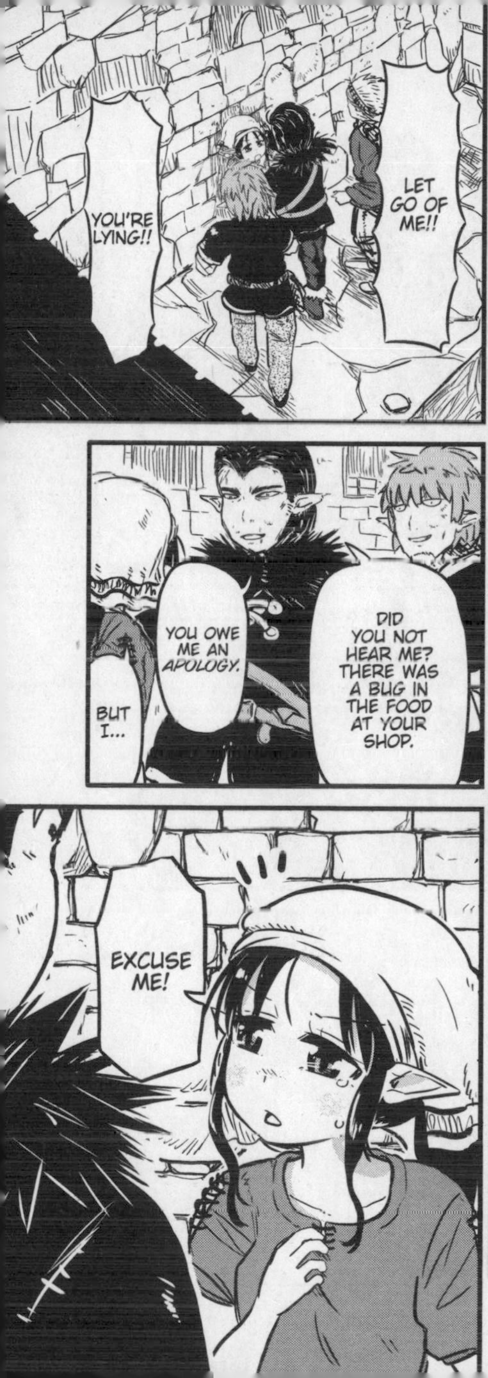
LET GO OF ME!!
YOU'RE LYING!!
DID YOU NOT HEAR ME? THERE WAS A BUG IN THE FOOD AT YOUR SHOP.
YOU OWE ME AN *APOLOGY.*
BUT I...
EXCUSE ME!

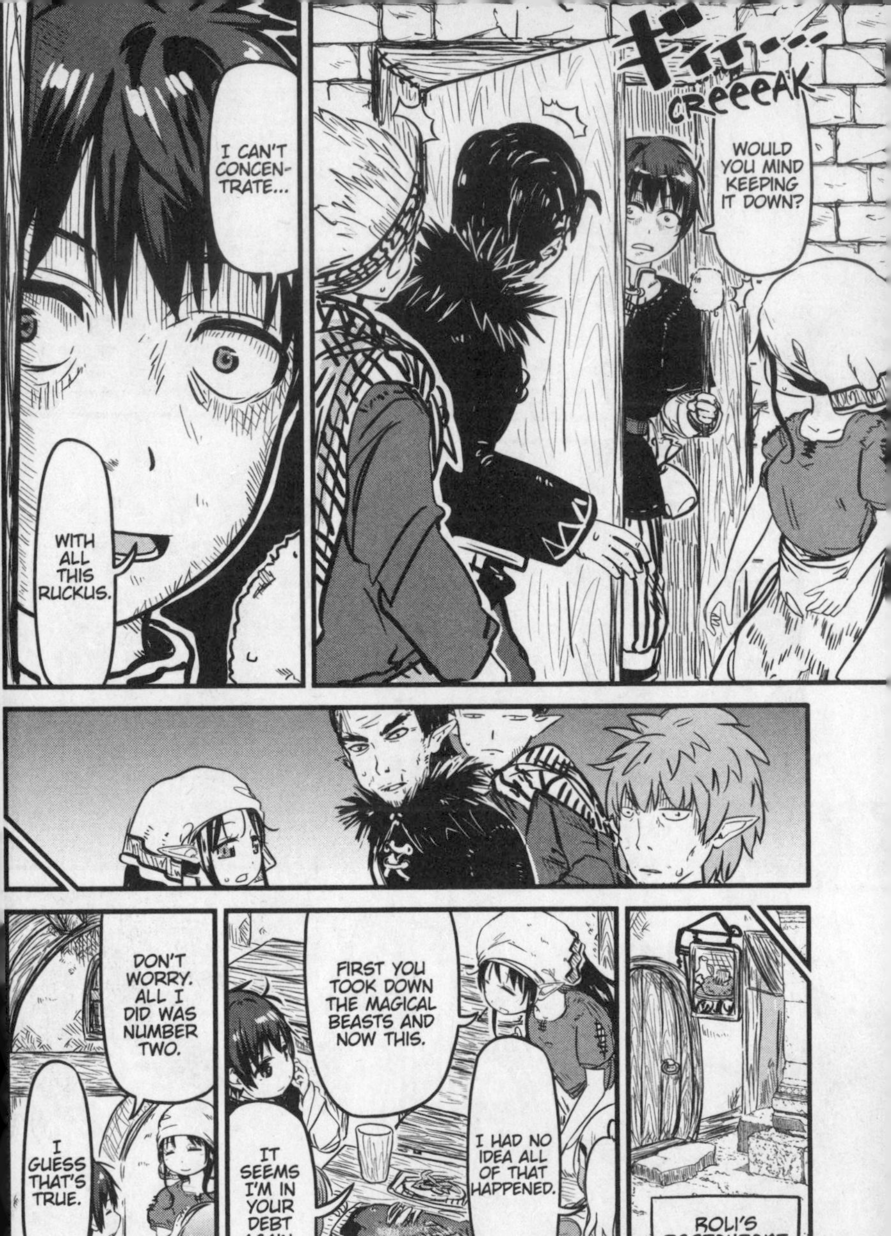
CREEEAK
WOULD YOU MIND KEEPING IT DOWN?
I CAN'T CONCENTRATE...
WITH ALL THIS RUCKUS.
ROLI'S RESTAURANT
FIRST YOU TOOK DOWN THE MAGICAL BEASTS AND NOW THIS.
I HAD NO IDEA ALL OF THAT HAPPENED.
IT SEEMS I'M IN YOUR DEBT AGAIN.
DON'T WORRY. ALL I DID WAS NUMBER TWO.
I GUESS THAT'S TRUE.

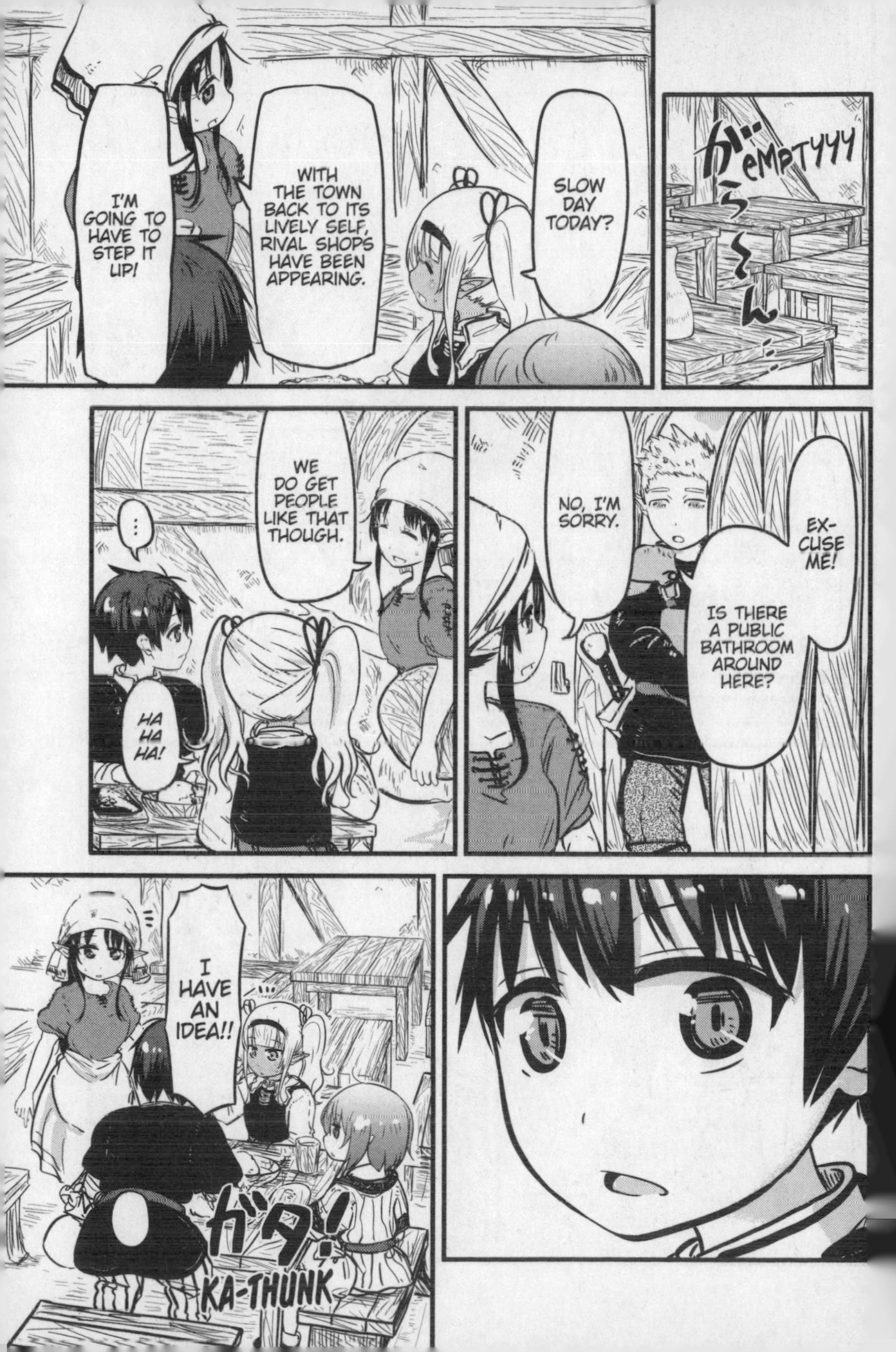
EMPTYYY
SLOW DAY TODAY?
WITH THE TOWN BACK TO ITS LIVELY SELF, RIVAL SHOPS HAVE BEEN APPEARING.
I'M GOING TO HAVE TO STEP IT UP!
EX-CUSE ME!
IS THERE A PUBLIC BATHROOM AROUND HERE?
NO, I'M SORRY.
WE DO GET PEOPLE LIKE THAT THOUGH.
...
HA HA HA!
I HAVE AN IDEA!!
KA-THUNK

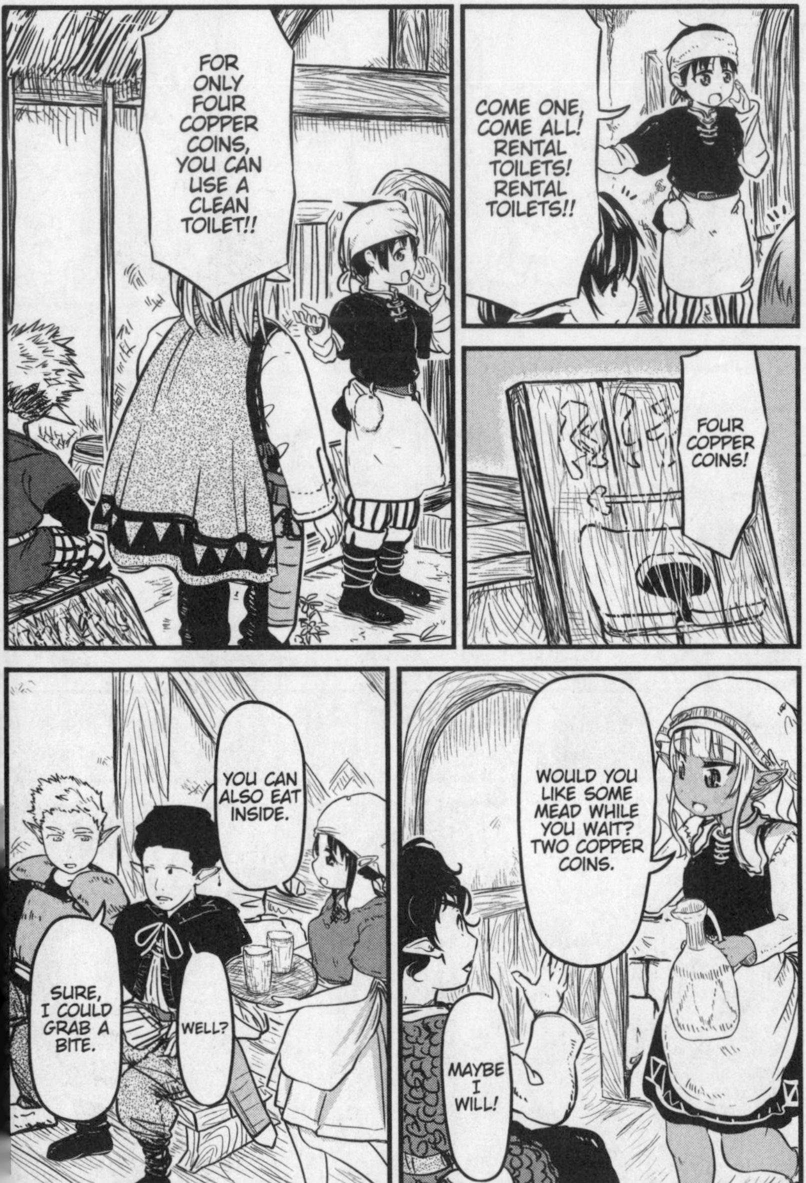
COME ONE, COME ALL! RENTAL TOILETS! RENTAL TOILETS!!
FOUR COPPER COINS!
FOR ONLY FOUR COPPER COINS, YOU CAN USE A CLEAN TOILET!!
WOULD YOU LIKE SOME MEAD WHILE YOU WAIT? TWO COPPER COINS.
MAYBE I WILL!
YOU CAN ALSO EAT INSIDE.
WELL?
SURE, I COULD GRAB A BITE.

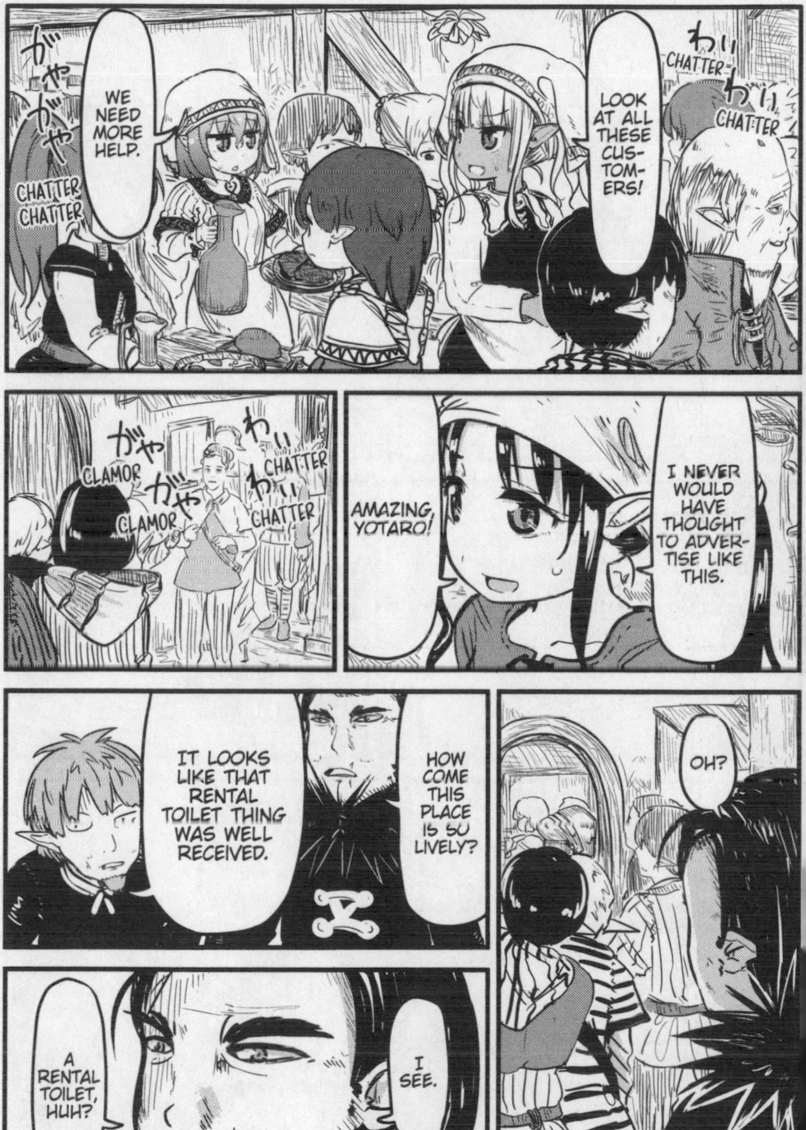
わい
CHATTER
わい
CHATTER
LOOK AT ALL THESE CUS-TOM-ERS!
WE NEED MORE HELP.
がやがや
CHATTER CHATTER
I NEVER WOULD HAVE THOUGHT TO ADVER-TISE LIKE THIS.
AMAZING, YOTARO!
わい
CHATTER
わい
CHATTER
がや
CLAMOR
がや
CLAMOR
OH?
HOW COME THIS PLACE IS SO LIVELY?
IT LOOKS LIKE THAT RENTAL TOILET THING WAS WELL RECEIVED.
I SEE.
A RENTAL TOILET, HUH?

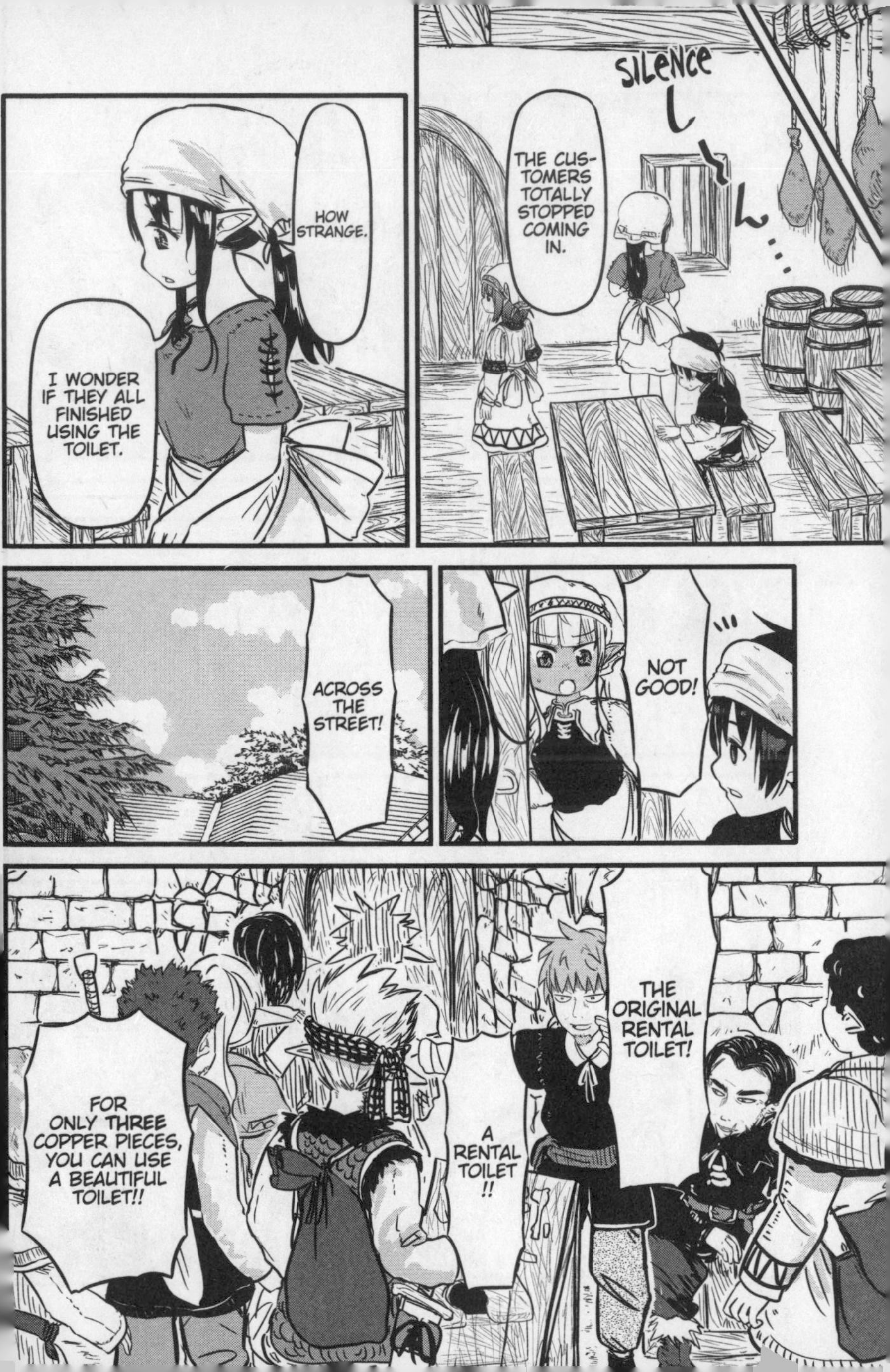
SILENCE
THE CUSTOMERS TOTALLY STOPPED COMING IN.
HOW STRANGE.
I WONDER IF THEY ALL FINISHED USING THE TOILET.
NOT GOOD!
ACROSS THE STREET!
THE ORIGINAL RENTAL TOILET!
A RENTAL TOILET!!
FOR ONLY THREE COPPER PIECES, YOU CAN USE A BEAUTIFUL TOILET!!

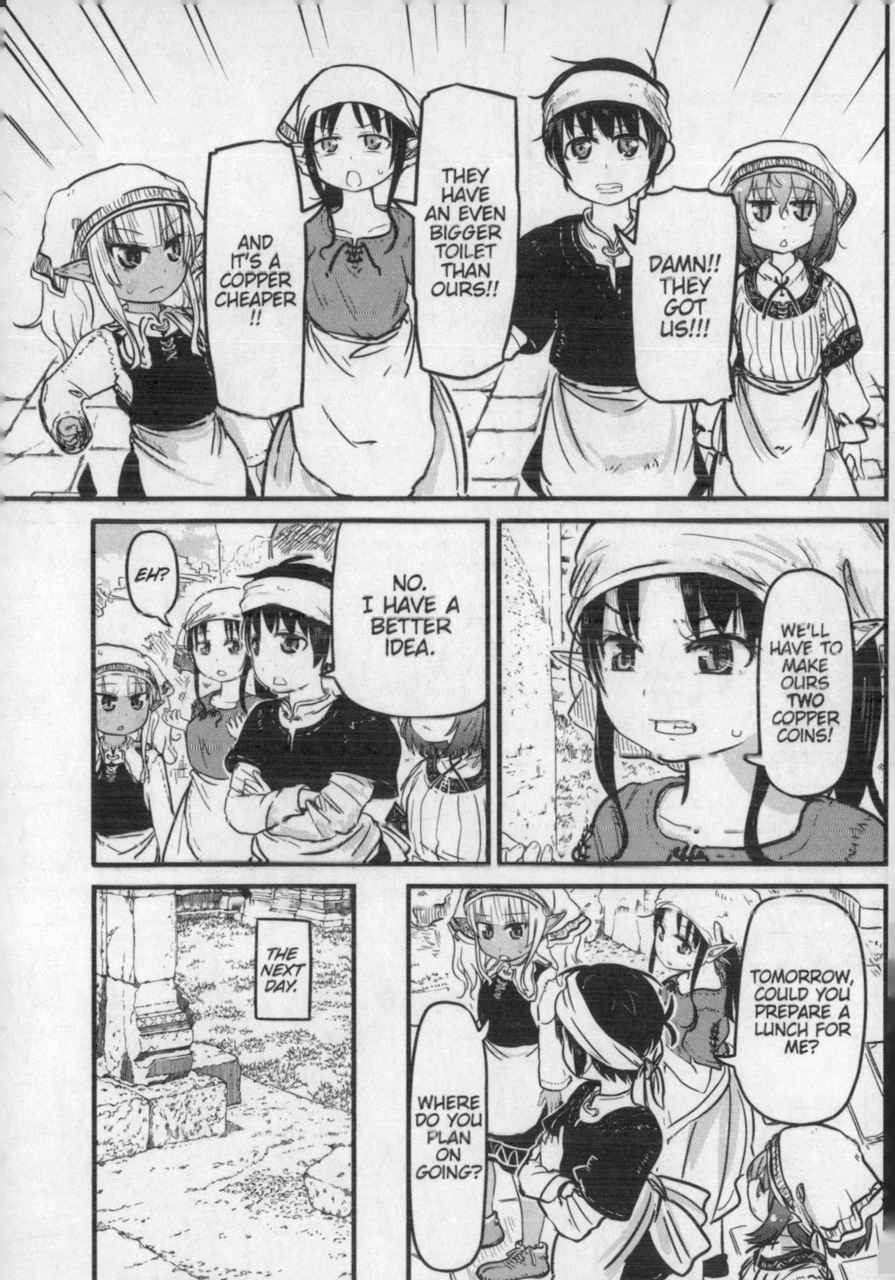
DAMN!! THEY GOT US!!!
THEY HAVE AN EVEN BIGGER TOILET THAN OURS!!
AND IT'S A COPPER CHEAPER!!
WE'LL HAVE TO MAKE OURS TWO COPPER COINS!
NO. I HAVE A BETTER IDEA.
EH?
TOMORROW, COULD YOU PREPARE A LUNCH FOR ME?
WHERE DO YOU PLAN ON GOING?
THE NEXT DAY.

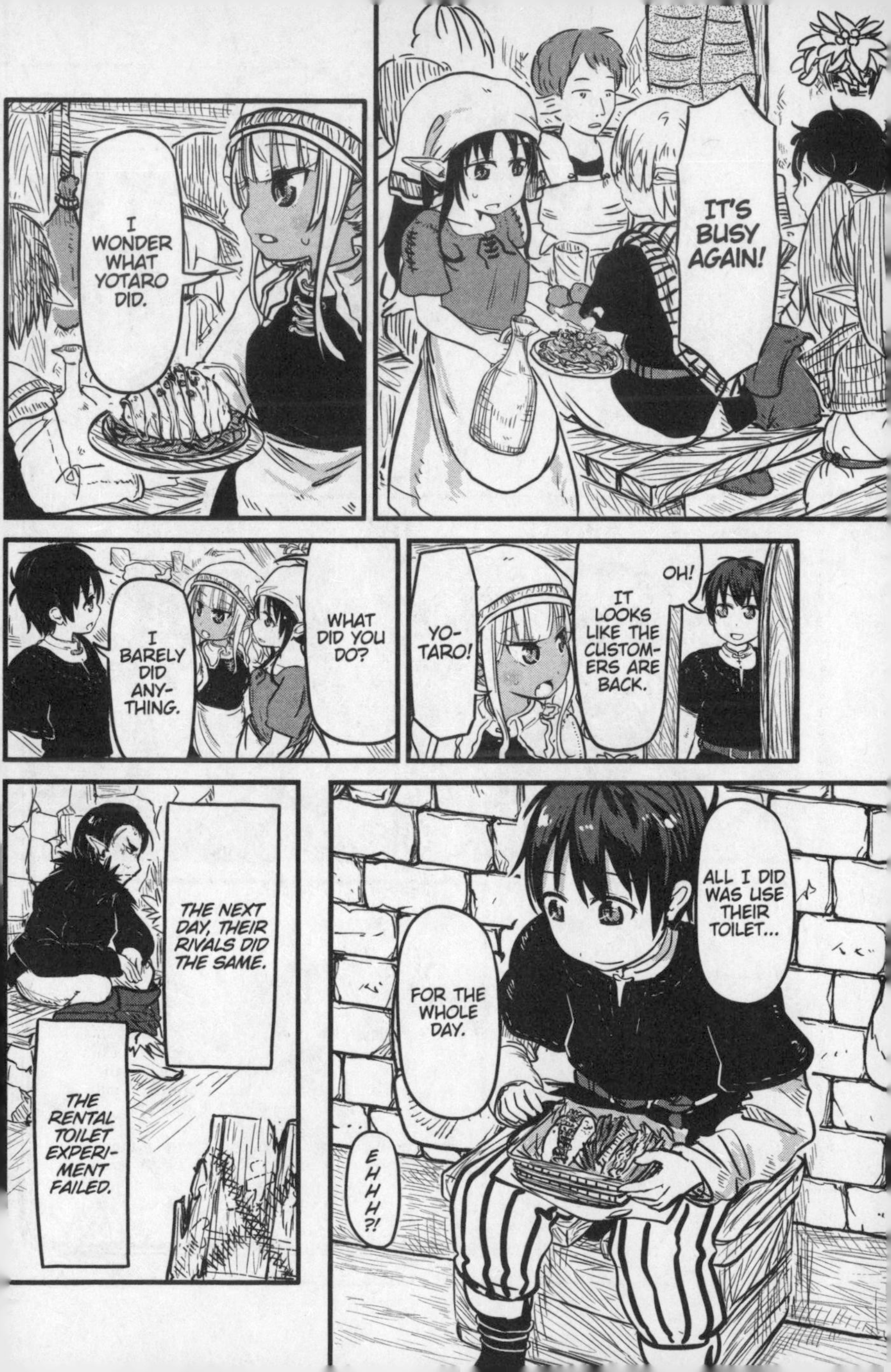
IT'S BUSY AGAIN!
I WONDER WHAT YOTARO DID.
OH!
IT LOOKS LIKE THE CUSTOM-ERS ARE BACK.
YO-TARO!
WHAT DID YOU DO?
I BARELY DID ANY-THING.
ALL I DID WAS USE THEIR TOILET...
FOR THE WHOLE DAY.
EHHH?!
THE NEXT DAY, THEIR RIVALS DID THE SAME.
THE RENTAL TOILET EXPERI-MENT FAILED.

ROOTS

PEOPLE WHO DON'T VALUE TOILET TIME ARE NO GOOD.

THIRTEENTH TOILET TIME

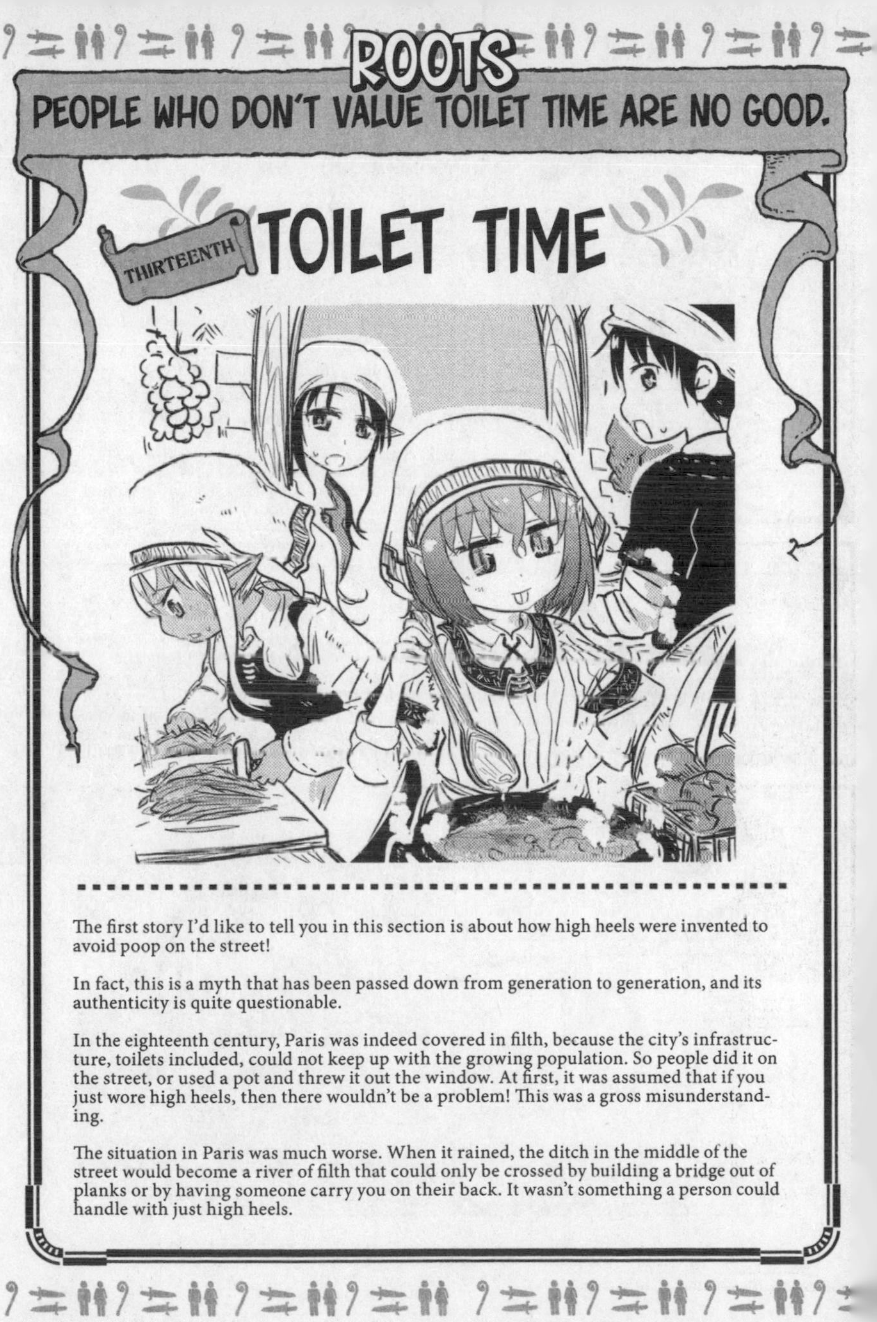

The first story I'd like to tell you in this section is about how high heels were invented to avoid poop on the street!

In fact, this is a myth that has been passed down from generation to generation, and its authenticity is quite questionable.

In the eighteenth century, Paris was indeed covered in filth, because the city's infrastructure, toilets included, could not keep up with the growing population. So people did it on the street, or used a pot and threw it out the window. At first, it was assumed that if you just wore high heels, then there wouldn't be a problem! This was a gross misunderstanding.

The situation in Paris was much worse. When it rained, the ditch in the middle of the street would become a river of filth that could only be crossed by building a bridge out of planks or by having someone carry you on their back. It wasn't something a person could handle with just high heels.

So, what are the origins of today's high heels? Well, there are pattens, which were worn over shoes, and chopines, which are like thick-soled sandals. There are also heels for riding. They were all made to protect shoes and roads, to make people look taller, or to make it easier to ride a horse, and they have nothing to do with poop.

As the creator of a poop manga, I find this quite unfortunate.

Similarly, silk hats and coats don't have much to do with toilets, either. But Yotaro insists that *everything* is due to toilets.

The second story is based on a classic rakugo story called *Kaicho no Toilet*. The content of the story is basically the same as this one. It's about a man who plans to make a fortune by renting out private toilets on the occasion of the opening of a temple (the day when a Buddha statue is unveiled). In the end, he takes over a rival's toilet.

The rental toilet was an actual business that existed. There were various types, from luxurious ones where you could have tea and dumplings while waiting, to simple toilets surrounded by boards, to straw mattresses with a tub in the middle. There were even portable toilets that one could offer as "on the spot" toilets.

IN OTHER WORDS

THIS MAXIM

"HE SQUATTED ON THE TOILET OVER THERE UNTIL THE SUN ROSE."

-FROM *KAICHO NO TOILET*

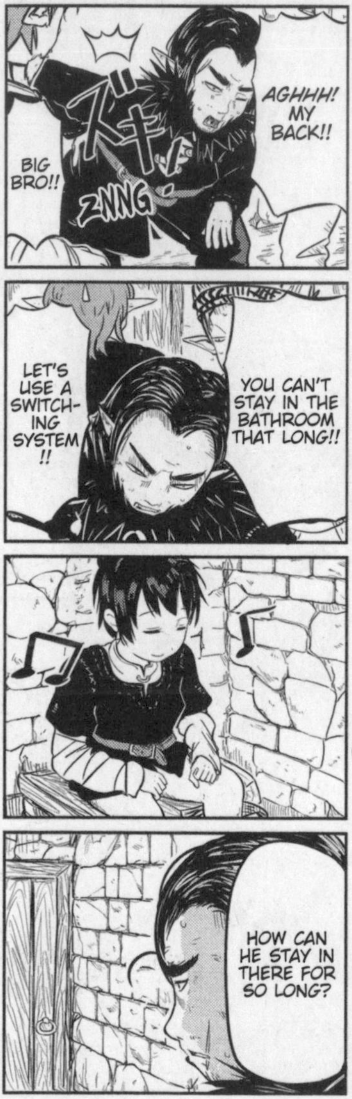
AGHHH! MY BACK!!
ZNNG
BIG BRO!!
YOU CAN'T STAY IN THE BATHROOM THAT LONG!!
LET'S USE A SWITCHING SYSTEM!!
HOW CAN HE STAY IN THERE FOR SO LONG?

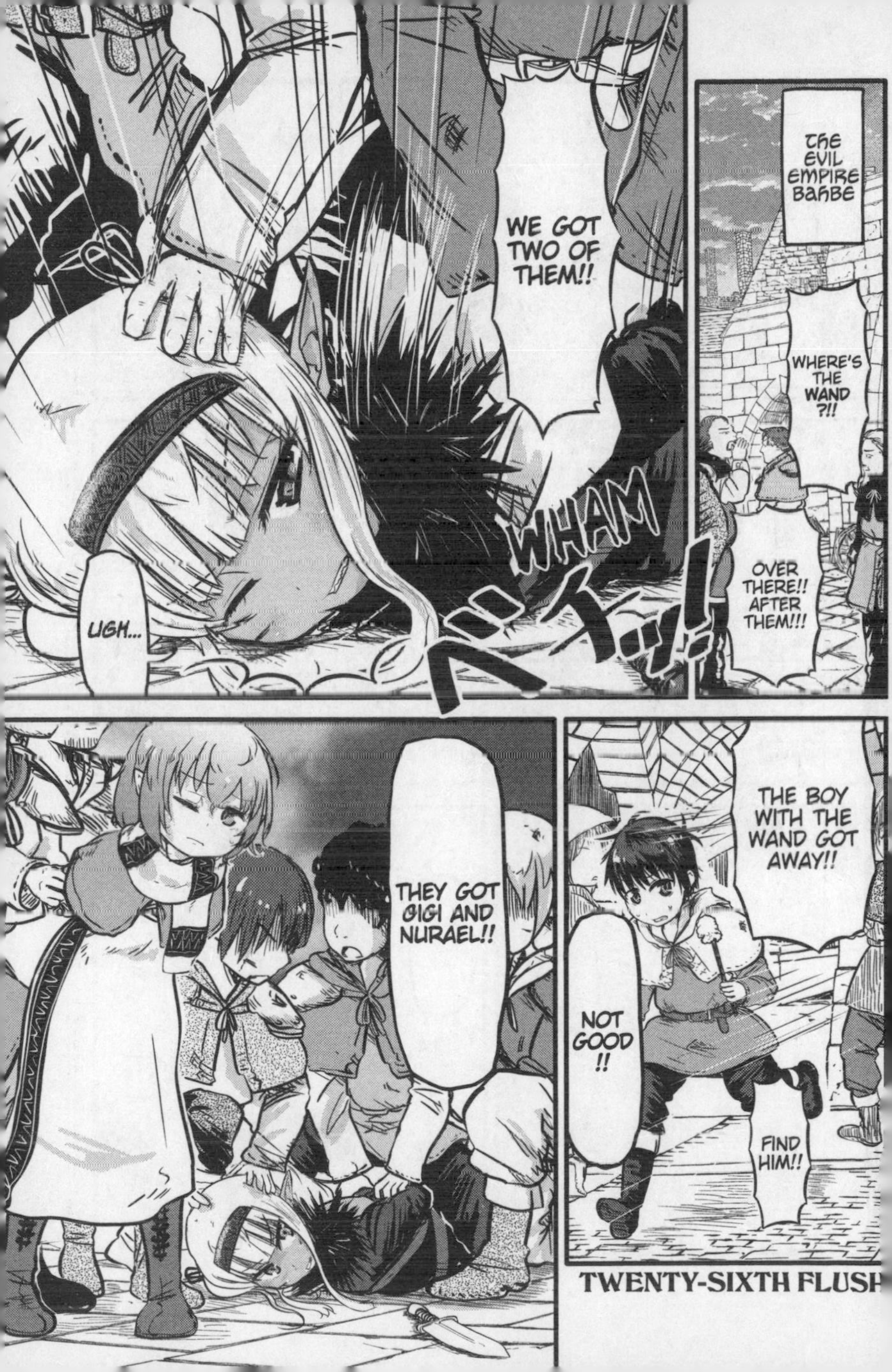
THE EVIL EMPIRE BAHBE
WHERE'S THE WAND ?!!
OVER THERE!! AFTER THEM!!!
WE GOT TWO OF THEM!!
WHAM
UGH...
THE BOY WITH THE WAND GOT AWAY!!
NOT GOOD !!
FIND HIM!!
THEY GOT GIGI AND NURAEL!!

TWENTY-SIXTH FLUSH

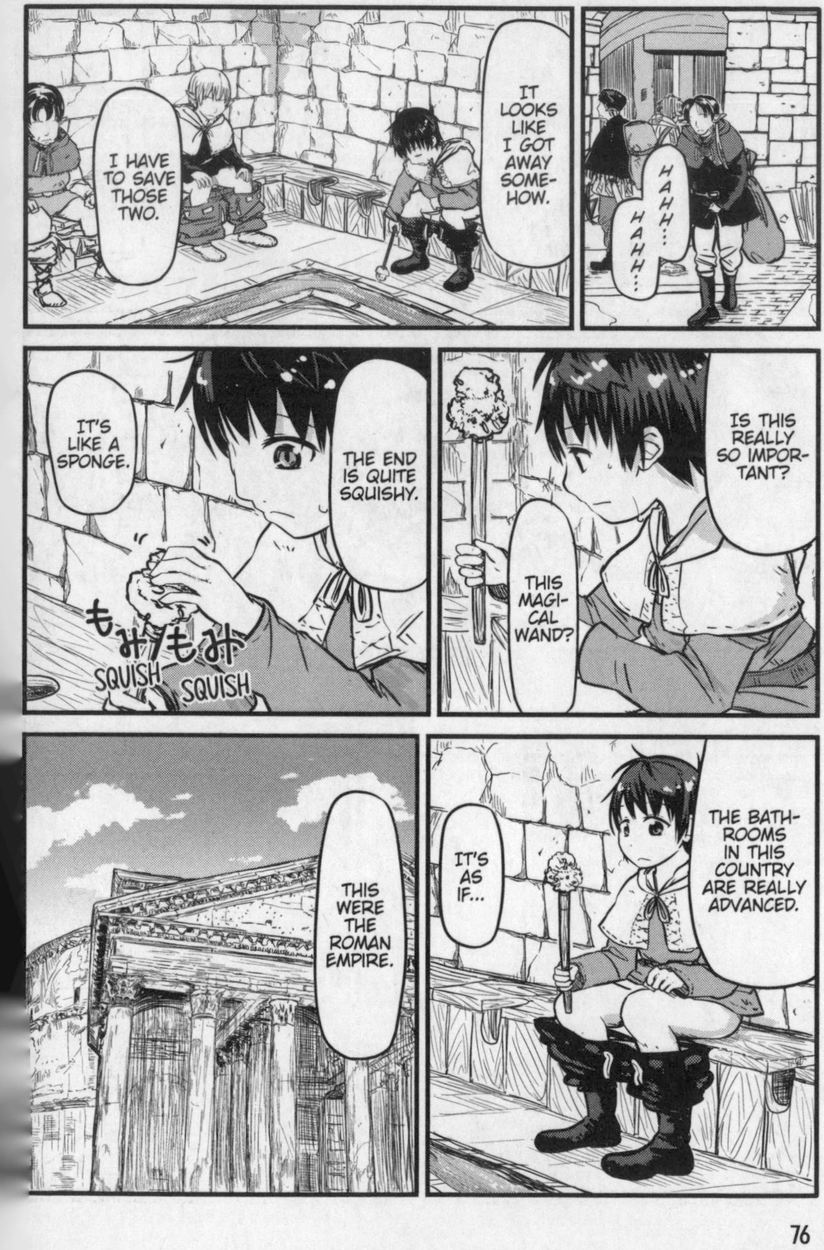
HAHH... HAHH...
IT LOOKS LIKE I GOT AWAY SOMEHOW.
I HAVE TO SAVE THOSE TWO.
IS THIS REALLY SO IMPORTANT?
THIS MAGICAL WAND?
THE END IS QUITE SQUISHY.
IT'S LIKE A SPONGE.
もみもみ
SQUISH SQUISH
THE BATHROOMS IN THIS COUNTRY ARE REALLY ADVANCED.
IT'S AS IF...
THIS WERE THE ROMAN EMPIRE.

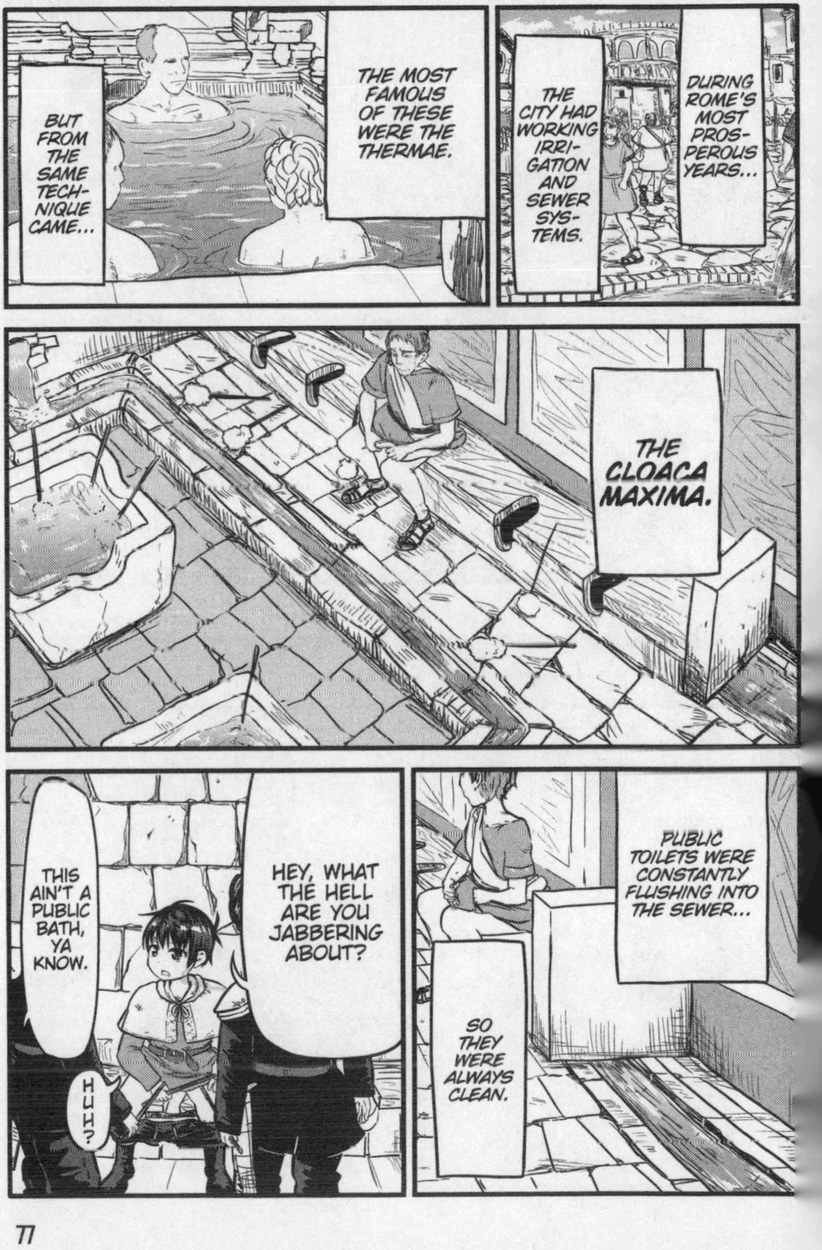
DURING ROME'S MOST PROSPEROUS YEARS...
THE CITY HAD WORKING IRRIGATION AND SEWER SYSTEMS.
THE MOST FAMOUS OF THESE WERE THE THERMAE.
BUT FROM THE SAME TECHNIQUE CAME...
THE CLOACA MAXIMA.
PUBLIC TOILETS WERE CONSTANTLY FLUSHING INTO THE SEWER...
SO THEY WERE ALWAYS CLEAN.
HEY, WHAT THE HELL ARE YOU JABBERING ABOUT?
THIS AIN'T A PUBLIC BATH, YA KNOW.
HUH?

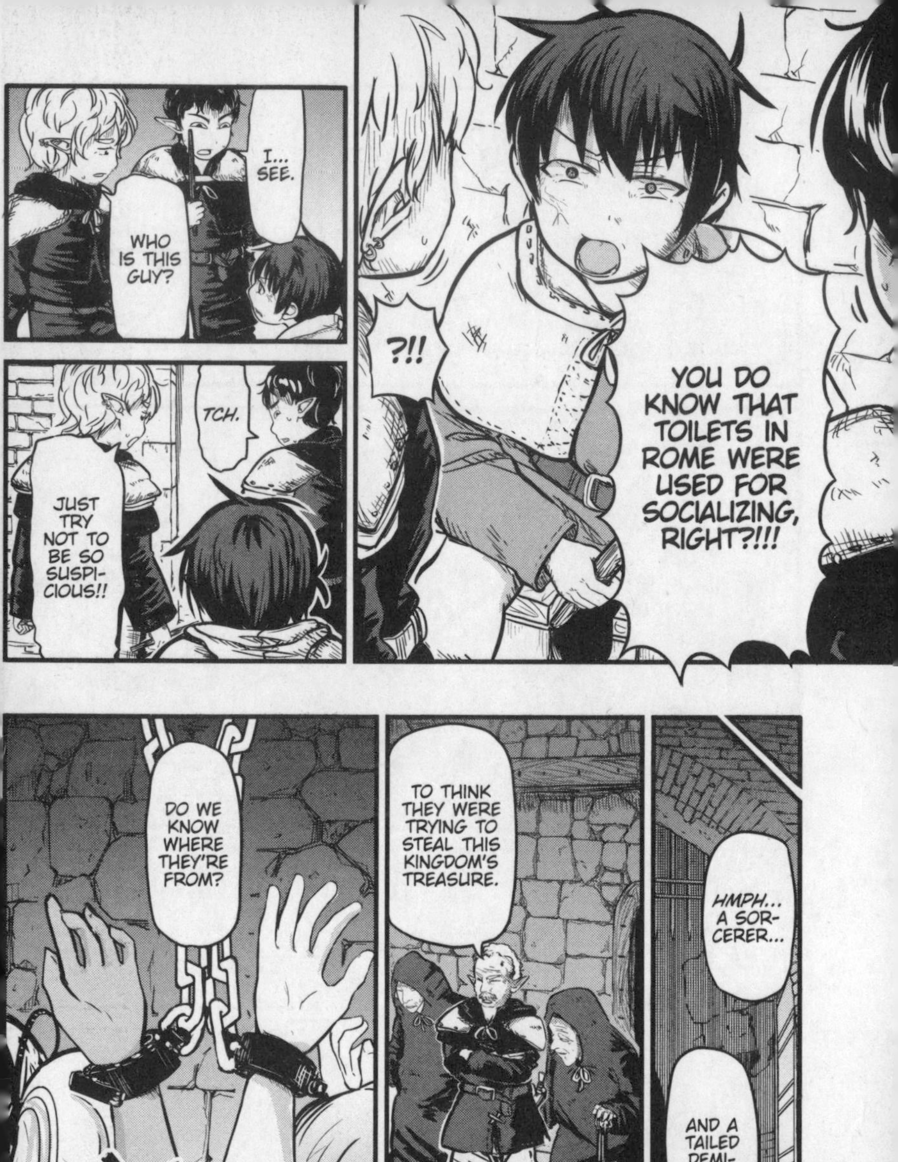
YOU DO KNOW THAT TOILETS IN ROME WERE USED FOR SOCIALIZING, RIGHT?!!!
?!!
I... SEE.
WHO IS THIS GUY?
TCH.
JUST TRY NOT TO BE SO SUSPICIOUS!!
HMPH... A SORCERER...
AND A TAILED DEMI-HUMAN.
TO THINK THEY WERE TRYING TO STEAL THIS KINGDOM'S TREASURE.
DO WE KNOW WHERE THEY'RE FROM?
KA-CLANK

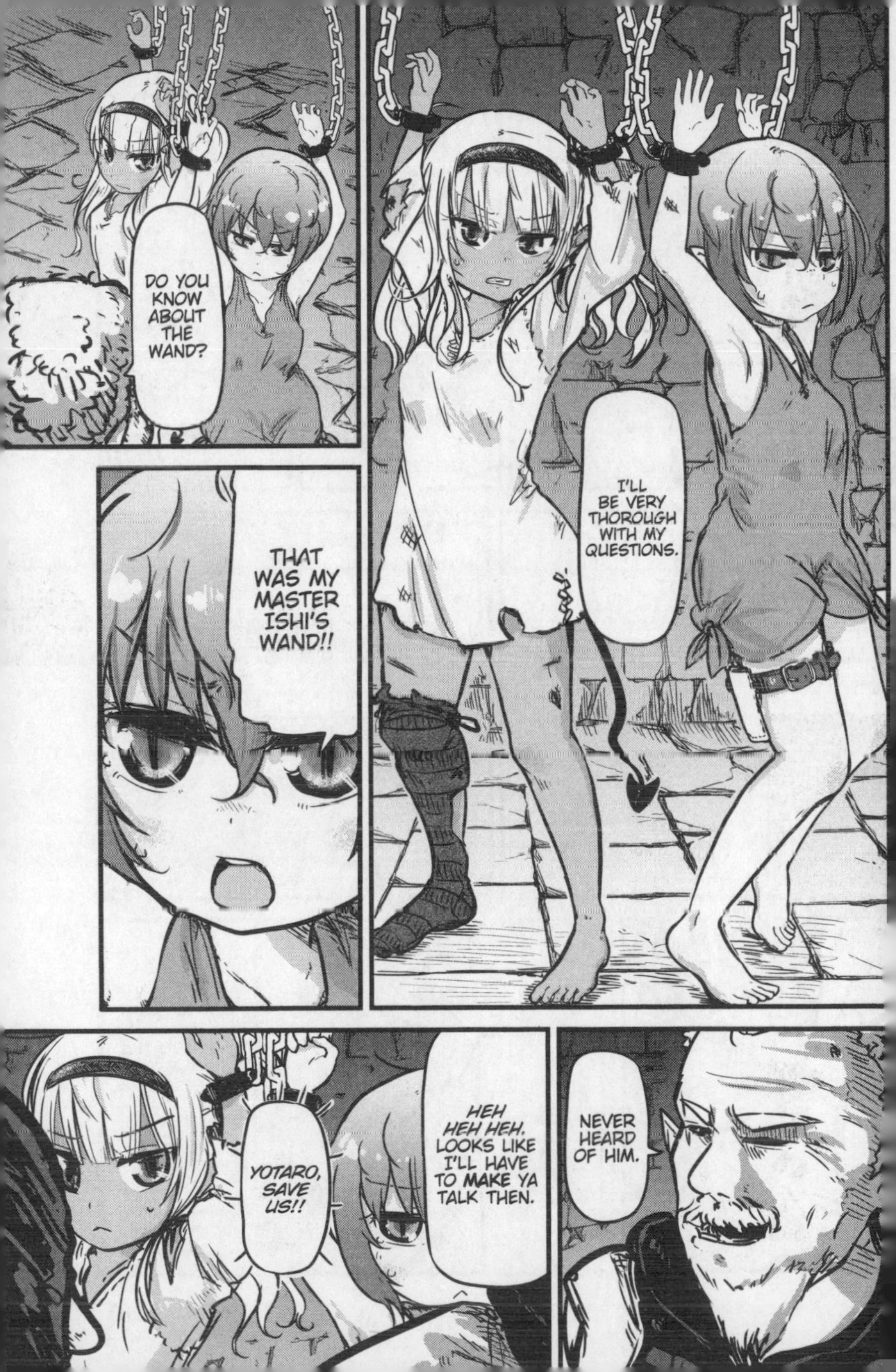
I'LL BE VERY THOROUGH WITH MY QUESTIONS.
DO YOU KNOW ABOUT THE WAND?
THAT WAS MY MASTER ISHI'S WAND!!
NEVER HEARD OF HIM.
HEH HEH HEH. LOOKS LIKE I'LL HAVE TO MAKE YA TALK THEN.
YOTARO, SAVE US!!

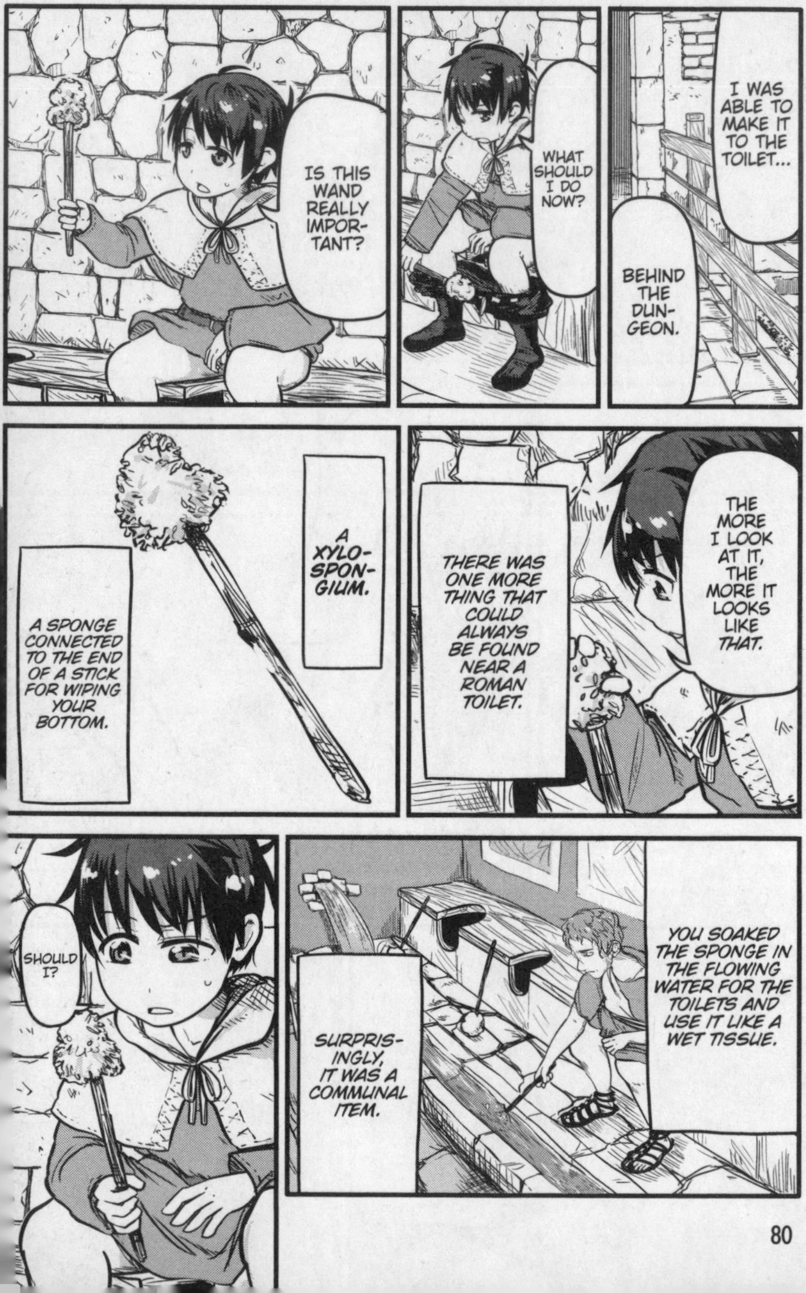
I WAS ABLE TO MAKE IT TO THE TOILET...
BEHIND THE DUN-GEON.
WHAT SHOULD I DO NOW?
IS THIS WAND REALLY IMPOR-TANT?
THE MORE I LOOK AT IT, THE MORE IT LOOKS LIKE THAT.
THERE WAS ONE MORE THING THAT COULD ALWAYS BE FOUND NEAR A ROMAN TOILET.
A XYLO-SPON-GIUM.
A SPONGE CONNECTED TO THE END OF A STICK FOR WIPING YOUR BOTTOM.
YOU SOAKED THE SPONGE IN THE FLOWING WATER FOR THE TOILETS AND USE IT LIKE A WET TISSUE.
SURPRIS-INGLY, IT WAS A COMMUNAL ITEM.
SHOULD I?

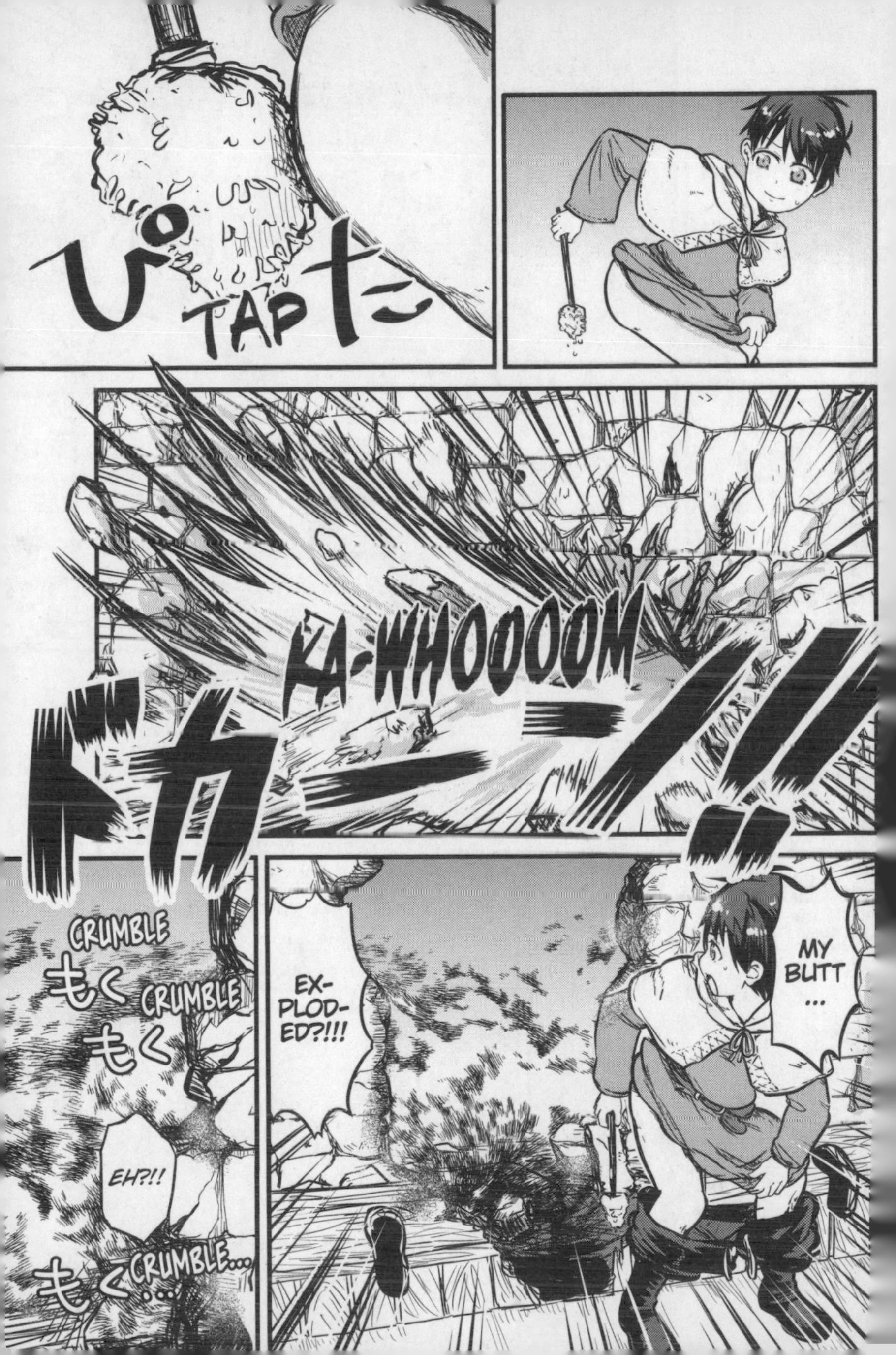

ぴ
TAP
たっ
KA-WHOOOOM
ドカーー!!
MY BUTT ...
EX-PLOD-ED?!!!
CRUMBLE
もく
CRUMBLE
もく
EH?!!
もく...
CRUMBLE...

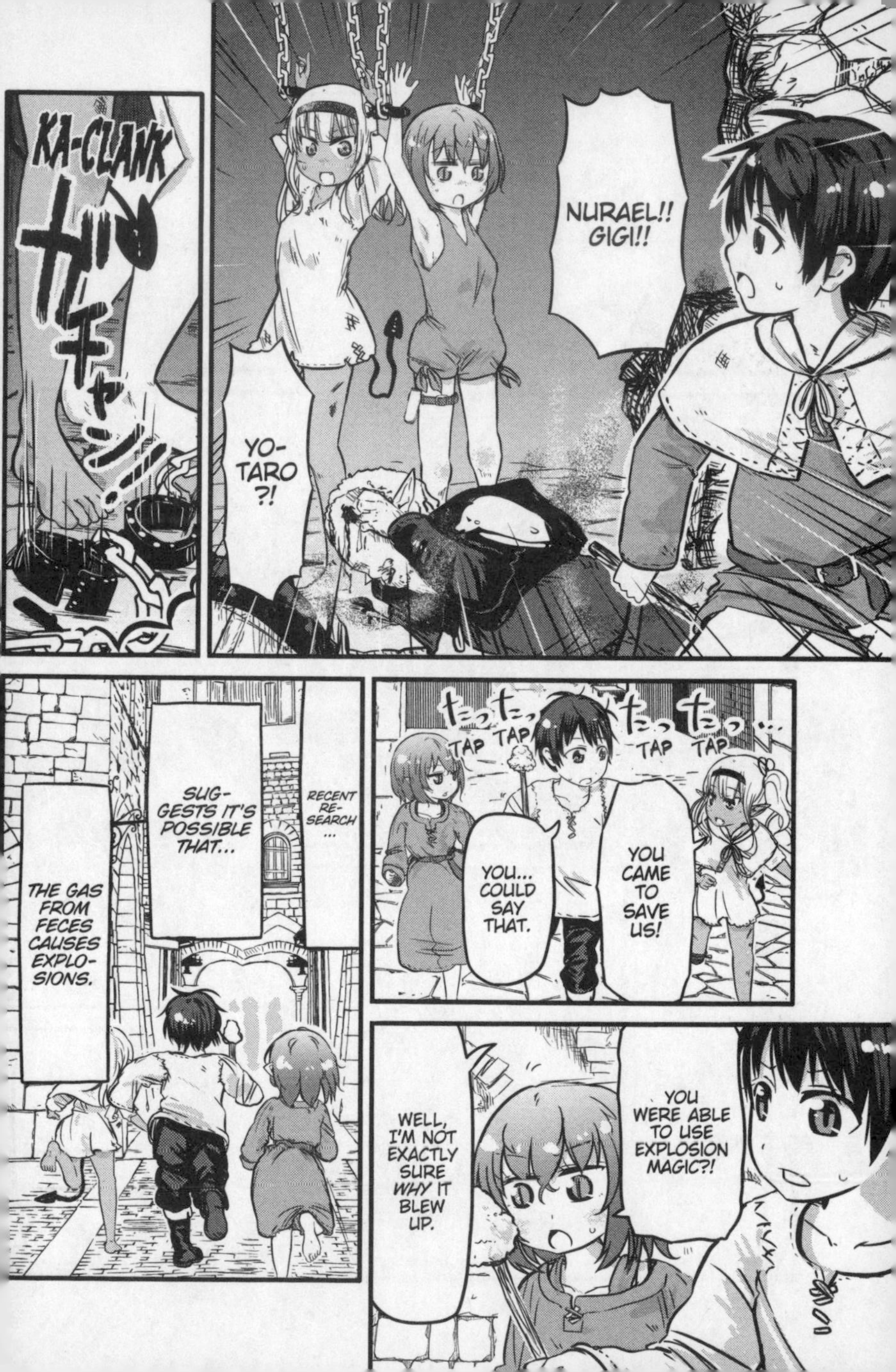
NURAEL!! GIGI!!
YO-TARO?!
KA-CLANK
ガチャン
たったっ TAP TAP
たったっ… TAP TAP
YOU CAME TO SAVE US!
YOU... COULD SAY THAT.
YOU WERE ABLE TO USE EXPLOSION MAGIC?!
WELL, I'M NOT EXACTLY SURE *WHY* IT BLEW UP.
RECENT RE-SEARCH...
SUG-GESTS IT'S POSSIBLE THAT...
THE GAS FROM FECES CAUSES EXPLO-SIONS.

TWENTY-SEVENTH FLUSH

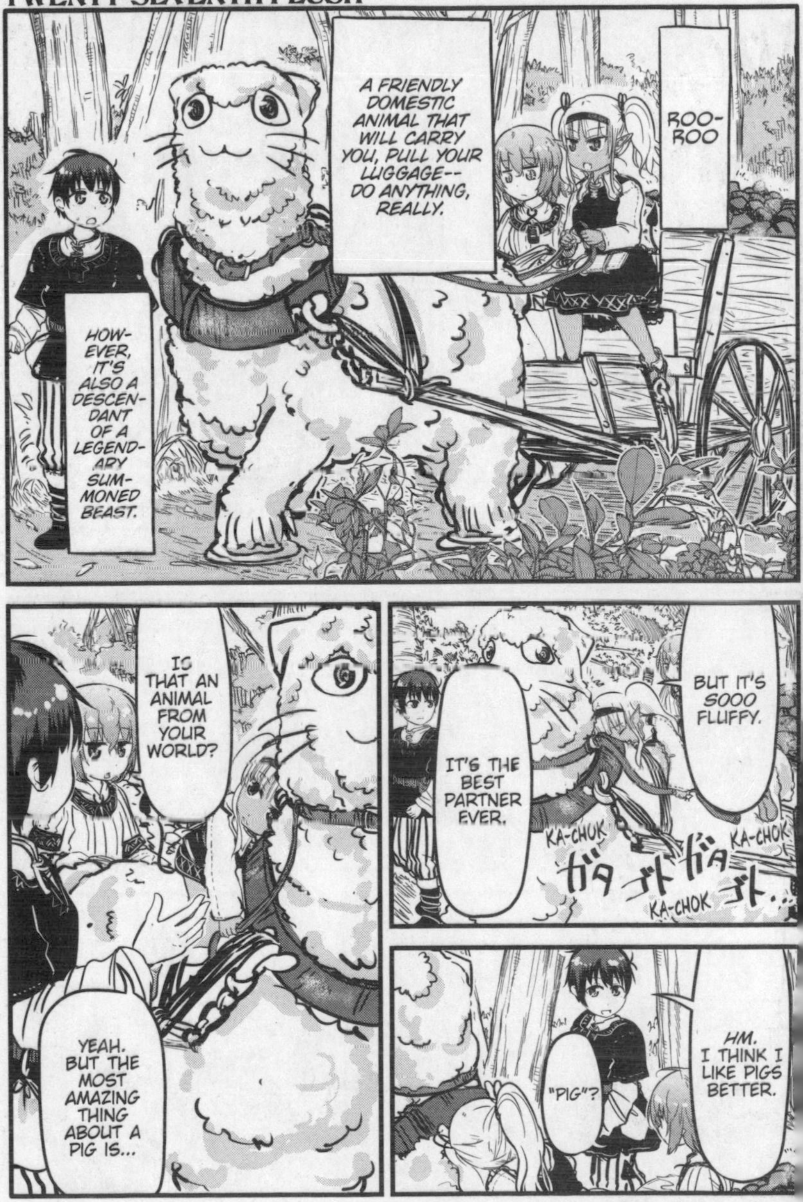
ROO-ROO
A FRIENDLY DOMESTIC ANIMAL THAT WILL CARRY YOU, PULL YOUR LUGGAGE-- DO ANYTHING, REALLY.
HOW-EVER, IT'S ALSO A DESCEN-DANT OF A LEGEND-ARY SUM-MONED BEAST.
BUT IT'S SOOO FLUFFY.
IT'S THE BEST PARTNER EVER.
ガタ ゴト ガタ ゴト…
KA-CHOK KA-CHOK KA-CHOK
HM. I THINK I LIKE PIGS BETTER.
"PIG"?
IS THAT AN ANIMAL FROM YOUR WORLD?
YEAH. BUT THE MOST AMAZING THING ABOUT A PIG IS...

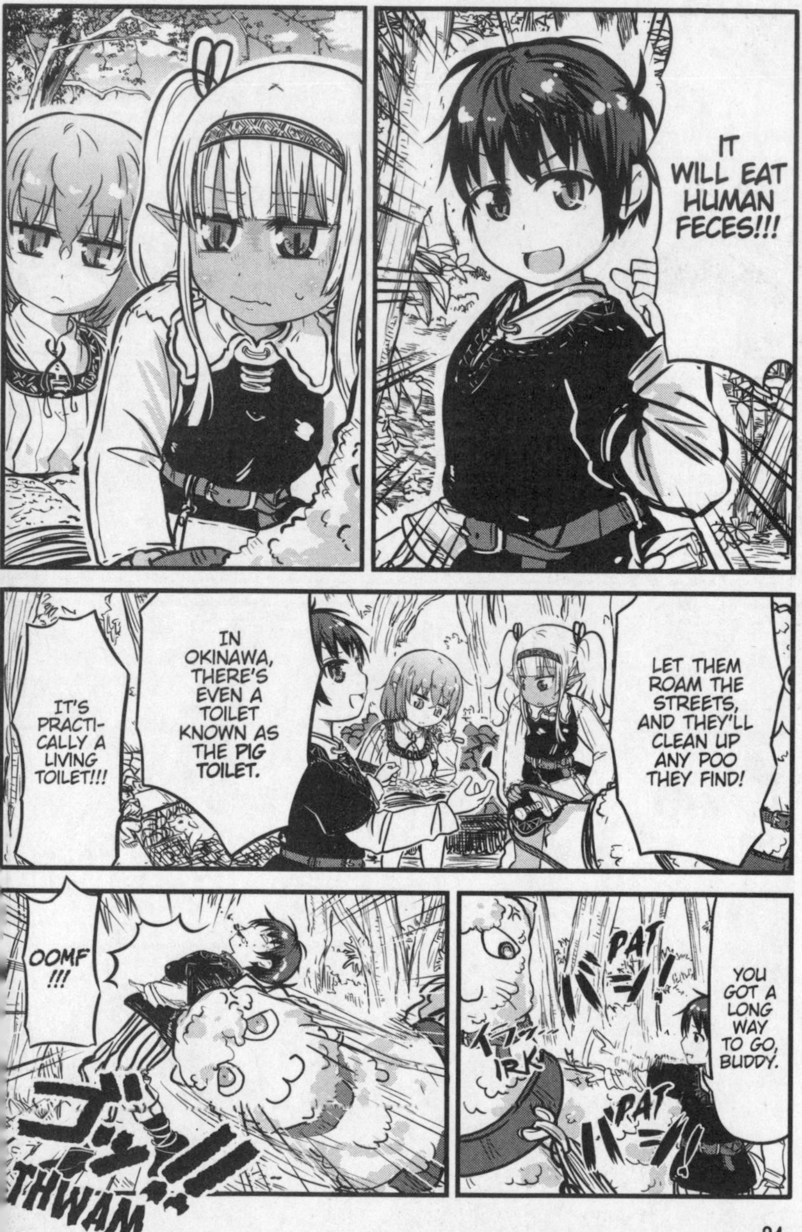
IT WILL EAT HUMAN FECES!!!
LET THEM ROAM THE STREETS, AND THEY'LL CLEAN UP ANY POO THEY FIND!
IN OKINAWA, THERE'S EVEN A TOILET KNOWN AS THE PIG TOILET.
IT'S PRACTI-CALLY A LIVING TOILET!!!
PAT
YOU GOT A LONG WAY TO GO, BUDDY.
IRK
PAT
OOMF!!!
THWAM

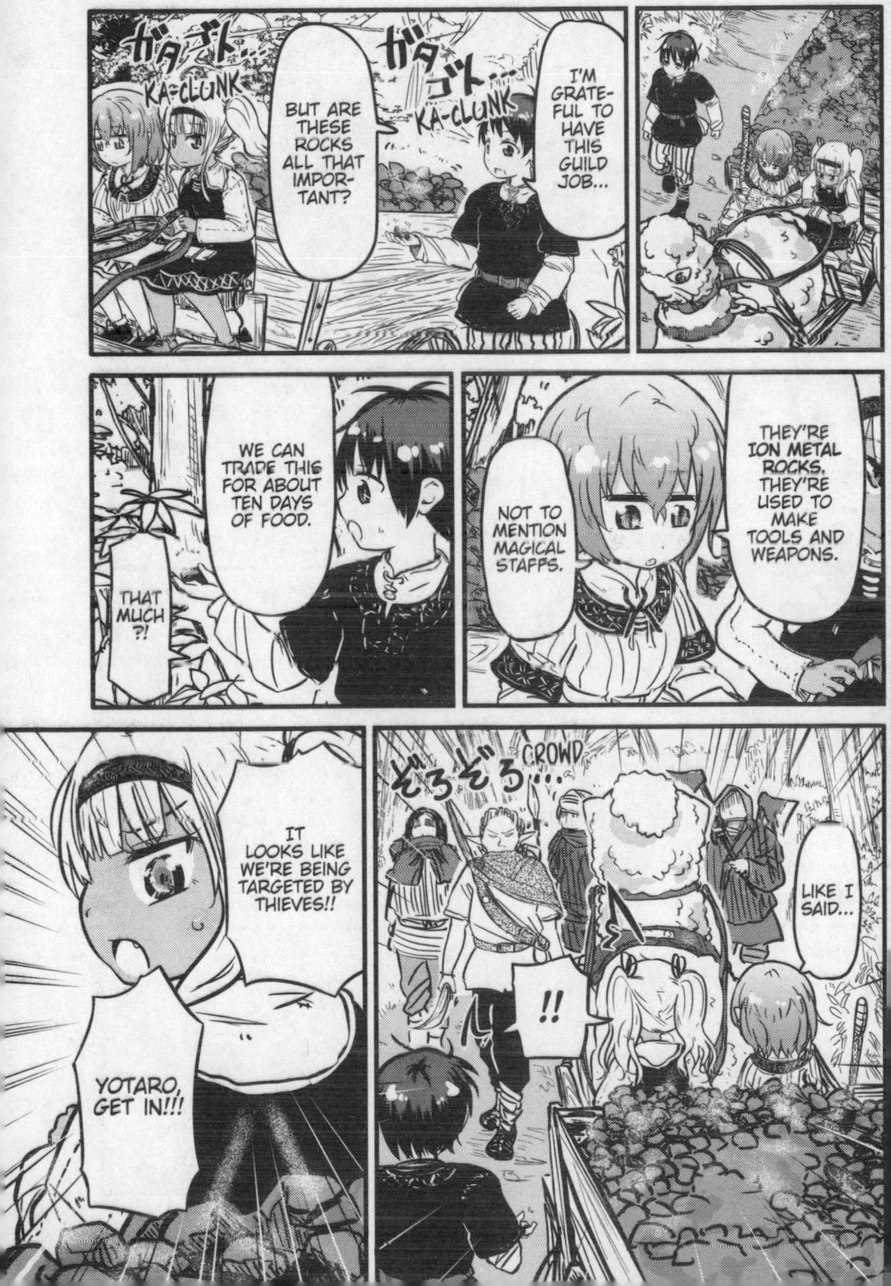
I'M GRATEFUL TO HAVE THIS GUILD JOB...
ガタゴト… KA-CLUNK
BUT ARE THESE ROCKS ALL THAT IMPORTANT?
ガタゴト… KA-CLUNK
THEY'RE ION METAL ROCKS. THEY'RE USED TO MAKE TOOLS AND WEAPONS.
NOT TO MENTION MAGICAL STAFFS.
WE CAN TRADE THIS FOR ABOUT TEN DAYS OF FOOD.
THAT MUCH?!
LIKE I SAID...
ぞろぞろ… CROWD
!!
IT LOOKS LIKE WE'RE BEING TARGETED BY THIEVES!!
YOTARO, GET IN!!!

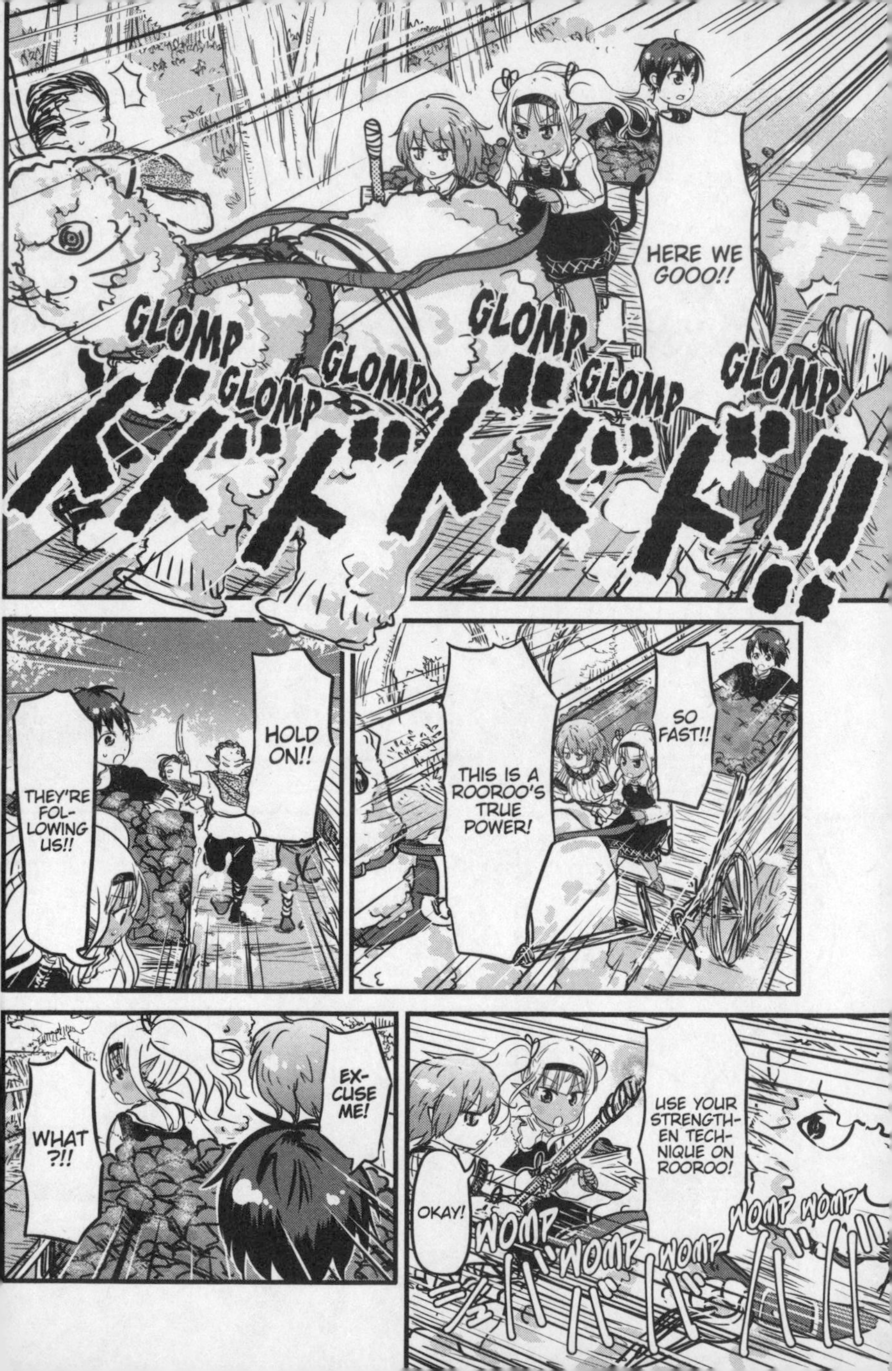
HERE WE GOOO!!
GLOMP GLOMP GLOMP GLOMP GLOMP GLOMP
SO FAST!!
THIS IS A ROOROO'S TRUE POWER!
HOLD ON!!
THEY'RE FOL-LOWING US!!
USE YOUR STRENGTH-EN TECH-NIQUE ON ROOROO!
OKAY!
WOMP WOMP WOMP WOMP WOMP
EX-CUSE ME!
WHAT?!!

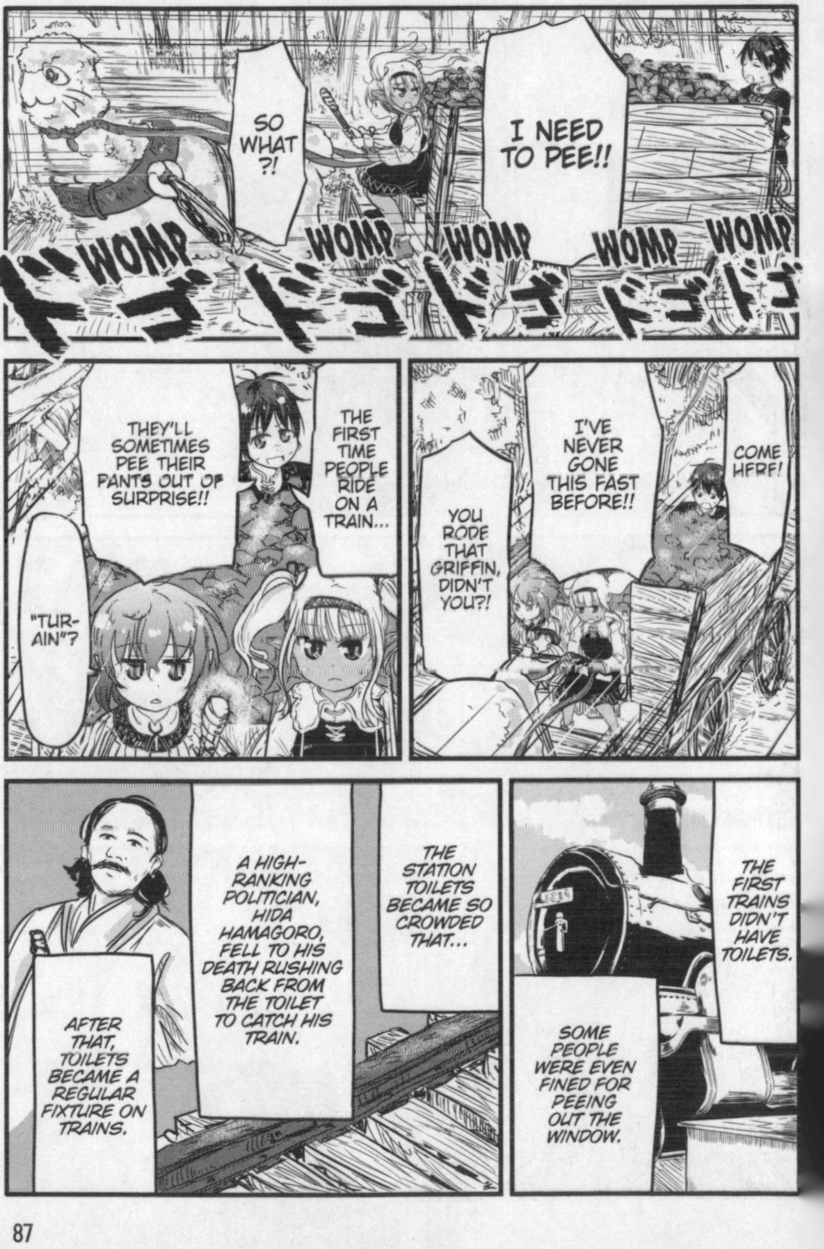
I NEED TO PEE!!
SO WHAT?!
WOMP WOMP WOMP WOMP WOMP
ドゴドゴドゴドゴドゴ
COME HERE!
I'VE NEVER GONE THIS FAST BEFORE!!
YOU RODE THAT GRIFFIN, DIDN'T YOU?!
THE FIRST TIME PEOPLE RIDE ON A TRAIN...
THEY'LL SOMETIMES PEE THEIR PANTS OUT OF SURPRISE!!
"TUR-AIN"?
THE FIRST TRAINS DIDN'T HAVE TOILETS.
SOME PEOPLE WERE EVEN FINED FOR PEEING OUT THE WINDOW.
THE STATION TOILETS BECAME SO CROWDED THAT...
A HIGH-RANKING POLITICIAN, HIDA HAMAGORO, FELL TO HIS DEATH RUSHING BACK FROM THE TOILET TO CATCH HIS TRAIN.
AFTER THAT, TOILETS BECAME A REGULAR FIXTURE ON TRAINS.

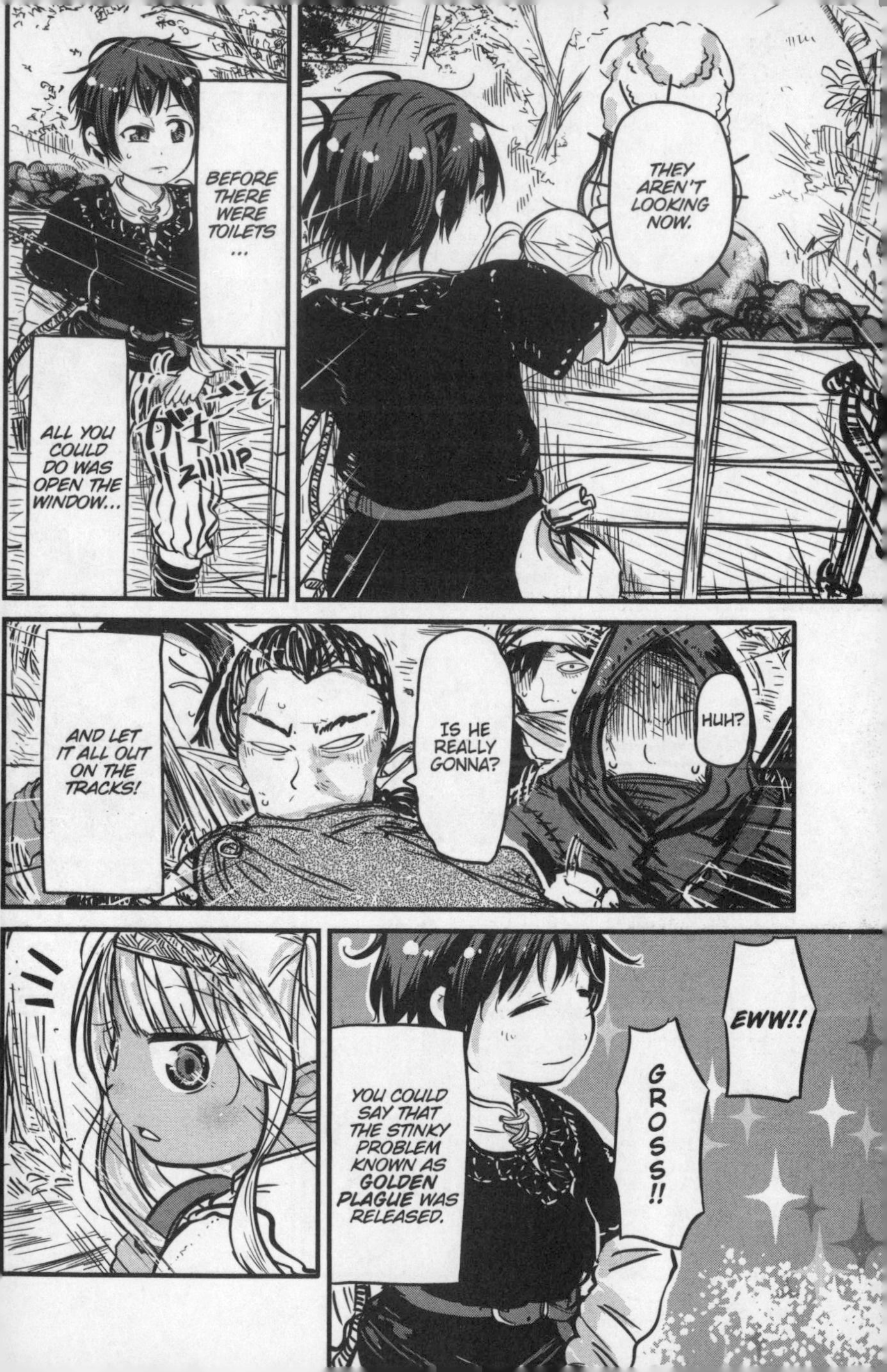
THEY AREN'T LOOKING NOW.
BEFORE THERE WERE TOILETS ...
ALL YOU COULD DO WAS OPEN THE WINDOW...
ZIIIIIP
HUH?
IS HE REALLY GONNA?
AND LET IT ALL OUT ON THE TRACKS!
EWW!!
GROSS!!
YOU COULD SAY THAT THE STINKY PROBLEM KNOWN AS GOLDEN PLAGUE WAS RELEASED.

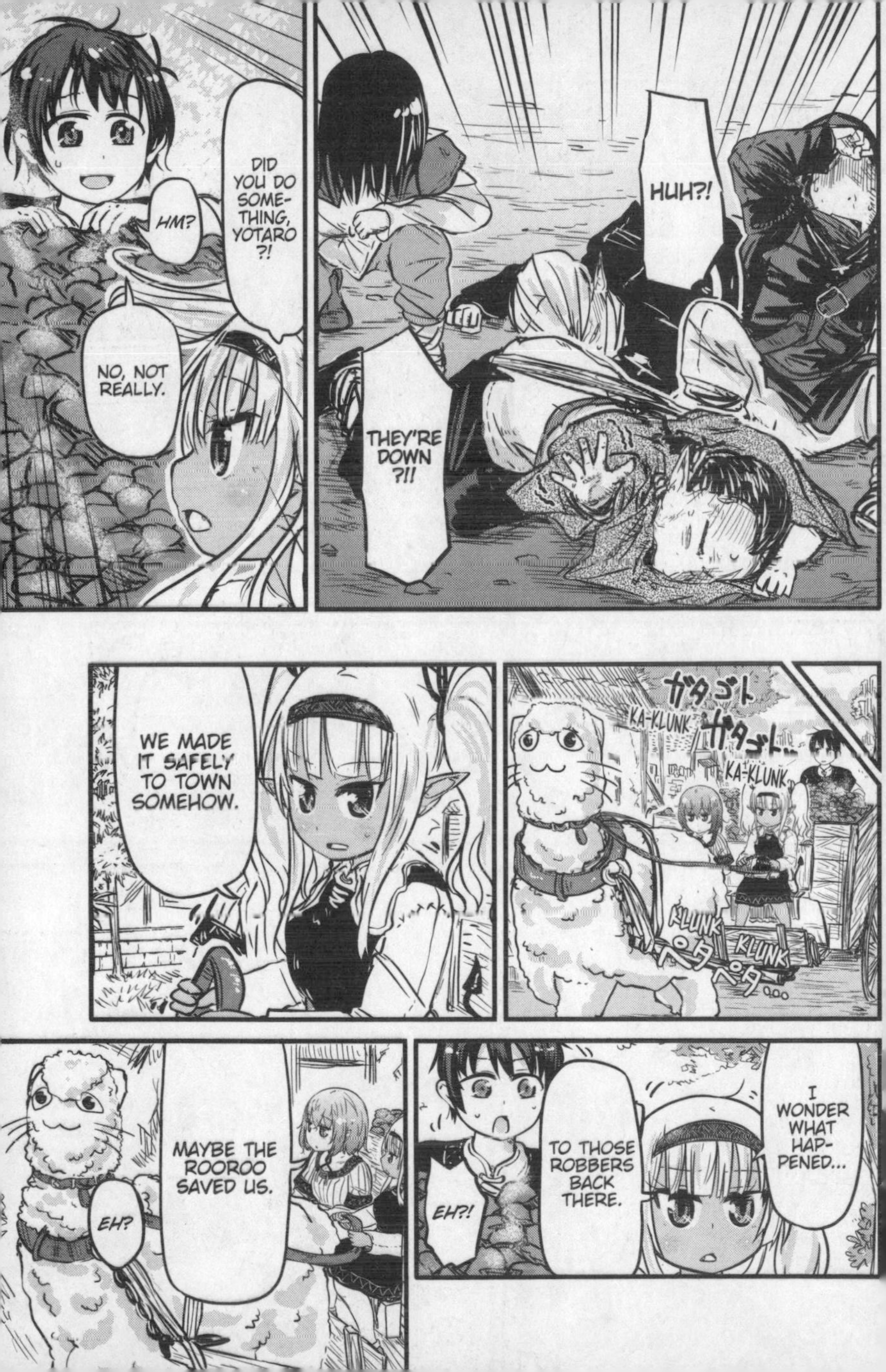
HUH?!
THEY'RE DOWN ?!!
DID YOU DO SOME-THING, YOTARO ?!
HM?
NO, NOT REALLY.
ガタゴト KA-KLUNK
ガタゴト KA-KLUNK
KLUNK KLUNK
ペタペタ
WE MADE IT SAFELY TO TOWN SOMEHOW.
I WONDER WHAT HAP-PENED...
TO THOSE ROBBERS BACK THERE.
EH?!
MAYBE THE ROOROO SAVED US.
EH?

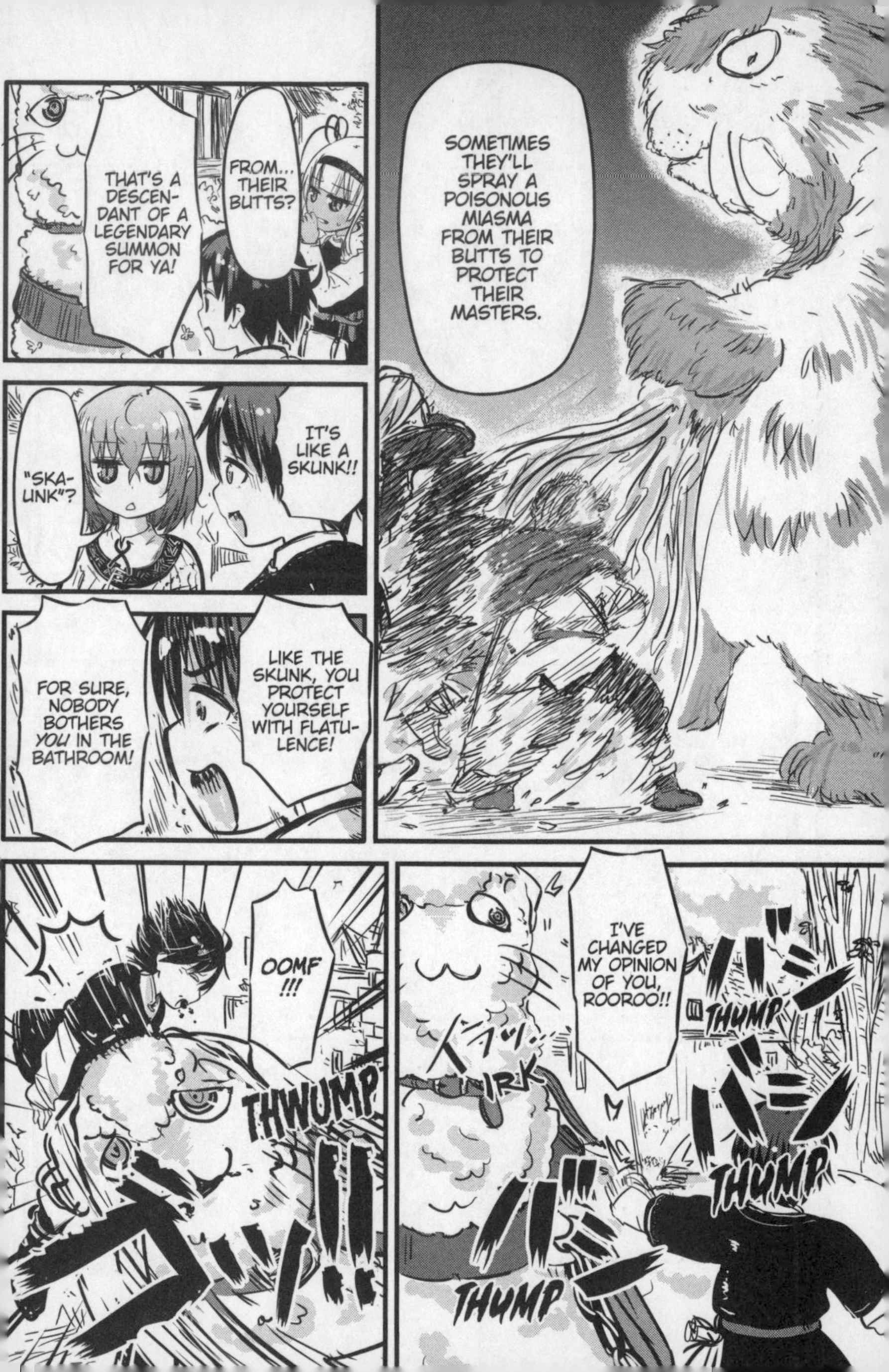
SOMETIMES THEY'LL SPRAY A POISONOUS MIASMA FROM THEIR BUTTS TO PROTECT THEIR MASTERS.
FROM... THEIR BUTTS?
THAT'S A DESCEN-DANT OF A LEGENDARY SUMMON FOR YA!
IT'S LIKE A SKUNK!!
"SKA-UNK"?
LIKE THE SKUNK, YOU PROTECT YOURSELF WITH FLATU-LENCE!
FOR SURE, NOBODY BOTHERS *YOU* IN THE BATHROOM!
I'VE CHANGED MY OPINION OF YOU, ROOROO!!
THUMP
IRK
THUMP
THUMP
OOMF !!!
THWUMP

ROOTS

PEOPLE WHO DON'T VALUE TOILET TIME ARE NO GOOD.

FOURTEENTH TOILET TIME

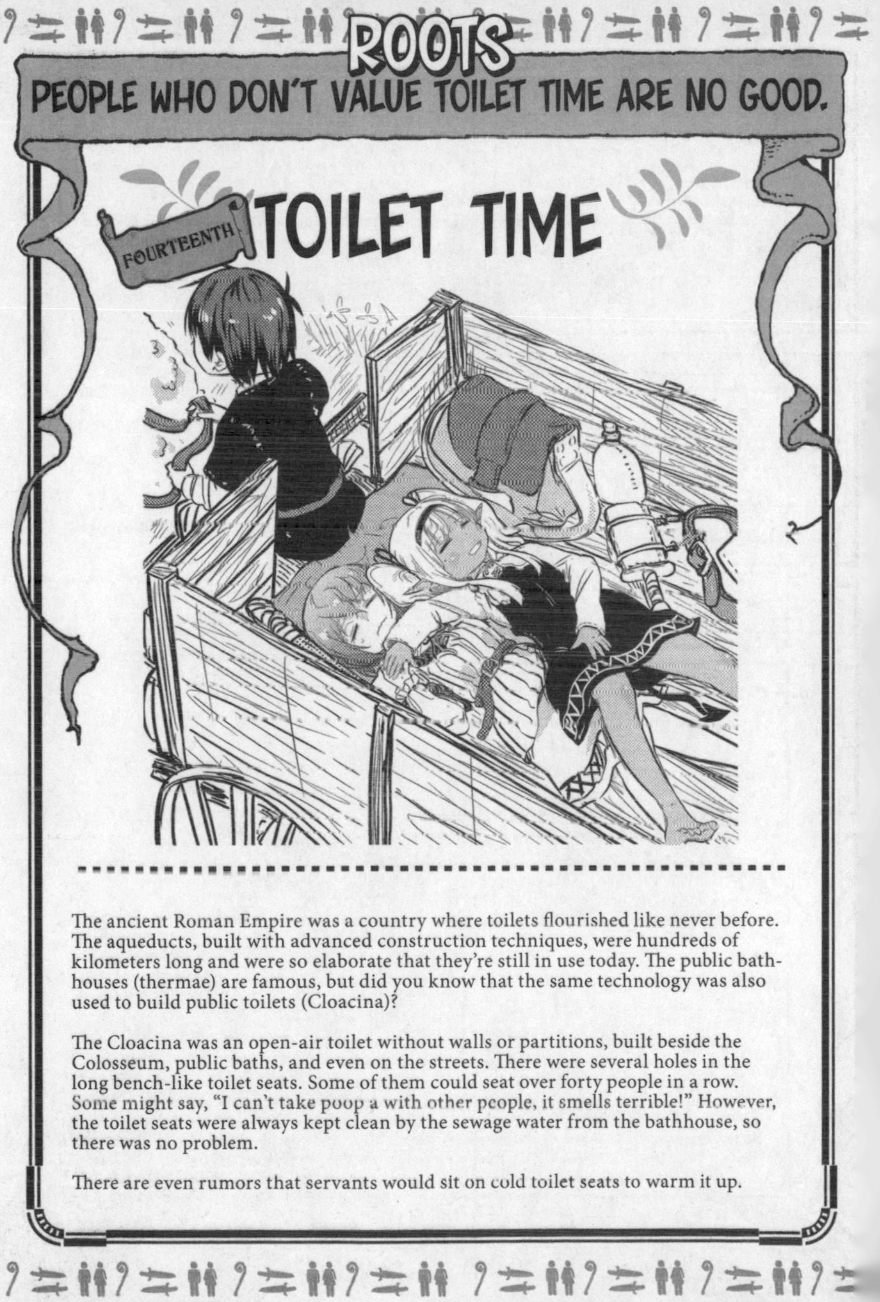

The ancient Roman Empire was a country where toilets flourished like never before. The aqueducts, built with advanced construction techniques, were hundreds of kilometers long and were so elaborate that they're still in use today. The public bathhouses (thermae) are famous, but did you know that the same technology was also used to build public toilets (Cloacina)?

The Cloacina was an open-air toilet without walls or partitions, built beside the Colosseum, public baths, and even on the streets. There were several holes in the long bench-like toilet seats. Some of them could seat over forty people in a row. Some might say, "I can't take poop a with other people, it smells terrible!" However, the toilet seats were always kept clean by the sewage water from the bathhouse, so there was no problem.

There are even rumors that servants would sit on cold toilet seats to warm it up.

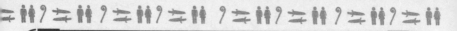

After using the toilet, it was time for the famous Cloacina "sponge sticks." This item was just as it sounds, a stick attached to a sponge, which are plentiful in the Mediterranean Sea. The etiquette was to take the sponge stick out of the bucket of salt water, wipe your bottom, and after using it, wash it again and put it back.

The Romans seemed to think this was hygienic. However, to modern sensibilities, it would seem quite disgusting. In fact, public use of this tool led to outbreaks of the plague. In addition, methane gas from feces and urine accumulated in the sewer system and sometimes caused explosions.

The Romans were also clever enough to install pump toilets instead of flush toilets. Feces and urine could be reused in many ways, so pots used by pee collectors and large pots and barrels for storing poop have been discovered.

Unfortunately, this toilet technology disappeared with the fall of the Roman Empire. It wasn't until nearly a thousand years later that public toilets were built again in the same area. Let us be thankful for our modern toilets, and do our business with this in mind!

IN OTHER WORDS

THIS MAXIM

"... A SPONGE FILLED WITH SOUR WINE AND ATTACHED TO A REED STICK ..."

–FROM THE GOSPEL OF MARK (A SECTION ABOUT THE SPONGE AND STICK)

YOU! YOU DID WELL BRINGING ME MY FREIGHT!
IT WASN'T EASY.
THIS ...
DO YOU MIND IF I HAVE A FEW OF THESE ION METAL ROCKS?
YOU CAN HAVE THEM AS PART OF YOUR PAYMENT!
WHAT ARE YOU GOING TO USE THOSE FOR?
WELL...
I THINK I'LL PLACE THEM ABOVE MY WATER TANK.
WATER TANK?

TWENTY-EIGHTH FLUSH

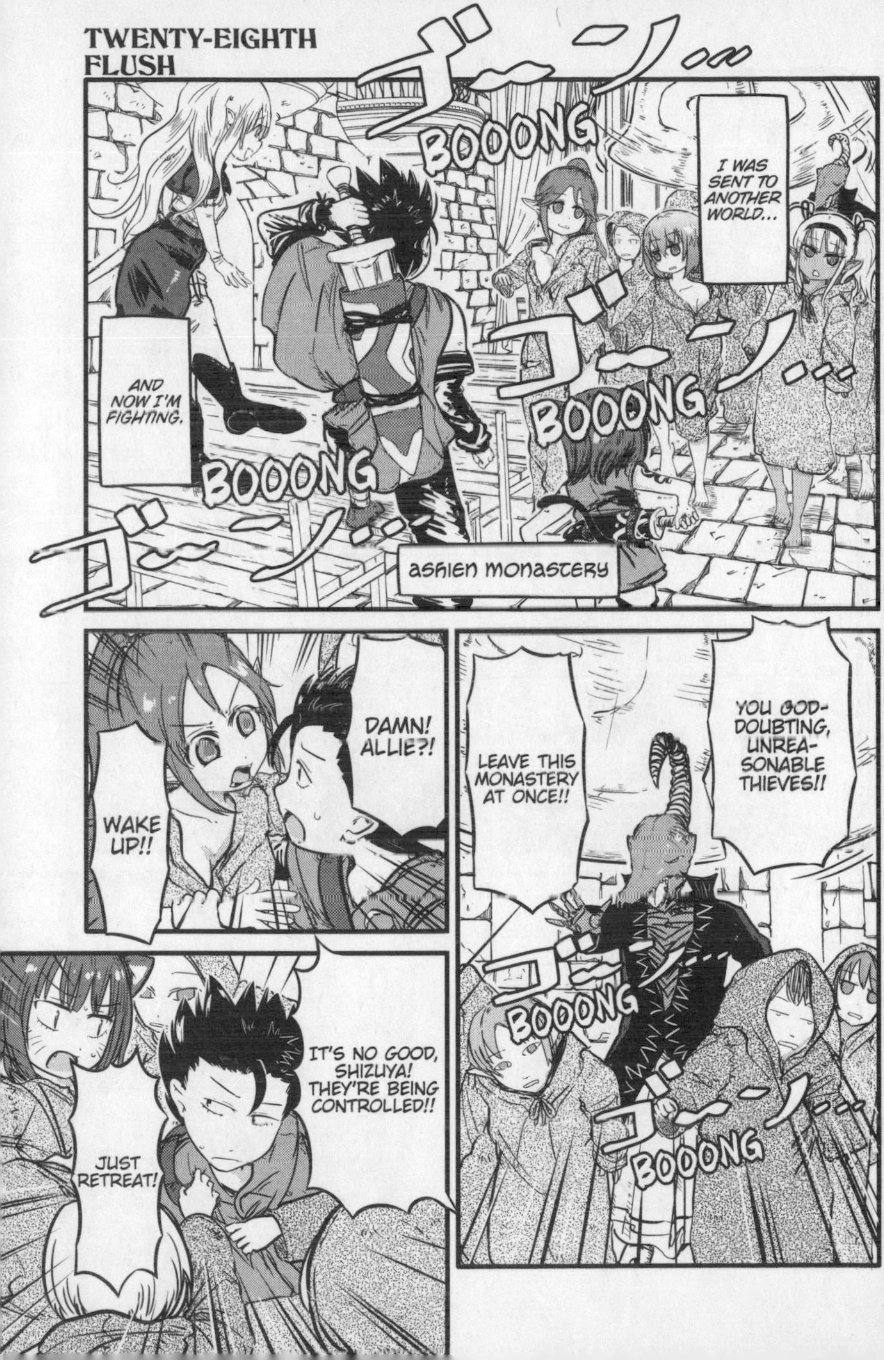

I WAS SENT TO ANOTHER WORLD...
BOOONG
BOOONG
AND NOW I'M FIGHTING.
BOOONG
ashien monastery
YOU GOD-DOUBTING, UNREA-SONABLE THIEVES!!
LEAVE THIS MONASTERY AT ONCE!!
BOOONG
BOOONG
DAMN! ALLIE?!
WAKE UP!!
IT'S NO GOOD, SHIZUYA! THEY'RE BEING CONTROLLED!!
JUST RETREAT!

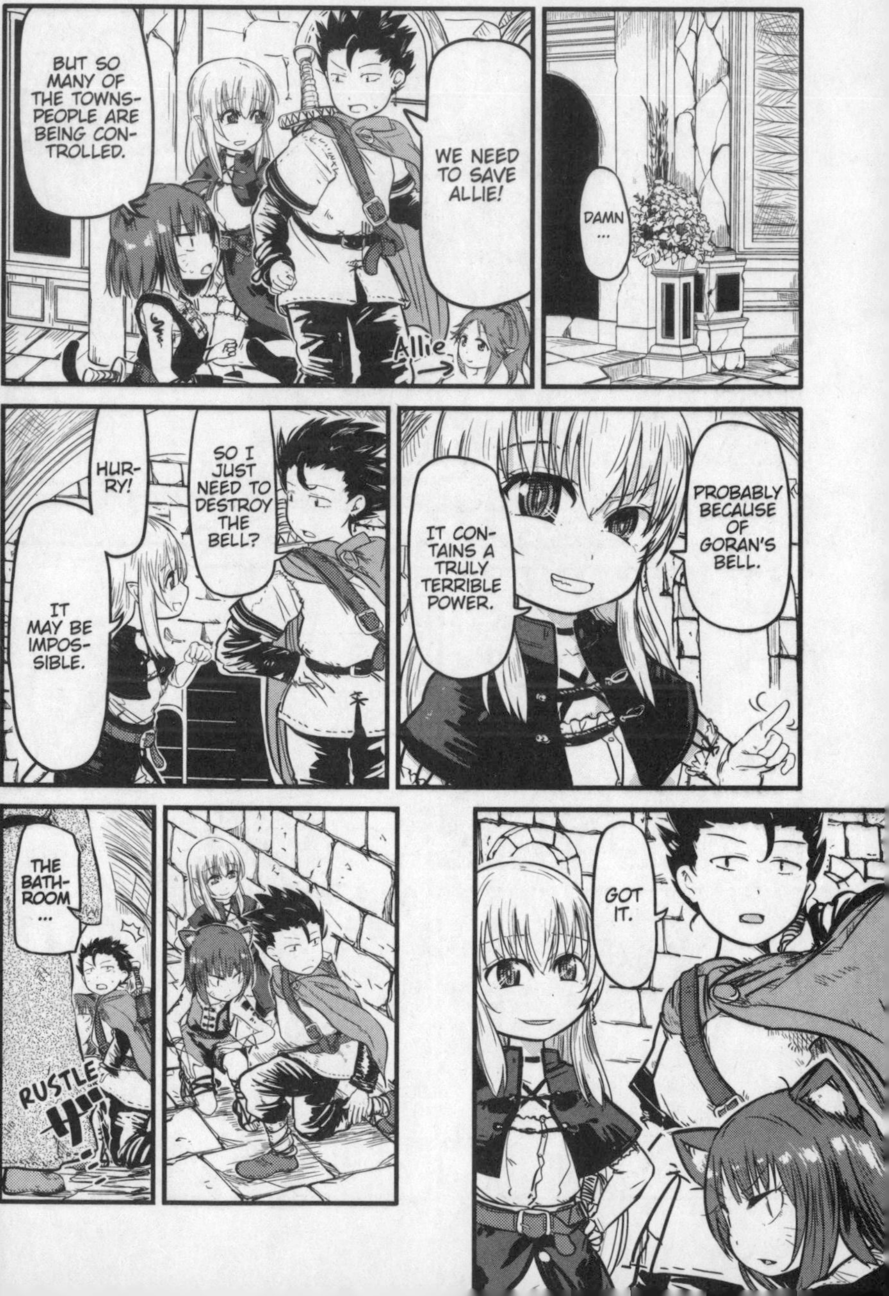
DAMN ...
WE NEED TO SAVE ALLIE!
BUT SO MANY OF THE TOWNS-PEOPLE ARE BEING CON-TROLLED.
Allie
PROBABLY BECAUSE OF GORAN'S BELL.
IT CON-TAINS A TRULY TERRIBLE POWER.
SO I JUST NEED TO DESTROY THE BELL?
HUR-RY!
IT MAY BE IMPOS-SIBLE.
GOT IT.
THE BATH-ROOM ...
RUSTLE

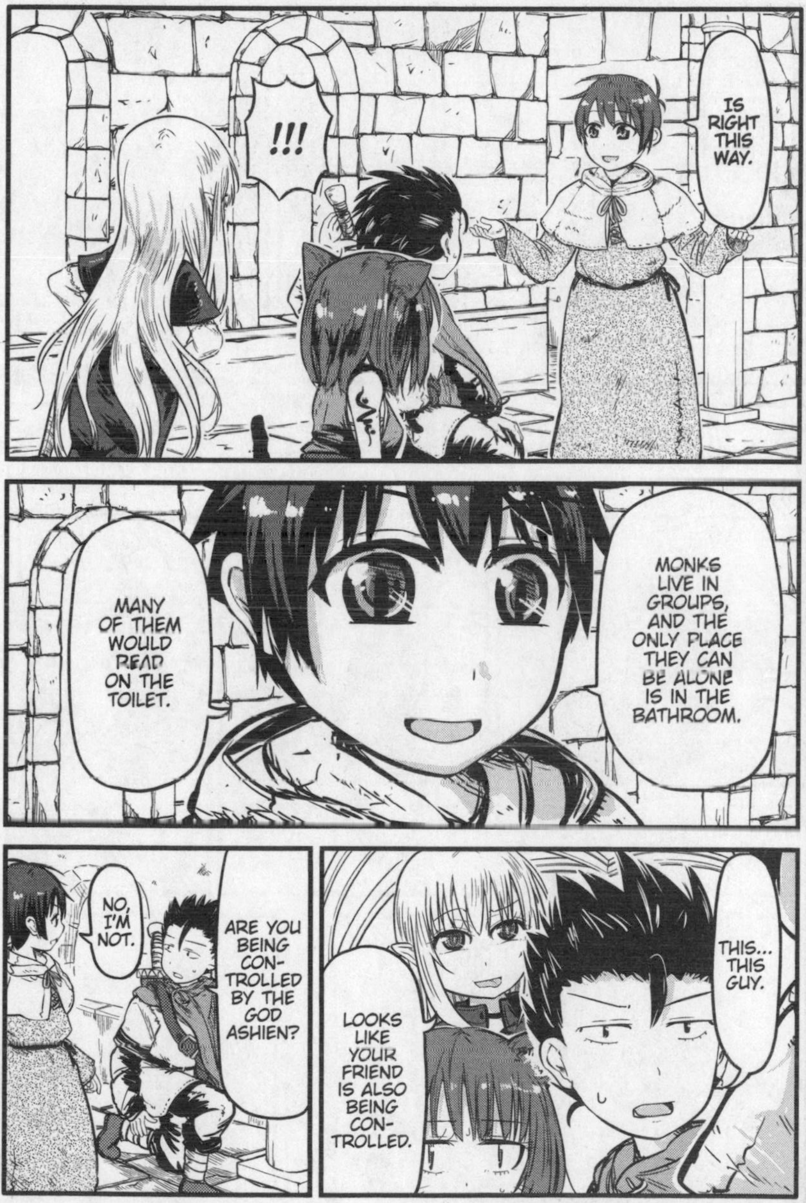
IS RIGHT THIS WAY.
!!!
MONKS LIVE IN GROUPS, AND THE ONLY PLACE THEY CAN BE ALONE IS IN THE BATHROOM.
MANY OF THEM WOULD READ ON THE TOILET.
THIS... THIS GUY.
LOOKS LIKE YOUR FRIEND IS ALSO BEING CON-TROLLED.
ARE YOU BEING CON-TROLLED BY THE GOD ASHIEN?
NO, I'M NOT.

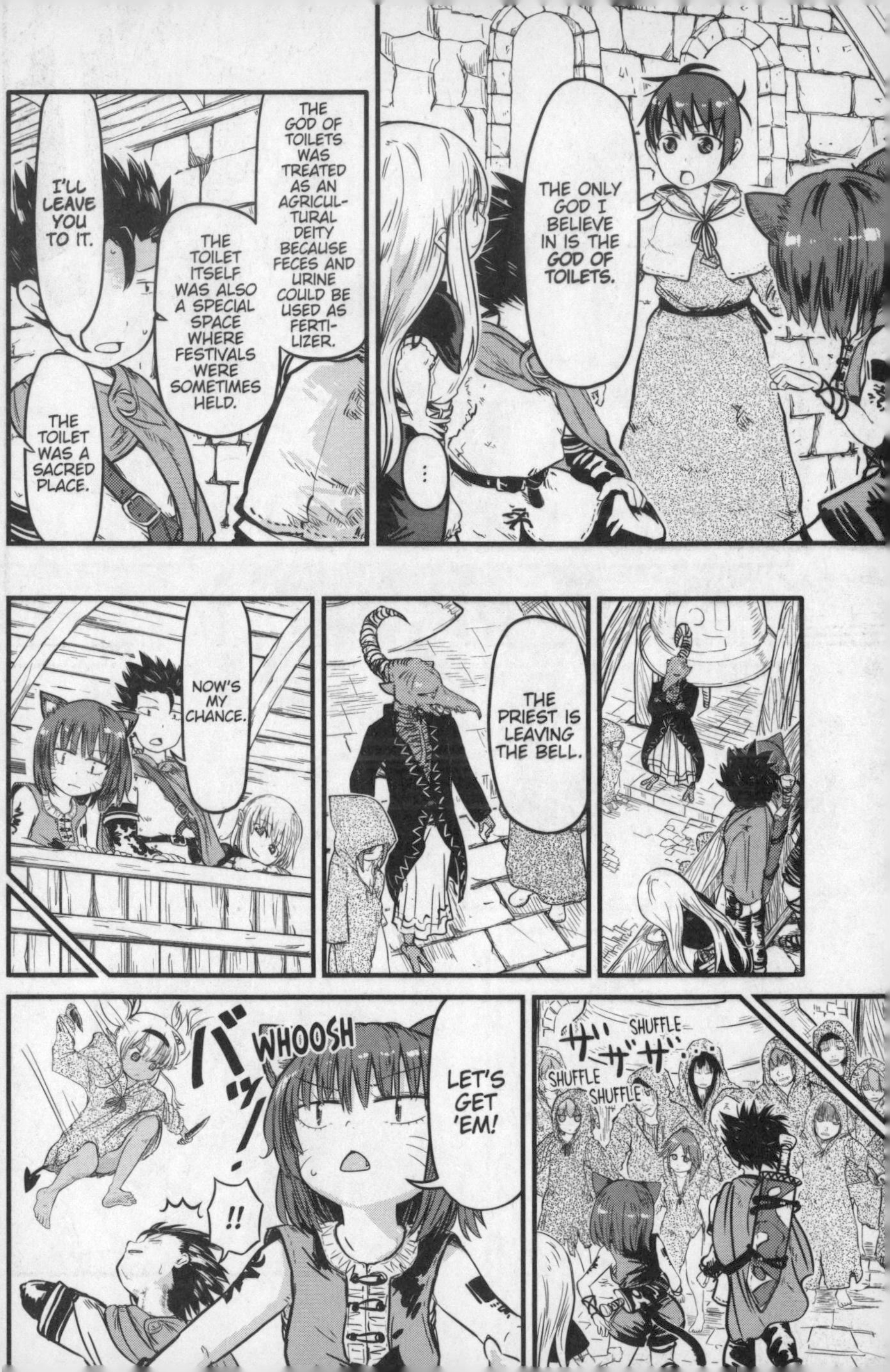
THE ONLY GOD I BELIEVE IN IS THE GOD OF TOILETS.
...
THE GOD OF TOILETS WAS TREATED AS AN AGRICULTURAL DEITY BECAUSE FECES AND URINE COULD BE USED AS FERTILIZER.
I'LL LEAVE YOU TO IT.
THE TOILET ITSELF WAS ALSO A SPECIAL SPACE WHERE FESTIVALS WERE SOMETIMES HELD.
THE TOILET WAS A SACRED PLACE.
THE PRIEST IS LEAVING THE BELL.
NOW'S MY CHANCE.
SHUFFLE
ザッザザ
SHUFFLE
SHUFFLE
LET'S GET 'EM!
WHOOSH
バッ
!!

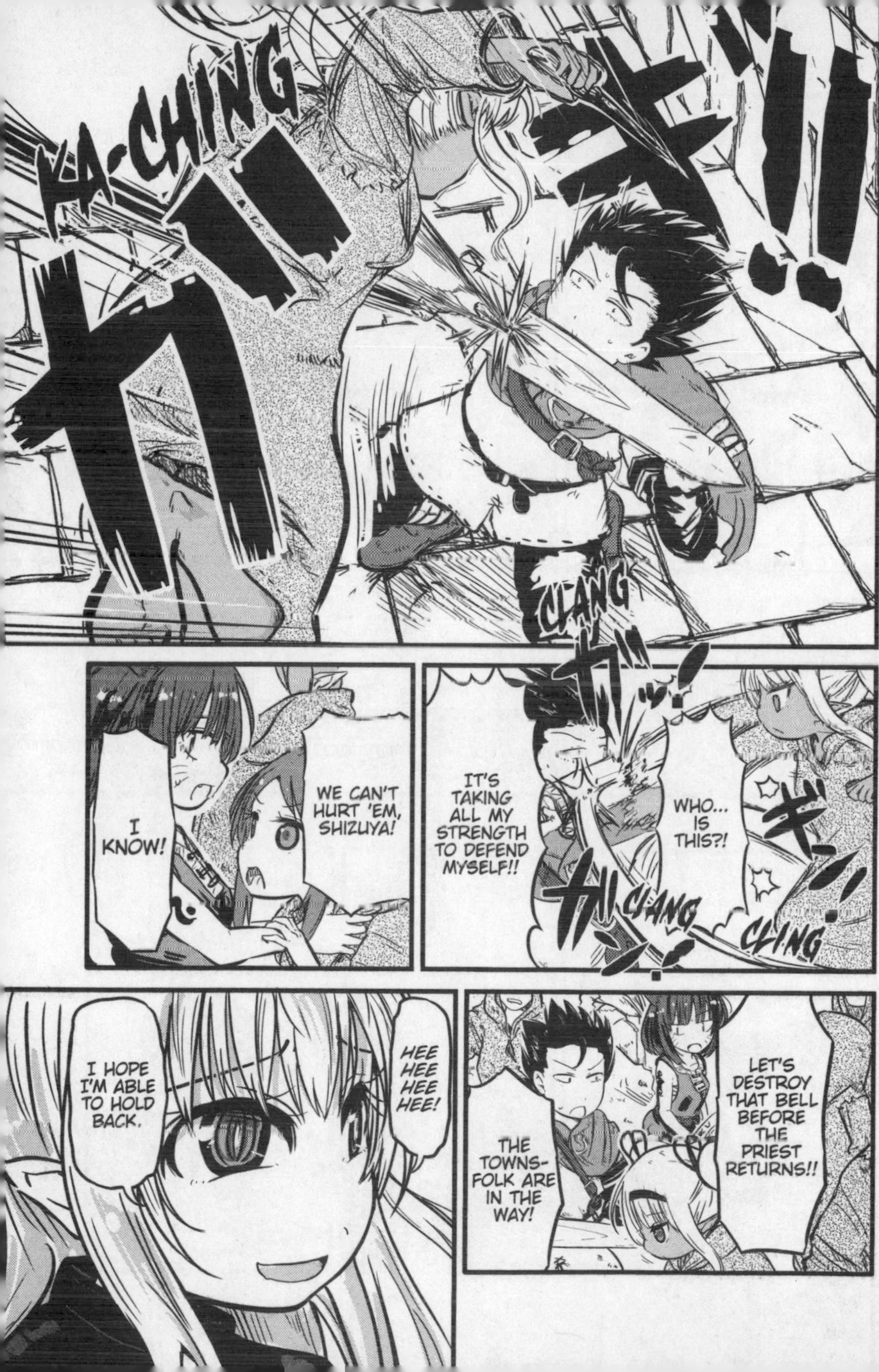

KA-CHING
CLANG
WHO... IS THIS?!
IT'S TAKING ALL MY STRENGTH TO DEFEND MYSELF!!
CLING
CLANG
WE CAN'T HURT 'EM, SHIZUYA!
I KNOW!
LET'S DESTROY THAT BELL BEFORE THE PRIEST RETURNS!!
THE TOWNS-FOLK ARE IN THE WAY!
HEE HEE HEE HEE!
I HOPE I'M ABLE TO HOLD BACK.

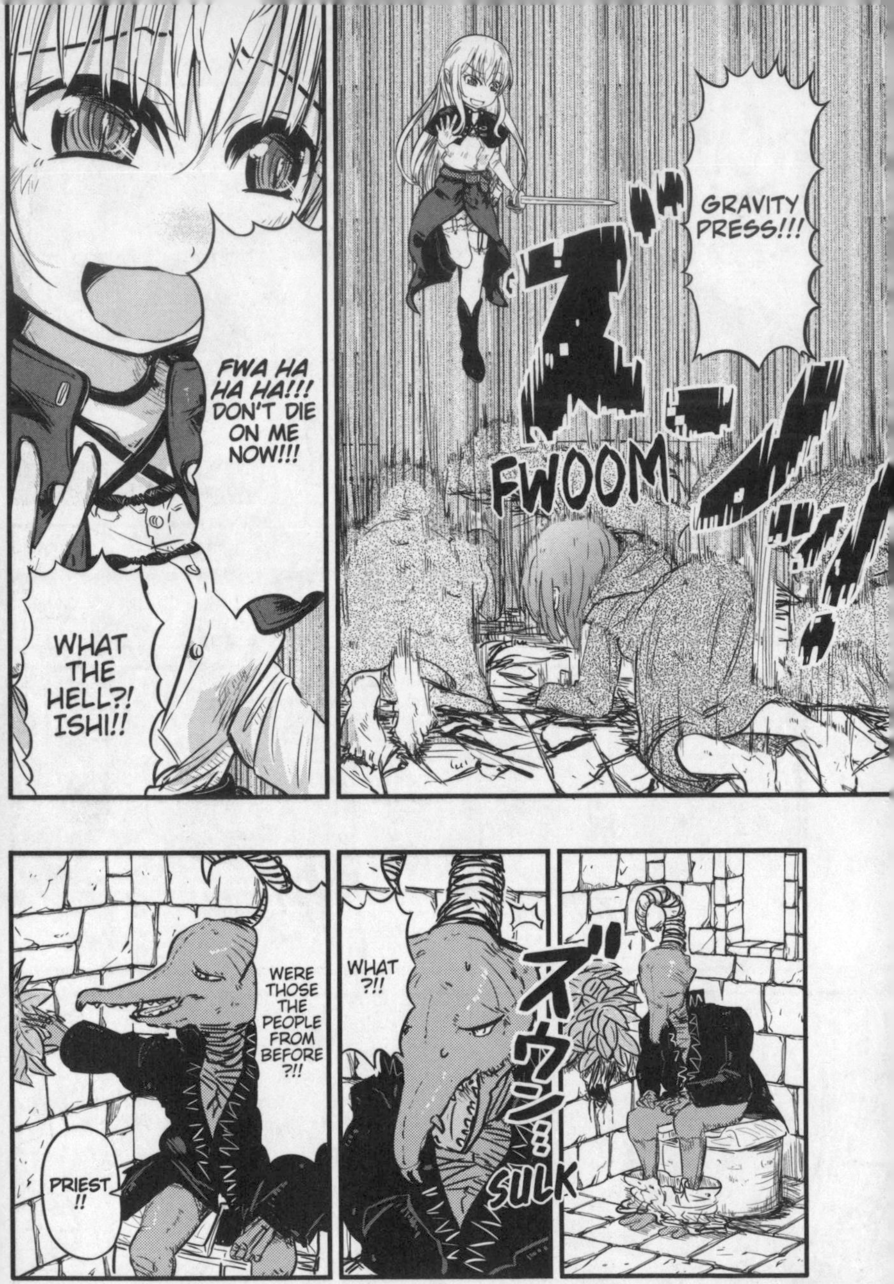
GRAVITY PRESS!!!
FWOOM
FWA HA HA HA!!! DON'T DIE ON ME NOW!!!
WHAT THE HELL?! ISHI!!
SULK
WHAT ?!!
WERE THOSE THE PEOPLE FROM BEFORE ?!!
PRIEST !!

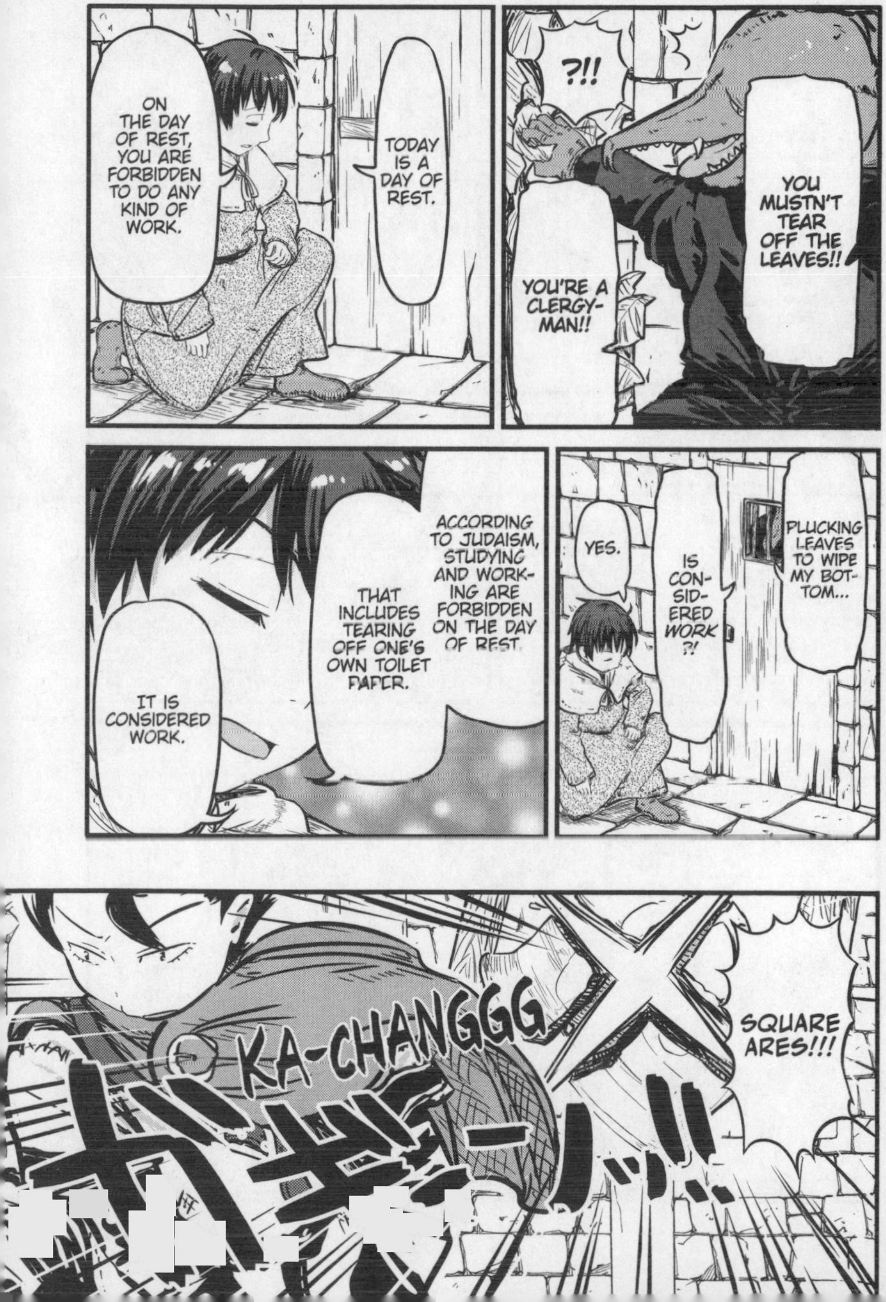
?!!
YOU MUSTN'T TEAR OFF THE LEAVES!!
YOU'RE A CLERGY-MAN!!
TODAY IS A DAY OF REST.
ON THE DAY OF REST, YOU ARE FORBIDDEN TO DO ANY KIND OF WORK.
PLUCKING LEAVES TO WIPE MY BOT-TOM...
IS CON-SID-ERED *WORK* ?!
YES.
ACCORDING TO JUDAISM, STUDYING AND WORK-ING ARE FORBIDDEN ON THE DAY OF REST.
THAT INCLUDES TEARING OFF ONE'S OWN TOILET PAPER.
IT IS CONSIDERED WORK.
SQUARE ARES!!!
KA-CHANGGG

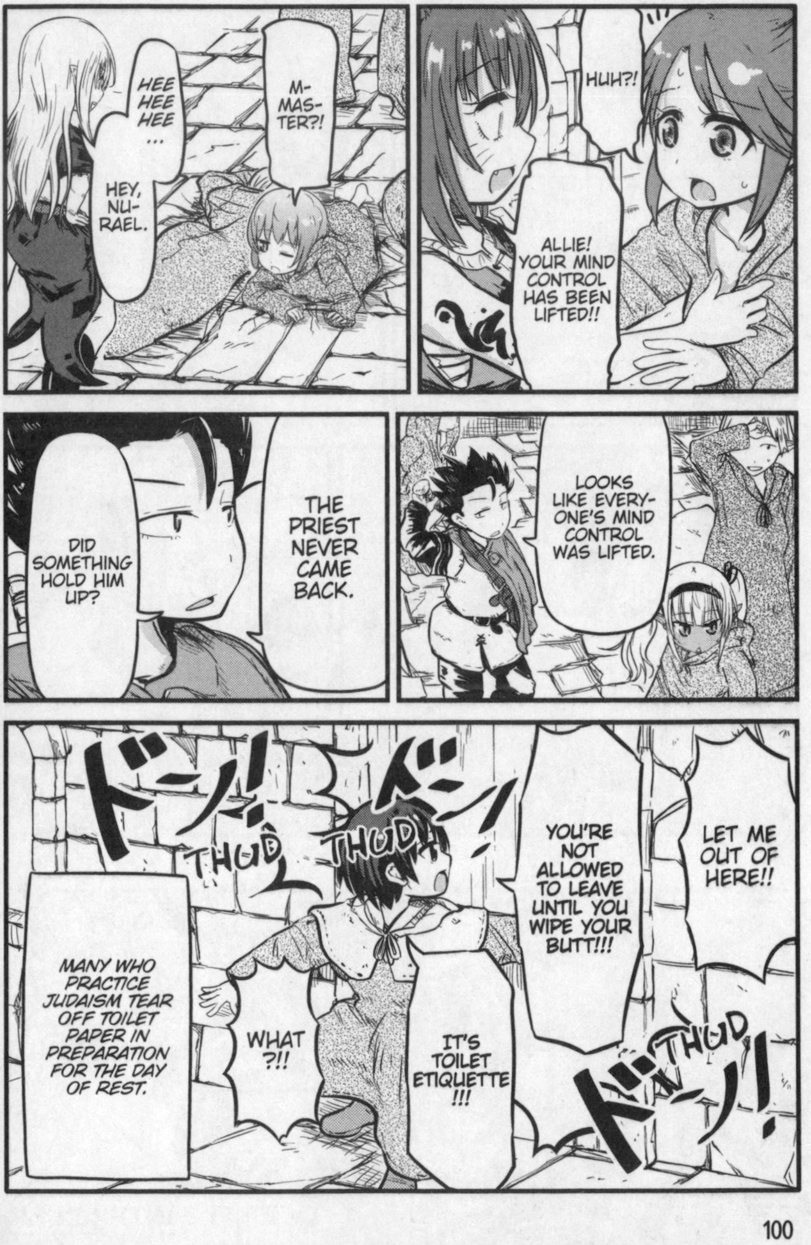
HUH?!
ALLIE! YOUR MIND CONTROL HAS BEEN LIFTED!!
M-MAS-TER?!
HEE HEE HEE ...
HEY, NU-RAEL.
LOOKS LIKE EVERY-ONE'S MIND CONTROL WAS LIFTED.
THE PRIEST NEVER CAME BACK.
DID SOMETHING HOLD HIM UP?
LET ME OUT OF HERE!!
YOU'RE NOT ALLOWED TO LEAVE UNTIL YOU WIPE YOUR BUTT!!!
THUD
THUD
THUD
IT'S TOILET ETIQUETTE!!!
WHAT?!!
MANY WHO PRACTICE JUDAISM TEAR OFF TOILET PAPER IN PREPARATION FOR THE DAY OF REST.

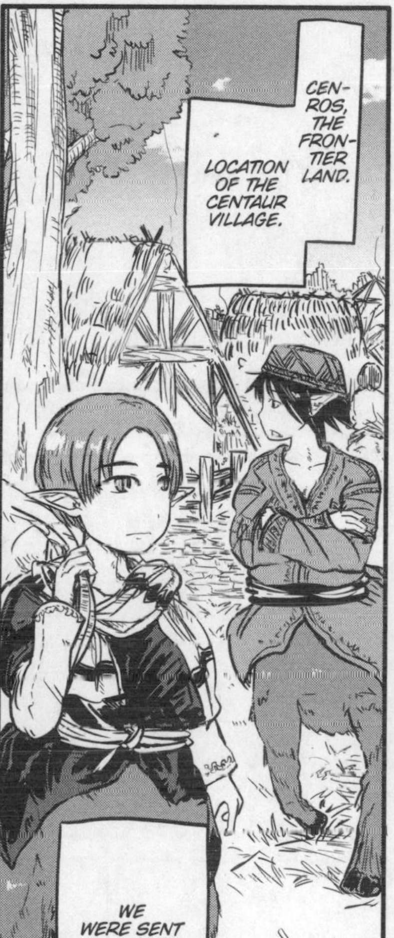
CENROS, THE FRONTIER LAND.
LOCATION OF THE CENTAUR VILLAGE.
WE WERE SENT ON A GUILD MISSION TO RETRIEVE AN ITEM.

TWENTY-NINTH FLUSH

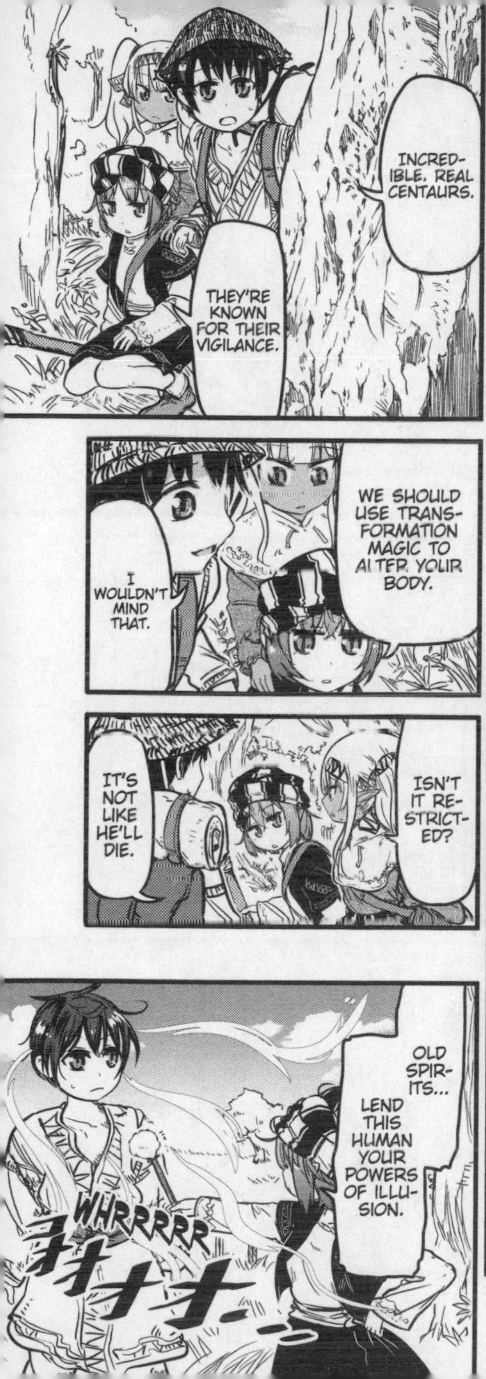
INCREDIBLE. REAL CENTAURS.
THEY'RE KNOWN FOR THEIR VIGILANCE.
WE SHOULD USE TRANSFORMATION MAGIC TO ALTER YOUR BODY.
I WOULDN'T MIND THAT.
ISN'T IT RESTRICTED?
IT'S NOT LIKE HE'LL DIE.
OLD SPIRITS... LEND THIS HUMAN YOUR POWERS OF ILLUSION.
WHRRRRR

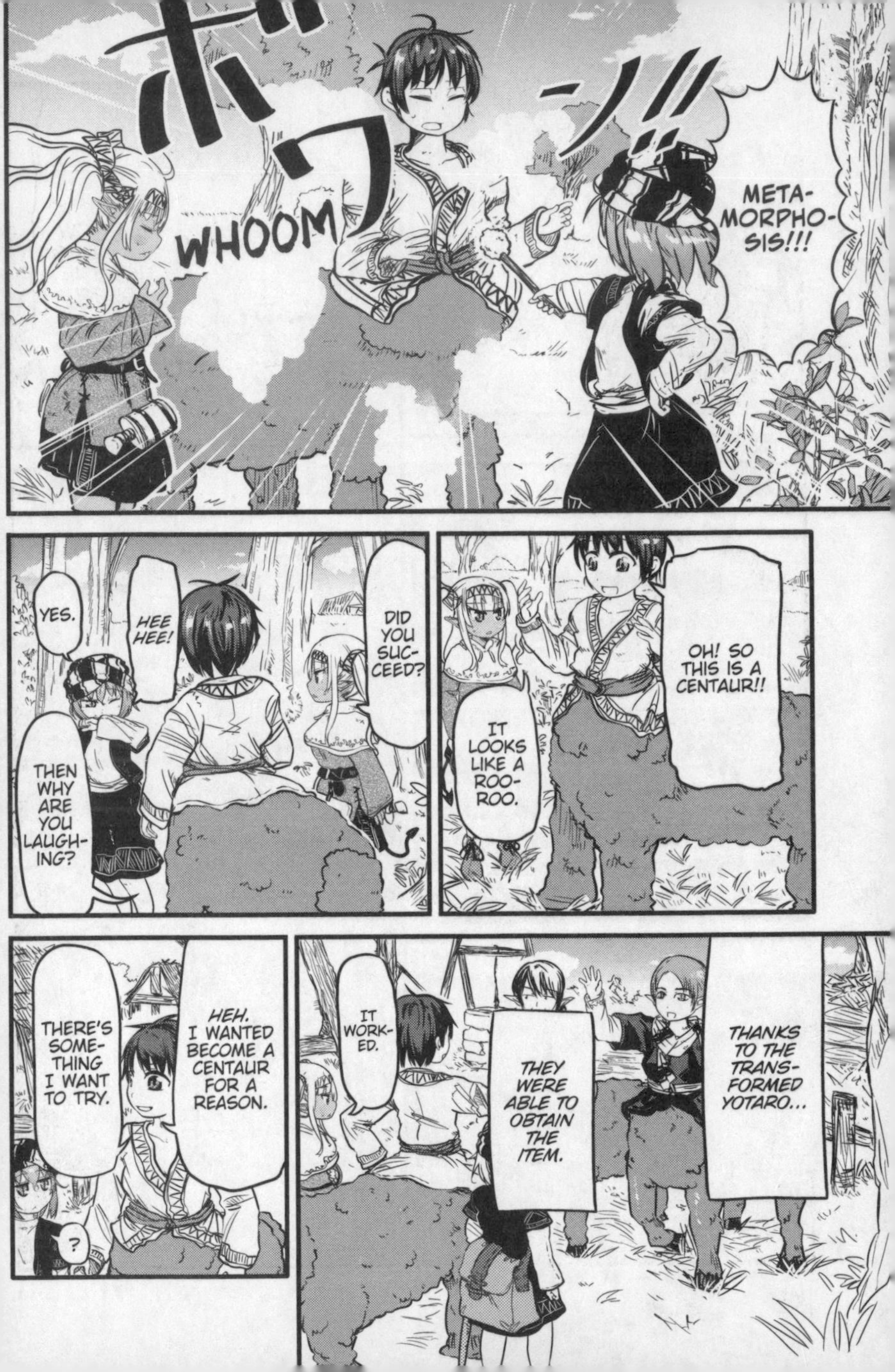
METAMORPHOSIS!!!
ボワーン!!
WHOOM
OH! SO THIS IS A CENTAUR!!
IT LOOKS LIKE A ROO-ROO.
DID YOU SUCCEED?
HEE HEE!
YES.
THEN WHY ARE YOU LAUGHING?
THANKS TO THE TRANSFORMED YOTARO...
THEY WERE ABLE TO OBTAIN THE ITEM.
IT WORKED.
HEH. I WANTED BECOME A CENTAUR FOR A REASON.
THERE'S SOMETHING I WANT TO TRY.
?

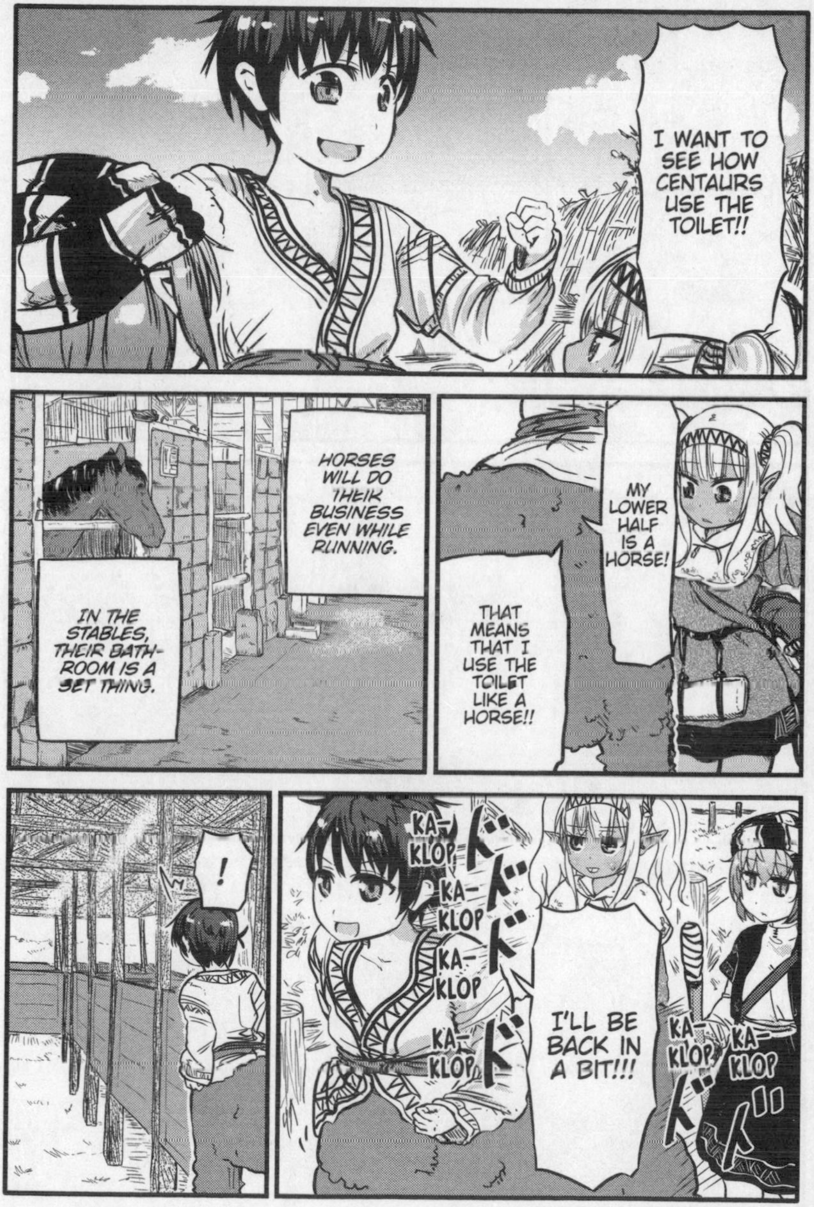
I WANT TO SEE HOW CENTAURS USE THE TOILET!!
MY LOWER HALF IS A HORSE!
THAT MEANS THAT I USE THE TOILET LIKE A HORSE!!
HORSES WILL DO THEIR BUSINESS EVEN WHILE RUNNING.
IN THE STABLES, THEIR BATHROOM IS A SET THING.
KA-KLOP
KA-KLOP
I'LL BE BACK IN A BIT!!!
KA-KLOP
KA-KLOP
KA-KLOP
KA-KLOP
!

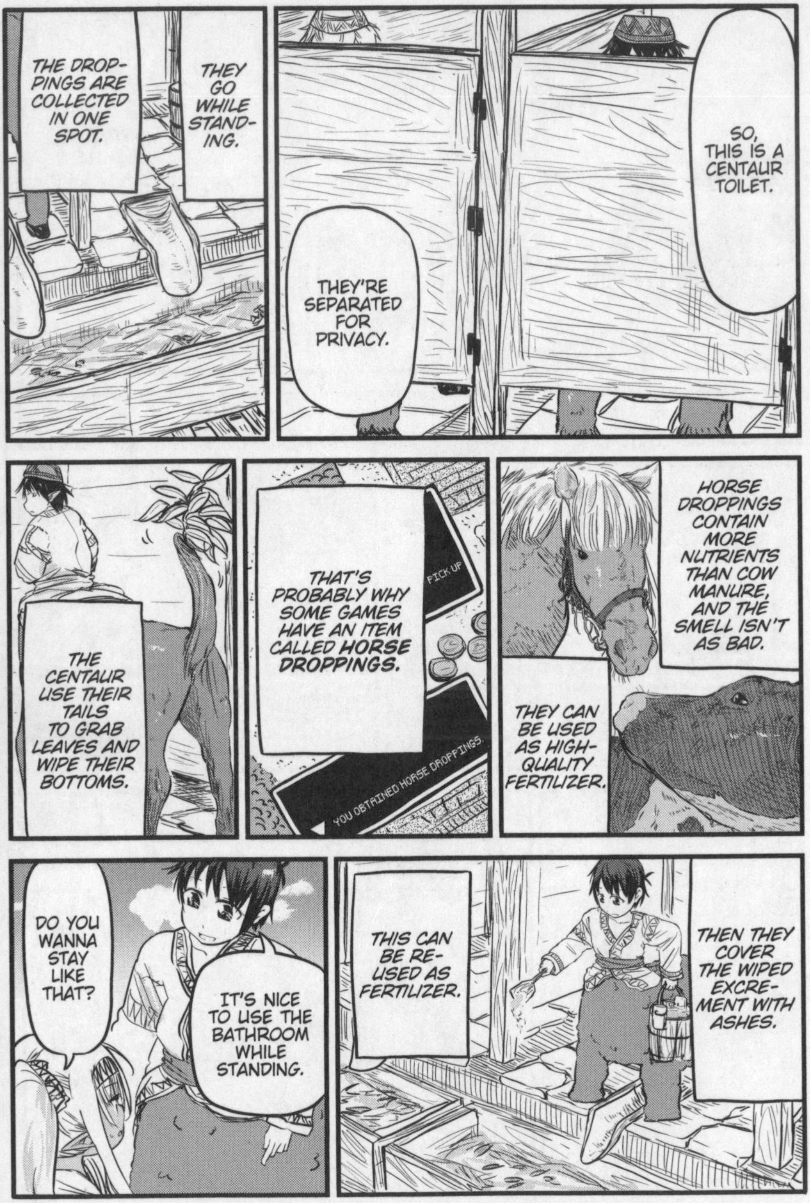
SO, THIS IS A CENTAUR TOILET.
THEY'RE SEPARATED FOR PRIVACY.
THEY GO WHILE STANDING.
THE DROPPINGS ARE COLLECTED IN ONE SPOT.
HORSE DROPPINGS CONTAIN MORE NUTRIENTS THAN COW MANURE, AND THE SMELL ISN'T AS BAD.
THEY CAN BE USED AS HIGH-QUALITY FERTILIZER.
THAT'S PROBABLY WHY SOME GAMES HAVE AN ITEM CALLED **HORSE DROPPINGS.**
PICK UP
YOU OBTAINED HORSE DROPPINGS.
THE CENTAUR USE THEIR TAILS TO GRAB LEAVES AND WIPE THEIR BOTTOMS.
THEN THEY COVER THE WIPED EXCREMENT WITH ASHES.
THIS CAN BE RE-USED AS FERTILIZER.
IT'S NICE TO USE THE BATHROOM WHILE STANDING.
DO YOU WANNA STAY LIKE THAT?

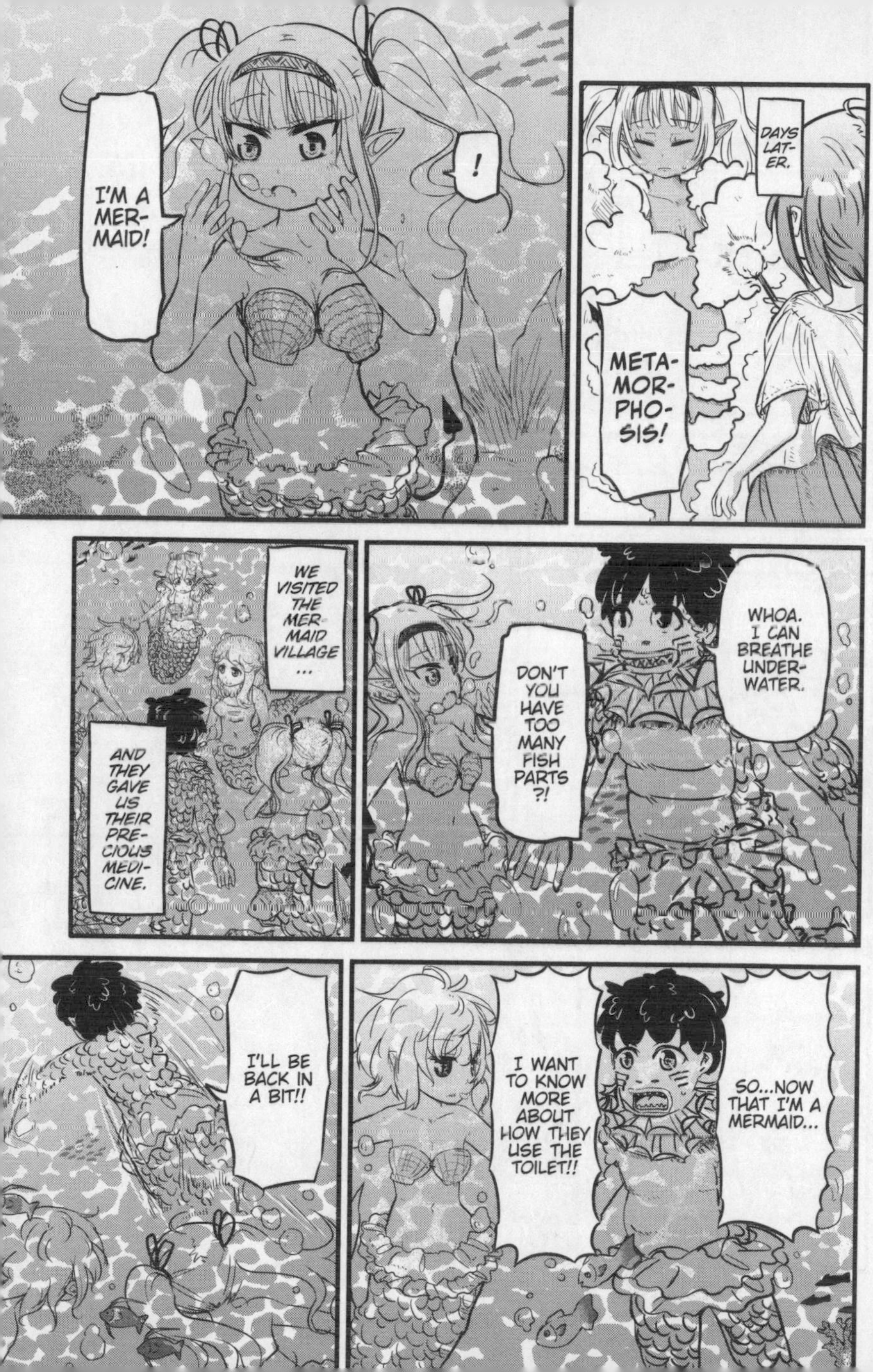
DAYS LATER.
METAMORPHOSIS!
!
I'M A MERMAID!
WHOA. I CAN BREATHE UNDERWATER.
DON'T YOU HAVE TOO MANY FISH PARTS?!
WE VISITED THE MERMAID VILLAGE...
AND THEY GAVE US THEIR PRECIOUS MEDICINE.
SO...NOW THAT I'M A MERMAID...
I WANT TO KNOW MORE ABOUT HOW THEY USE THE TOILET!!
I'LL BE BACK IN A BIT!!

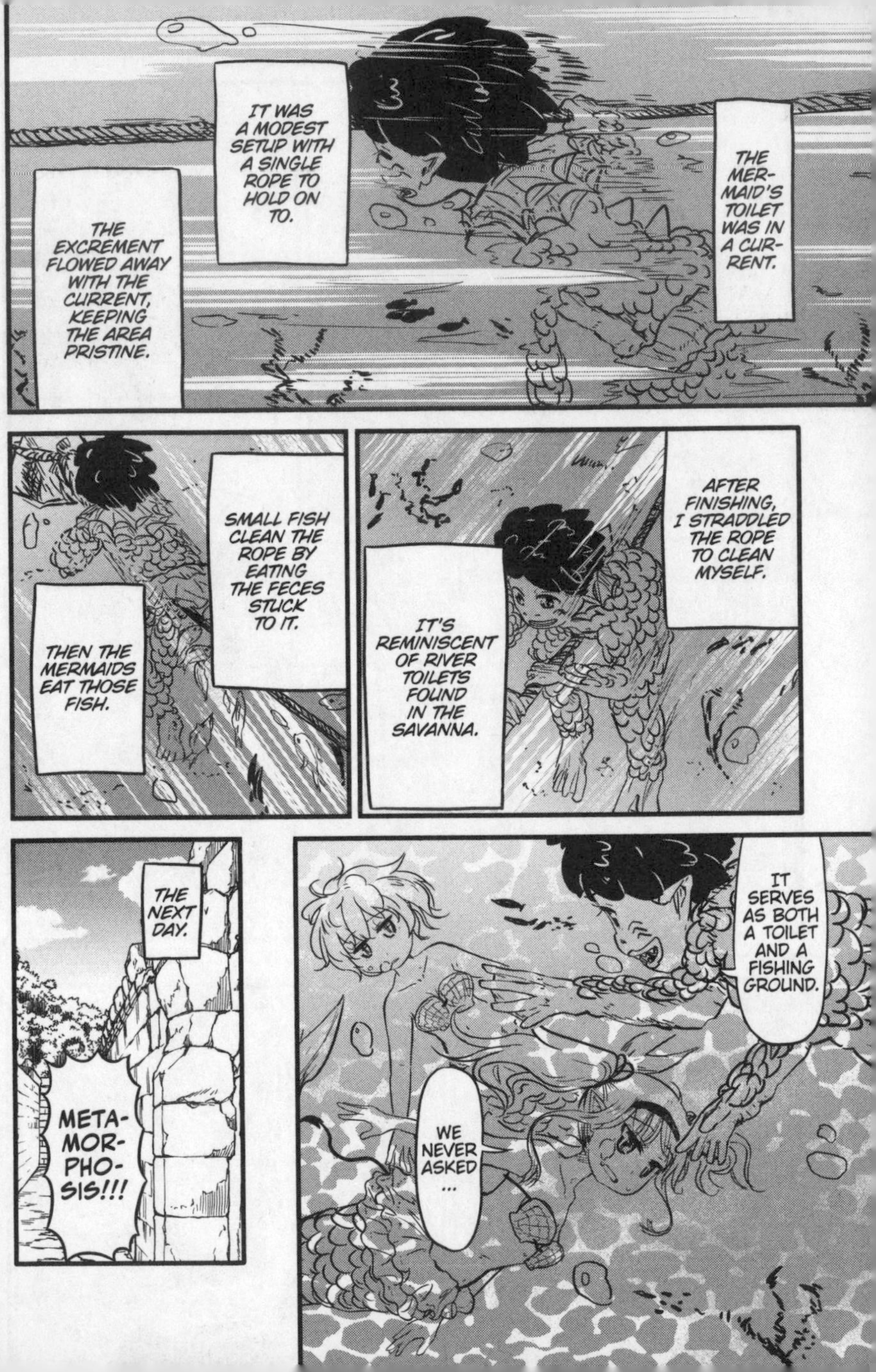
THE MER-MAID'S TOILET WAS IN A CUR-RENT.
IT WAS A MODEST SETUP WITH A SINGLE ROPE TO HOLD ON TO.
THE EXCREMENT FLOWED AWAY WITH THE CURRENT, KEEPING THE AREA PRISTINE.
AFTER FINISHING, I STRADDLED THE ROPE TO CLEAN MYSELF.
IT'S REMINISCENT OF RIVER TOILETS FOUND IN THE SAVANNA.
SMALL FISH CLEAN THE ROPE BY EATING THE FECES STUCK TO IT.
THEN THE MERMAIDS EAT THOSE FISH.
IT SERVES AS BOTH A TOILET AND A FISHING GROUND.
WE NEVER ASKED ...
THE NEXT DAY.
META-MOR-PHO-SIS!!!

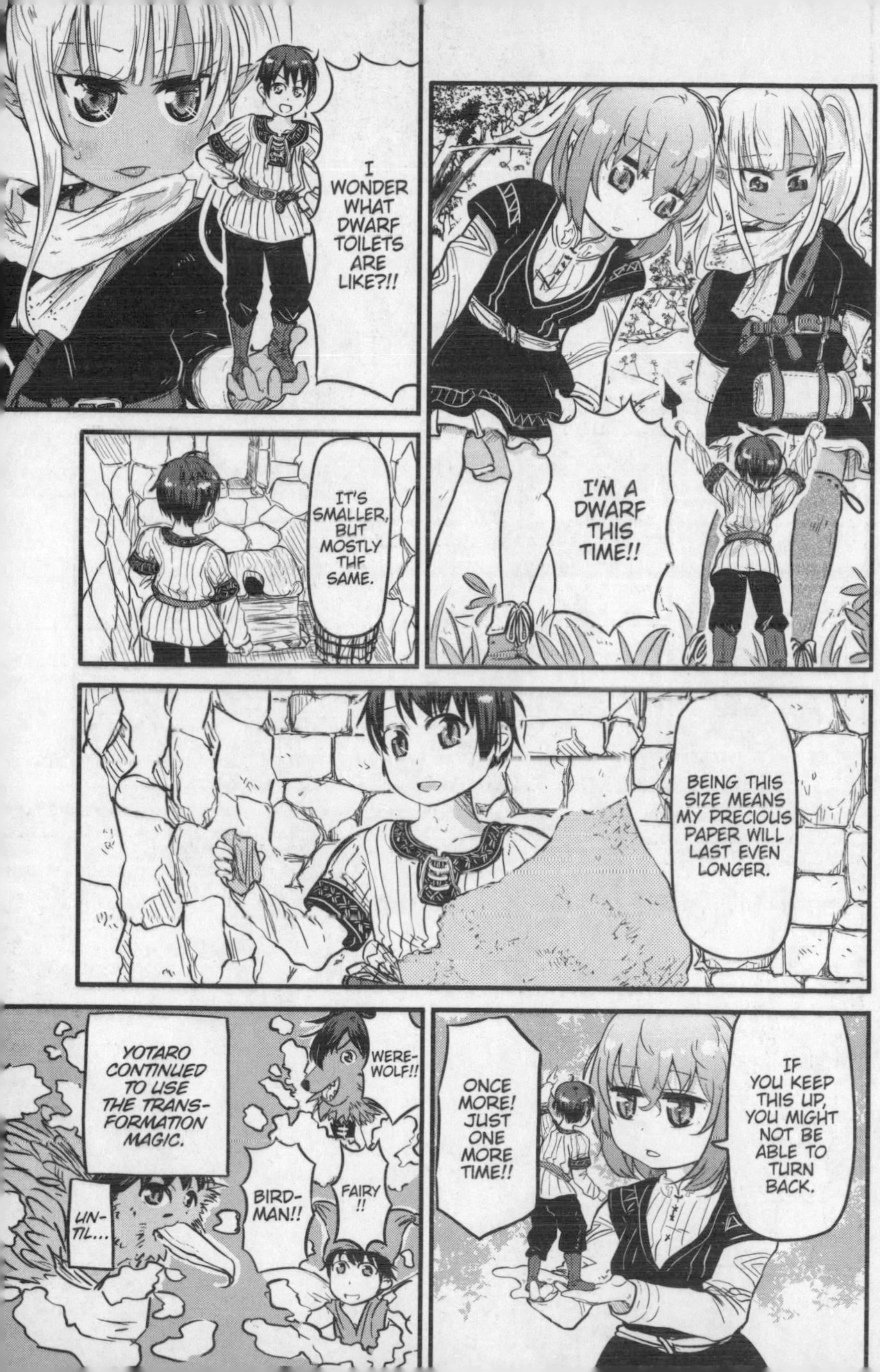
I'M A DWARF THIS TIME!!
I WONDER WHAT DWARF TOILETS ARE LIKE?!!
IT'S SMALLER, BUT MOSTLY THF SAME.
BEING THIS SIZE MEANS MY PRECIOUS PAPER WILL LAST EVEN LONGER.
IF YOU KEEP THIS UP, YOU MIGHT NOT BE ABLE TO TURN BACK.
ONCE MORE! JUST ONE MORE TIME!!
YOTARO CONTINUED TO USE THE TRANSFORMATION MAGIC.
WERE-WOLF!!
FAIRY!!
BIRD-MAN!!
UN-TIL...

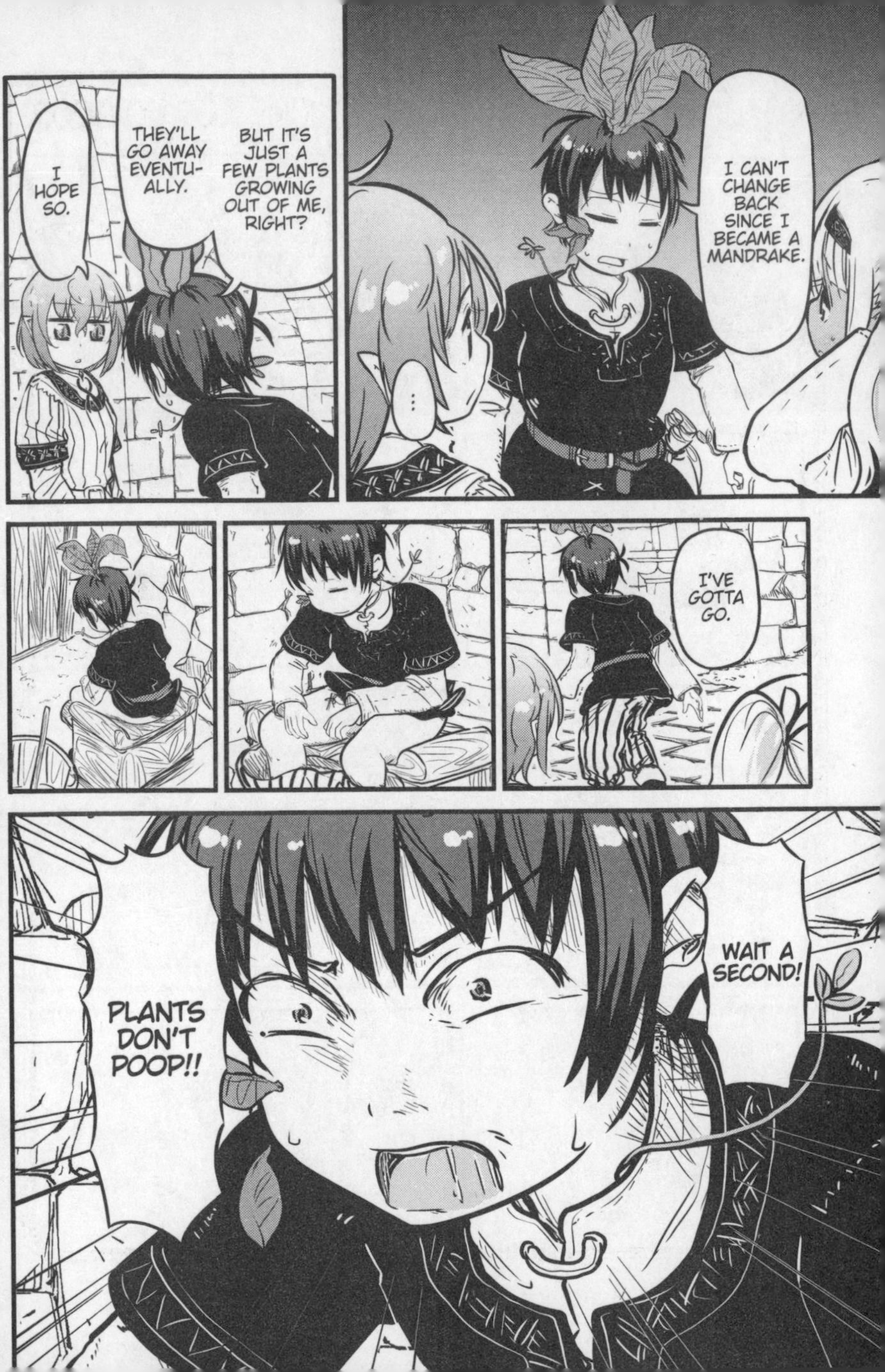
I CAN'T CHANGE BACK SINCE I BECAME A MANDRAKE.
...
BUT IT'S JUST A FEW PLANTS GROWING OUT OF ME, RIGHT?
THEY'LL GO AWAY EVENTUALLY.
I HOPE SO.
I'VE GOTTA GO.
WAIT A SECOND!
PLANTS DON'T POOP!!

ROOTS

PEOPLE WHO DON'T VALUE TOILET TIME ARE NO GOOD.

FIFTEENTH

TOILET TIME

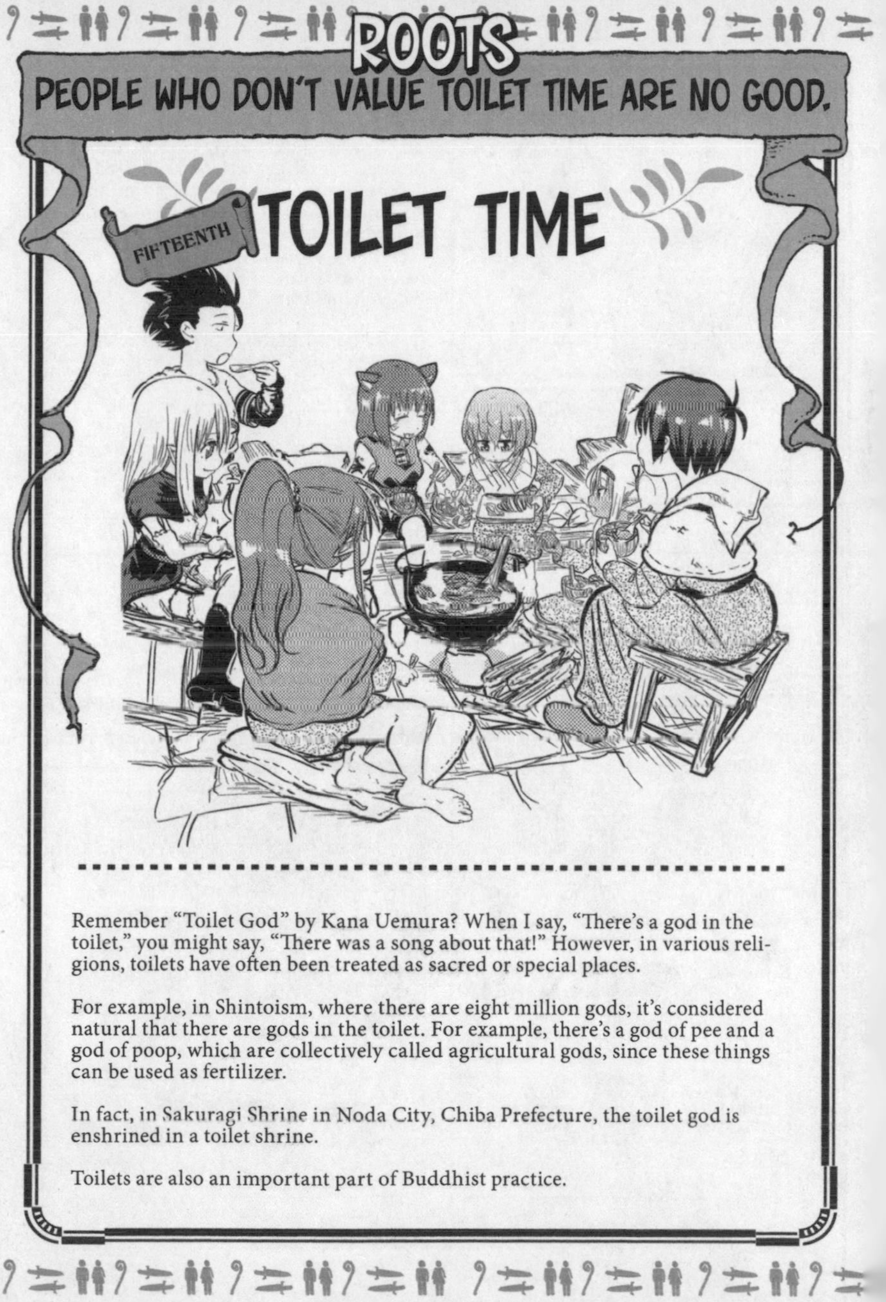

Remember "Toilet God" by Kana Uemura? When I say, "There's a god in the toilet," you might say, "There was a song about that!" However, in various religions, toilets have often been treated as sacred or special places.

For example, in Shintoism, where there are eight million gods, it's considered natural that there are gods in the toilet. For example, there's a god of pee and a god of poop, which are collectively called agricultural gods, since these things can be used as fertilizer.

In fact, in Sakuragi Shrine in Noda City, Chiba Prefecture, the toilet god is enshrined in a toilet shrine.

Toilets are also an important part of Buddhist practice.

As I've mentioned before, according to a book written by Dogen, the famous monk, graffiti is not allowed in the bathroom, and the body, mind, and toilet itself must be clean after pooping. Dogen's teacher, Zen Master Tendo Nyojo, also struggled with the deeper meaning of cleaning the toilet when he was young.

In Orthodox Judaism, it is forbidden to bring books into the bathroom or to tear toilet paper on Shabbat (because tearing toilet paper is considered work). Similarly, in Islam, it is forbidden to use your unclean hand for eating or other activities (you are only allowed to use your left hand after doing your business). These customs are treated as something special in many religions.

Cherish your precious time on the toilet.

IN OTHER WORDS

THIS MAXIM

"THEREFORE, EVEN THOUGH OUR BODIES AND MINDS ARE UNSTAINED, THERE IS A METHOD FOR CLEANSING THE BODY, WHICH IS ALSO A METHOD FOR CLEANSING THE MIND. NOT ONLY WILL IT PURIFY BODY AND MIND, IT WILL ALSO PURIFY THOSE IN OUR NATION AND THOSE WHO TRAIN 'UNDER A TREE'."

-FROM *SHOBOGENZO*, BY DOGEN

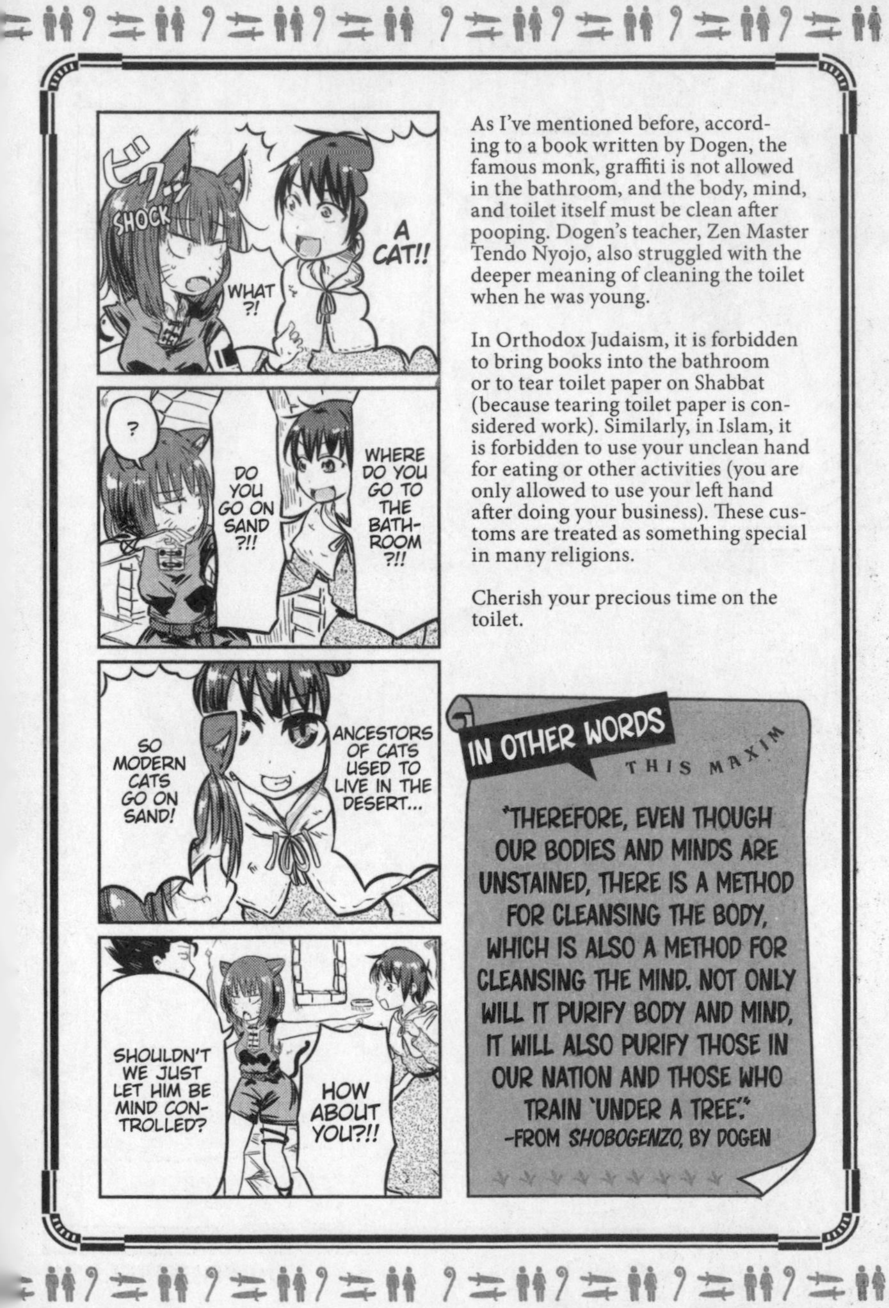
A CAT!!
SHOCK
WHAT ?!
WHERE DO YOU GO TO THE BATH-ROOM ?!!
DO YOU GO ON SAND ?!!
?
ANCESTORS OF CATS USED TO LIVE IN THE DESERT...
SO MODERN CATS GO ON SAND!
HOW ABOUT YOU?!!
SHOULDN'T WE JUST LET HIM BE MIND CON-TROLLED?

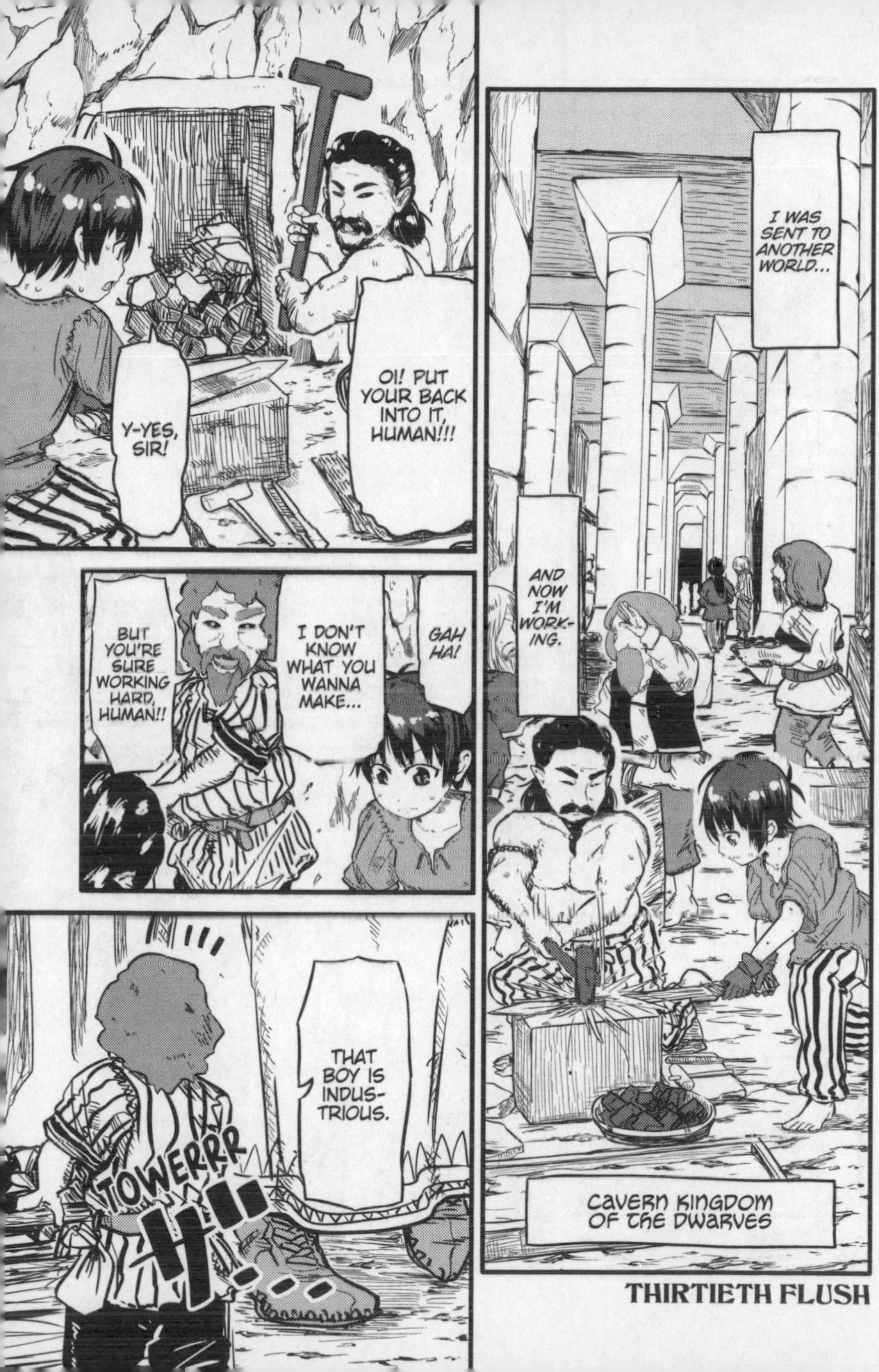
I WAS SENT TO ANOTHER WORLD...
AND NOW I'M WORKING.
CAVERN KINGDOM OF THE DWARVES
OI! PUT YOUR BACK INTO IT, HUMAN!!!
Y-YES, SIR!
GAH HA!
I DON'T KNOW WHAT YOU WANNA MAKE...
BUT YOU'RE SURE WORKING HARD, HUMAN!!
THAT BOY IS INDUSTRIOUS.
TOWERRR

THIRTIETH FLUSH

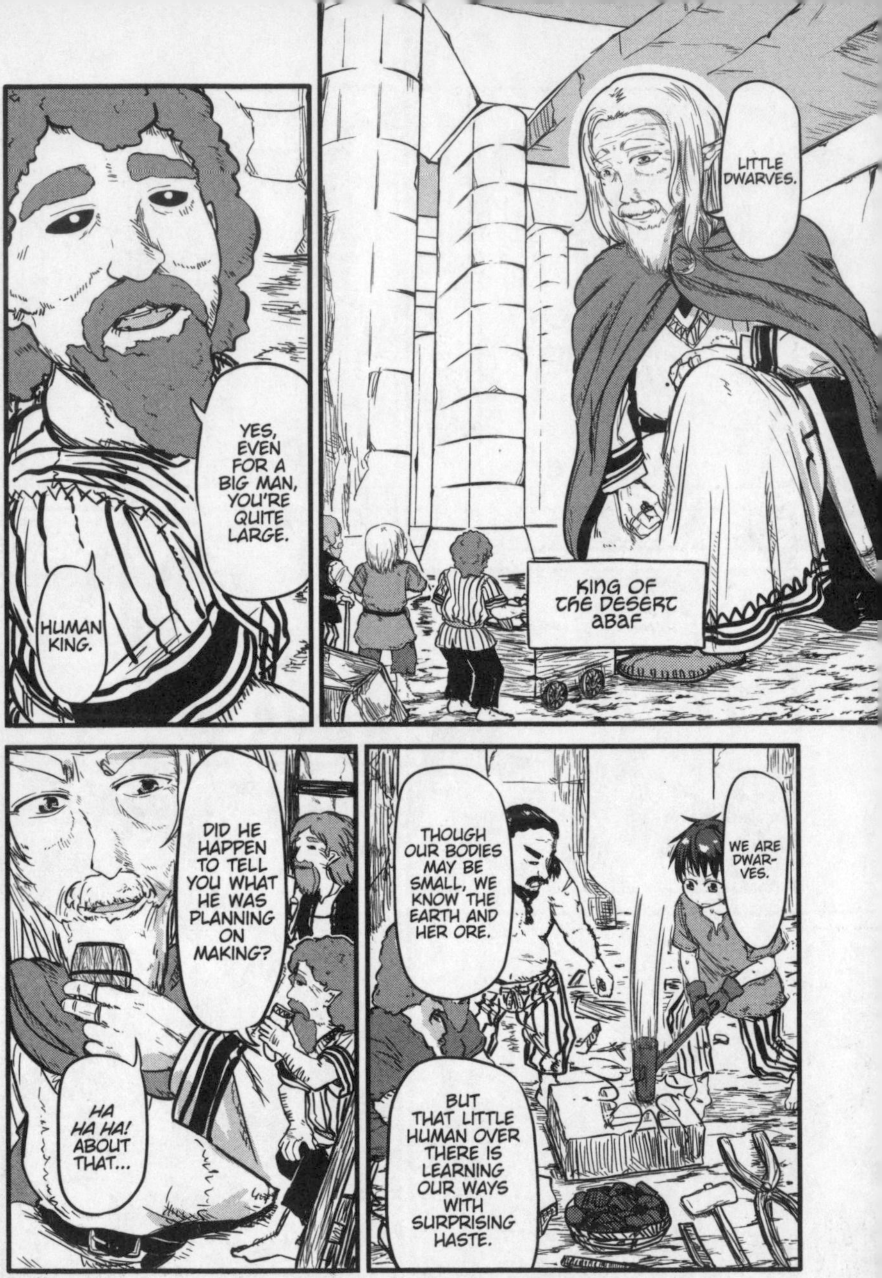
LITTLE DWARVES.
KING OF THE DESERT ABAF
YES, EVEN FOR A BIG MAN, YOU'RE QUITE LARGE.
HUMAN KING.
WE ARE DWARVES.
THOUGH OUR BODIES MAY BE SMALL, WE KNOW THE EARTH AND HER ORE.
BUT THAT LITTLE HUMAN OVER THERE IS LEARNING OUR WAYS WITH SURPRISING HASTE.
DID HE HAPPEN TO TELL YOU WHAT HE WAS PLANNING ON MAKING?
HA HA HA! ABOUT THAT...

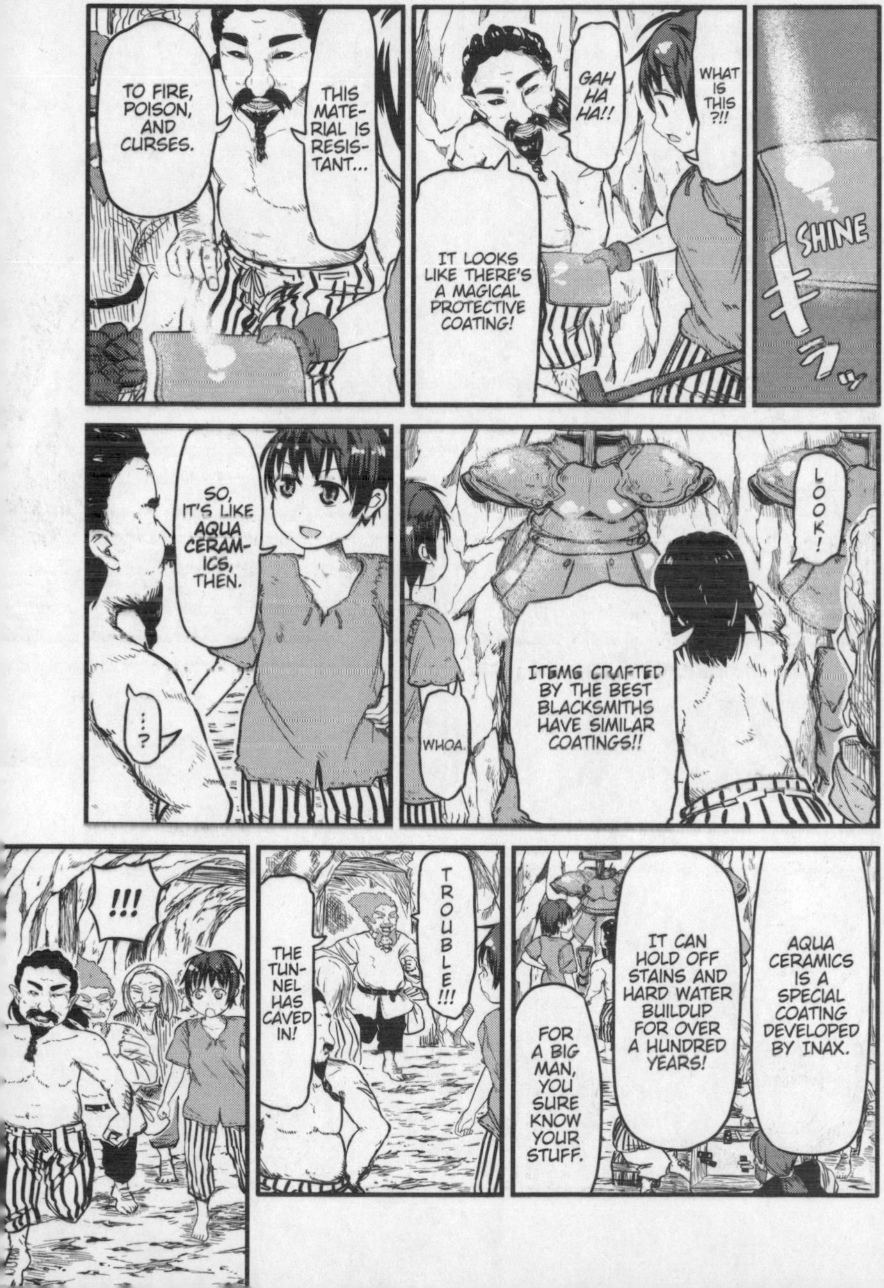
SHINE
キラッ
WHAT IS THIS?!!
GAH HA HA!!
IT LOOKS LIKE THERE'S A MAGICAL PROTECTIVE COATING!
THIS MATERIAL IS RESISTANT...
TO FIRE, POISON, AND CURSES.
LOOK!
ITEMS CRAFTED BY THE BEST BLACKSMITHS HAVE SIMILAR COATINGS!!
WHOA.
SO, IT'S LIKE AQUA CERAMICS, THEN.
...?
AQUA CERAMICS IS A SPECIAL COATING DEVELOPED BY INAX.
IT CAN HOLD OFF STAINS AND HARD WATER BUILDUP FOR OVER A HUNDRED YEARS!
FOR A BIG MAN, YOU SURE KNOW YOUR STUFF.
TROUBLE!!!
THE TUNNEL HAS CAVED IN!
!!!

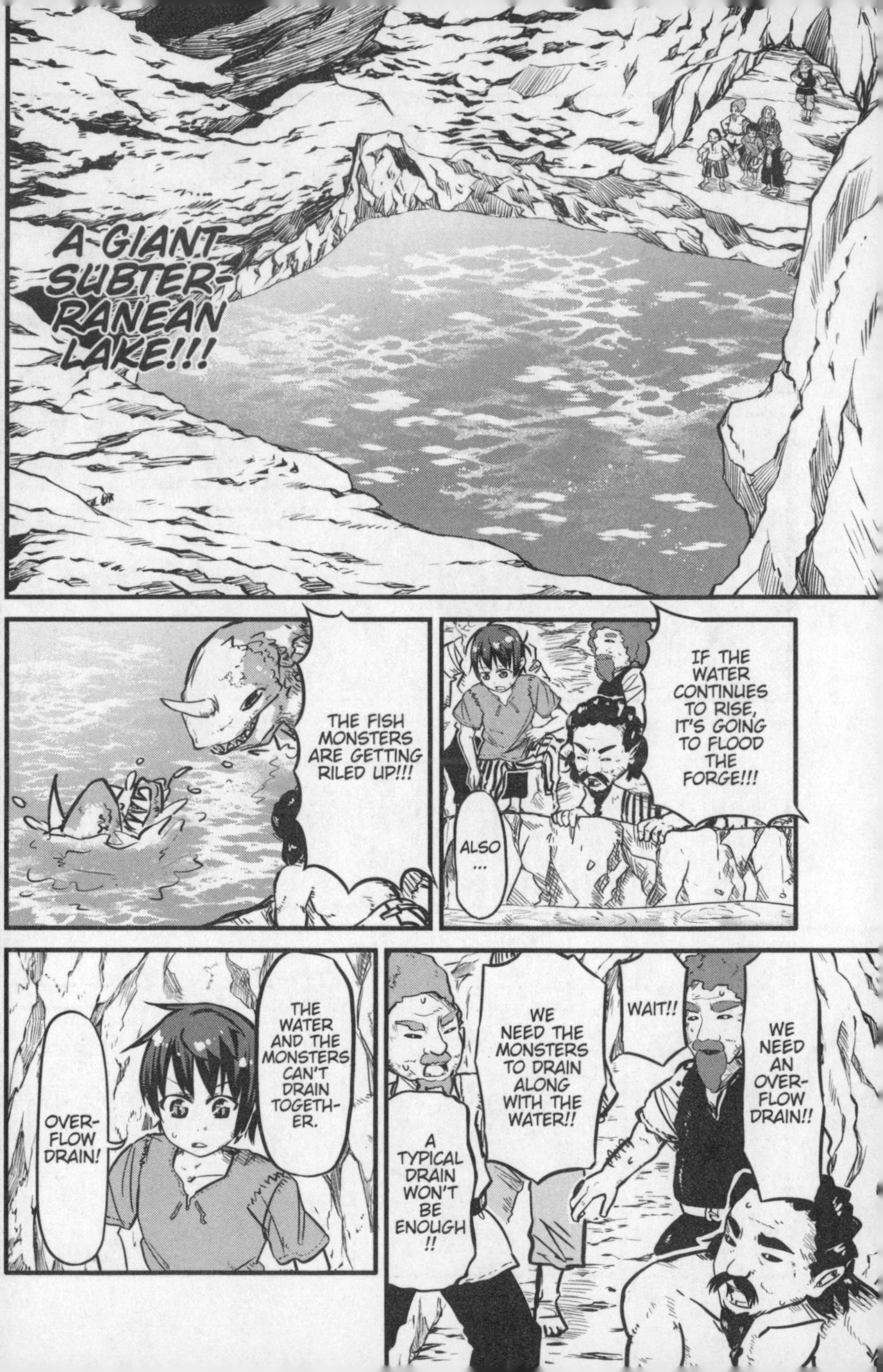
A GIANT SUBTERRANEAN LAKE!!!
IF THE WATER CONTINUES TO RISE, IT'S GOING TO FLOOD THE FORGE!!!
ALSO ...
THE FISH MONSTERS ARE GETTING RILED UP!!!
WE NEED AN OVERFLOW DRAIN!!
WAIT!!
WE NEED THE MONSTERS TO DRAIN ALONG WITH THE WATER!!
A TYPICAL DRAIN WON'T BE ENOUGH!!
THE WATER AND THE MONSTERS CAN'T DRAIN TOGETHER.
OVERFLOW DRAIN!

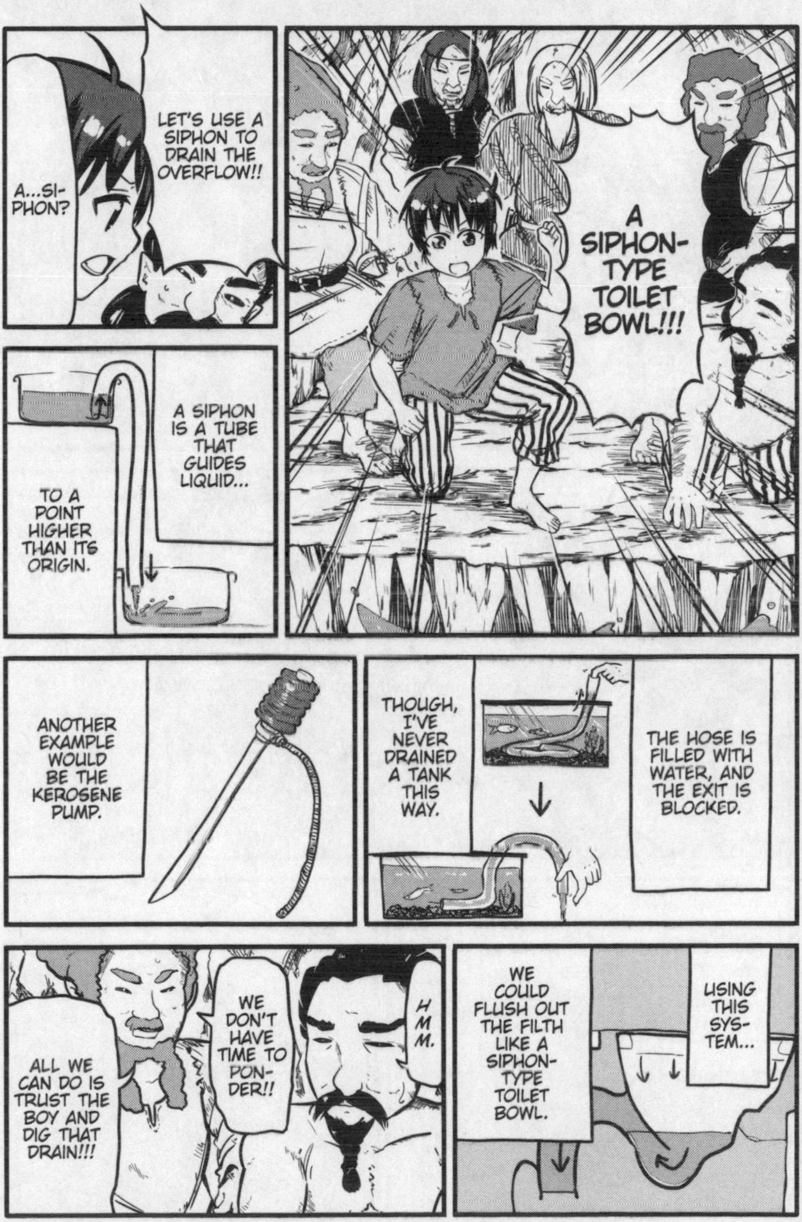
A SIPHON-TYPE TOILET BOWL!!!
LET'S USE A SIPHON TO DRAIN THE OVERFLOW!!
A...SI-PHON?
A SIPHON IS A TUBE THAT GUIDES LIQUID...
TO A POINT HIGHER THAN ITS ORIGIN.
THE HOSE IS FILLED WITH WATER, AND THE EXIT IS BLOCKED.
THOUGH, I'VE NEVER DRAINED A TANK THIS WAY.
ANOTHER EXAMPLE WOULD BE THE KEROSENE PUMP.
USING THIS SYS-TEM...
WE COULD FLUSH OUT THE FILTH LIKE A SIPHON-TYPE TOILET BOWL.
HMM.
WE DON'T HAVE TIME TO PON-DER!!
ALL WE CAN DO IS TRUST THE BOY AND DIG THAT DRAIN!!!

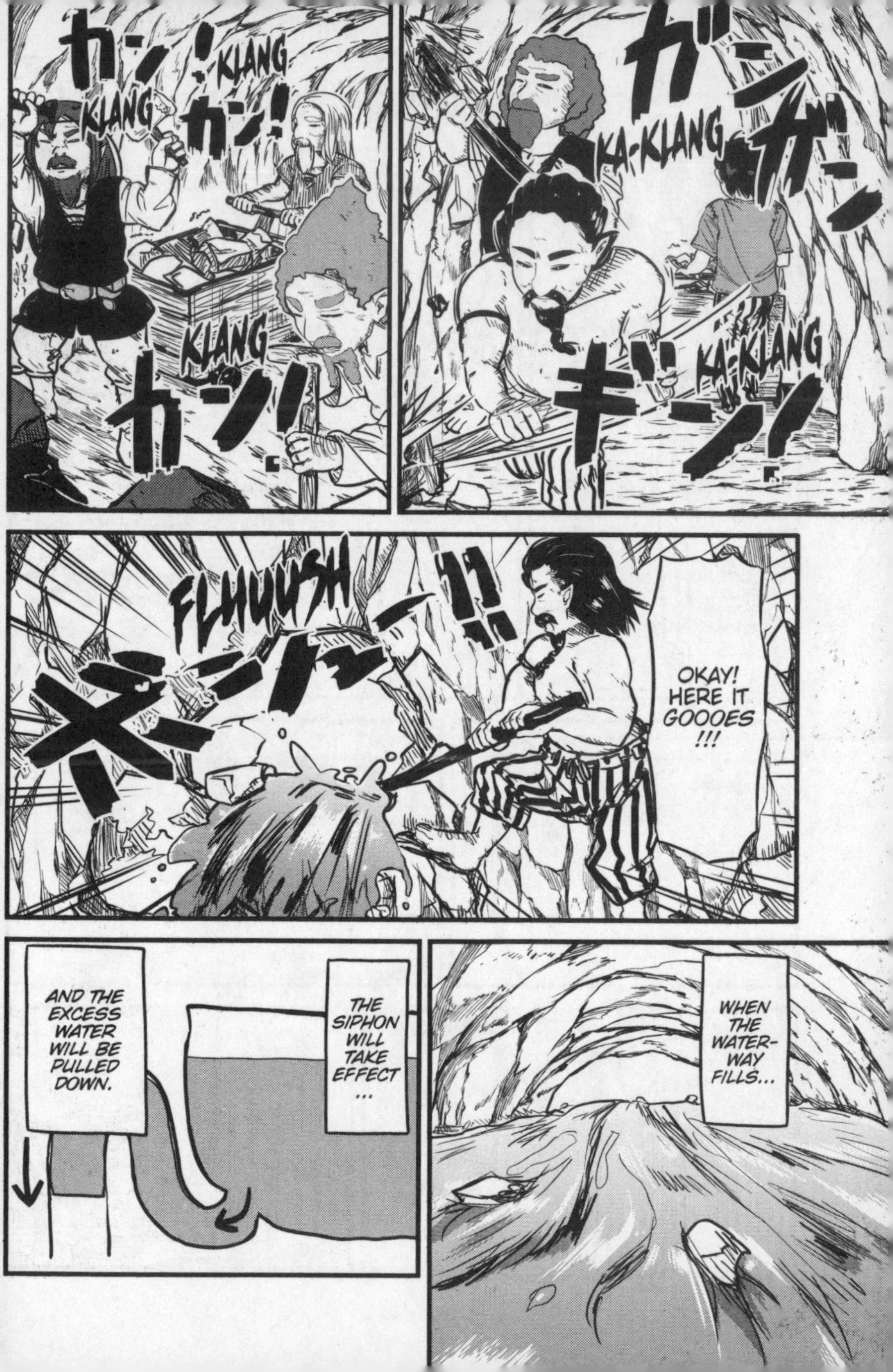
KA-KLANG
KA-KLANG
KLANG
KLANG
KLANG
FLHUUSH
OKAY! HERE IT GOOOES!!!
WHEN THE WATER-WAY FILLS...
THE SIPHON WILL TAKE EFFECT...
AND THE EXCESS WATER WILL BE PULLED DOWN.

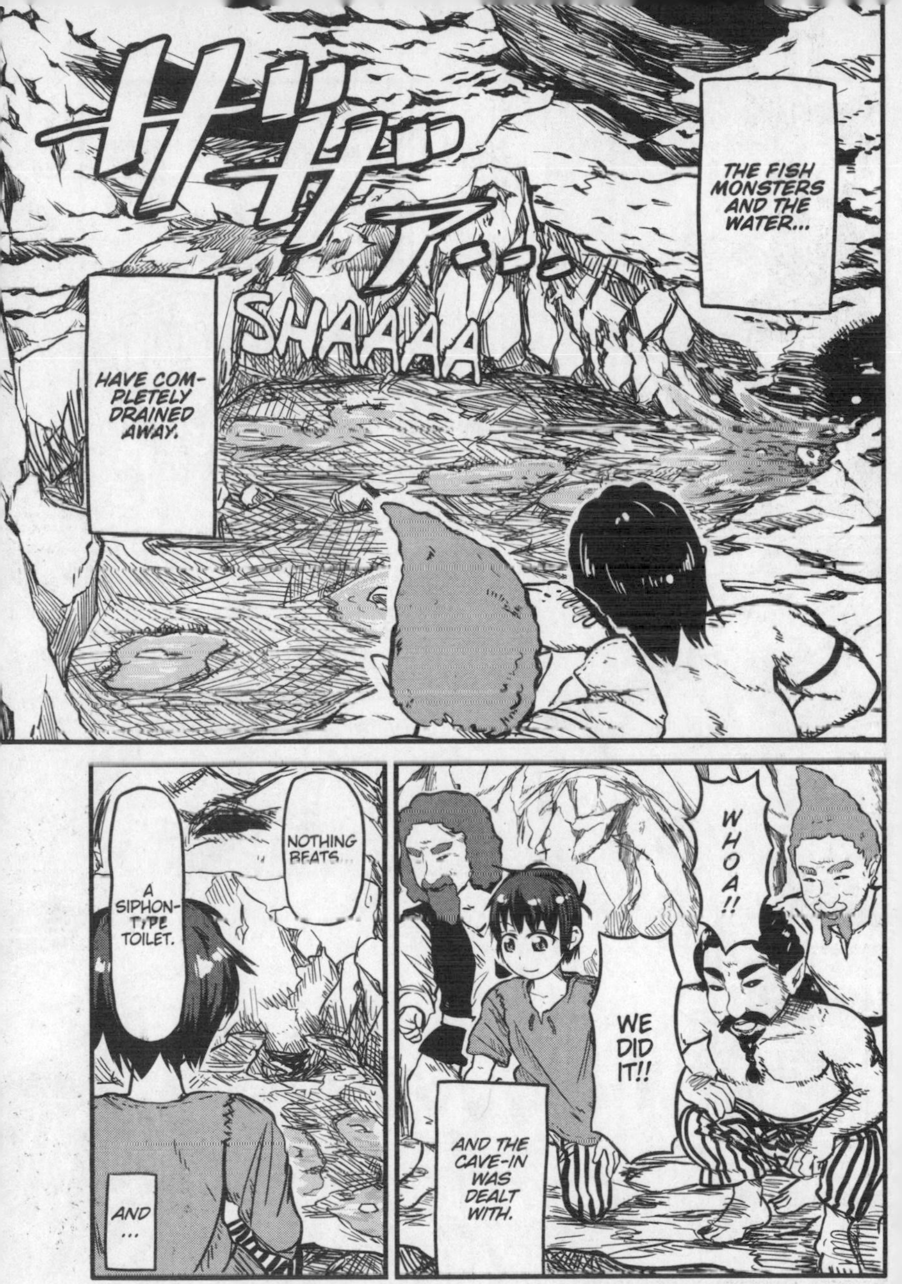
THE FISH MONSTERS AND THE WATER...
SHAAAA
HAVE COMPLETELY DRAINED AWAY.
WHOA!!
WE DID IT!!
AND THE CAVE-IN WAS DEALT WITH.
NOTHING BEATS...
A SIPHON-TYPE TOILET.
AND ...

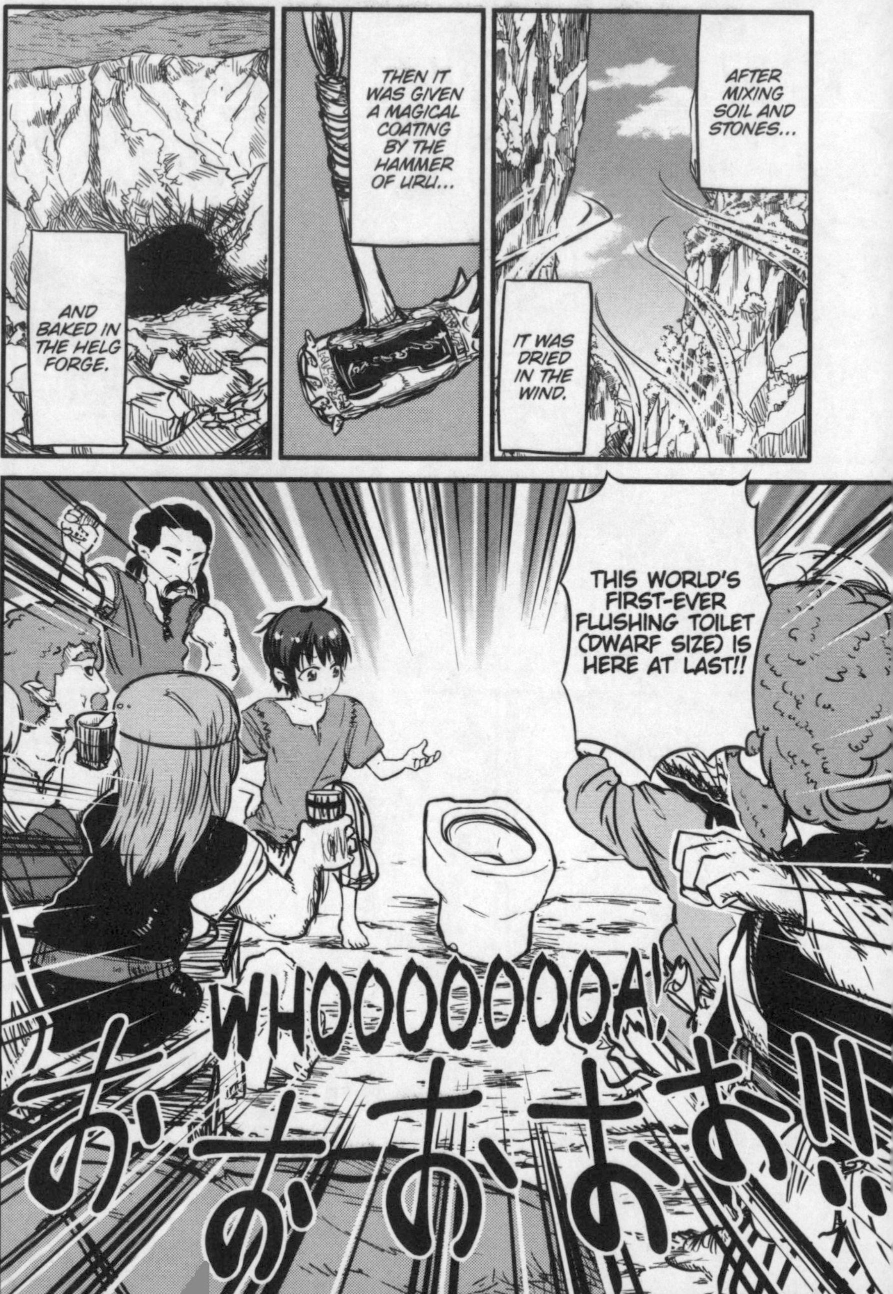
AFTER MIXING SOIL AND STONES...
IT WAS DRIED IN THE WIND.
THEN IT WAS GIVEN A MAGICAL COATING BY THE HAMMER OF URU...
AND BAKED IN THE HELG FORGE.
THIS WORLD'S FIRST-EVER FLUSHING TOILET (DWARF SIZE) IS HERE AT LAST!!
WHOOOOOOOA!
おおおおお!!

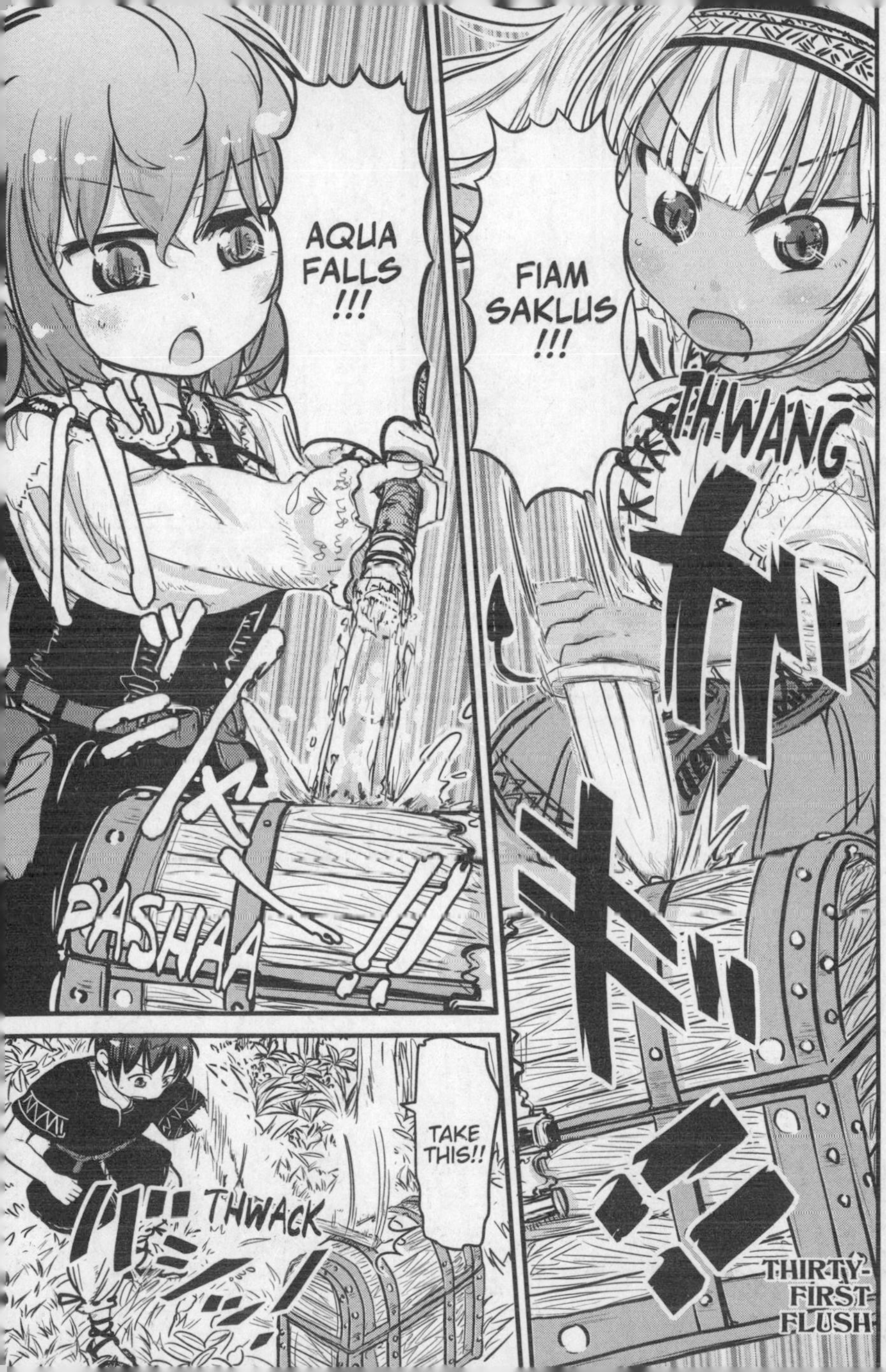
FIAM SAKLUS !!!
THWANG
THIRTY-FIRST FLUSH
AQUA FALLS !!!
PASHAA
TAKE THIS!!
THWACK

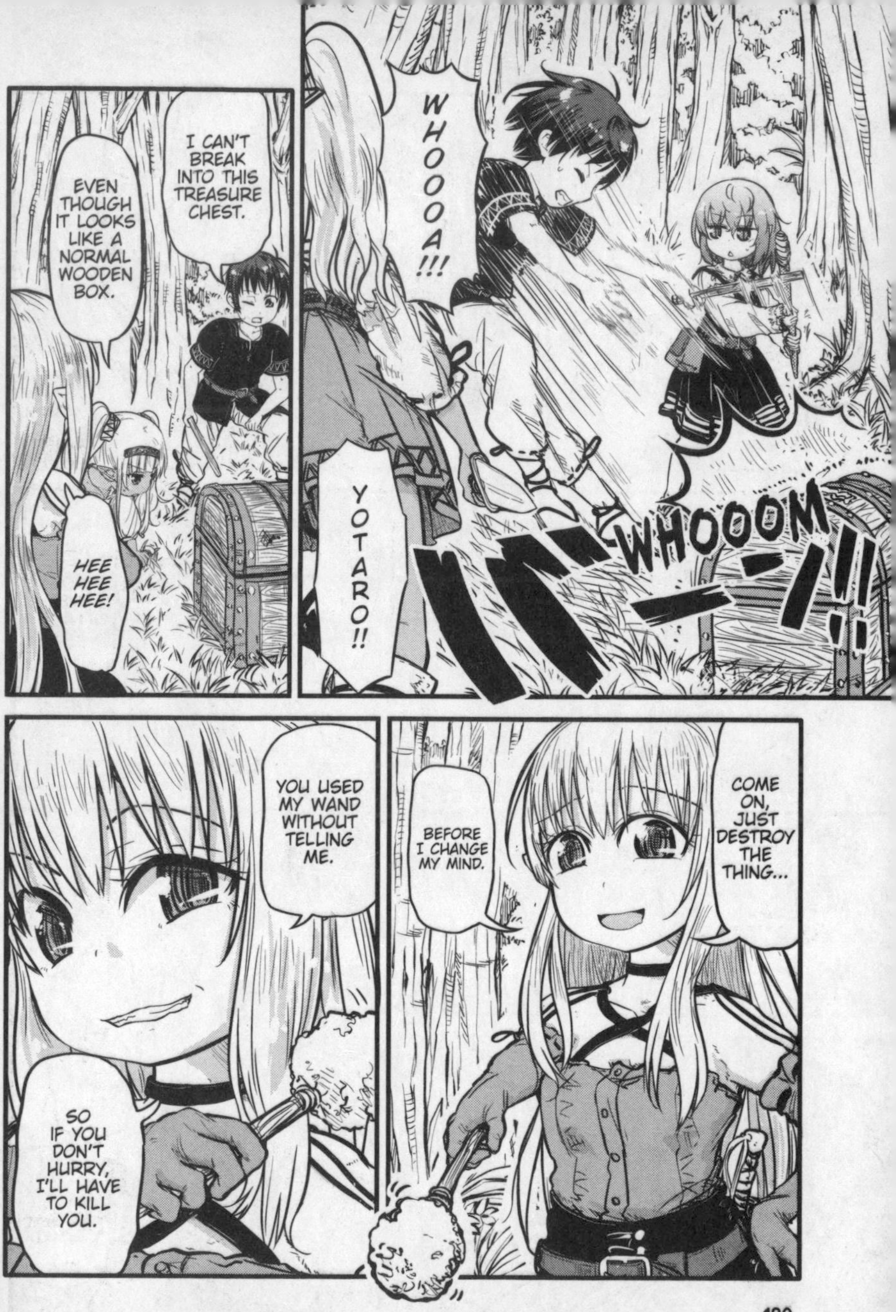
WHOOOOA!!!
WHOOOM!!
YOTARO!!
I CAN'T BREAK INTO THIS TREASURE CHEST.
EVEN THOUGH IT LOOKS LIKE A NORMAL WOODEN BOX.
HEE HEE HEE!
COME ON, JUST DESTROY THE THING...
BEFORE I CHANGE MY MIND.
YOU USED MY WAND WITHOUT TELLING ME.
SO IF YOU DON'T HURRY, I'LL HAVE TO KILL YOU.

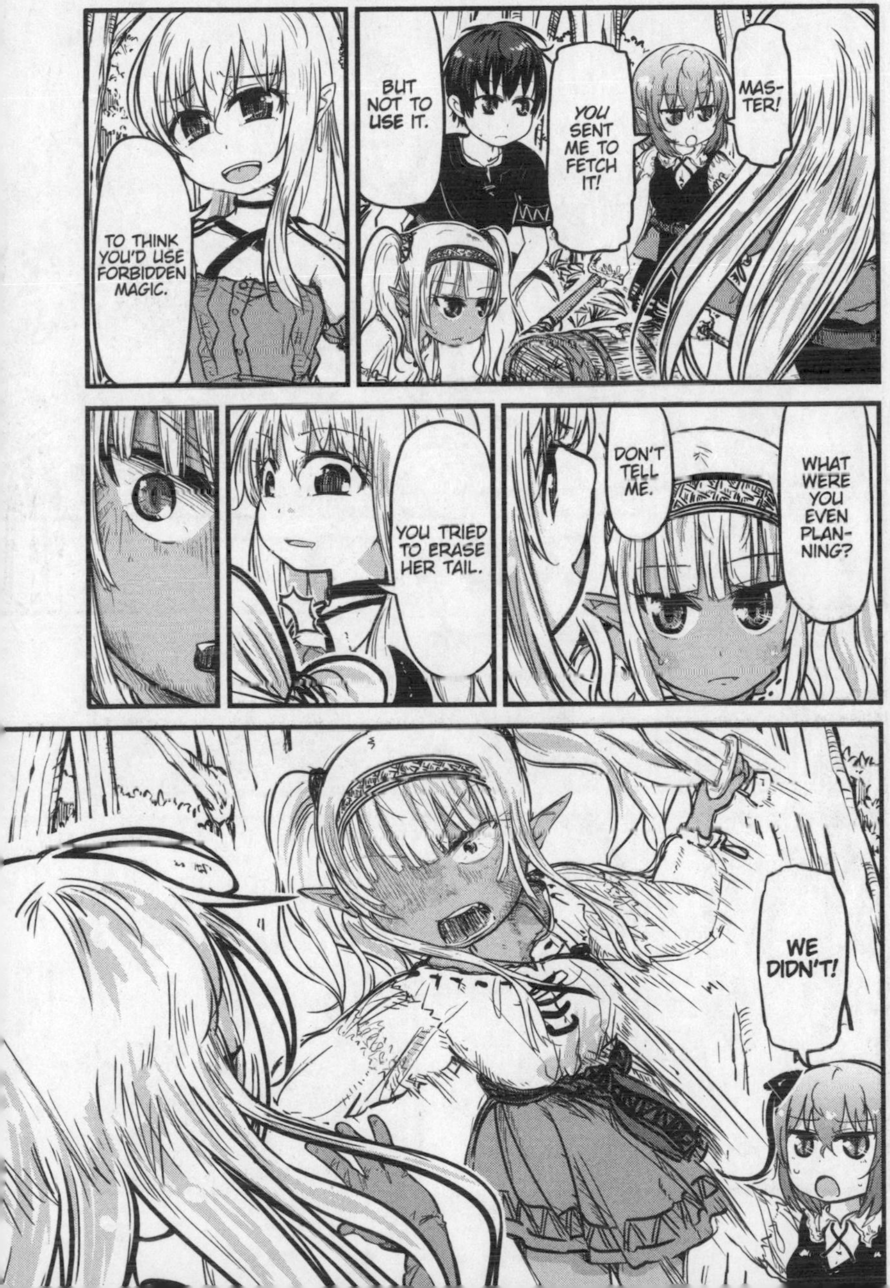
MAS-TER!
YOU SENT ME TO FETCH IT!
BUT NOT TO USE IT.
TO THINK YOU'D USE FORBIDDEN MAGIC.
WHAT WERE YOU EVEN PLAN-NING?
DON'T TELL ME.
YOU TRIED TO ERASE HER TAIL.
WE DIDN'T!

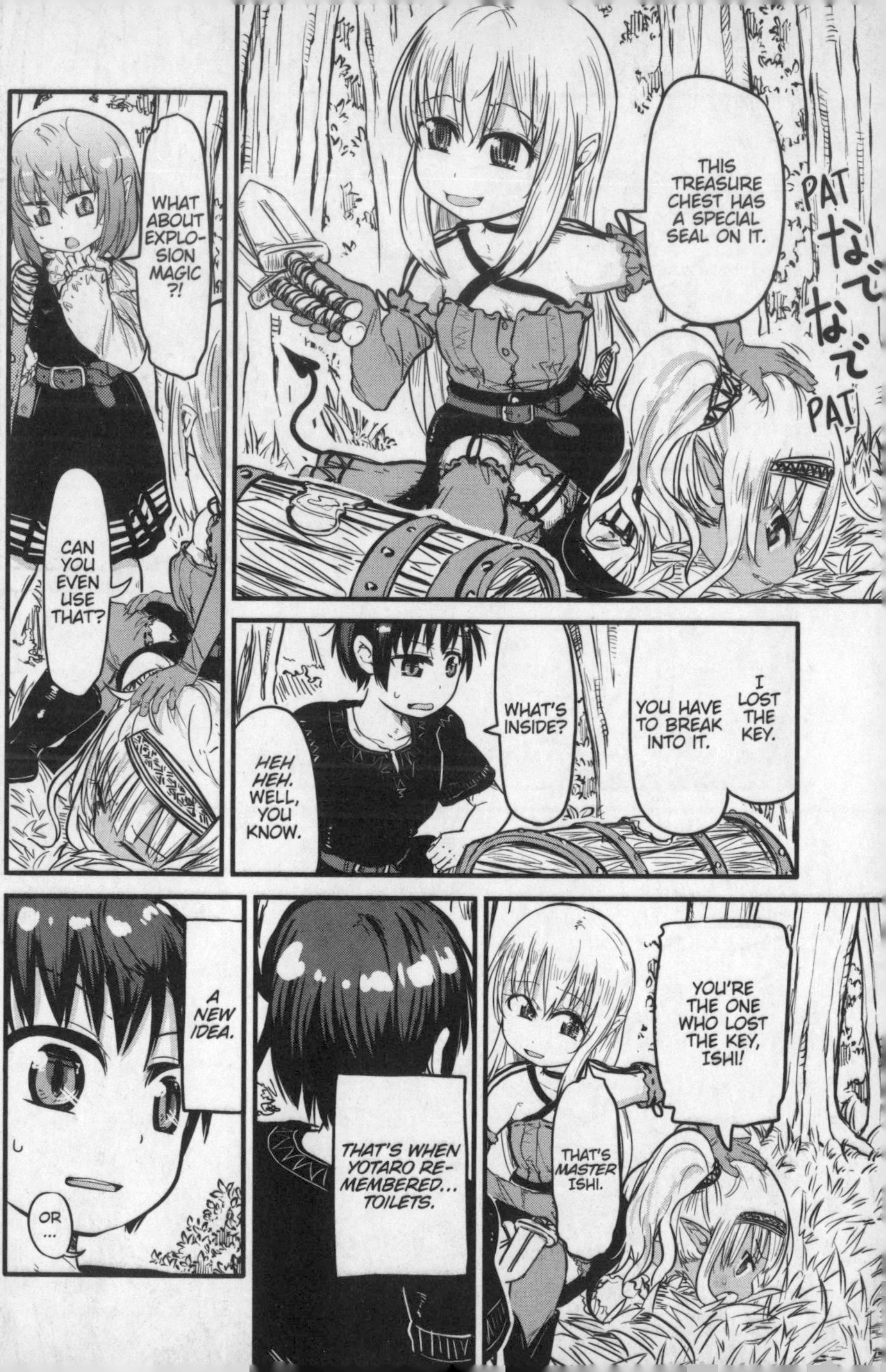
THIS TREASURE CHEST HAS A SPECIAL SEAL ON IT.
PAT なで なで PAT
I LOST THE KEY.
YOU HAVE TO BREAK INTO IT.
WHAT'S INSIDE?
HEH HEH. WELL, YOU KNOW.
WHAT ABOUT EXPLOSION MAGIC?!
CAN YOU EVEN USE THAT?
YOU'RE THE ONE WHO LOST THE KEY, ISHI!
THAT'S MASTER ISHI.
THAT'S WHEN YOTARO REMEMBERED... TOILETS.
A NEW IDEA.
OR ...

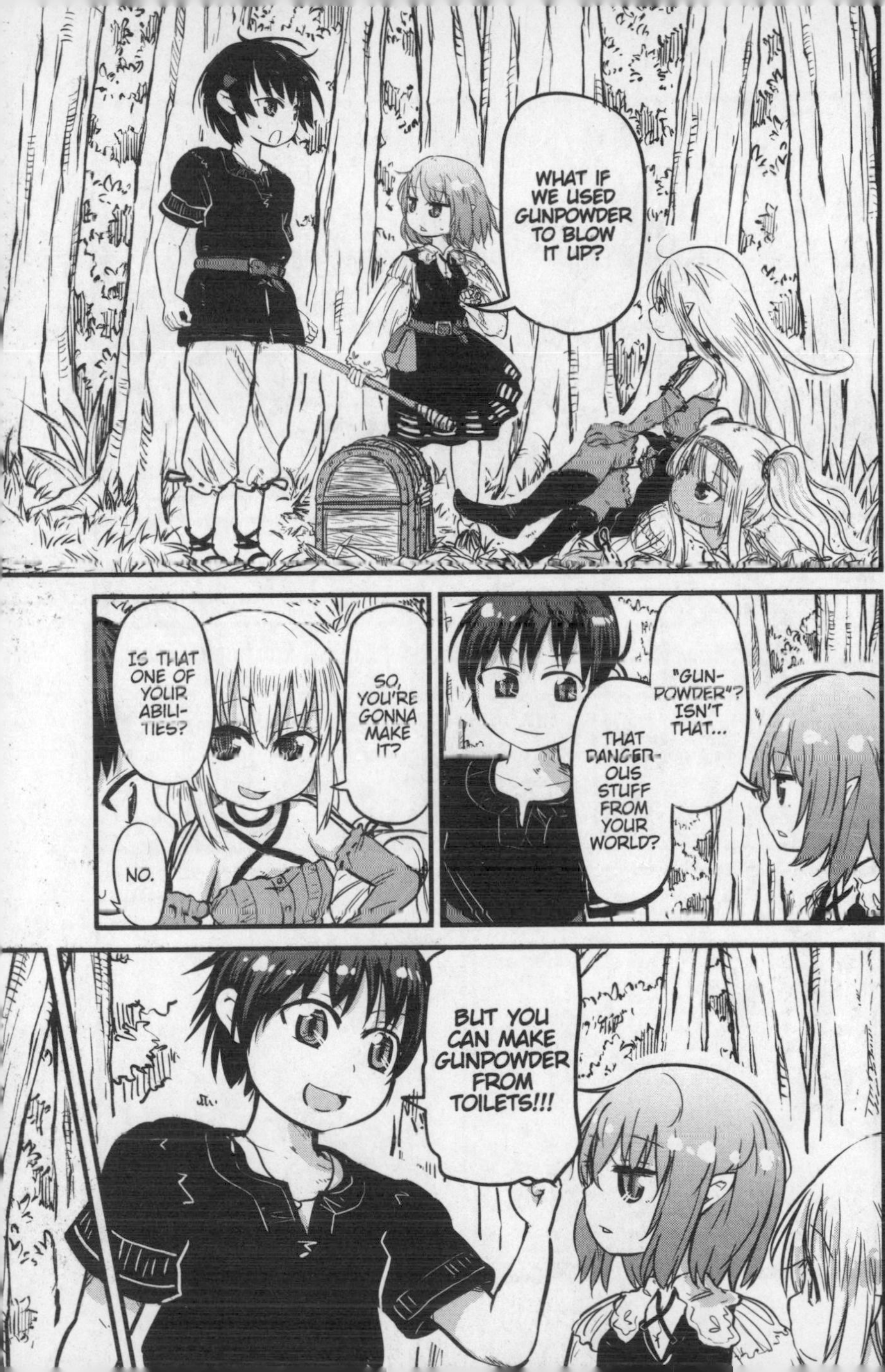
WHAT IF WE USED GUNPOWDER TO BLOW IT UP?
"GUN-POWDER"? ISN'T THAT...
THAT DANGER-OUS STUFF FROM YOUR WORLD?
SO, YOU'RE GONNA MAKE IT?
IS THAT ONE OF YOUR ABILI-TIES?
NO.
BUT YOU CAN MAKE GUNPOWDER FROM TOILETS!!!

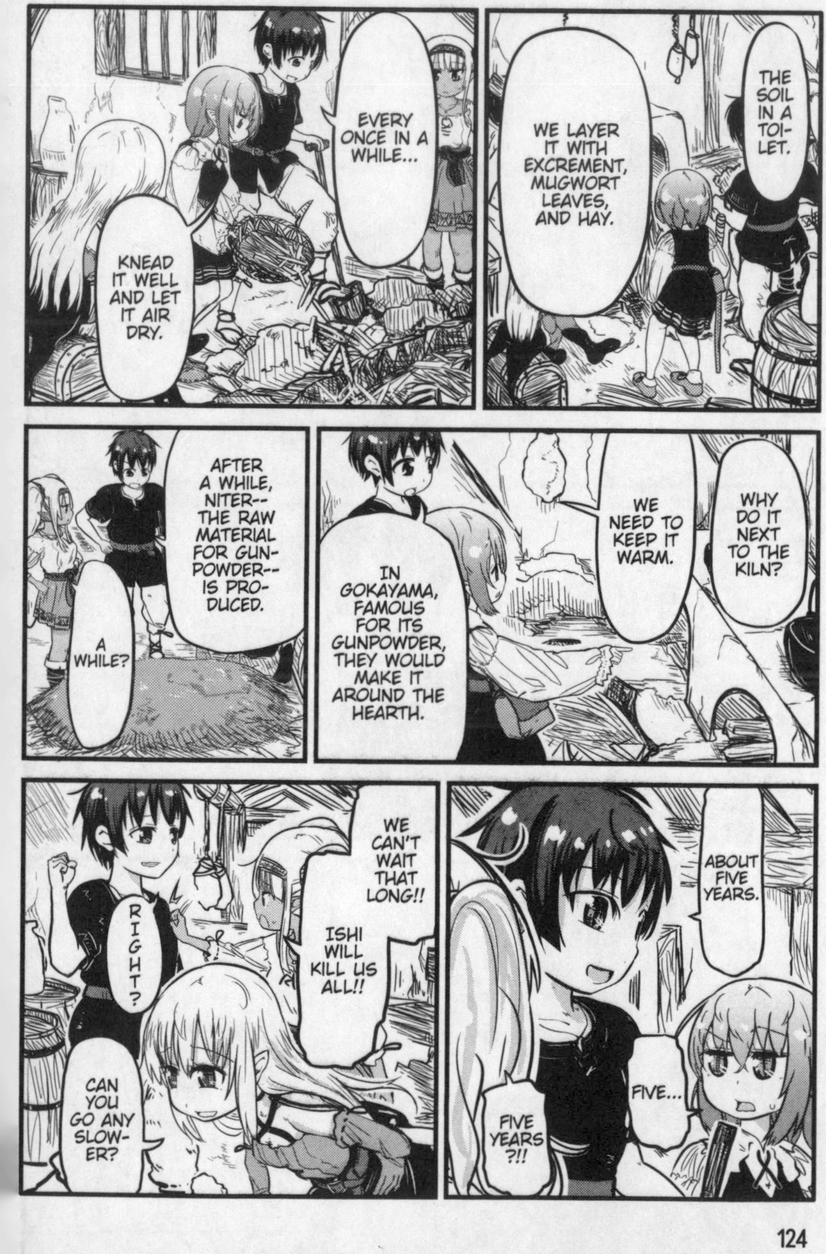
THE SOIL IN A TOILET.
WE LAYER IT WITH EXCREMENT, MUGWORT LEAVES, AND HAY.
EVERY ONCE IN A WHILE...
KNEAD IT WELL AND LET IT AIR DRY.
WHY DO IT NEXT TO THE KILN?
WE NEED TO KEEP IT WARM.
IN GOKAYAMA, FAMOUS FOR ITS GUNPOWDER, THEY WOULD MAKE IT AROUND THE HEARTH.
AFTER A WHILE, NITER--THE RAW MATERIAL FOR GUNPOWDER--IS PRODUCED.
A WHILE?
ABOUT FIVE YEARS.
FIVE...
FIVE YEARS?!!
WE CAN'T WAIT THAT LONG!!
ISHI WILL KILL US ALL!!
RIGHT?
CAN YOU GO ANY SLOWER?

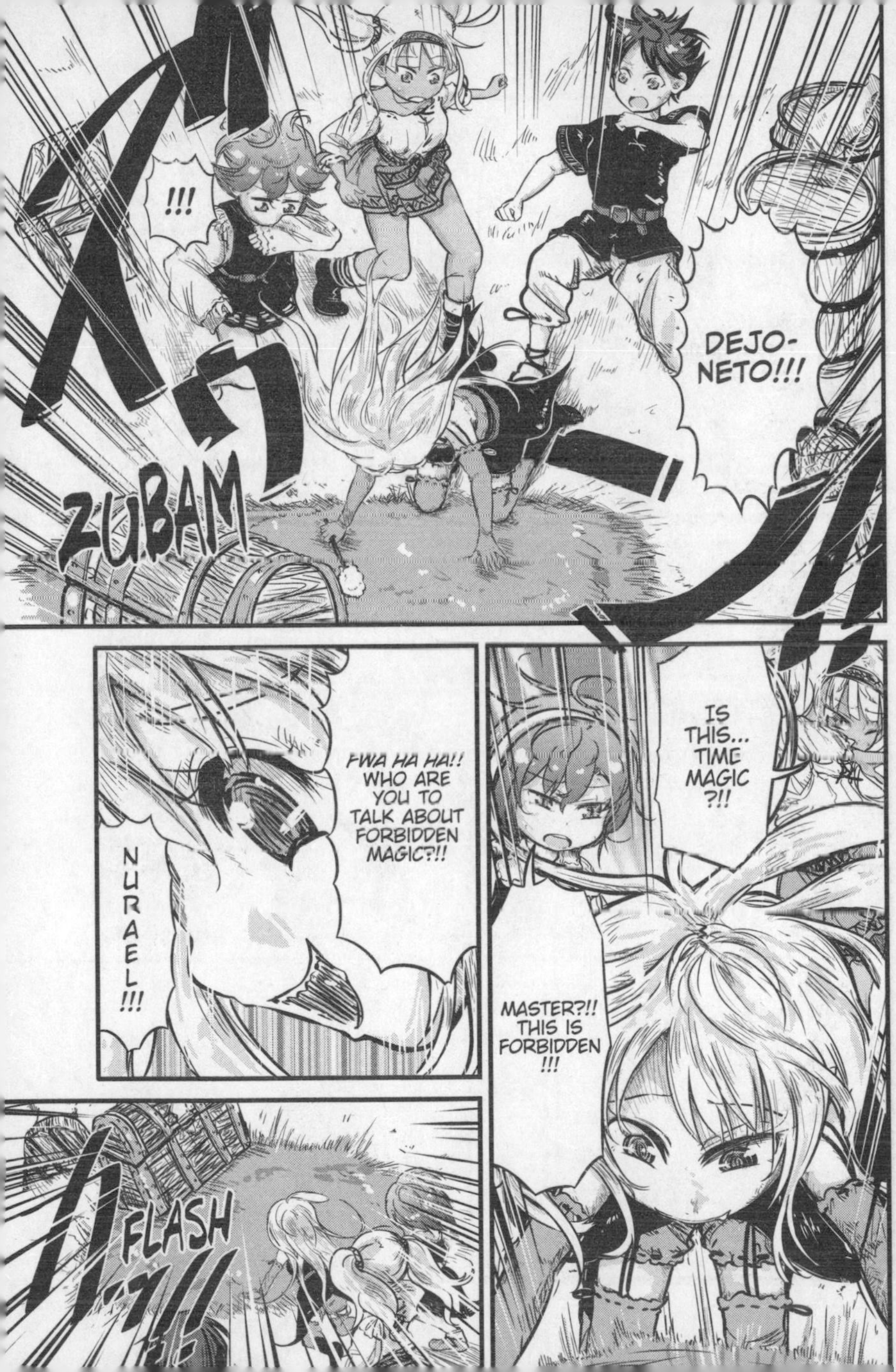
DEJO-NETO!!!
!!!
ZUBAM
IS THIS... TIME MAGIC?!!
MASTER?!! THIS IS FORBIDDEN!!!
FWA HA HA!! WHO ARE YOU TO TALK ABOUT FORBIDDEN MAGIC?!!
NURAEL!!!
FLASH

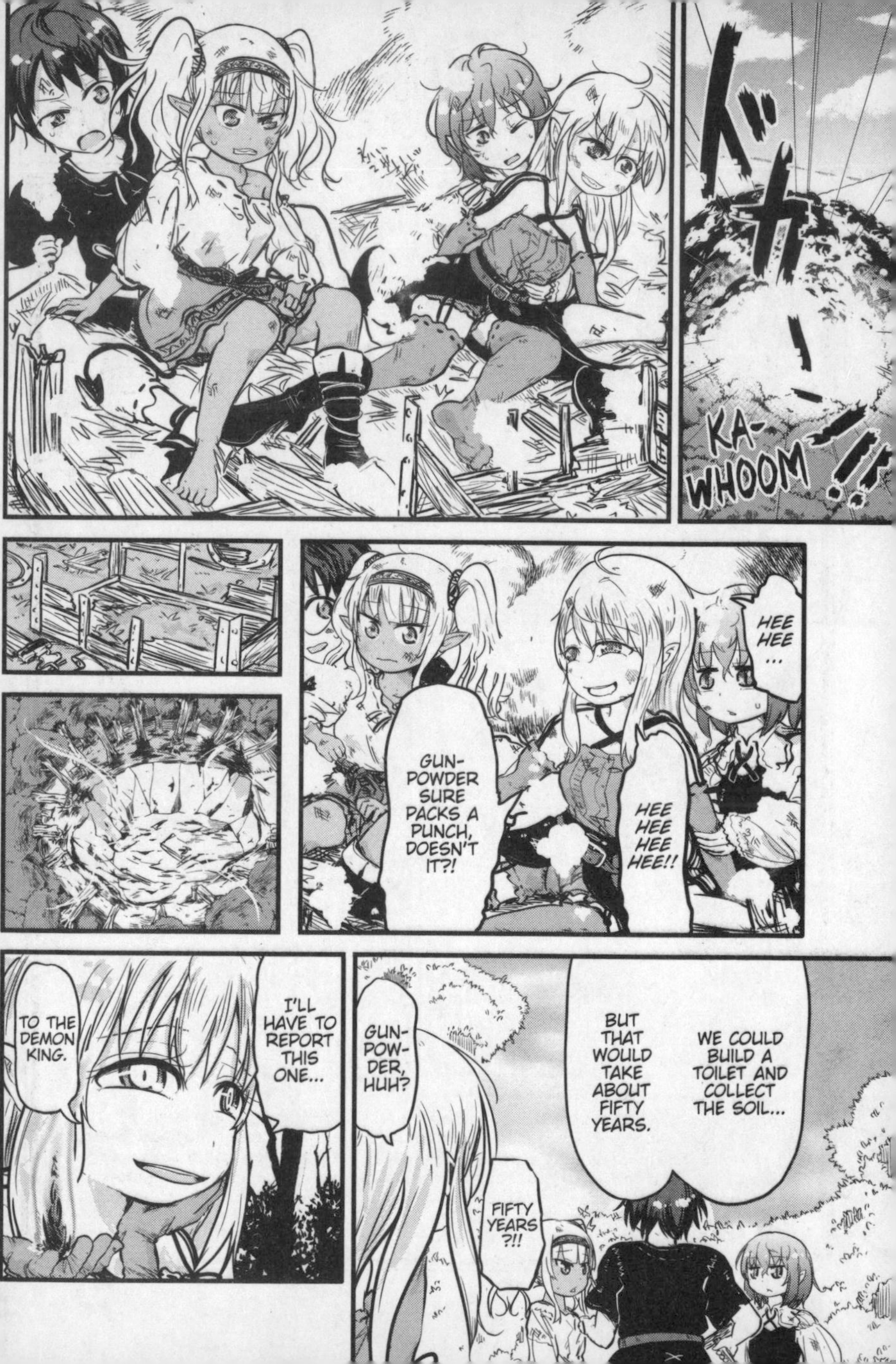
KA-WHOOM!!
HEE HEE...
HEE HEE HEE HEE!!
GUN-POWDER SURE PACKS A PUNCH, DOESN'T IT?!
WE COULD BUILD A TOILET AND COLLECT THE SOIL...
BUT THAT WOULD TAKE ABOUT FIFTY YEARS.
GUN-POW-DER, HUH?
FIFTY YEARS?!!
I'LL HAVE TO REPORT THIS ONE...
TO THE DEMON KING.

ROOTS

PEOPLE WHO DON'T VALUE TOILET TIME ARE NO GOOD.

SIXTEENTH TOILET TIME

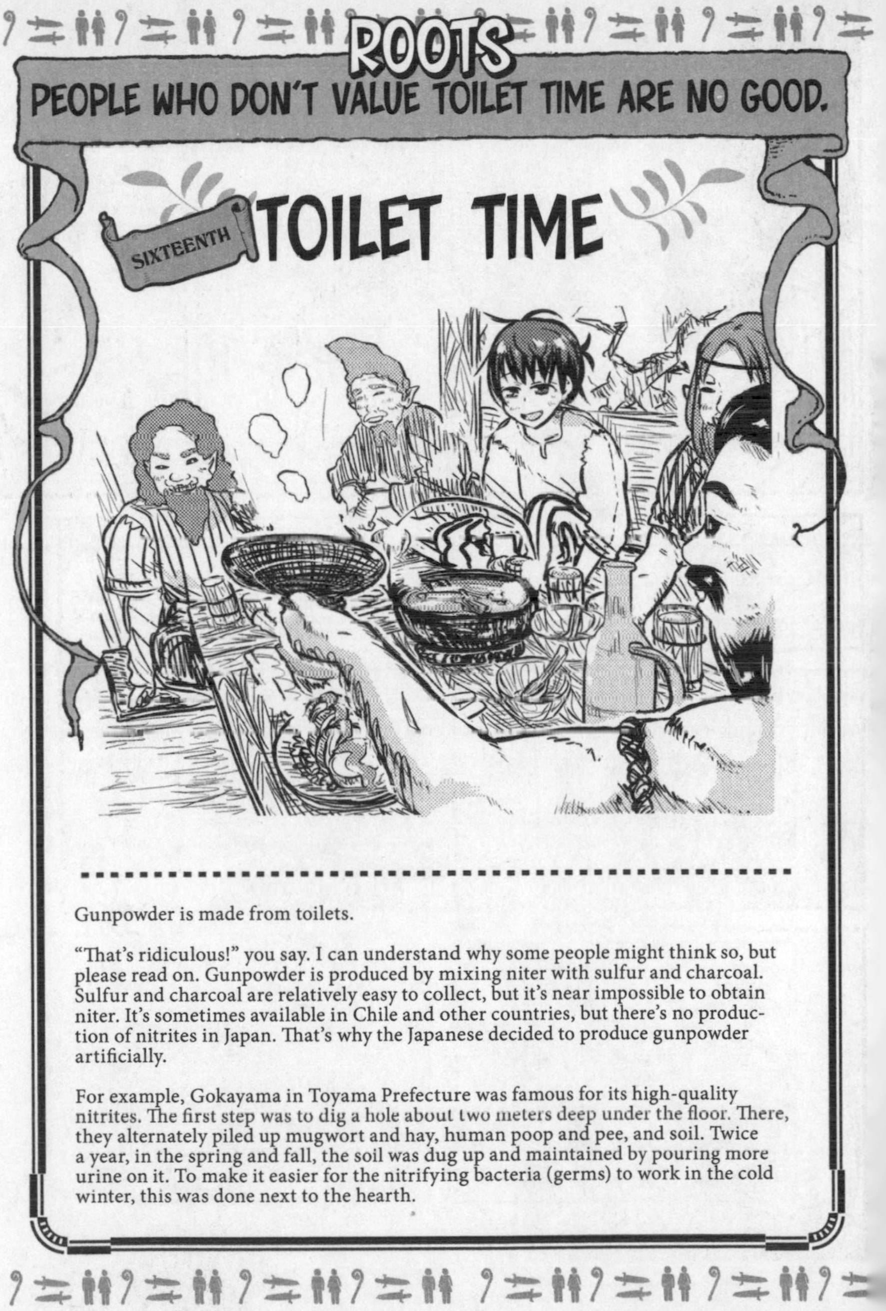

Gunpowder is made from toilets.

"That's ridiculous!" you say. I can understand why some people might think so, but please read on. Gunpowder is produced by mixing niter with sulfur and charcoal. Sulfur and charcoal are relatively easy to collect, but it's near impossible to obtain niter. It's sometimes available in Chile and other countries, but there's no production of nitrites in Japan. That's why the Japanese decided to produce gunpowder artificially.

For example, Gokayama in Toyama Prefecture was famous for its high-quality nitrites. The first step was to dig a hole about two meters deep under the floor. There, they alternately piled up mugwort and hay, human poop and pee, and soil. Twice a year, in the spring and fall, the soil was dug up and maintained by pouring more urine on it. To make it easier for the nitrifying bacteria (germs) to work in the cold winter, this was done next to the hearth.

After four or five years, the nitrifying bacteria would cause the soil to create gunpowder. Water was poured into the clay, boiled down with lye, and the supernatant was scooped out. The supernatant was then boiled and filtered. Water was added, then heated. Debris was removed, and the mixture was evaporated, concentrated, and left to crystallize. Thus was saltpeter, one of the key ingredients in gunpowder, made.

It's natural to say, "I don't understand what you're talking about at all!" But all I want you to know is that they actually made gunpowder from toilets.

Gokayama is a rugged area surrounded by mountains, and the people worked hard to keep the secret from leaking out. This method of producing nitrites made the local economy prosperous. The relationship between toilets and gunpowder is a story that should be passed down through the generations.

But what happened next in the history of gunpowder production?

By the end of the Edo period (1603-1868), more efficient methods had been introduced, and during the Meiji Restoration (1868-1912), gunpowder was imported from overseas. The gunpowder industry in Gokayama and other areas disappeared.

However, there's an interesting story behind this story. At the end of the Pacific War, the government asked Gokayama if it was possible to produce nitrites again, but Gokayama refused, saying that it would take five years.

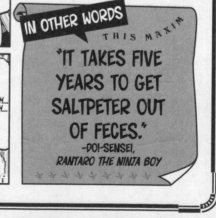

IN OTHER WORDS

THIS MAXIM

"IT TAKES FIVE YEARS TO GET SALTPETER OUT OF FECES."

-DOI-SENSEI, *RANTARO THE NINJA BOY*

PLEASE GIVE ME MY WAND.
MY SEA SPONGE ON A STICK?
NOT A CHANCE!
DASH
OH?
GRAVITY PRESS!!
WHUD
OOH... AGH...
H-HELP ME!
OHH!
WHOOOOO

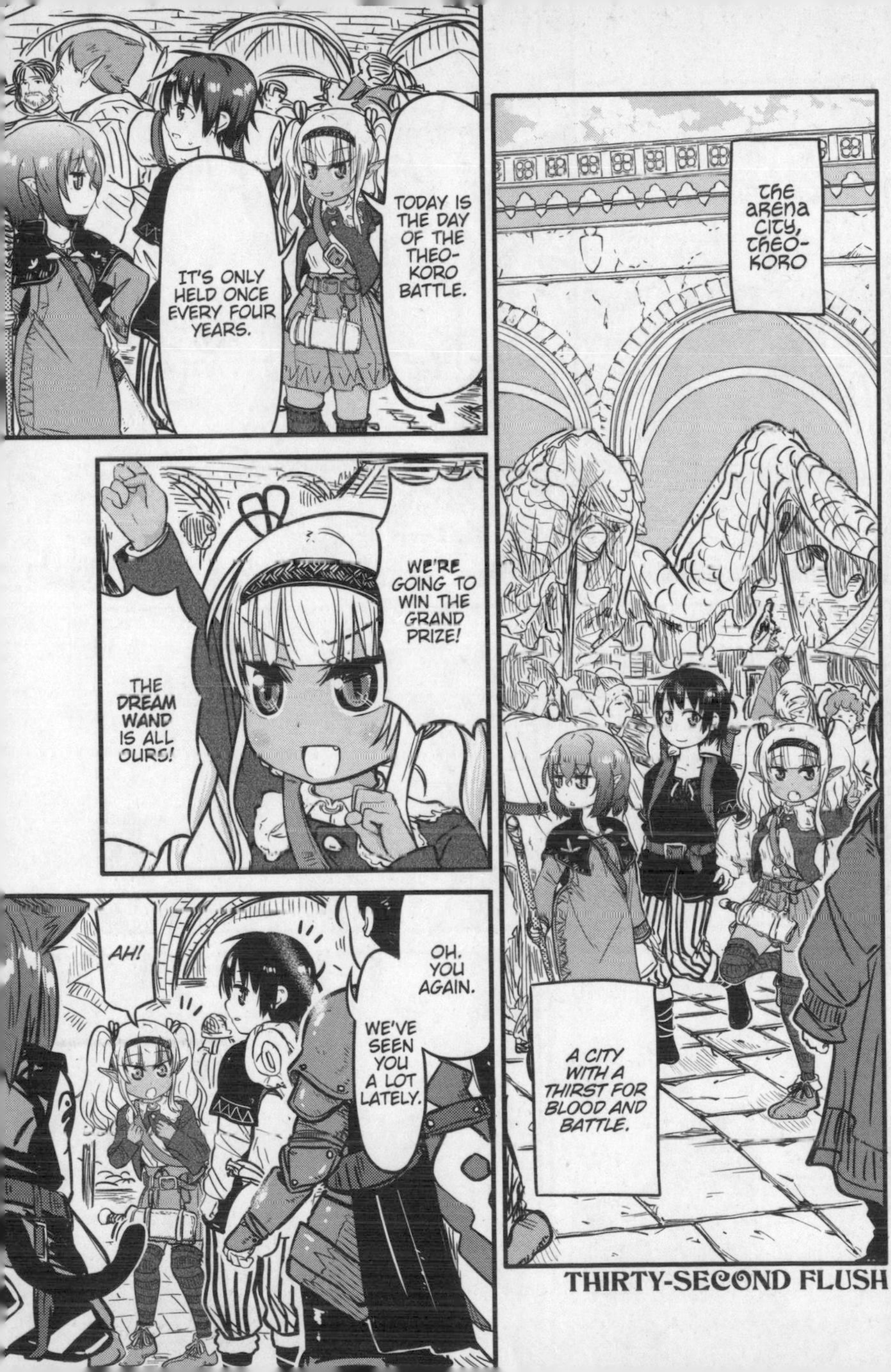
THE ARENA CITY, THEO-KORO
A CITY WITH A THIRST FOR BLOOD AND BATTLE.
TODAY IS THE DAY OF THE THEO-KORO BATTLE.
IT'S ONLY HELD ONCE EVERY FOUR YEARS.
WE'RE GOING TO WIN THE GRAND PRIZE!
THE DREAM WAND IS ALL OURS!
OH. YOU AGAIN.
WE'VE SEEN YOU A LOT LATELY.
AH!

THIRTY-SECOND FLUSH

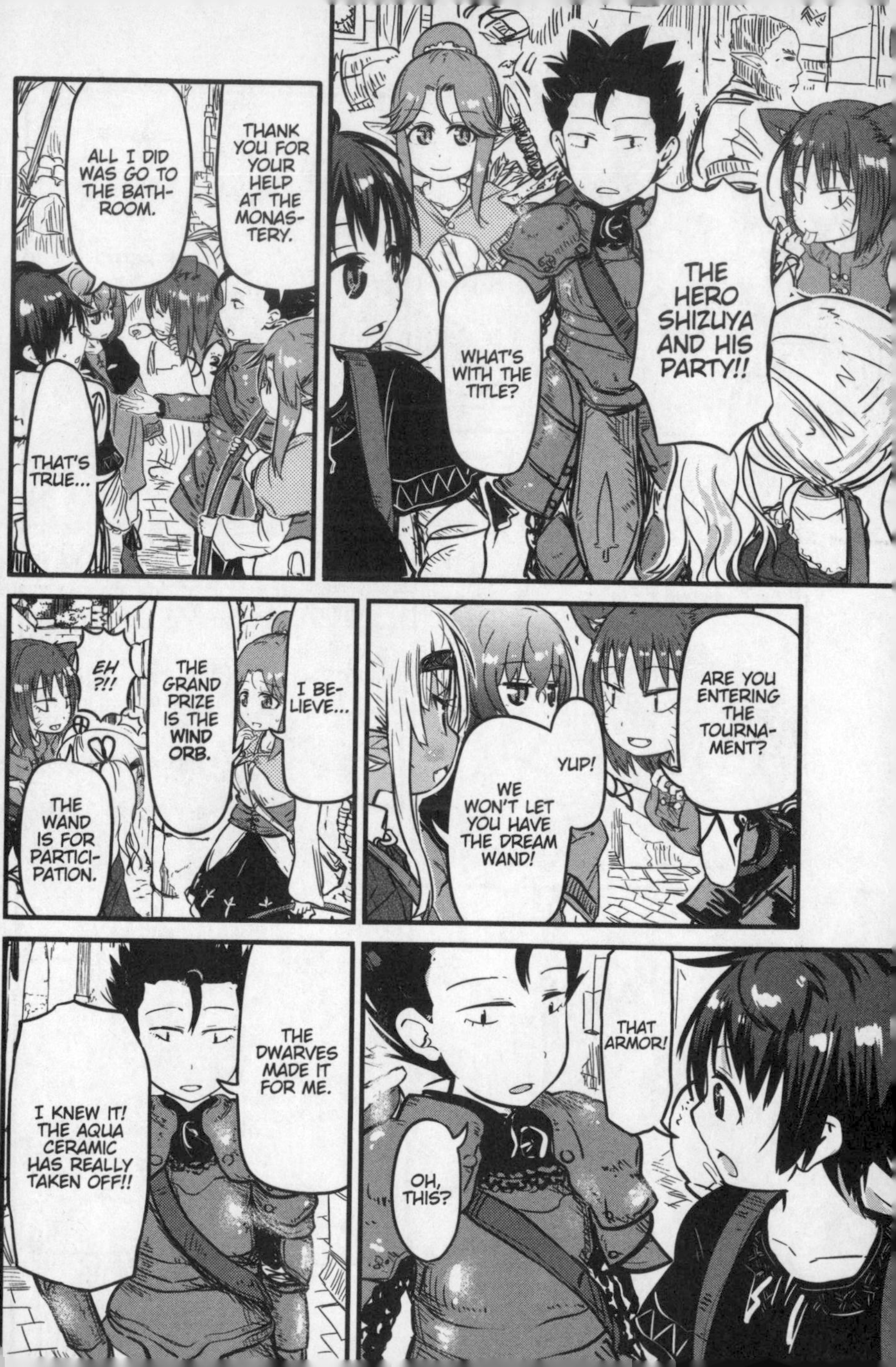
THE HERO SHIZUYA AND HIS PARTY!!
WHAT'S WITH THE TITLE?
THANK YOU FOR YOUR HELP AT THE MONASTERY.
ALL I DID WAS GO TO THE BATHROOM.
THAT'S TRUE...
ARE YOU ENTERING THE TOURNAMENT?
YUP!
WE WON'T LET YOU HAVE THE DREAM WAND!
I BELIEVE...
THE GRAND PRIZE IS THE WIND ORB.
EH ?!!
THE WAND IS FOR PARTICIPATION.
THAT ARMOR!
OH, THIS?
THE DWARVES MADE IT FOR ME.
I KNEW IT! THE AQUA CERAMIC HAS REALLY TAKEN OFF!!

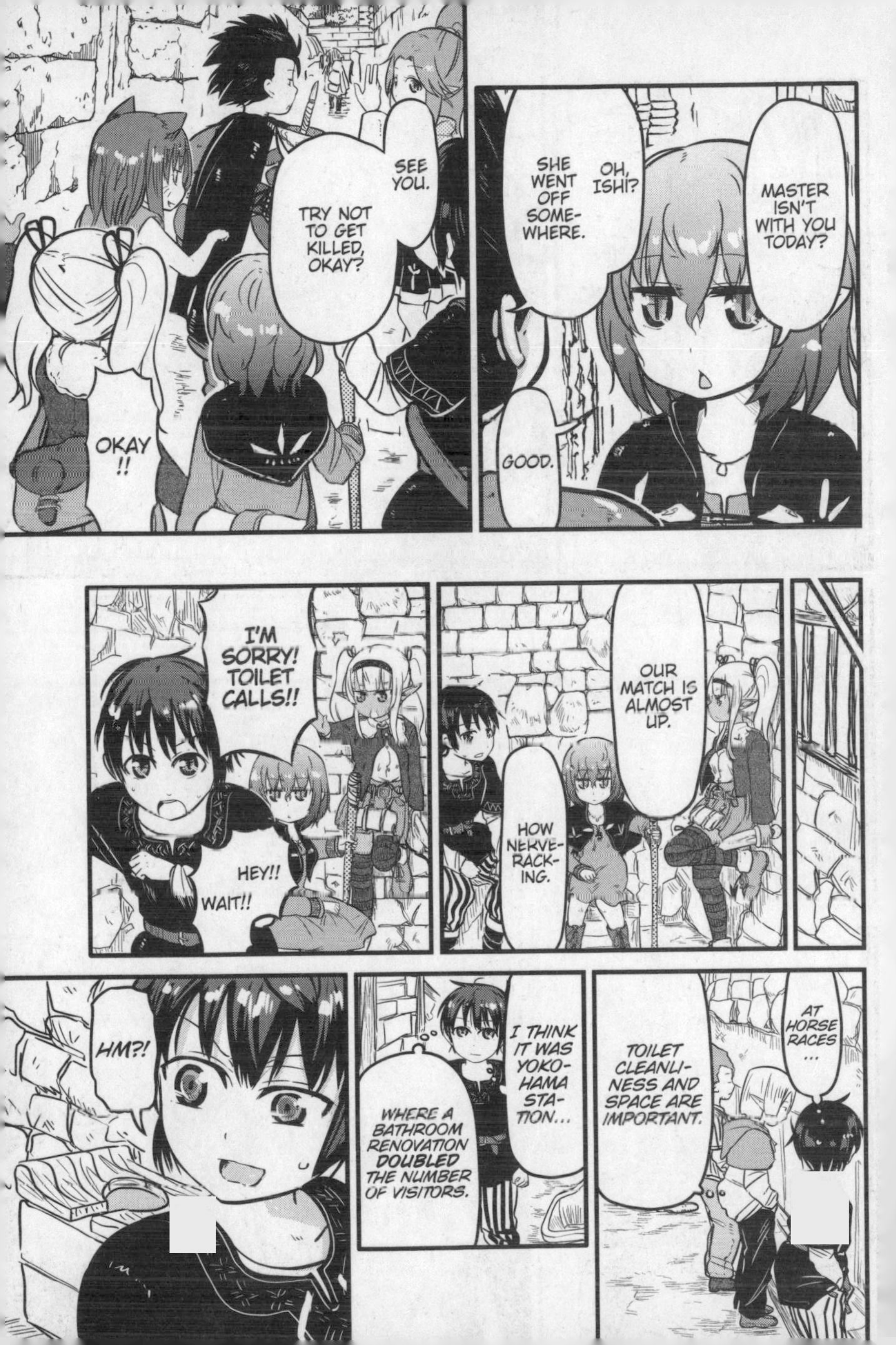
MASTER ISN'T WITH YOU TODAY?
OH, ISHI?
SHE WENT OFF SOME-WHERE.
GOOD.
SEE YOU.
TRY NOT TO GET KILLED, OKAY?
OKAY !!
OUR MATCH IS ALMOST UP.
HOW NERVE-RACK-ING.
I'M SORRY! TOILET CALLS!!
HEY!!
WAIT!!
AT HORSE RACES ...
TOILET CLEANLI-NESS AND SPACE ARE IMPORTANT.
I THINK IT WAS YOKO-HAMA STA-TION...
WHERE A BATHROOM RENOVATION **DOUBLED** THE NUMBER OF VISITORS.
HM?!

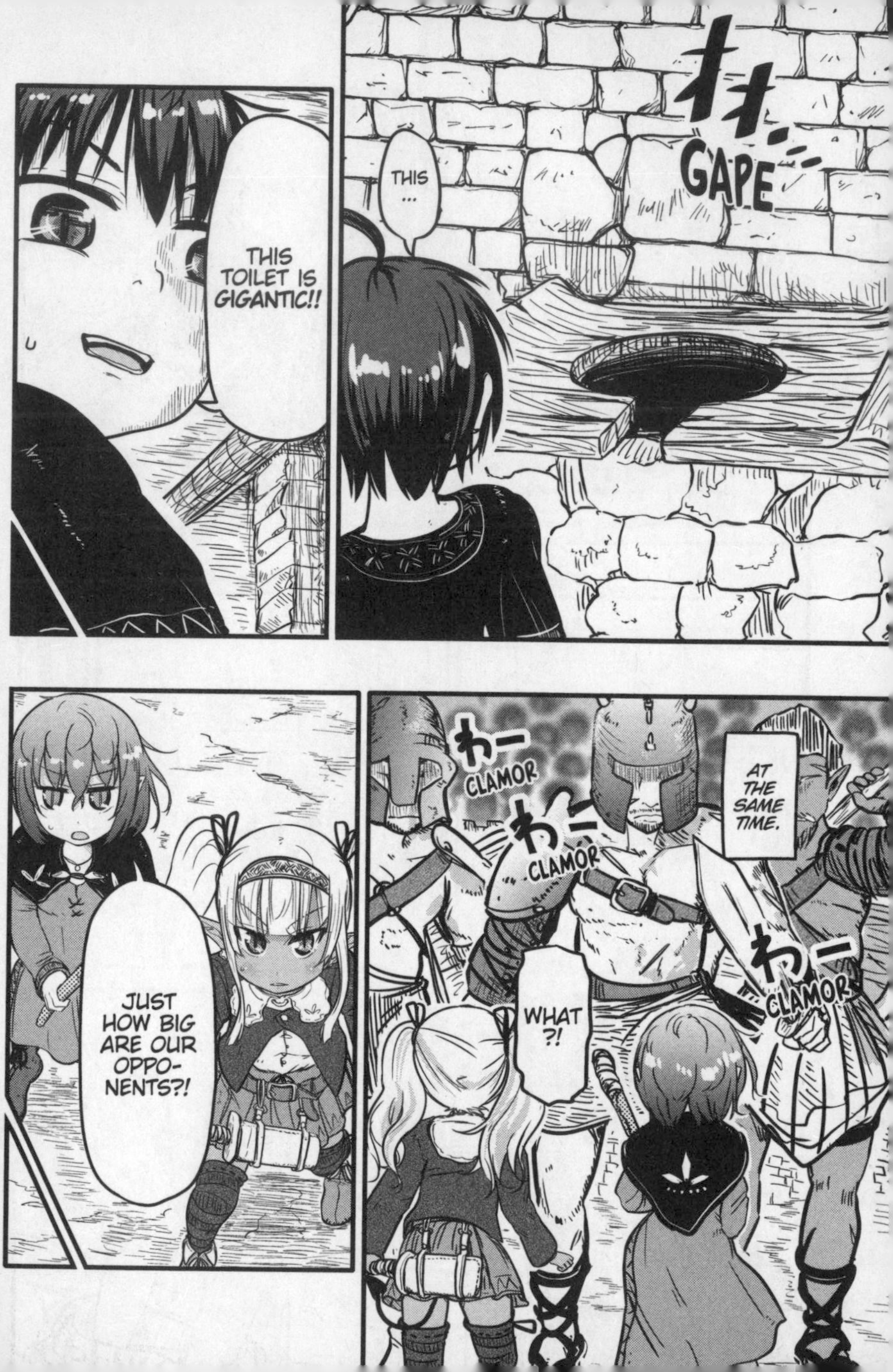
GAPE
THIS ...
THIS TOILET IS GIGANTIC!!
AT THE SAME TIME.
わー CLAMOR
わー CLAMOR
わー CLAMOR
WHAT?!
JUST HOW BIG ARE OUR OPPO-NENTS?!

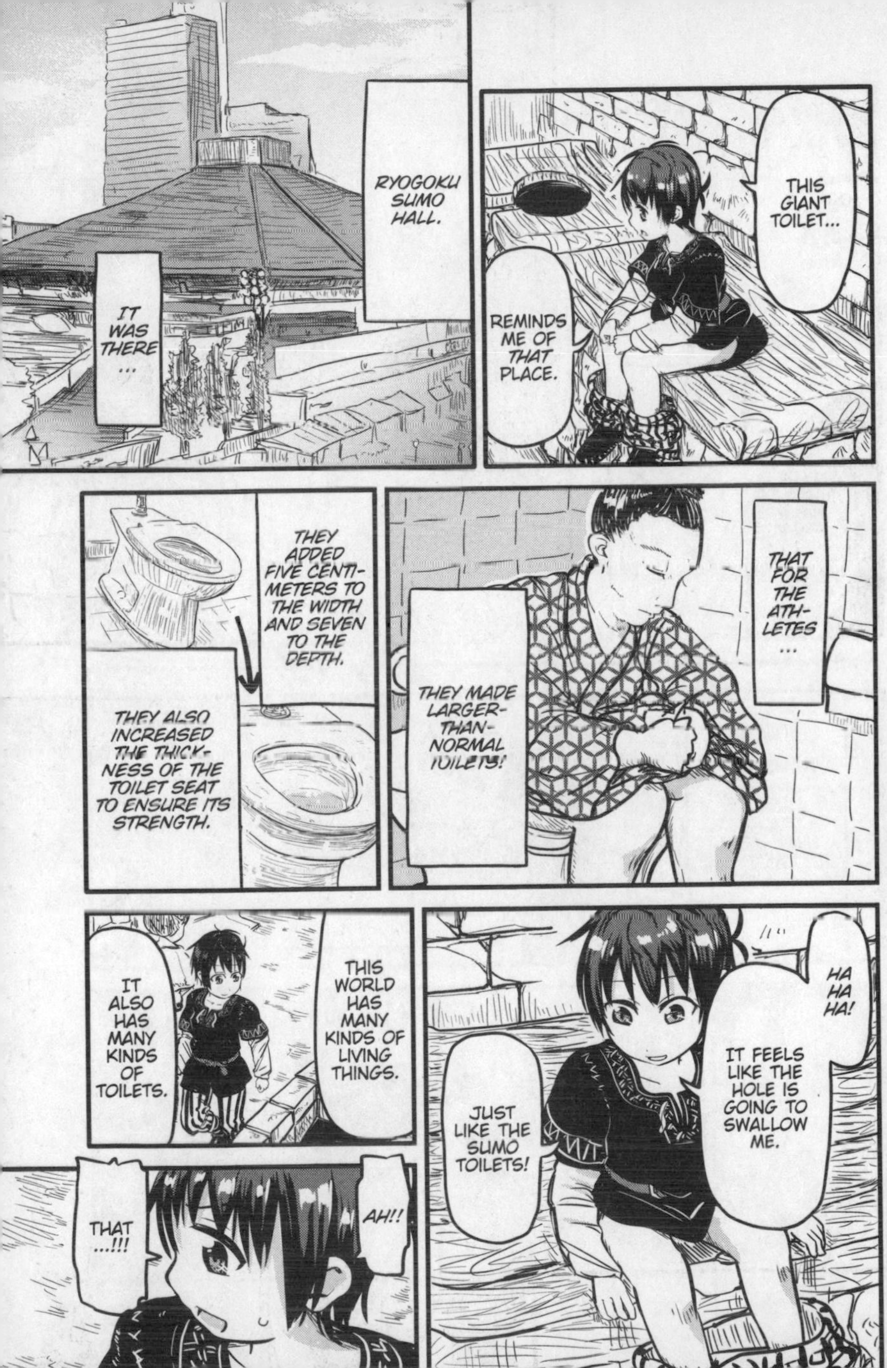
THIS GIANT TOILET...
REMINDS ME OF THAT PLACE.
RYOGOKU SUMO HALL.
IT WAS THERE...
THAT FOR THE ATHLETES...
THEY MADE LARGER-THAN-NORMAL TOILETS!
THEY ADDED FIVE CENTIMETERS TO THE WIDTH AND SEVEN TO THE DEPTH.
THEY ALSO INCREASED THE THICKNESS OF THE TOILET SEAT TO ENSURE ITS STRENGTH.
HA HA HA!
IT FEELS LIKE THE HOLE IS GOING TO SWALLOW ME.
JUST LIKE THE SUMO TOILETS!
THIS WORLD HAS MANY KINDS OF LIVING THINGS.
IT ALSO HAS MANY KINDS OF TOILETS.
AH!!
THAT...!!!

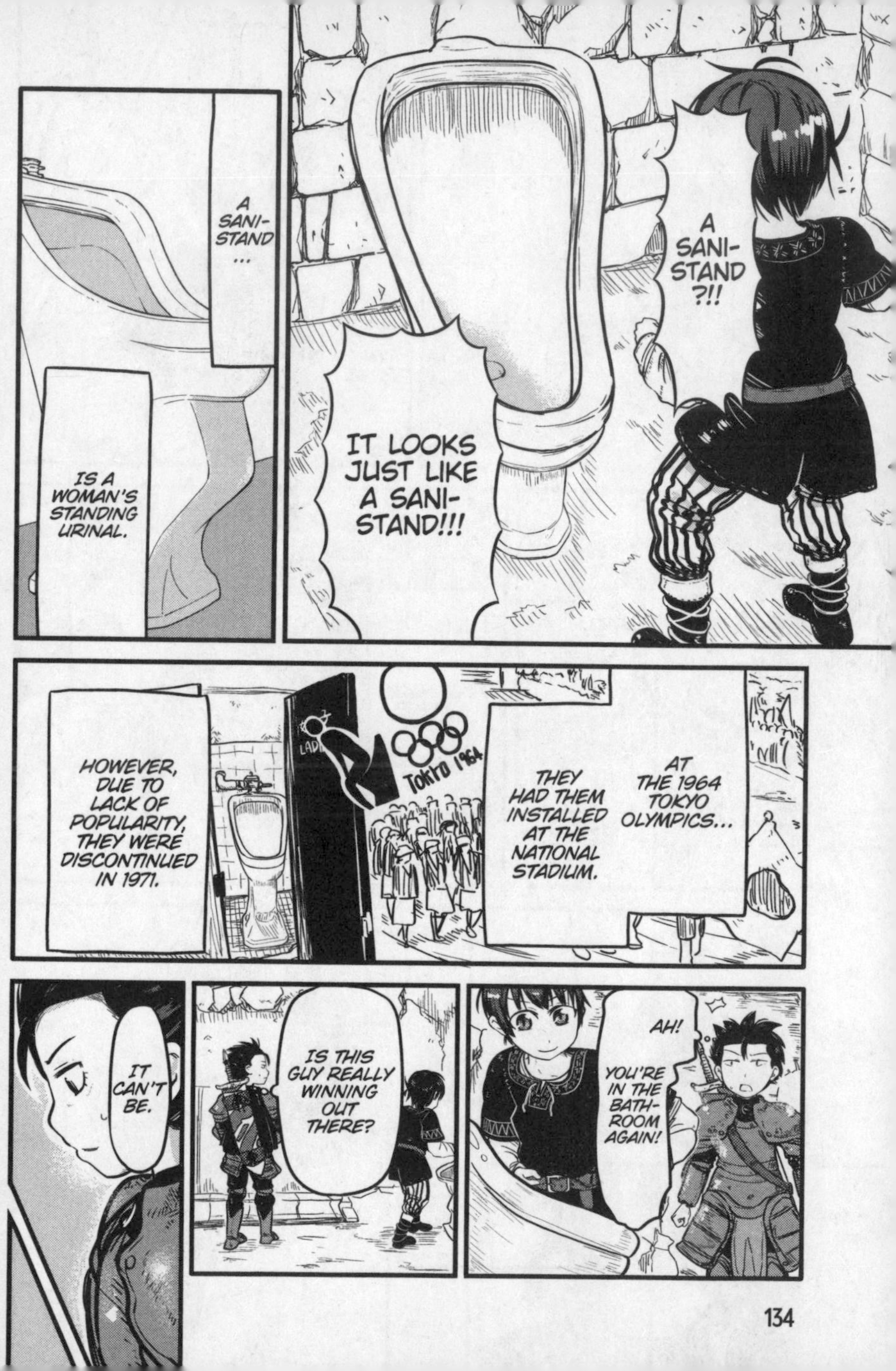
A SANI-STAND?!!
IT LOOKS JUST LIKE A SANI-STAND!!!
A SANI-STAND...
IS A WOMAN'S STANDING URINAL.
AT THE 1964 TOKYO OLYMPICS...
THEY HAD THEM INSTALLED AT THE NATIONAL STADIUM.
TOKYO 1964
HOWEVER, DUE TO LACK OF POPULARITY, THEY WERE DISCONTINUED IN 1971.
AH!
YOU'RE IN THE BATHROOM AGAIN!
IS THIS GUY REALLY WINNING OUT THERE?
IT CAN'T BE.

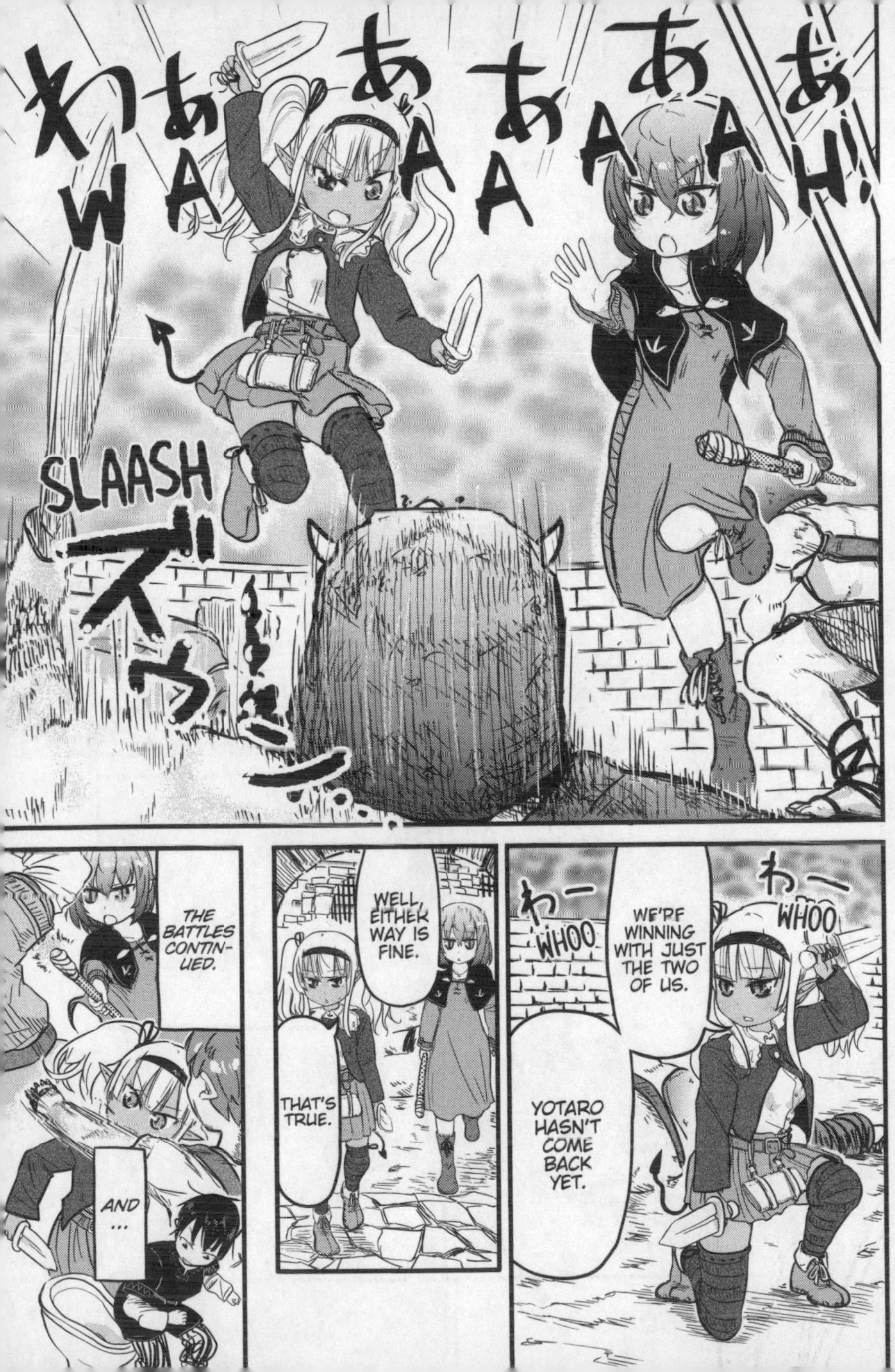
わあああああ
WAAAAAH!!
SLAASH
ズヴ
わー
WHOO
わー
WHOO
WE'RF WINNING WITH JUST THE TWO OF US.
YOTARO HASN'T COME BACK YET.
WELL, EITHEK WAY IS FINE.
THAT'S TRUE.
THE BATTLES CONTINUED.
AND ...

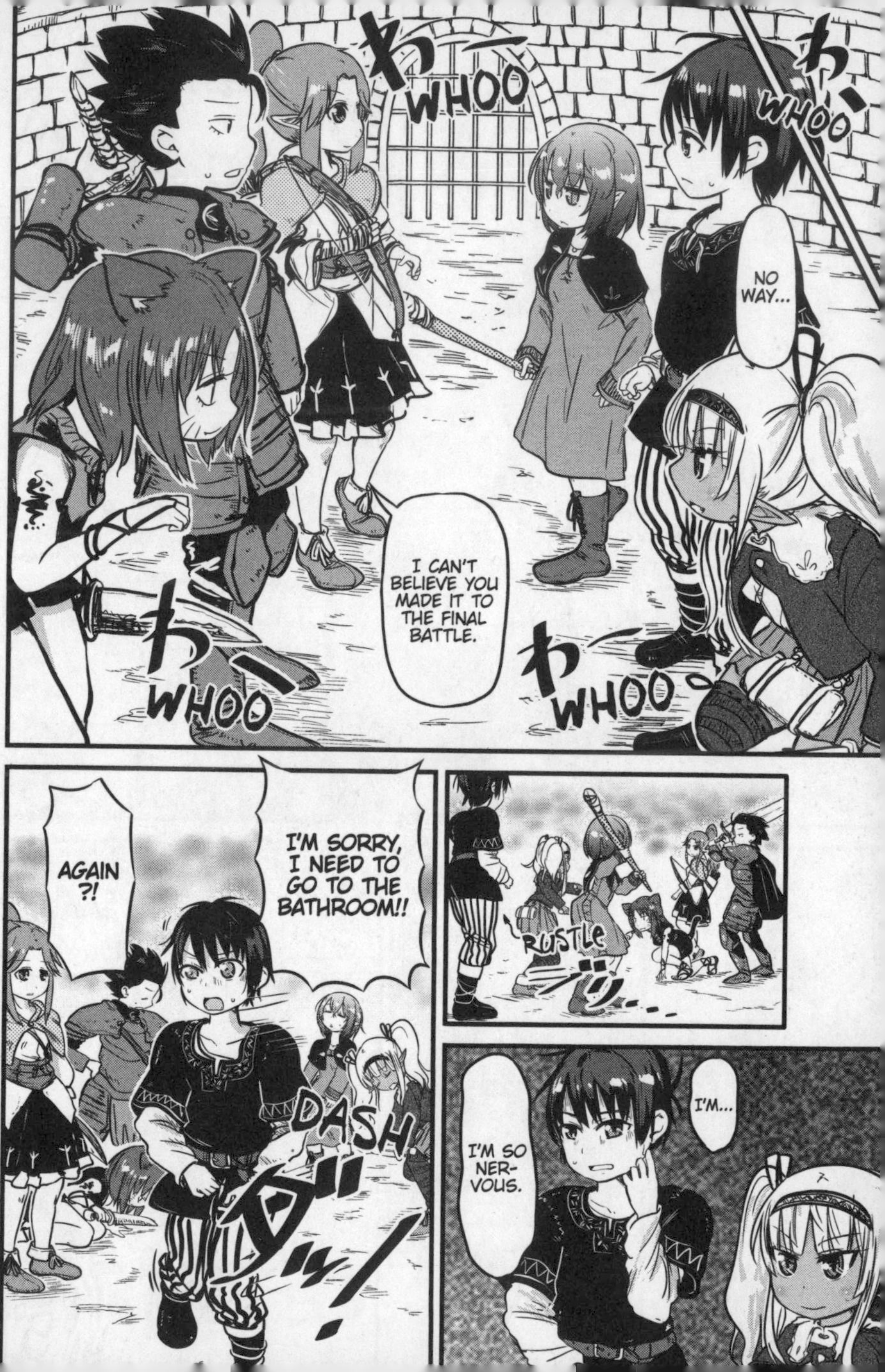

わ、
WHOO
わー
WHOO
NO WAY...
I CAN'T BELIEVE YOU MADE IT TO THE FINAL BATTLE.
わー
WHOO
わー
WHOO
RUSTLE
I'M...
I'M SO NER-VOUS.
I'M SORRY, I NEED TO GO TO THE BATHROOM!!
AGAIN ?!
DASH

THIRTY-THIRD FLUSH

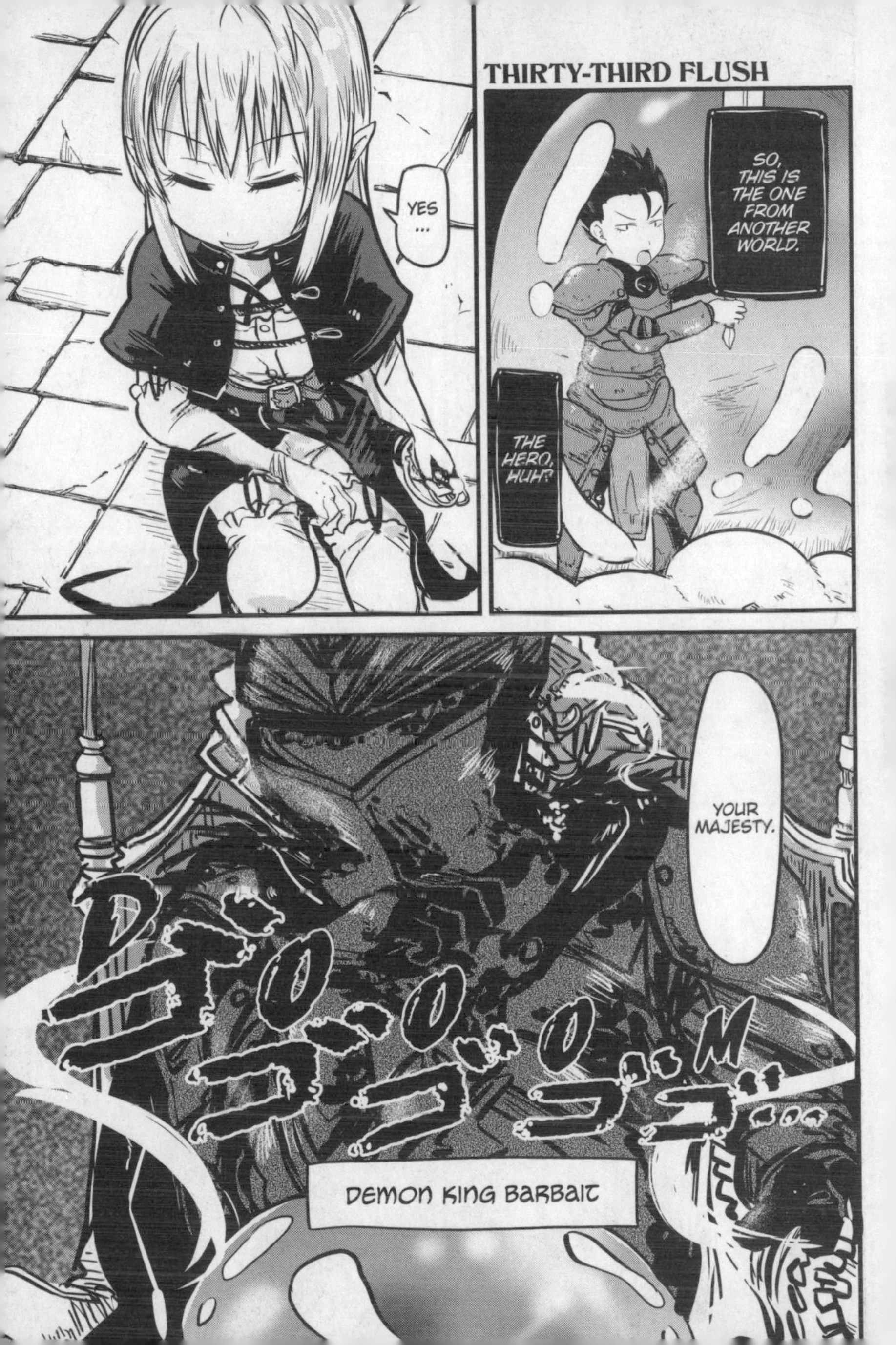
SO, THIS IS THE ONE FROM ANOTHER WORLD.
THE HERO, HUH?
YES ...
YOUR MAJESTY.
DOOO...M
DEMON KING BARBAIT

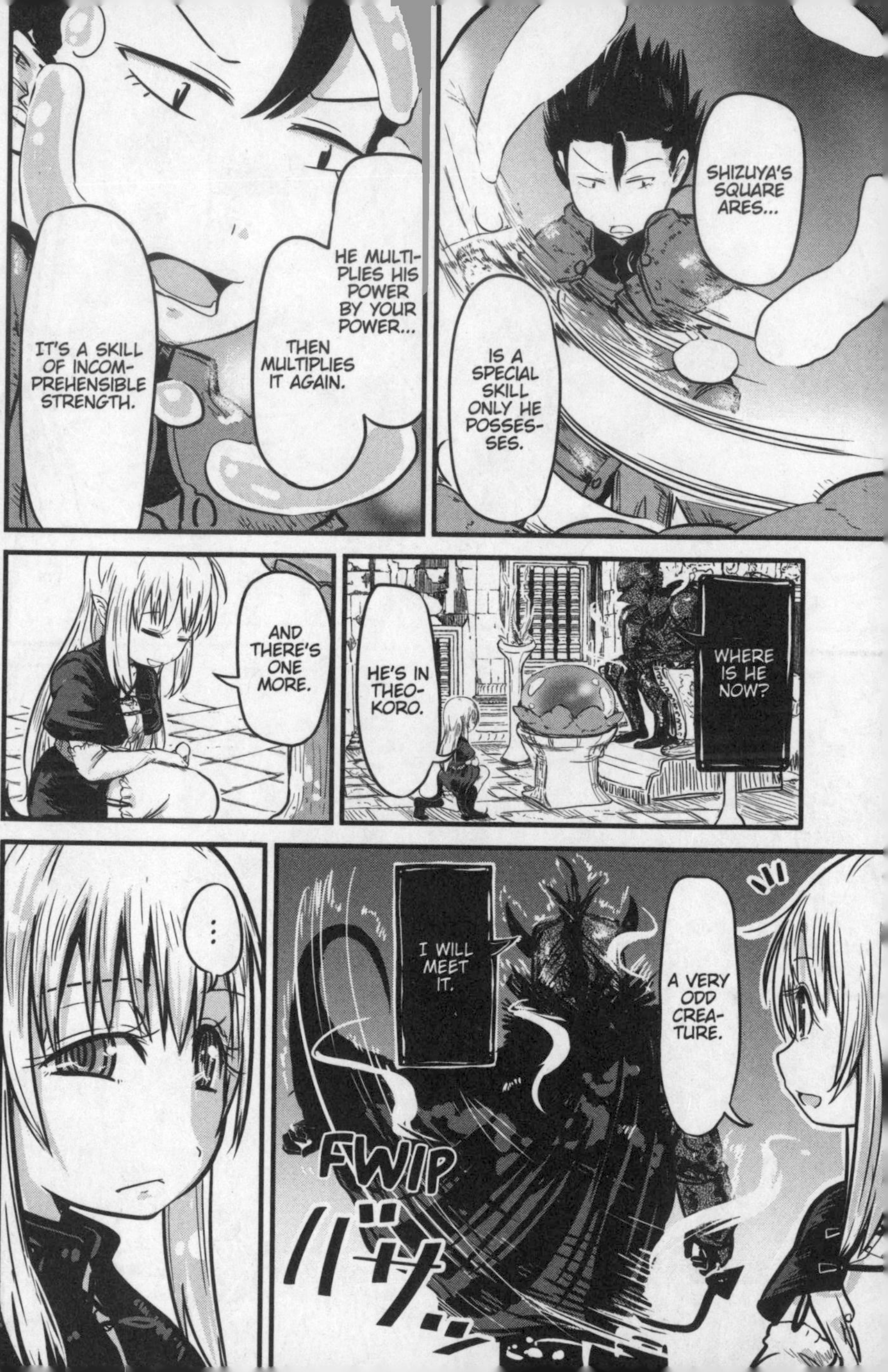
SHIZUYA'S SQUARE ARES...
IS A SPECIAL SKILL ONLY HE POSSESSES.
HE MULTIPLIES HIS POWER BY YOUR POWER...
THEN MULTIPLIES IT AGAIN.
IT'S A SKILL OF INCOMPREHENSIBLE STRENGTH.
WHERE IS HE NOW?
HE'S IN THEOKORO.
AND THERE'S ONE MORE.
A VERY ODD CREATURE.
I WILL MEET IT.
FWIP
バサッ
...

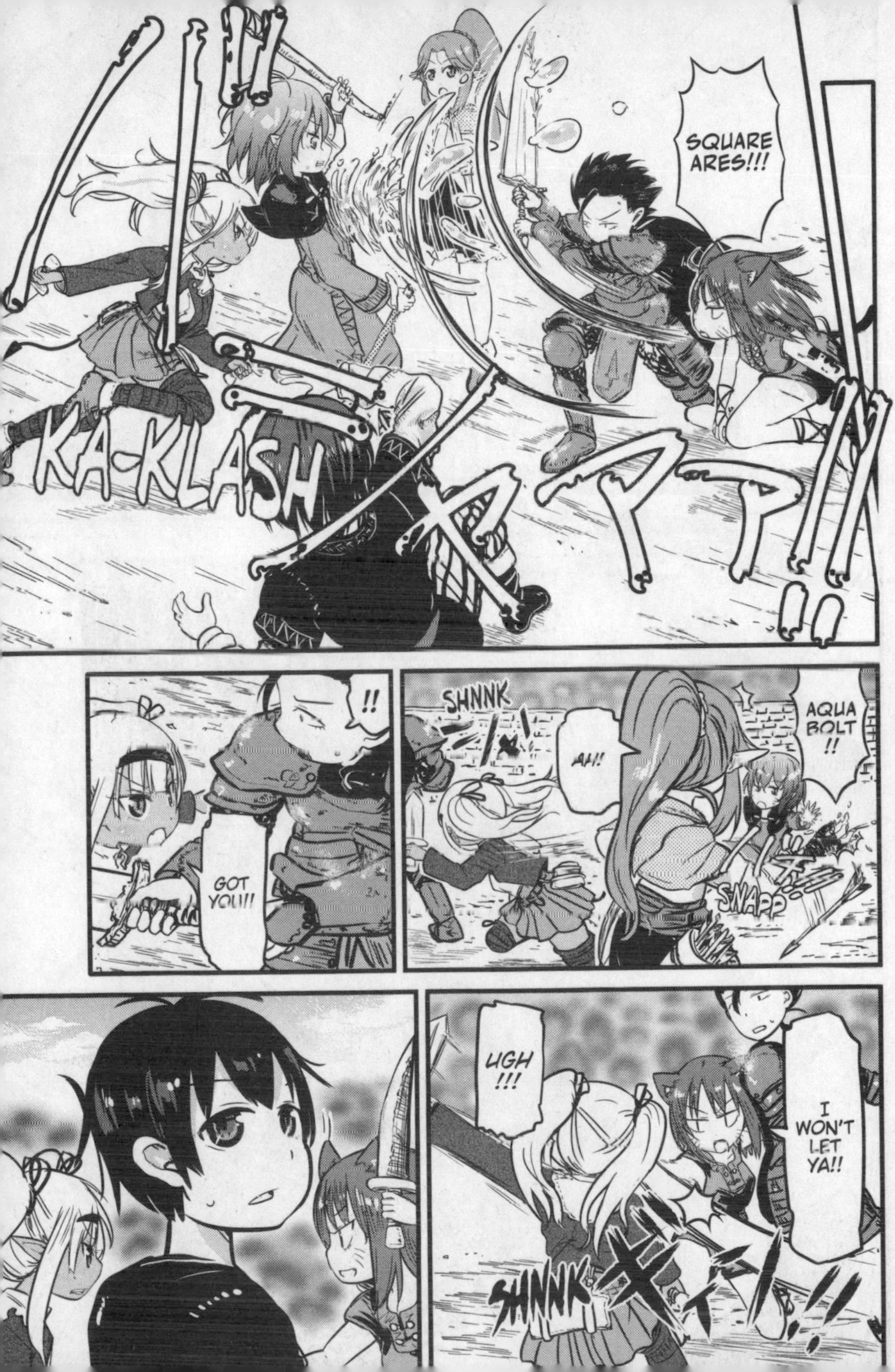
SQUARE ARES!!!
KA-KLASH
AQUA BOLT !!
!
AH!
SHNNK
SNAPP
!!
GOT YOU!!!
I WON'T LET YA!!
UGH !!!
SHNNK

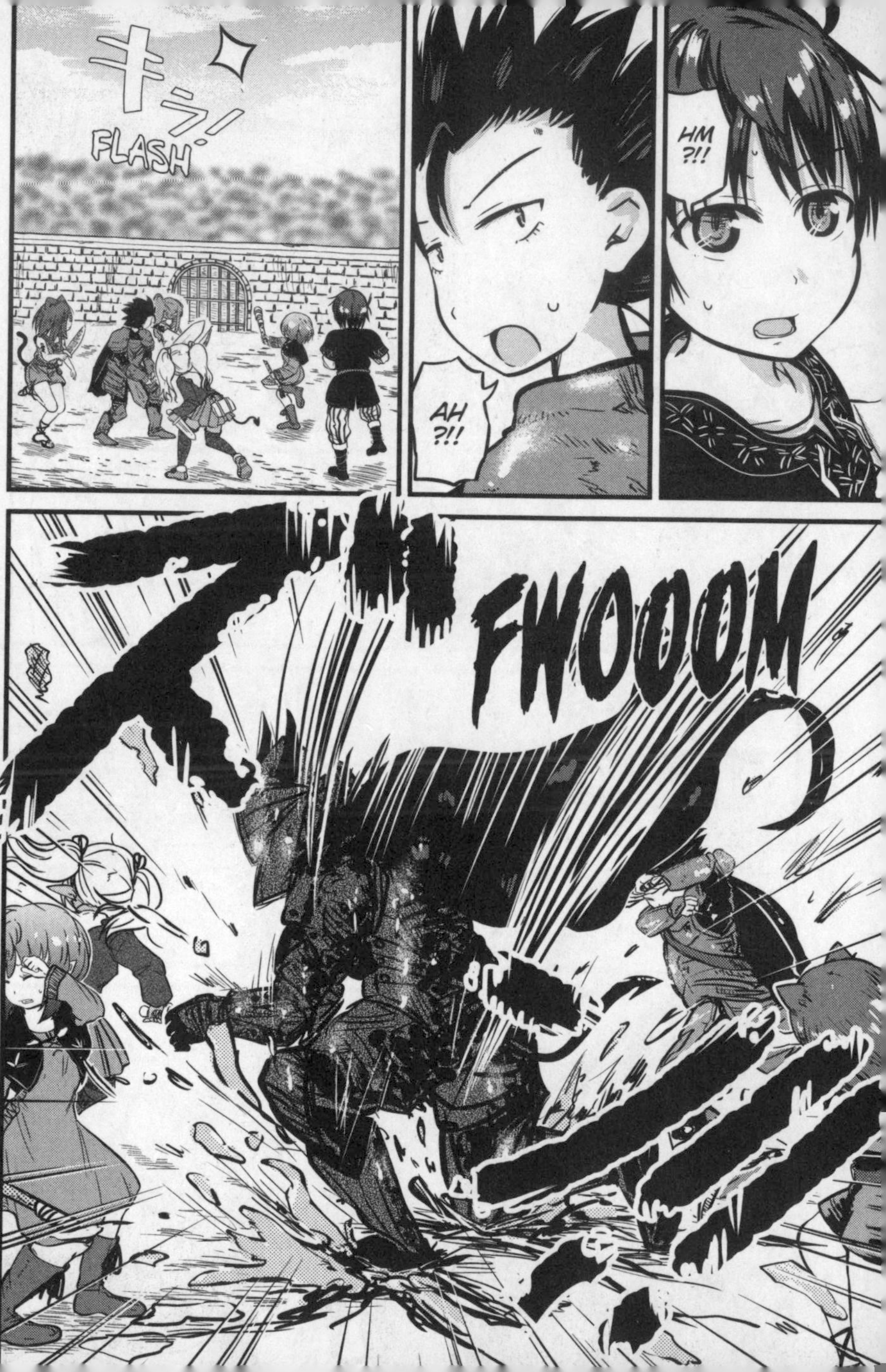
HM ?!!
AH ?!!
キラ!
FLASH
FWOOOM

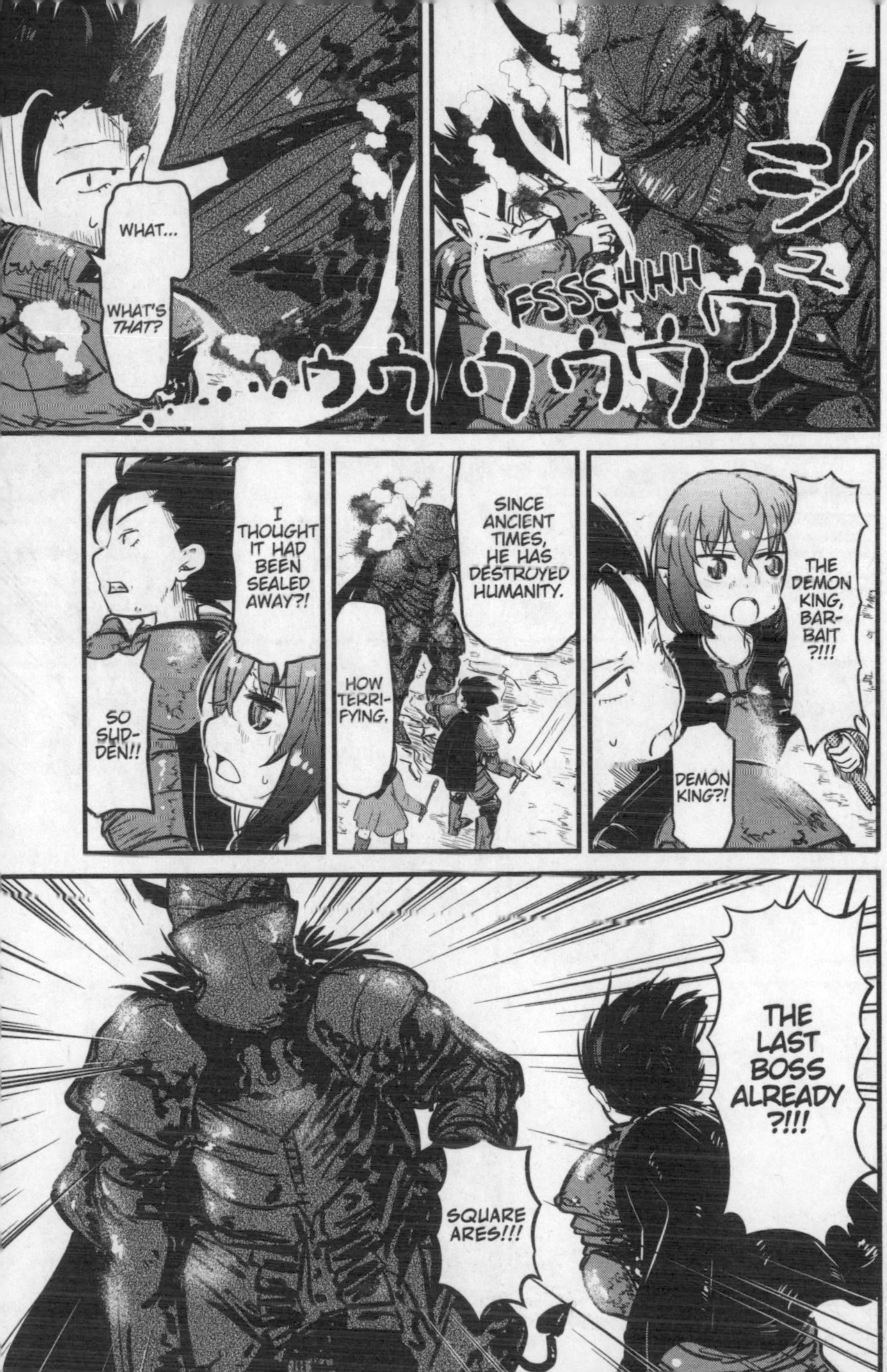
FSSSHHH
WHAT...
WHAT'S *THAT*?
THE DEMON KING, BAR-BAIT?!!!
DEMON KING?!
SINCE ANCIENT TIMES, HE HAS DESTROYED HUMANITY.
HOW TERRI-FYING.
I THOUGHT IT HAD BEEN SEALED AWAY?!
SO SUD-DEN!!
THE LAST BOSS ALREADY?!!!
SQUARE ARES!!!

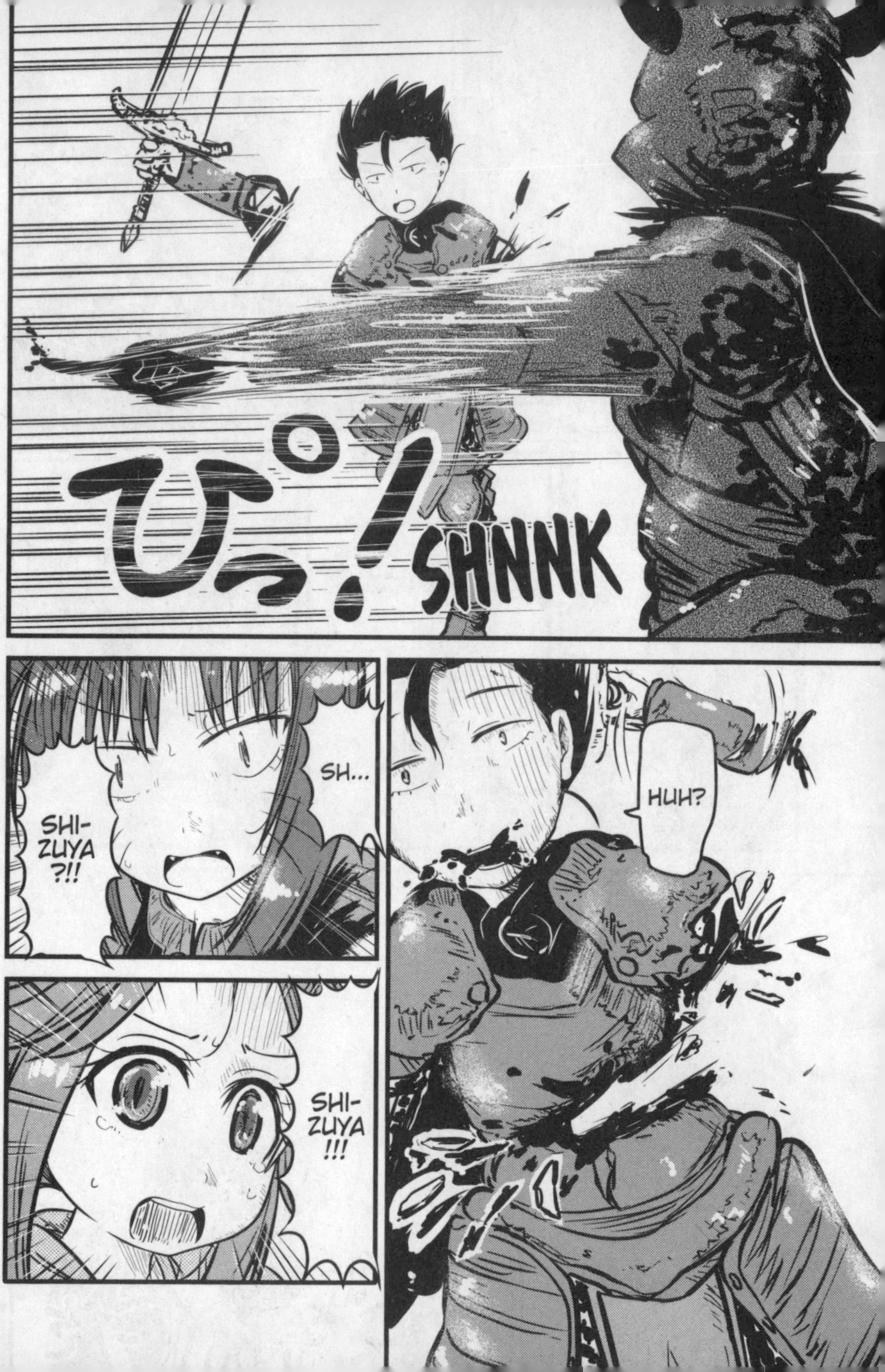
SHNNK
ひっ!
HUH?
SH...
SHI-ZUYA?!!
SHI-ZUYA!!!

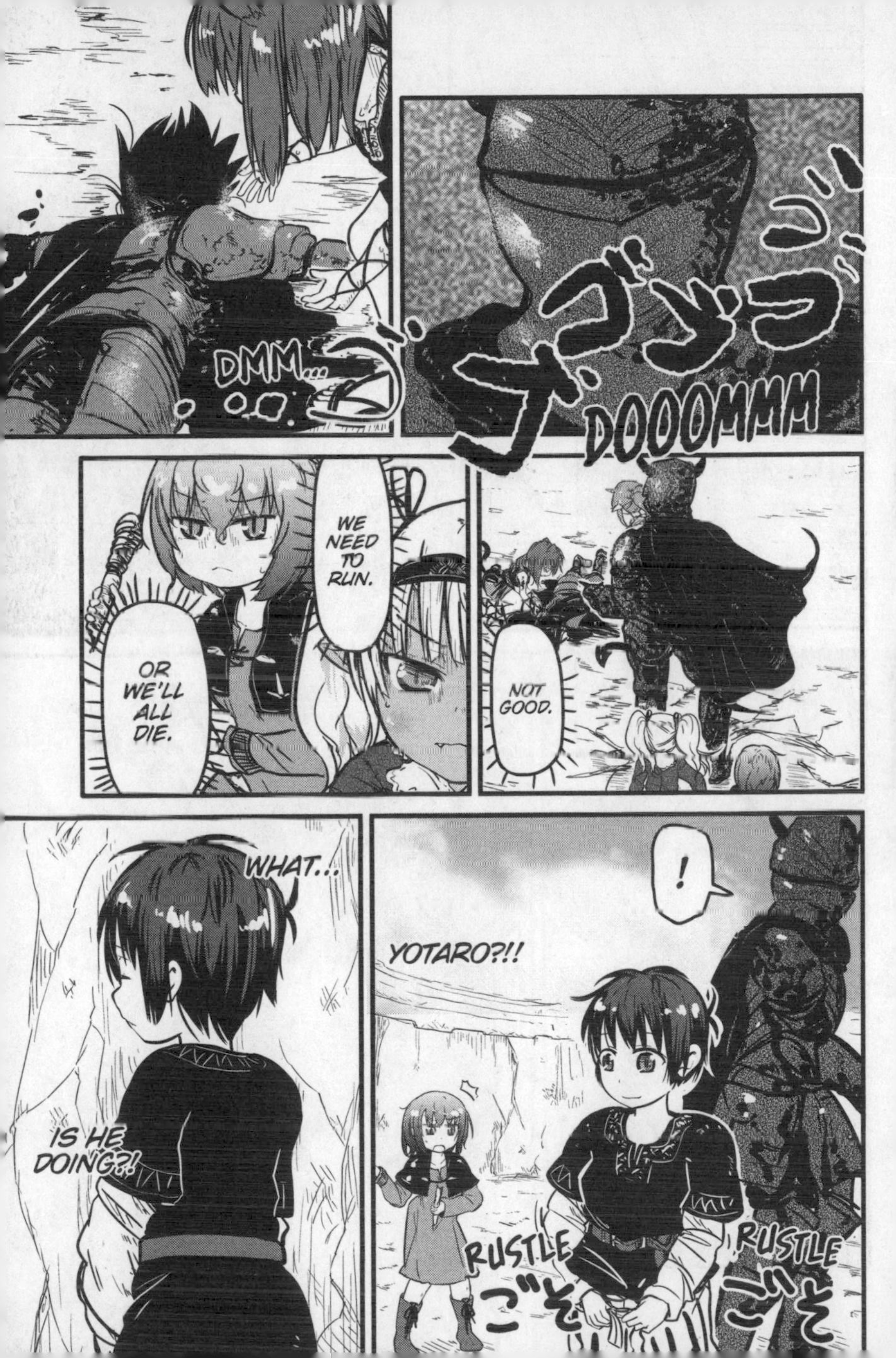

DOOOMMM
DMM...
NOT GOOD.
WE NEED TO RUN.
OR WE'LL ALL DIE.
!
YOTARO?!!
RUSTLE
ごそ
RUSTLE
ごそ
WHAT...
IS HE DOING?!

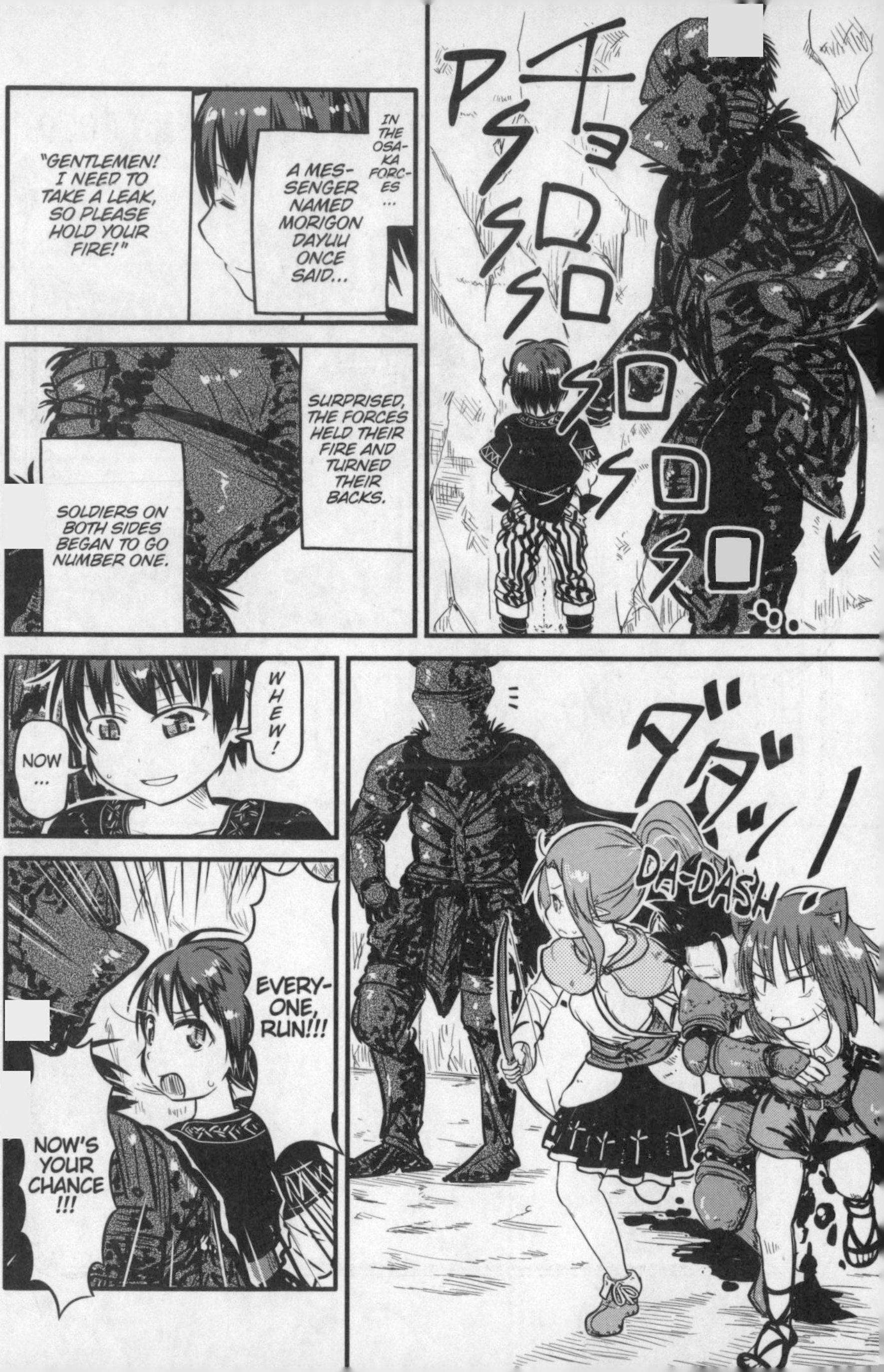
IN THE OSAKA FORCES...
A MESSENGER NAMED MORIGON DAYUU ONCE SAID...
"GENTLEMEN! I NEED TO TAKE A LEAK, SO PLEASE HOLD YOUR FIRE!"
SURPRISED, THE FORCES HELD THEIR FIRE AND TURNED THEIR BACKS.
SOLDIERS ON BOTH SIDES BEGAN TO GO NUMBER ONE.
ダダッ
DA-DASH
WHEW!
NOW...
EVERYONE, RUN!!!
NOW'S YOUR CHANCE!!!

ROOTS

PEOPLE WHO DON'T VALUE TOILET TIME ARE NO GOOD.

SEVETEENTH TOILET TIME

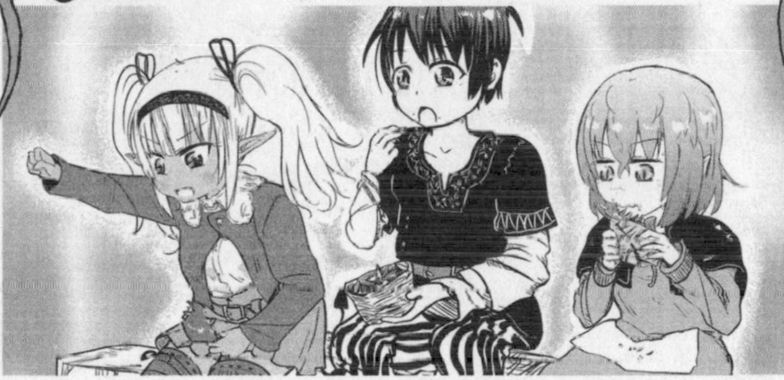

I'm always excited to write this column, where I introduce ways to make your toilet experience more comfortable.

This time, I'm back with the second installment of "The End all of Butts in the East and West"! Among all the various human civilizations, the use of paper is very recent. Let's revisit the act of wiping by examining the tools used in toilets, and clean our minds while we clean our butts!

No. 5: Clay Cake
A triangular stone excavated in the ruins of Mohenjo Daro. This is the world's oldest tool for wiping one's bottom. It's about the size of a rice ball and has rounded corners to make it comfortable. Another advantage is that it's made of clay, so it doesn't get hot. When it was first excavated, it was thought to have been used for rituals dedicated to the gods, hence the word "cake."

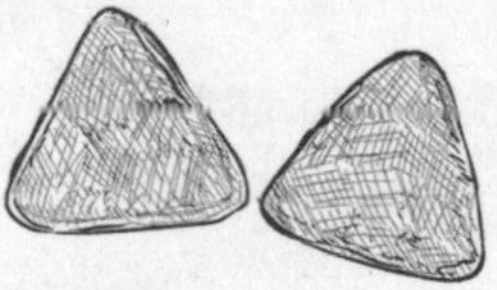

No. 6: Poop Stick
A dung spatula. A piece of wood used to write letters can be broken and reused as a poop stick. When a refuse site is excavated, whether it's a garbage dump or a toilet can be determined by whether or not this piece of wood is unearthed. I wonder if it hurts?

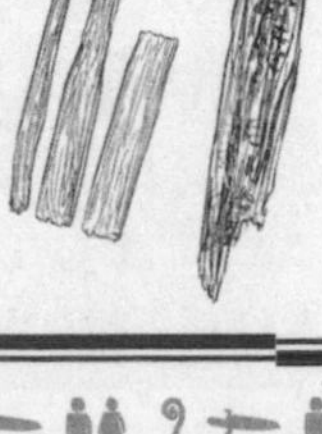

No. 7: Rope
In Africa, there was a method of straddling a rope in a river while facing upstream to do your business. Apparently, there was also a toilet in China that used a rope suspended from the ceiling to wipe.

No. 8: Sponge on a Stick
The sponge sticks that were used in public toilets in ancient Rome are as Roman as you can get. People would wet the sponge and wipe their buttocks with it. Honestly, it sounds quite nice. I've read various anecdotes, such as that it was dirty because it was used all the time, or that the nobles carried their own sponges with them. There are also anecdotes about them being used for cleaning. Even now, research into these tools continues.

No. 9: Not Wiping
There were many avant-garde people who chose not to wipe due to various factors, such as diet, climate, and culture.

Humans used a variety of tools to wipe their butts other than those introduced here. What we can say is that in a few hundred years, we may be using tools we can't even imagine. We must be more open-minded, because there are many things we can learn through poop.

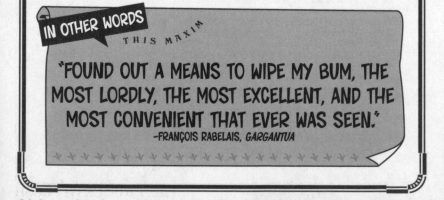

IN OTHER WORDS THIS MAXIM

"FOUND OUT A MEANS TO WIPE MY BUM, THE MOST LORDLY, THE MOST EXCELLENT, AND THE MOST CONVENIENT THAT EVER WAS SEEN."
–FRANÇOIS RABELAIS, *GARGANTUA*

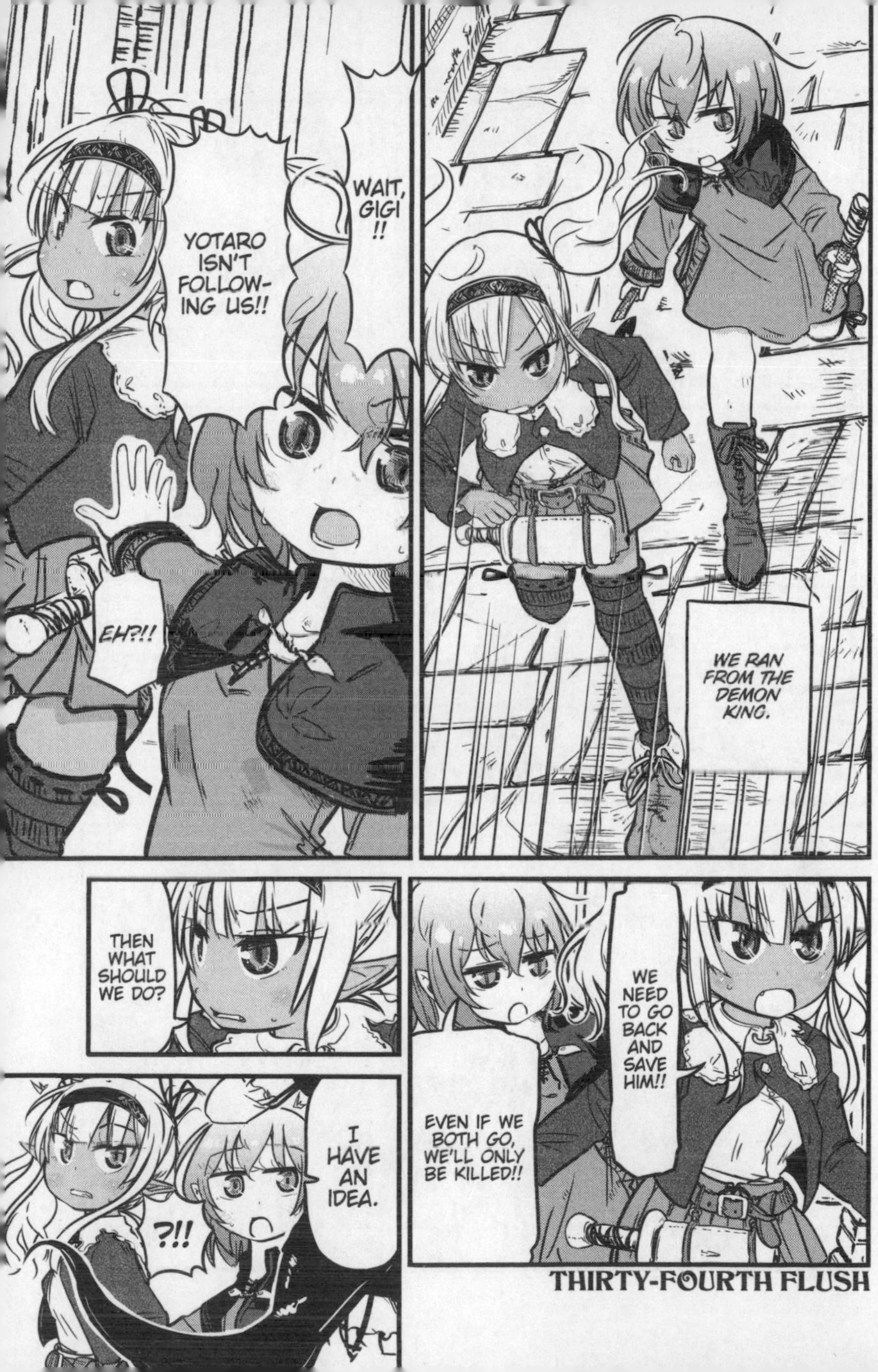
WE RAN FROM THE DEMON KING.
WAIT, GIGI!!
YOTARO ISN'T FOLLOWING US!!
EH?!!
WE NEED TO GO BACK AND SAVE HIM!!
EVEN IF WE BOTH GO, WE'LL ONLY BE KILLED!!
THEN WHAT SHOULD WE DO?
I HAVE AN IDEA.
?!!

THIRTY-FOURTH FLUSH

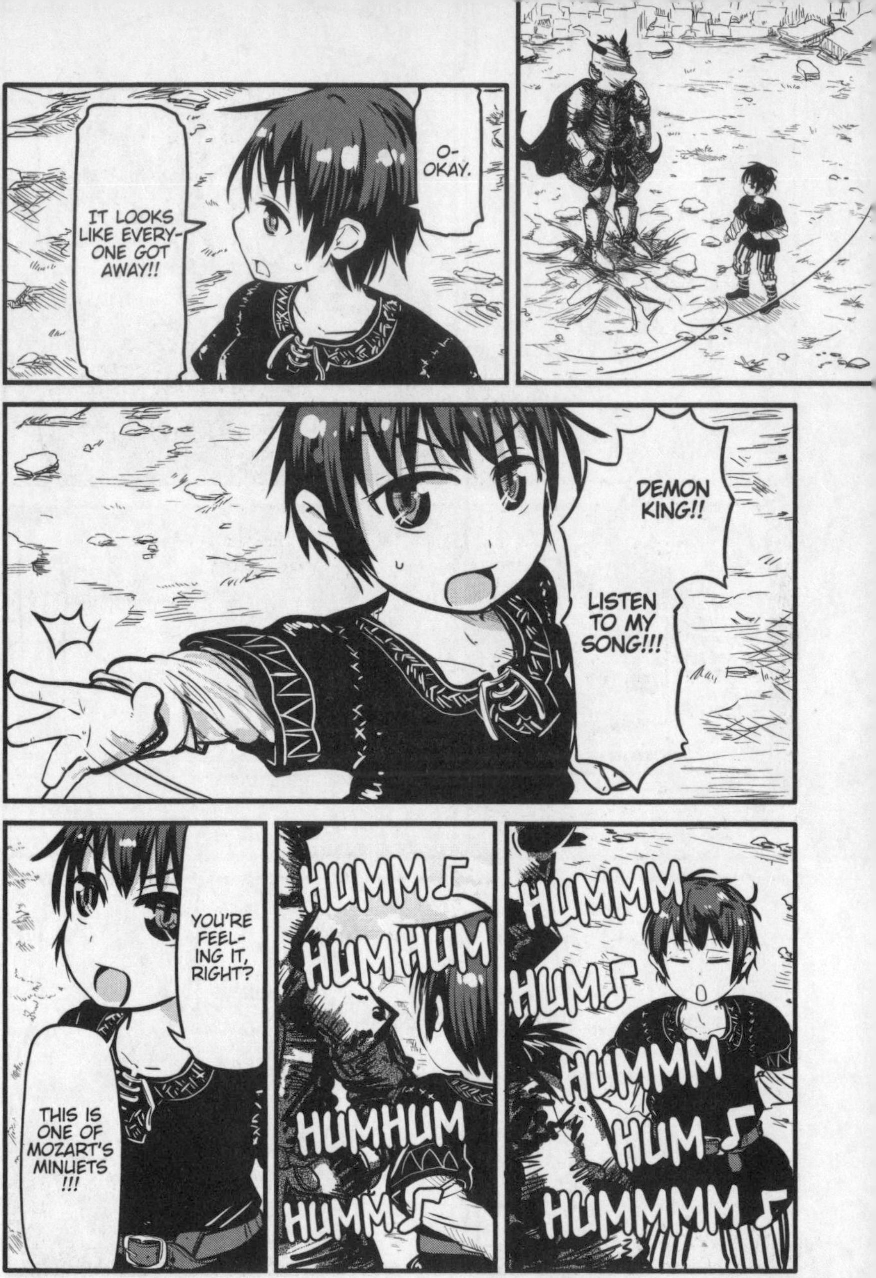
O-OKAY.
IT LOOKS LIKE EVERY-ONE GOT AWAY!!
DEMON KING!!
LISTEN TO MY SONG!!!
HUMMMM
HUM♪
HUMMMM
HUM♪
HUMMMMM♪
HUMM♪
HUM HUM
HUMHUM
HUMM♪
YOU'RE FEEL-ING IT, RIGHT?
THIS IS ONE OF MOZART'S MINUETS!!!

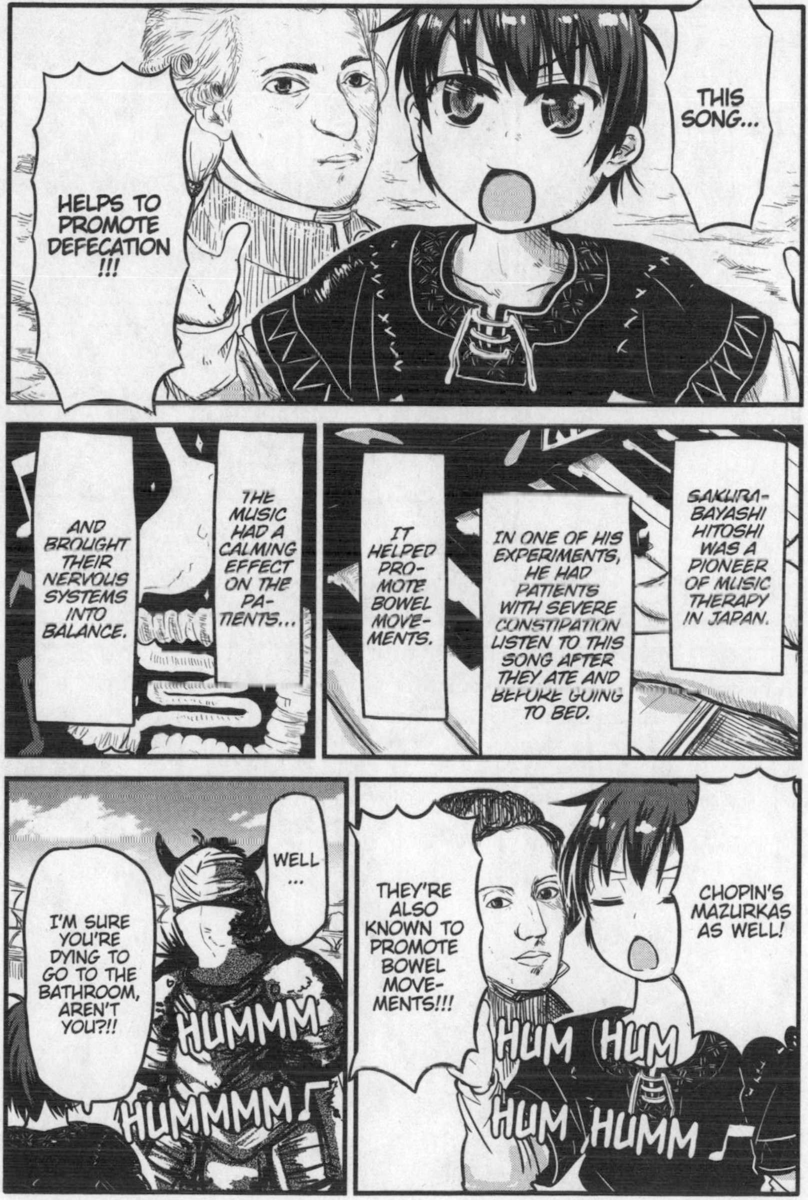
THIS SONG...
HELPS TO PROMOTE DEFECATION !!!
SAKURA-BAYASHI HITOSHI WAS A PIONEER OF MUSIC THERAPY IN JAPAN.
IN ONE OF HIS EXPERIMENTS, HE HAD PATIENTS WITH SEVERE CONSTIPATION LISTEN TO THIS SONG AFTER THEY ATE AND BEFORE GOING TO BED.
IT HELPED PRO-MOTE BOWEL MOVE-MENTS.
THE MUSIC HAD A CALMING EFFECT ON THE PA-TIENTS...
AND BROUGHT THEIR NERVOUS SYSTEMS INTO BALANCE.
CHOPIN'S MAZURKAS AS WELL!
THEY'RE ALSO KNOWN TO PROMOTE BOWEL MOVE-MENTS!!!
HUM HUM
HUM HUMM
WELL ...
I'M SURE YOU'RE DYING TO GO TO THE BATHROOM, AREN'T YOU?!!
HUMMM
HUMMMM

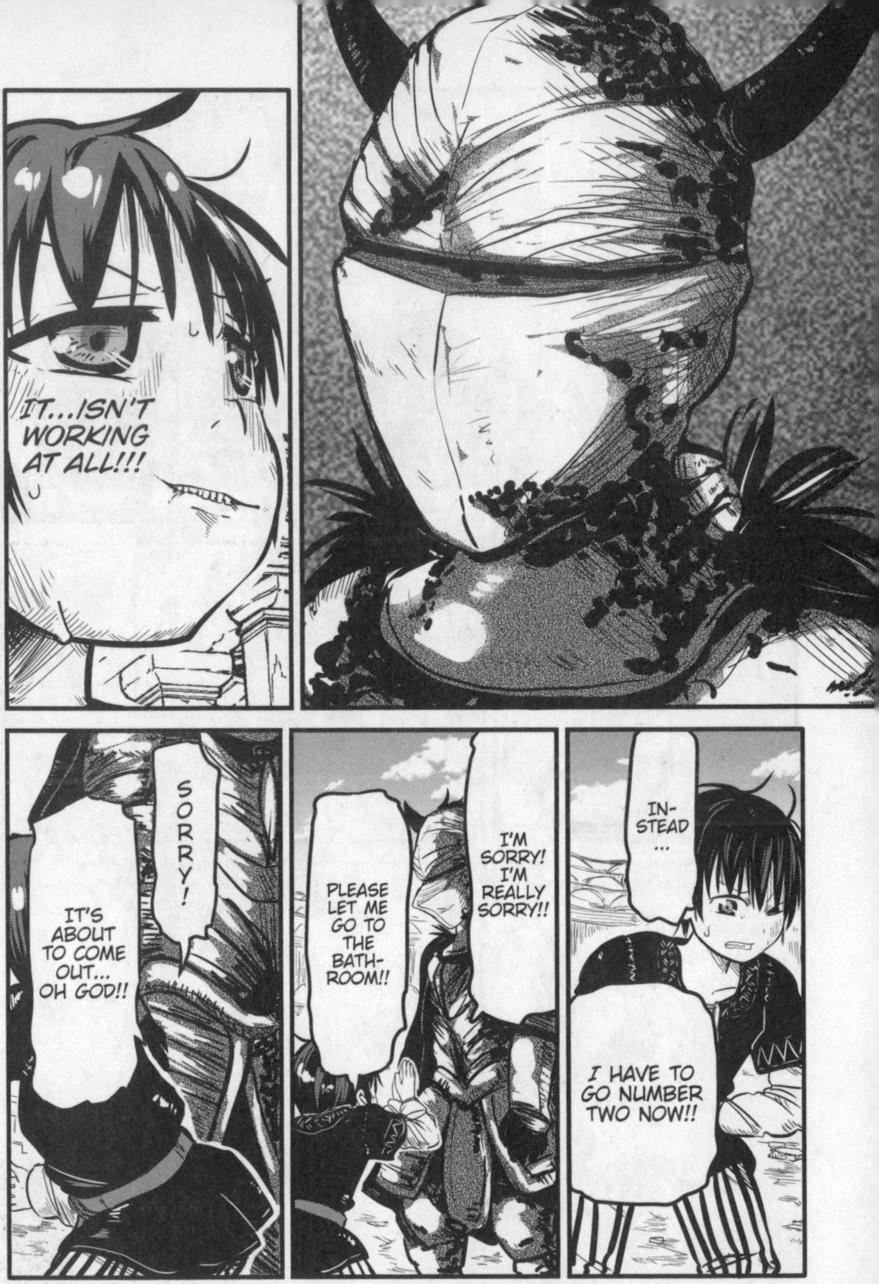
IT...ISN'T WORKING AT ALL!!!
IN-STEAD...
I HAVE TO GO NUMBER TWO NOW!!
I'M SORRY! I'M REALLY SORRY!!
PLEASE LET ME GO TO THE BATH-ROOM!!
SORRY!
IT'S ABOUT TO COME OUT... OH GOD!!

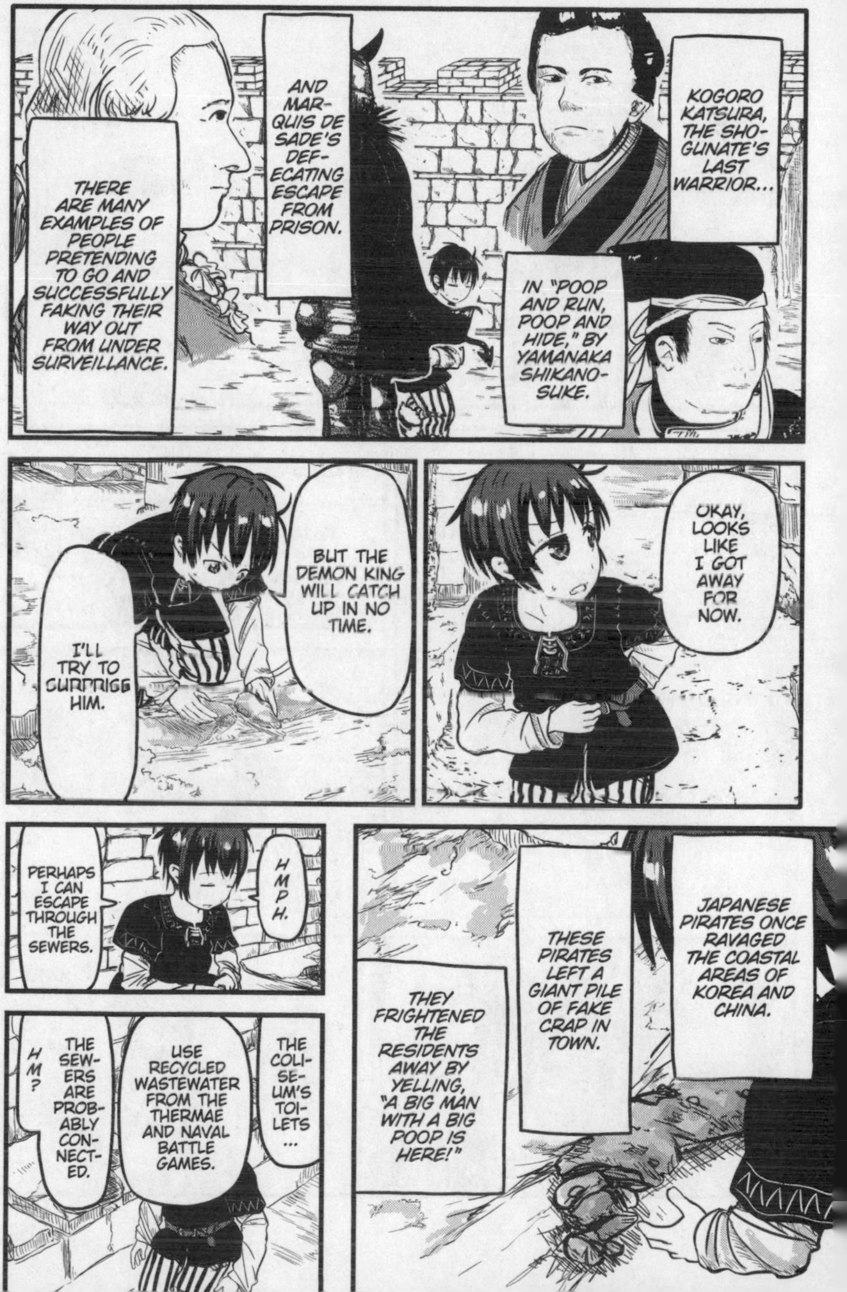
KOGORO KATSURA, THE SHOGUNATE'S LAST WARRIOR...
IN "POOP AND RUN, POOP AND HIDE," BY YAMANAKA SHIKANOSUKE.
AND MARQUIS DE SADE'S DEFECATING ESCAPE FROM PRISON.
THERE ARE MANY EXAMPLES OF PEOPLE PRETENDING TO GO AND SUCCESSFULLY FAKING THEIR WAY OUT FROM UNDER SURVEILLANCE.
OKAY, LOOKS LIKE I GOT AWAY FOR NOW.
BUT THE DEMON KING WILL CATCH UP IN NO TIME.
I'LL TRY TO SURPRISE HIM.
JAPANESE PIRATES ONCE RAVAGED THE COASTAL AREAS OF KOREA AND CHINA.
THESE PIRATES LEFT A GIANT PILE OF FAKE CRAP IN TOWN.
THEY FRIGHTENED THE RESIDENTS AWAY BY YELLING, "A BIG MAN WITH A BIG POOP IS HERE!"
HMPH.
PERHAPS I CAN ESCAPE THROUGH THE SEWERS.
THE COLISEUM'S TOILETS...
USE RECYCLED WASTEWATER FROM THE THERMAE AND NAVAL BATTLE GAMES.
THE SEWERS ARE PROBABLY CONNECTED.
HM?

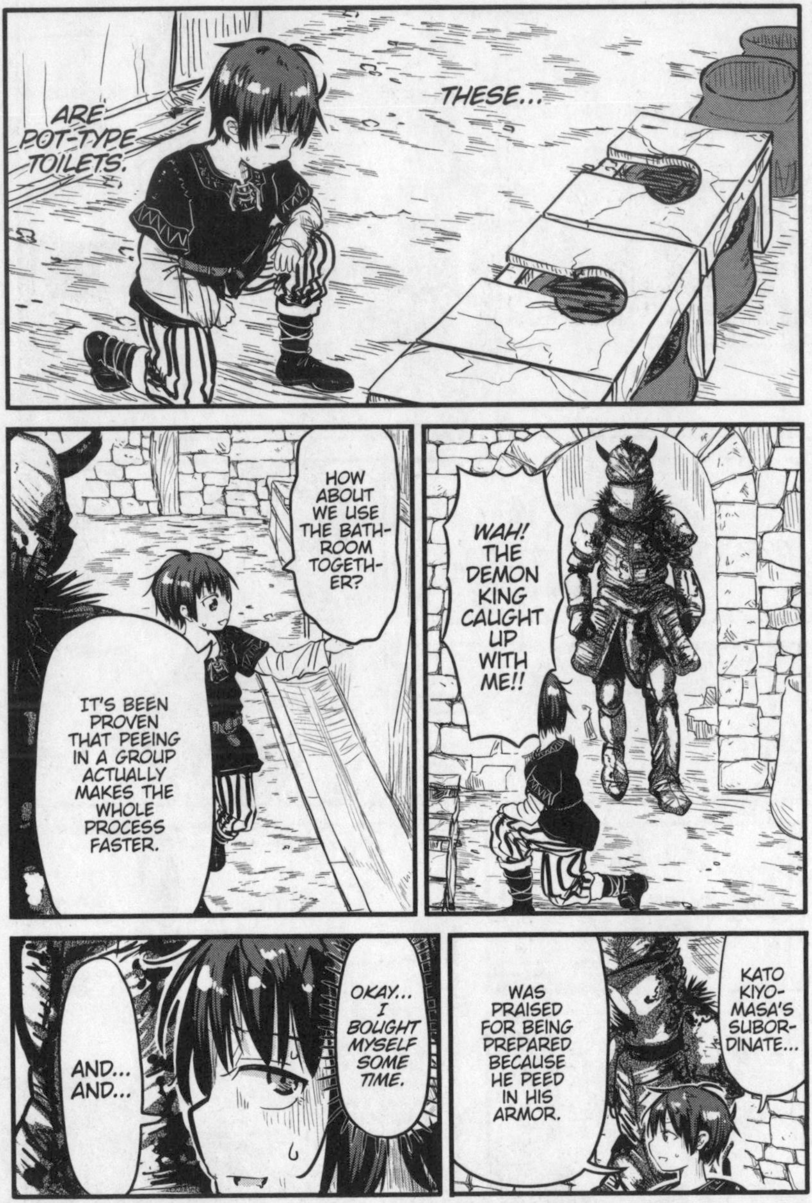
THESE...
ARE POT-TYPE TOILETS.
WAH! THE DEMON KING CAUGHT UP WITH ME!!
HOW ABOUT WE USE THE BATHROOM TOGETHER?
IT'S BEEN PROVEN THAT PEEING IN A GROUP ACTUALLY MAKES THE WHOLE PROCESS FASTER.
KATO KIYOMASA'S SUBORDINATE...
WAS PRAISED FOR BEING PREPARED BECAUSE HE PEED IN HIS ARMOR.
OKAY... I BOUGHT MYSELF SOME TIME.
AND... AND...

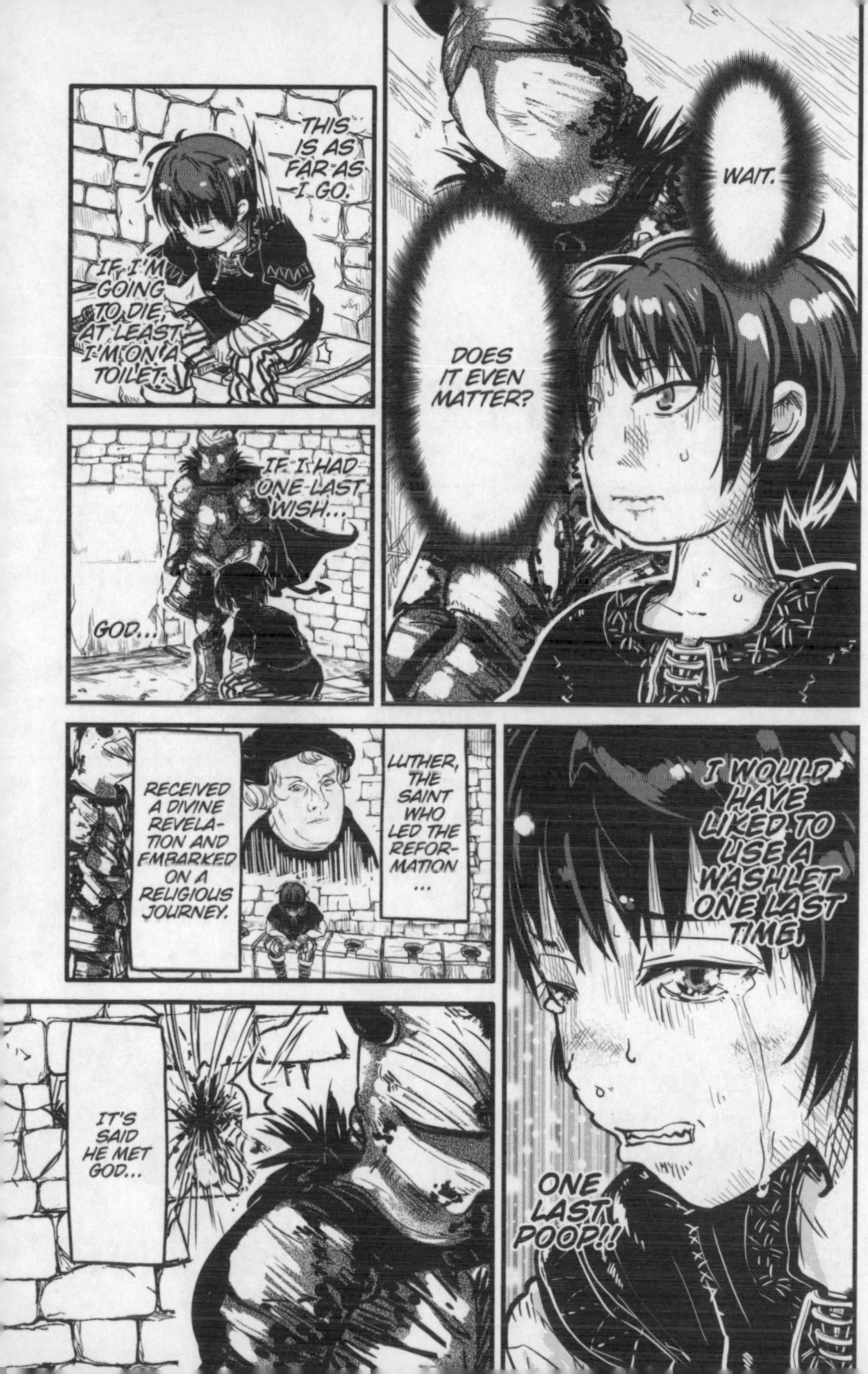
WAIT.
DOES IT EVEN MATTER?
THIS IS AS FAR AS I GO.
IF I'M GOING TO DIE, AT LEAST I'M ON A TOILET.
IF I HAD ONE LAST WISH...
GOD...
I WOULD HAVE LIKED TO USE A WASHLET ONE LAST TIME.
ONE LAST POOP!!
LUTHER, THE SAINT WHO LED THE REFOR-MATION...
RECEIVED A DIVINE REVELA-TION AND EMBARKED ON A RELIGIOUS JOURNEY.
IT'S SAID HE MET GOD...

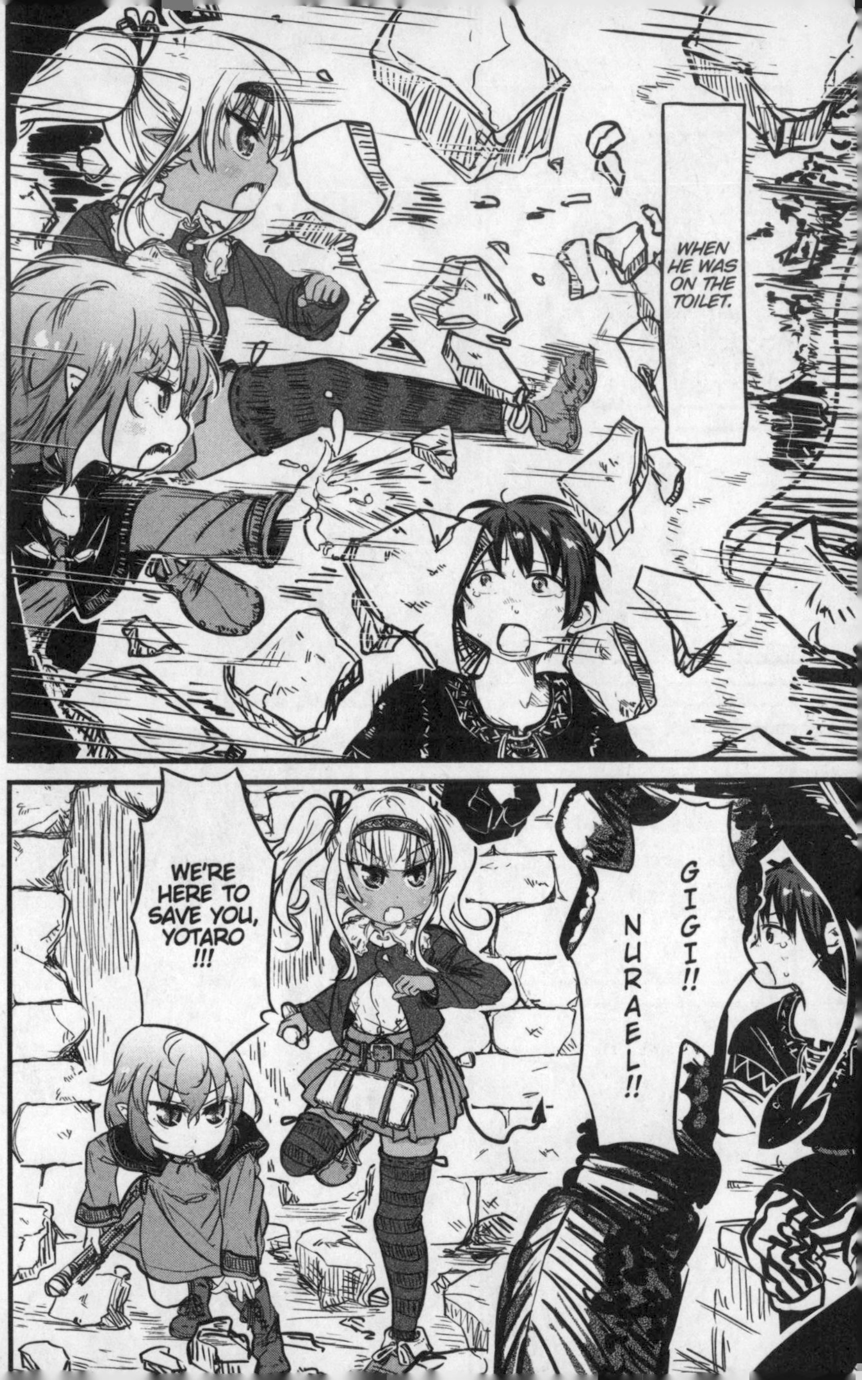
WHEN HE WAS ON THE TOILET.
GIGI!!
NURAEL!!
WE'RE HERE TO SAVE YOU, YOTARO!!!

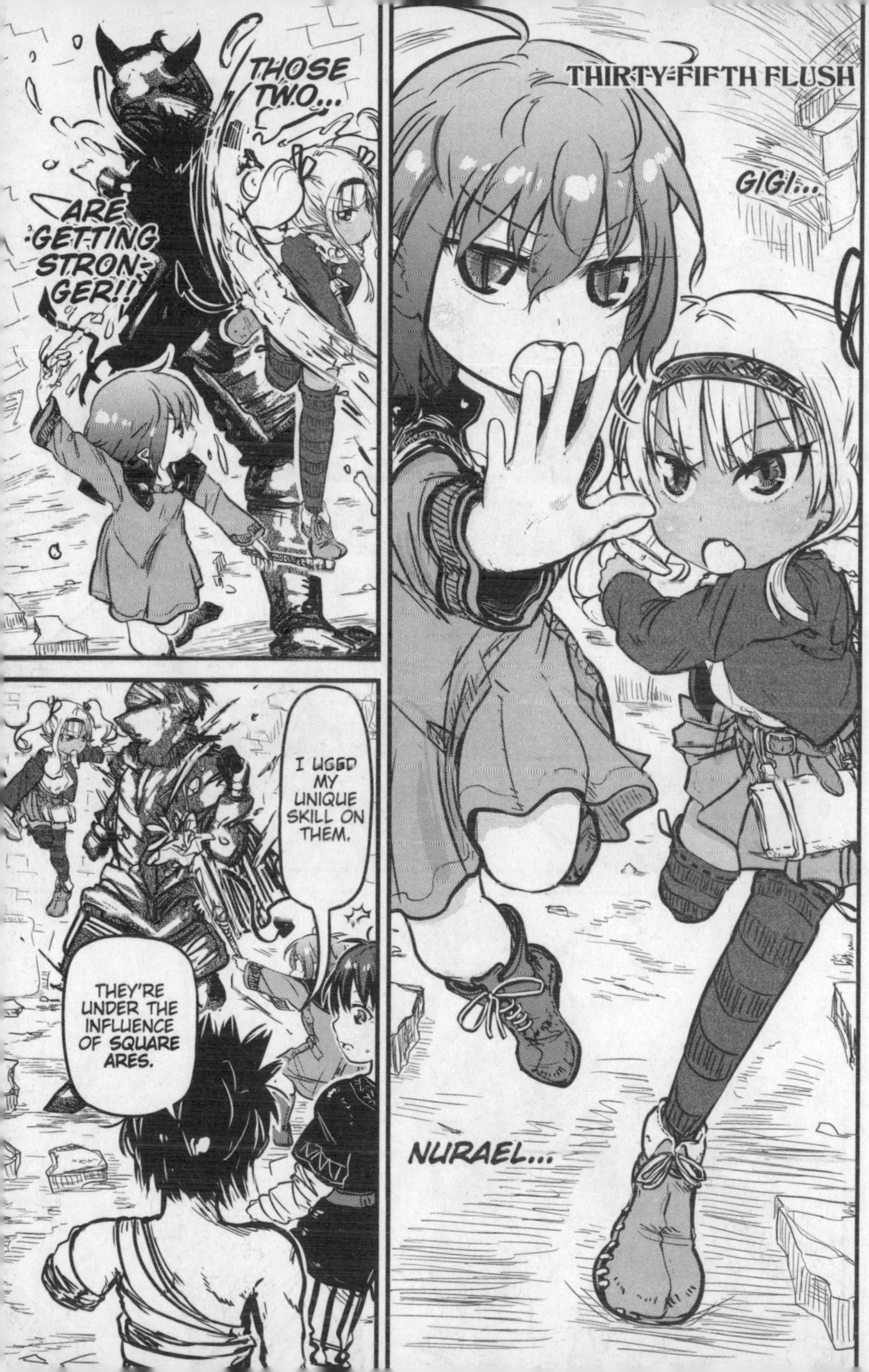
THIRTY-FIFTH FLUSH
GIGI...
NURAEL...
THOSE TWO...
ARE GETTING STRONGER!!
I USED MY UNIQUE SKILL ON THEM.
THEY'RE UNDER THE INFLUENCE OF SQUARE ARES.

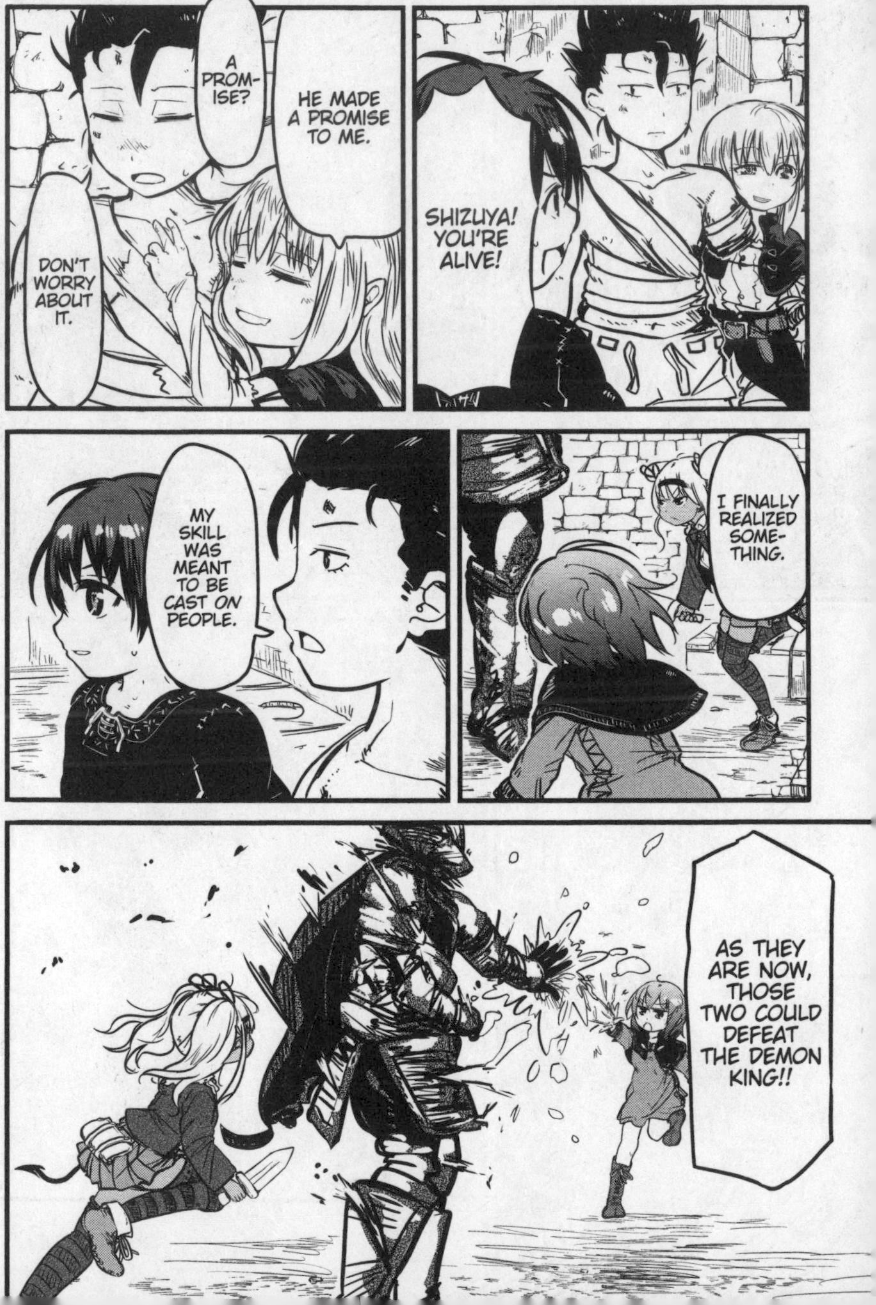
SHIZUYA! YOU'RE ALIVE!
HE MADE A PROMISE TO ME.
A PROMISE?
DON'T WORRY ABOUT IT.
I FINALLY REALIZED SOMETHING.
MY SKILL WAS MEANT TO BE CAST ON PEOPLE.
AS THEY ARE NOW, THOSE TWO COULD DEFEAT THE DEMON KING!!

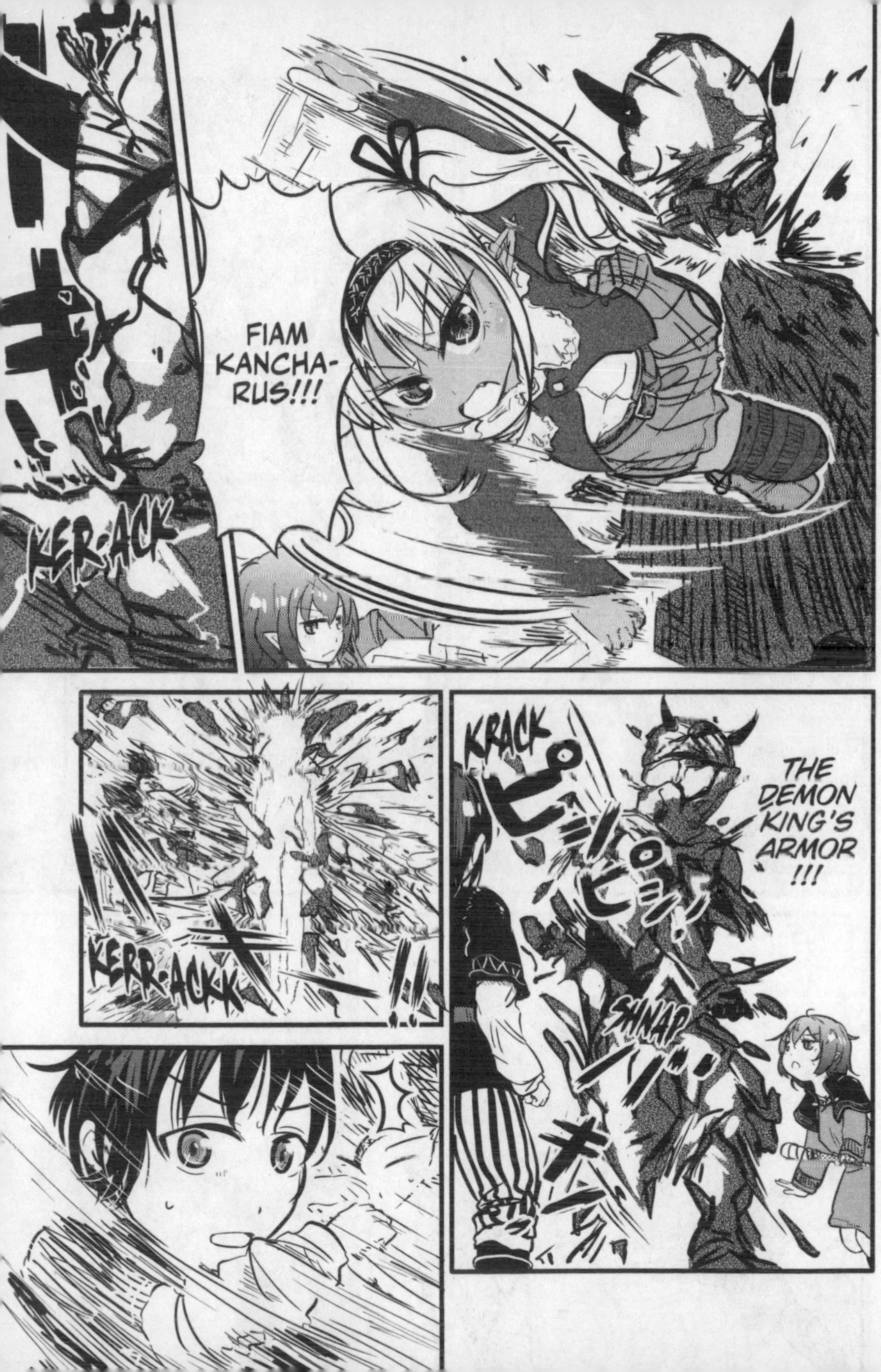
FIAM KANCHA-RUS!!!
KER-ACK
KRACK
THE DEMON KING'S ARMOR !!!
SNAP
KERR-ACKK

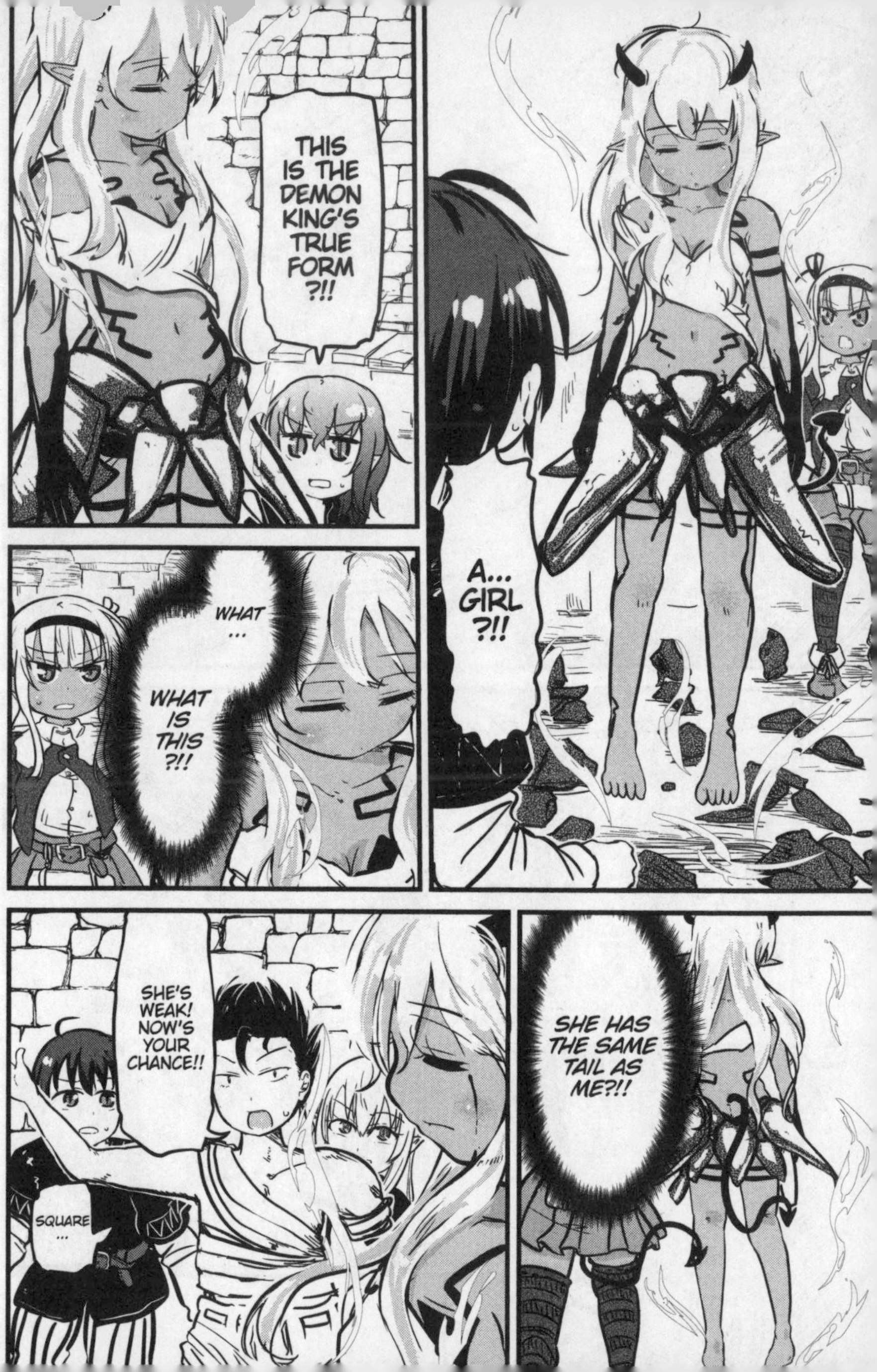
A... GIRL?!!
THIS IS THE DEMON KING'S TRUE FORM?!!
WHAT...
WHAT IS THIS?!!
SHE HAS THE SAME TAIL AS ME?!!
SHE'S WEAK! NOW'S YOUR CHANCE!!
SQUARE...

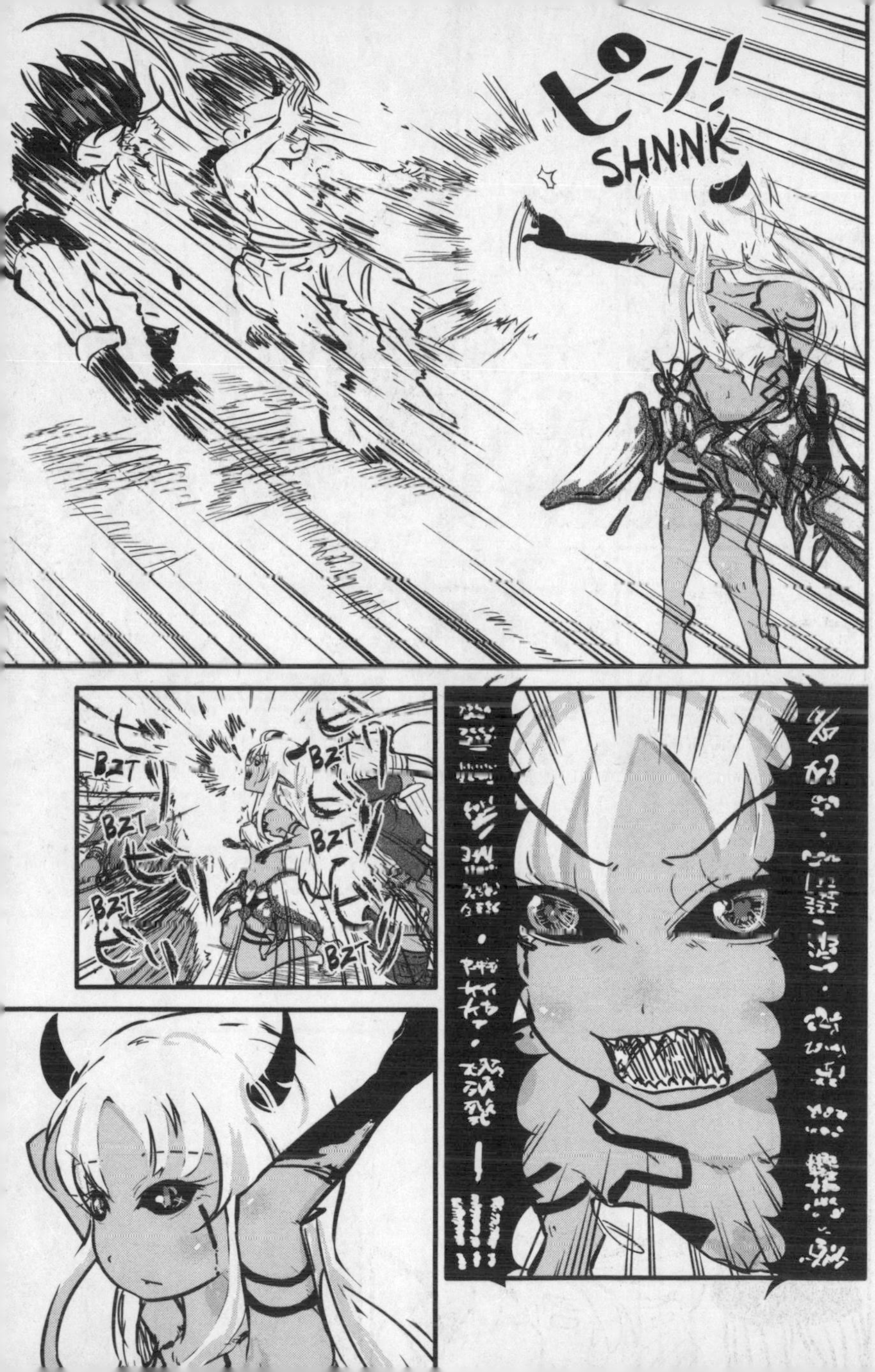
ピーン!
SHNNK
BZT
BZT
BZT
BZT
BZT

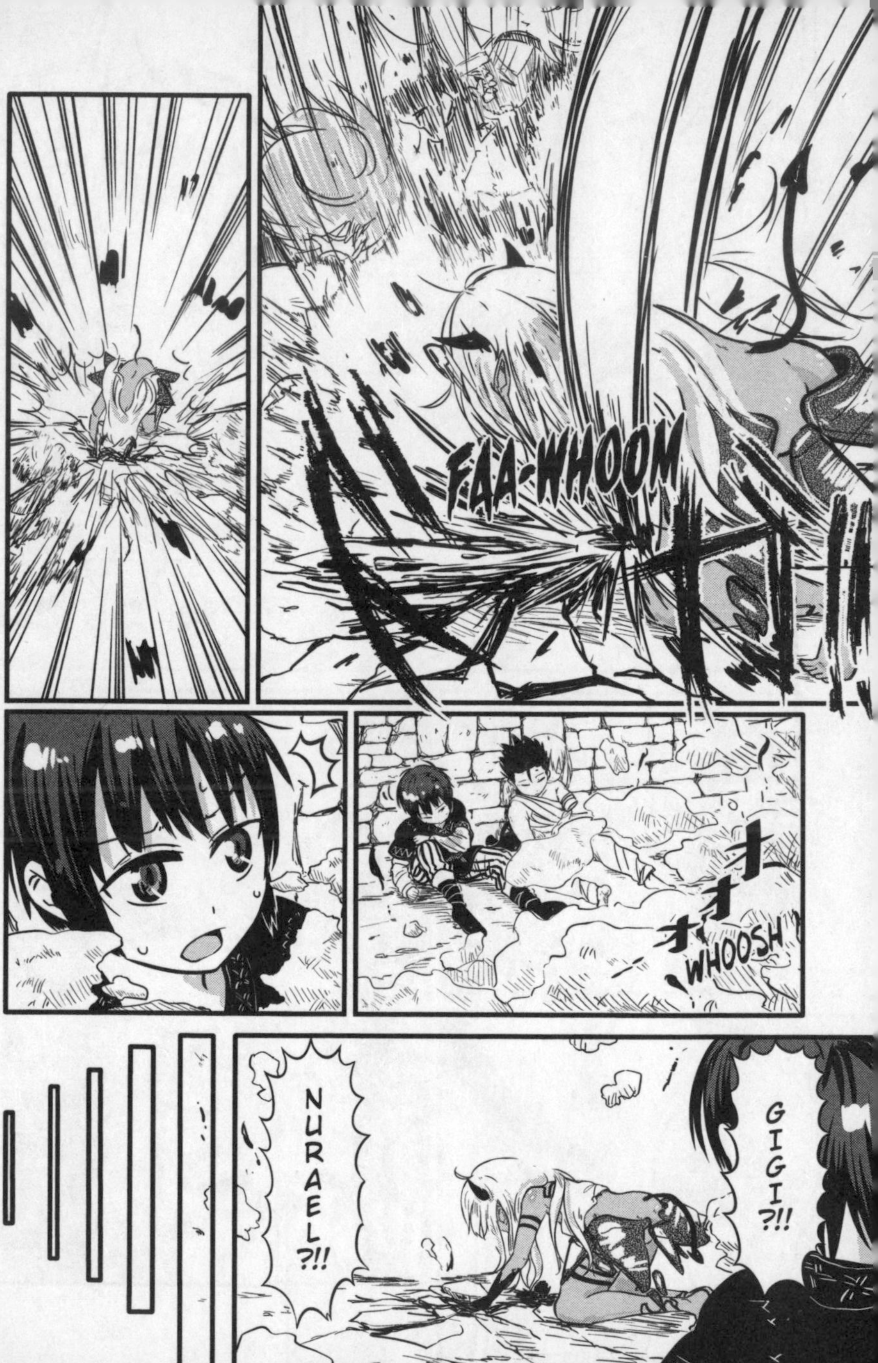
FAA-WHOOM
WHOOSH
GIGI?!!
NURAEL?!!

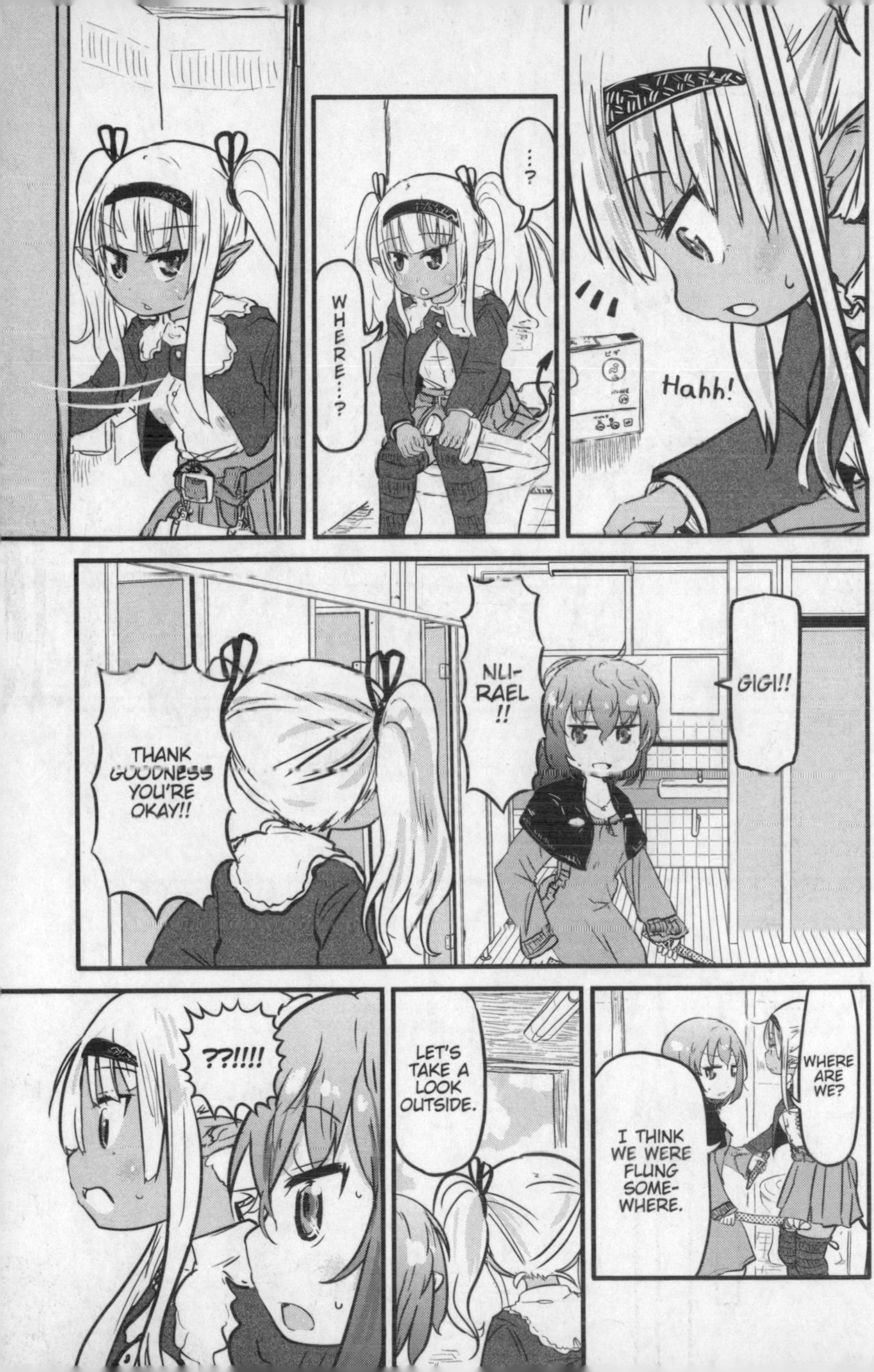
Hahh!
…?
WHERE…?
GIGI!!
NLI-RAEL!!
THANK GOODNESS YOU'RE OKAY!!
WHERE ARE WE?
I THINK WE WERE FLUNG SOME-WHERE.
LET'S TAKE A LOOK OUTSIDE.
??!!!!

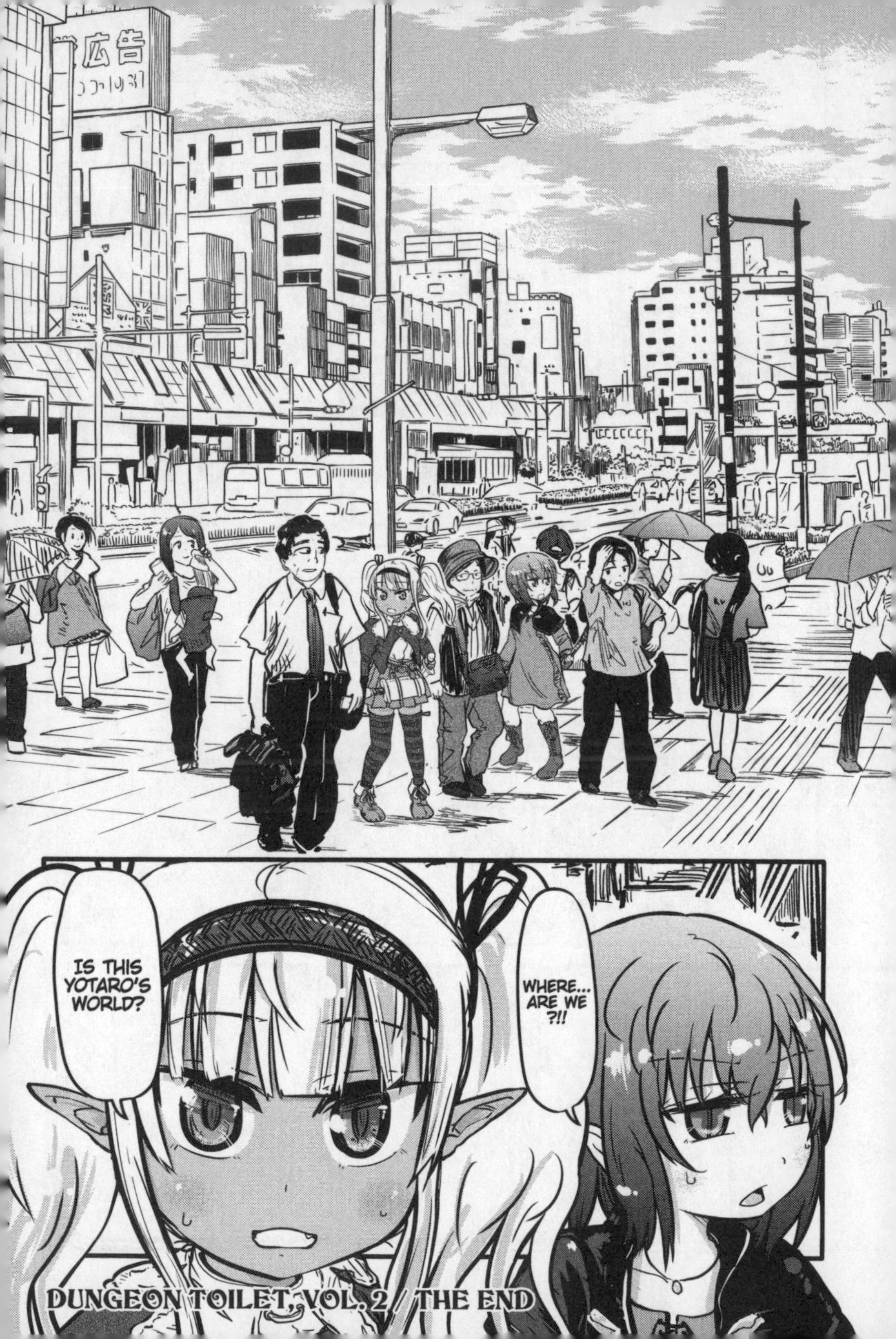
広告
WHERE... ARE WE ?!!
IS THIS YOTARO'S WORLD?
DUNGEON TOILET, VOL. 2 / THE END

ROOTS

PEOPLE WHO DON'T VALUE TOILET TIME ARE NO GOOD.

EIGHTEENTH TOILET TIME

Throughout history, there have been many famous people with stories related to toilets.

Kiyomasa Kato, the warlord who built Kumamoto Castle, was famous for hiding in the toilet for long periods. This may have been because he liked to use it, but it was also because he suffered from hemorrhoids. He often called his subordinates to the toilet to give them instructions because he was there for so long. One day, when Kiyomasa was holed up as usual, he suddenly remembered something.

"Call Hayato Shobayashi for me," he said.

Shobayashi, who'd been sick in bed with a cold, came to see what was the matter.

"One of your men, I think his name is Dekisuke," Kiyomasa said. "I saw him peeing while standing."

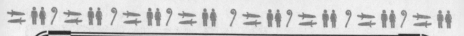

Shobayashi couldn't believe that one of his men would do such a rude thing in the presence of a daimyo.

"I see," he responded. "He was peeing in his armor. He is always ready for battle, which is a splendid attitude. I will reward him."

Kiyomasa also wore a pair of thirty-centimeter-high toilet sandals. Perhaps he didn't like dirty floors, or perhaps he feared getting splashed.

There have been many great military commanders who loved toilets.

IN OTHER WORDS

THIS MAXIM

"WHAT DO YOU THINK ABOUT DURING YOUR LONG BATHROOM BREAKS?"

-MORIKAWA KYORIKU

A GIRL?!
THAT MEANS...
I INVITED A *GIRL* TO STAND AND PEE WITH ME?!!
NO...
THERE WAS A SANI-STAND!!
Sani-stand. Where women can stand and pee, too.

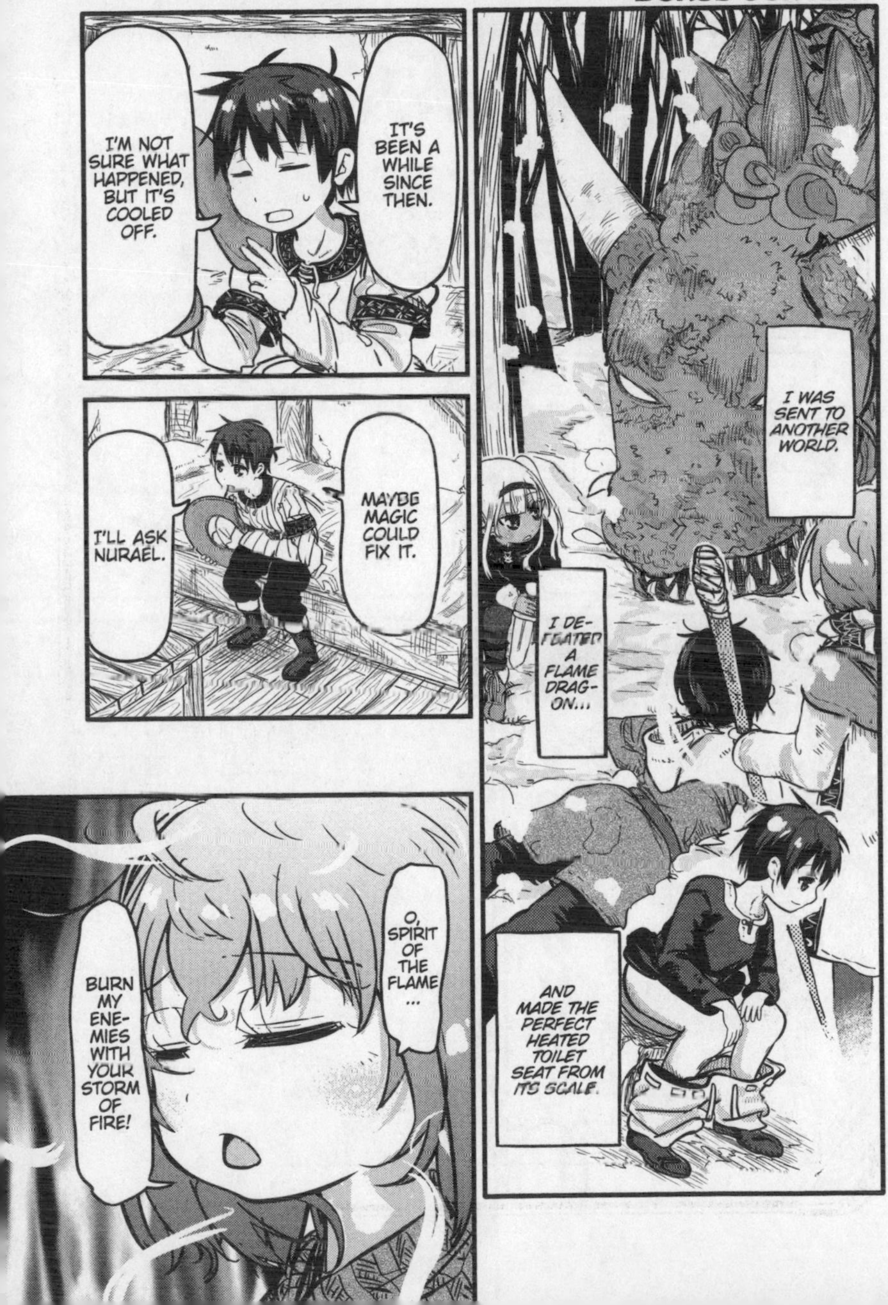
I WAS SENT TO ANOTHER WORLD.
I DE-FEATED A FLAME DRAG-ON...
AND MADE THE PERFECT HEATED TOILET SEAT FROM ITS SCALE.
IT'S BEEN A WHILE SINCE THEN.
I'M NOT SURE WHAT HAPPENED, BUT IT'S COOLED OFF.
MAYBE MAGIC COULD FIX IT.
I'LL ASK NURAEL.
O, SPIRIT OF THE FLAME...
BURN MY ENEMIES WITH YOUR STORM OF FIRE!

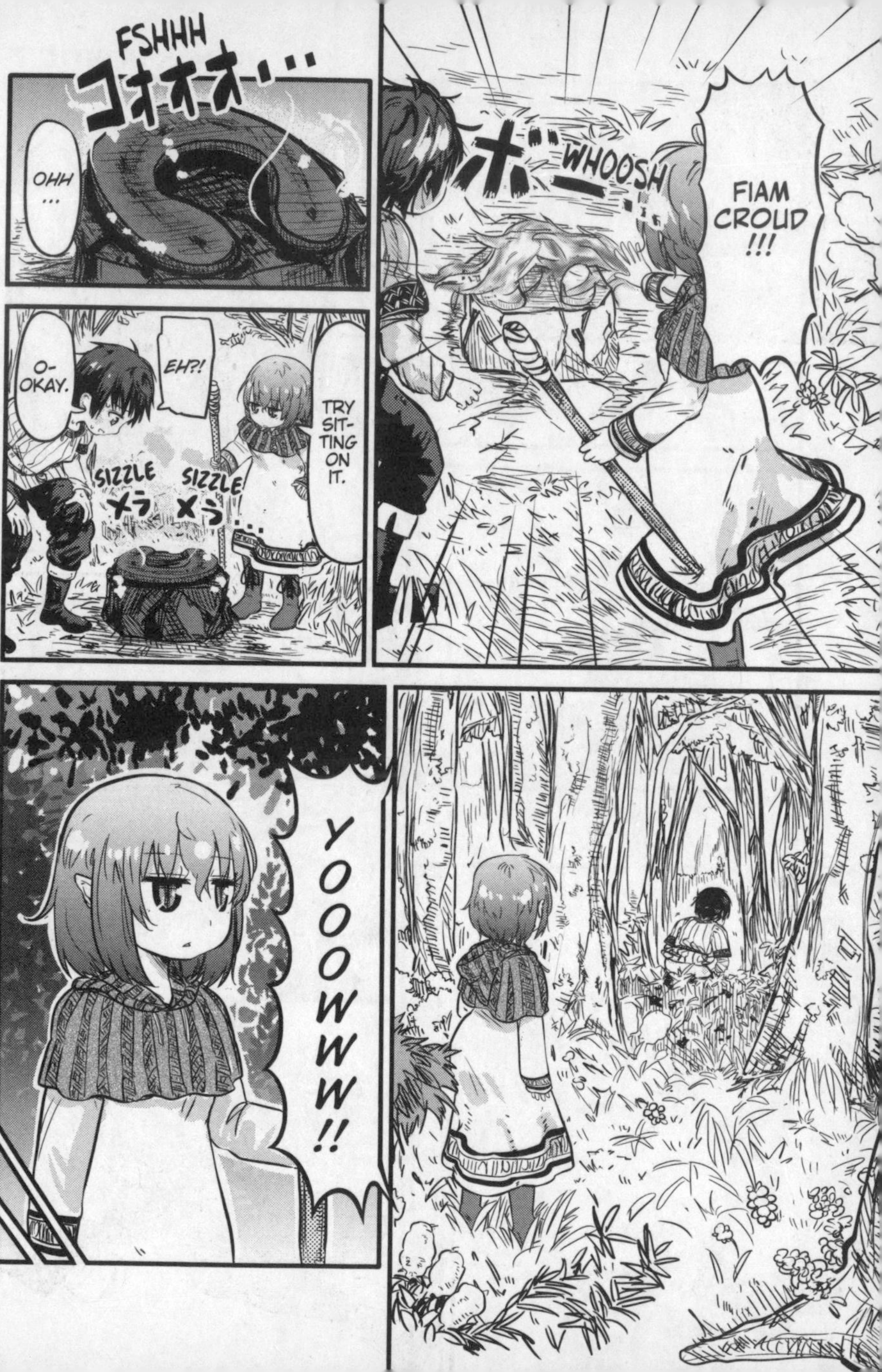
ボー WHOOSH
FIAM CROUD !!!
FSHHH コオオオ…
OHH ...
TRY SIT-TING ON IT.
EH?!
O-OKAY.
SIZZLE メラ SIZZLE メラ…
YOOOOWWW!!

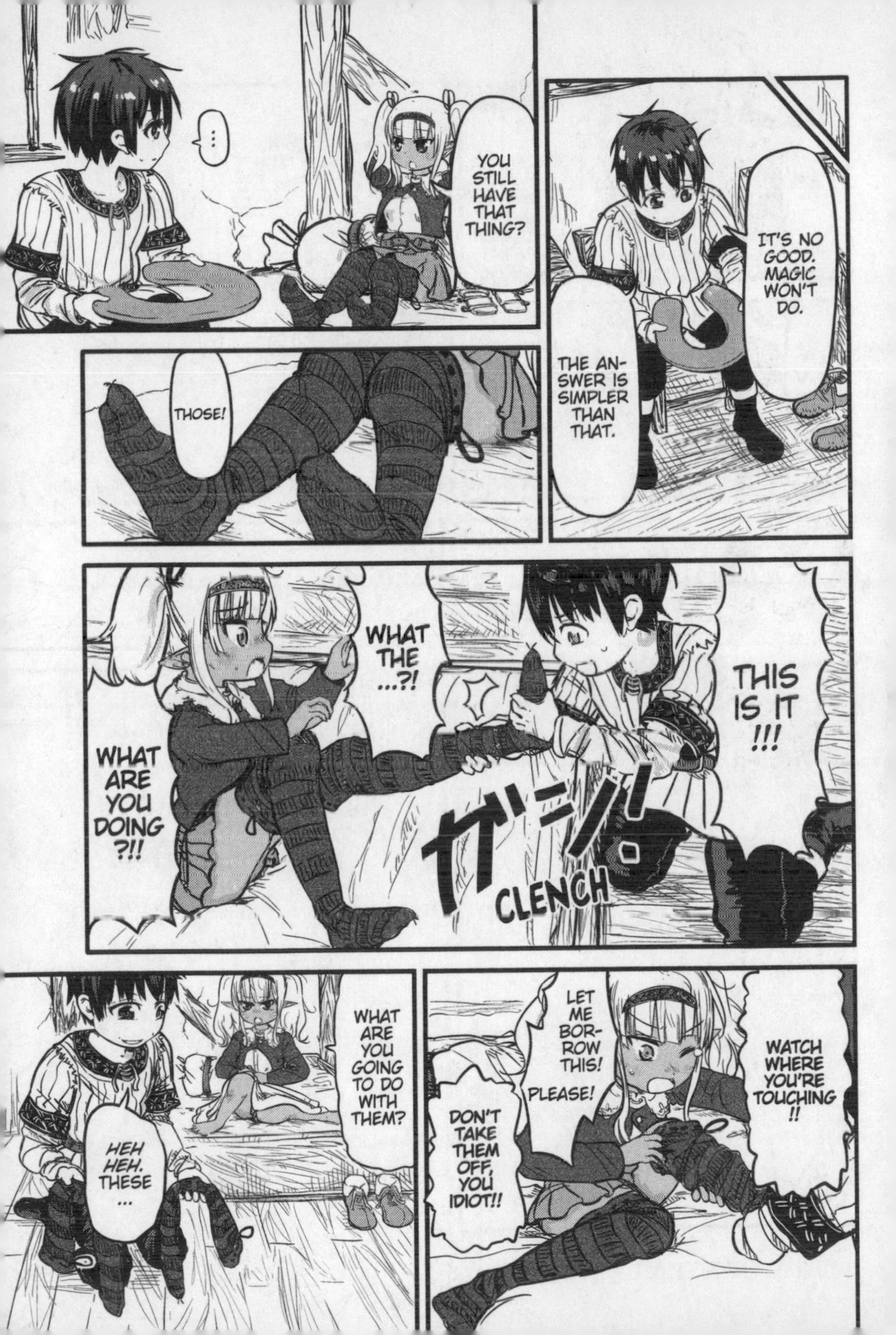
YOU STILL HAVE THAT THING?
...
IT'S NO GOOD. MAGIC WON'T DO.
THE AN- SWER IS SIMPLER THAN THAT.
THOSE!
THIS IS IT !!!
WHAT THE ...?!
WHAT ARE YOU DOING ?!!
ガシッ!
CLENCH
WATCH WHERE YOU'RE TOUCHING !!
LET ME BOR- ROW THIS!
PLEASE!
DON'T TAKE THEM OFF, YOU IDIOT!!
WHAT ARE YOU GOING TO DO WITH THEM?
HEH HEH. THESE ...

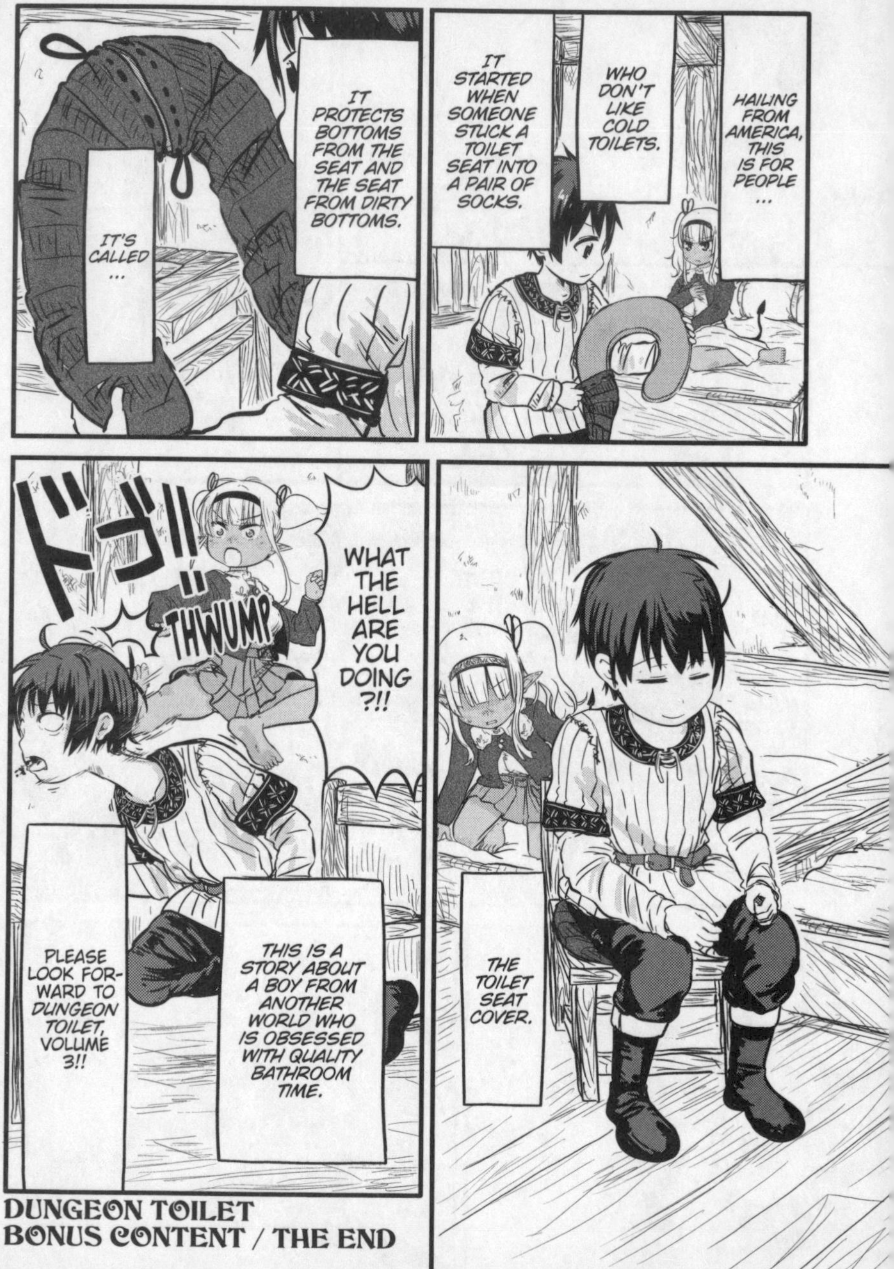
HAILING FROM AMERICA, THIS IS FOR PEOPLE ...
WHO DON'T LIKE COLD TOILETS.
IT STARTED WHEN SOMEONE STUCK A TOILET SEAT INTO A PAIR OF SOCKS.
IT PROTECTS BOTTOMS FROM THE SEAT AND THE SEAT FROM DIRTY BOTTOMS.
IT'S CALLED ...
THE TOILET SEAT COVER.
ドゴ!!
THWUMP
WHAT THE HELL ARE YOU DOING?!!
THIS IS A STORY ABOUT A BOY FROM ANOTHER WORLD WHO IS OBSESSED WITH QUALITY BATHROOM TIME.
PLEASE LOOK FOR-WARD TO DUNGEON TOILET, VOLUME 3!!

DUNGEON TOILET
BONUS CONTENT / THE END

Bibliography

Kawaya Kou by Rinoie Masafumi

Toilet Study Encyclopedia by the Japan Toilet Association

A Book of Funny Facts About Toilets by Planning OM

Let's Talk About Toilets: A Problem Spanning 6.5 Billion People by Rose George; translated by Ozawa Akiko

Water Flushing Toilets Have Been Around Since Ancient Times: An Introduction to Ancient Toilet Studies by Kurosaki Tadashi

Architecture Picture Book, Household Fire and Water: The History of the Kitchen, Bathroom, and Toilet by Mitsufuji Toshio and Nakayama Shigenobu

Bath Toilet Eulogy by Lawrence Wright

Toilet Studies with Sato Mitsuharu by Sato Mitsuharu

Let's Talk about Toilets: Dialogues with Rinoie Masafumi by Rinoie Masafumi

Manure and Culture of Life: Scatology in the 21st Century by Rinoie Masafumi

Toilet Cultural History by Roger-Henri Guerrand; translated by Ooya Takayasu

Diagram of the Privy Mandala by Rinoie Masafumi, Muramatsu Teijiro, Otomasu Shigetaka, Mitsuoka Tomotari, Miyazaki Akira, Fukuzumi Haruo, and INAX Gallery Planning Committee

Compost Philosophy Will Save the World: Let's Start Pooping in the Leaves by Izawa Masana

Everyone Poops by Gomi Taro

A Story About the World's Best Washlet Toilet by Hayashi Ryoyu

European Toilet Natural History by Unno Hiroshi, Nimi Ryu, and Fritz Lischka

Websites:

"The Pitfalls of the Toilet in Ancient Rome" by Koji Toyoda
http://pweb.sophia.ac.jp/k-toyota/atelier/column/column_roma_toilette1.html

"High Heels, the Middle Ages, and Dung: A Chronicle of the WTNB Agency" by Gregorius Yamada
http://www.wtnb-bnz.jp/blog/medieval/heels

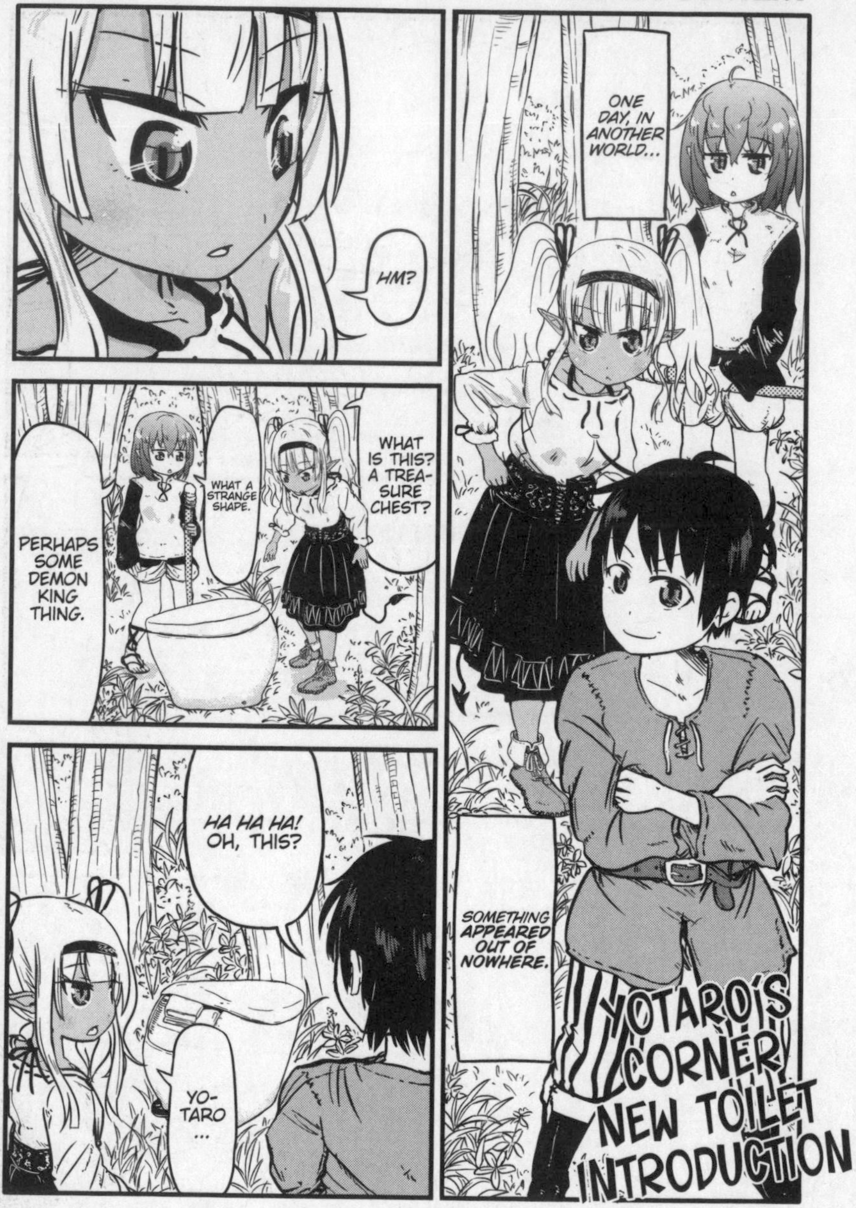
ONE DAY, IN ANOTHER WORLD...
SOMETHING APPEARED OUT OF NOWHERE.
YOTARO'S CORNER
NEW TOILET INTRODUCTION
HM?
WHAT IS THIS? A TREA-SURE CHEST?
WHAT A STRANGE SHAPE.
PERHAPS SOME DEMON KING THING.
HA HA HA! OH, THIS?
YO-TARO ...

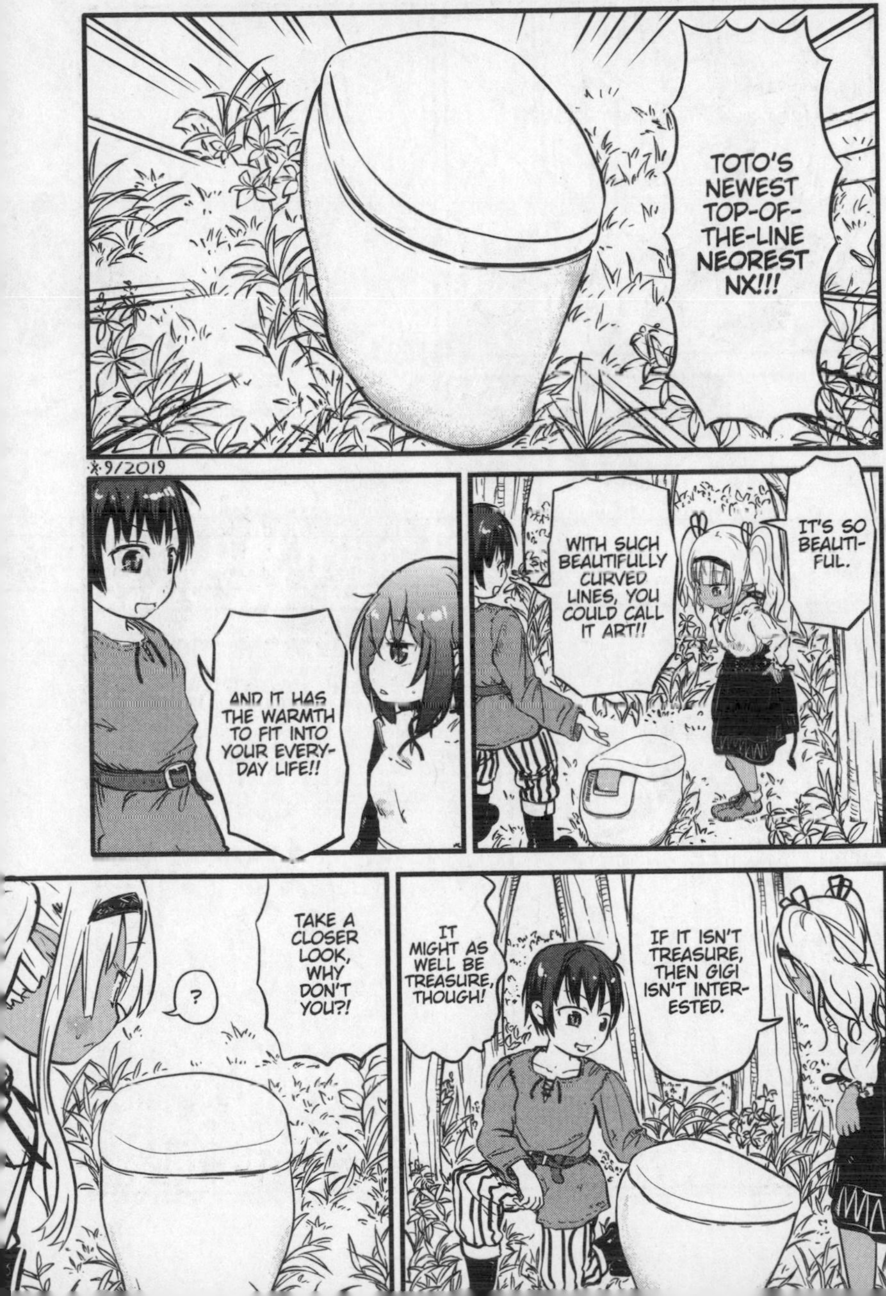
TOTO'S NEWEST TOP-OF-THE-LINE NEOREST NX!!!
※9/2019
IT'S SO BEAUTIFUL.
WITH SUCH BEAUTIFULLY CURVED LINES, YOU COULD CALL IT ART!!
AND IT HAS THE WARMTH TO FIT INTO YOUR EVERYDAY LIFE!!
IF IT ISN'T TREASURE, THEN GIGI ISN'T INTERESTED.
IT MIGHT AS WELL BE TREASURE, THOUGH!
TAKE A CLOSER LOOK, WHY DON'T YOU?!
?

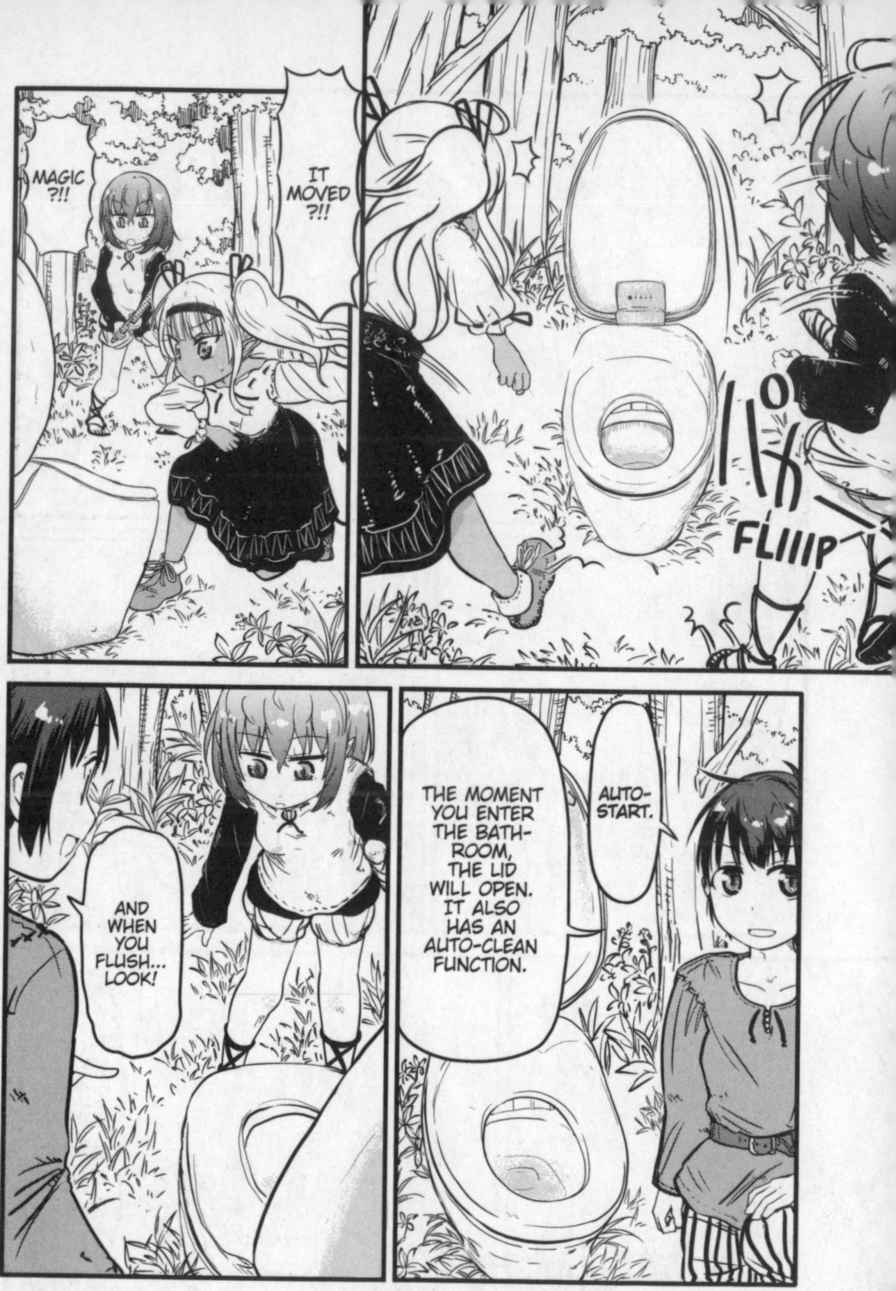
FLIIIP
IT MOVED ?!!
MAGIC ?!!
AUTO-START.
THE MOMENT YOU ENTER THE BATHROOM, THE LID WILL OPEN. IT ALSO HAS AN AUTO-CLEAN FUNCTION.
AND WHEN YOU FLUSH... LOOK!

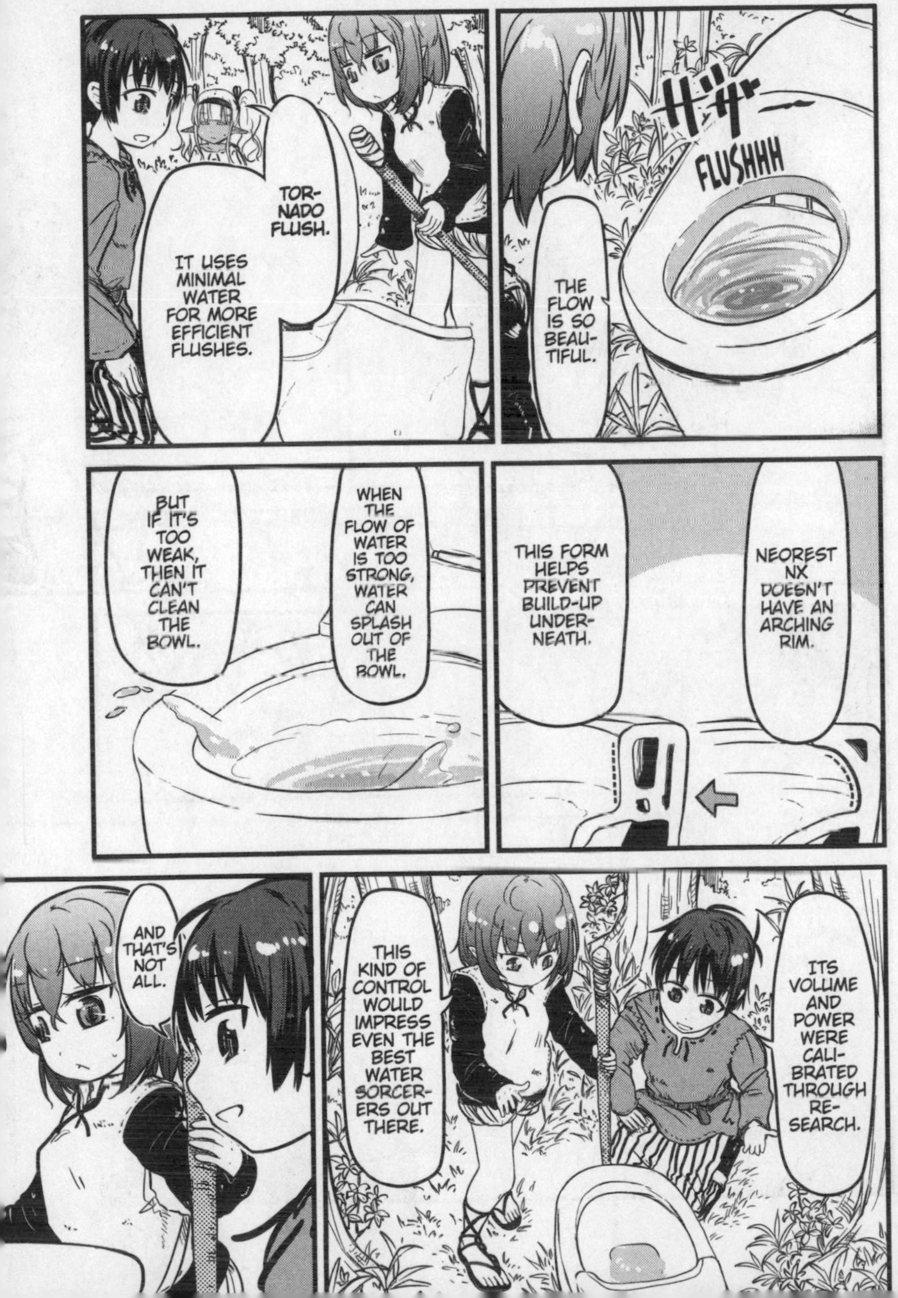
FLUSHHH
THE FLOW IS SO BEAUTIFUL.
TORNADO FLUSH.
IT USES MINIMAL WATER FOR MORE EFFICIENT FLUSHES.
NEOREST NX DOESN'T HAVE AN ARCHING RIM.
THIS FORM HELPS PREVENT BUILD-UP UNDERNEATH.
WHEN THE FLOW OF WATER IS TOO STRONG, WATER CAN SPLASH OUT OF THE BOWL.
BUT IF IT'S TOO WEAK, THEN IT CAN'T CLEAN THE BOWL.
ITS VOLUME AND POWER WERE CALIBRATED THROUGH RESEARCH.
THIS KIND OF CONTROL WOULD IMPRESS EVEN THE BEST WATER SORCERERS OUT THERE.
AND THAT'S NOT ALL.

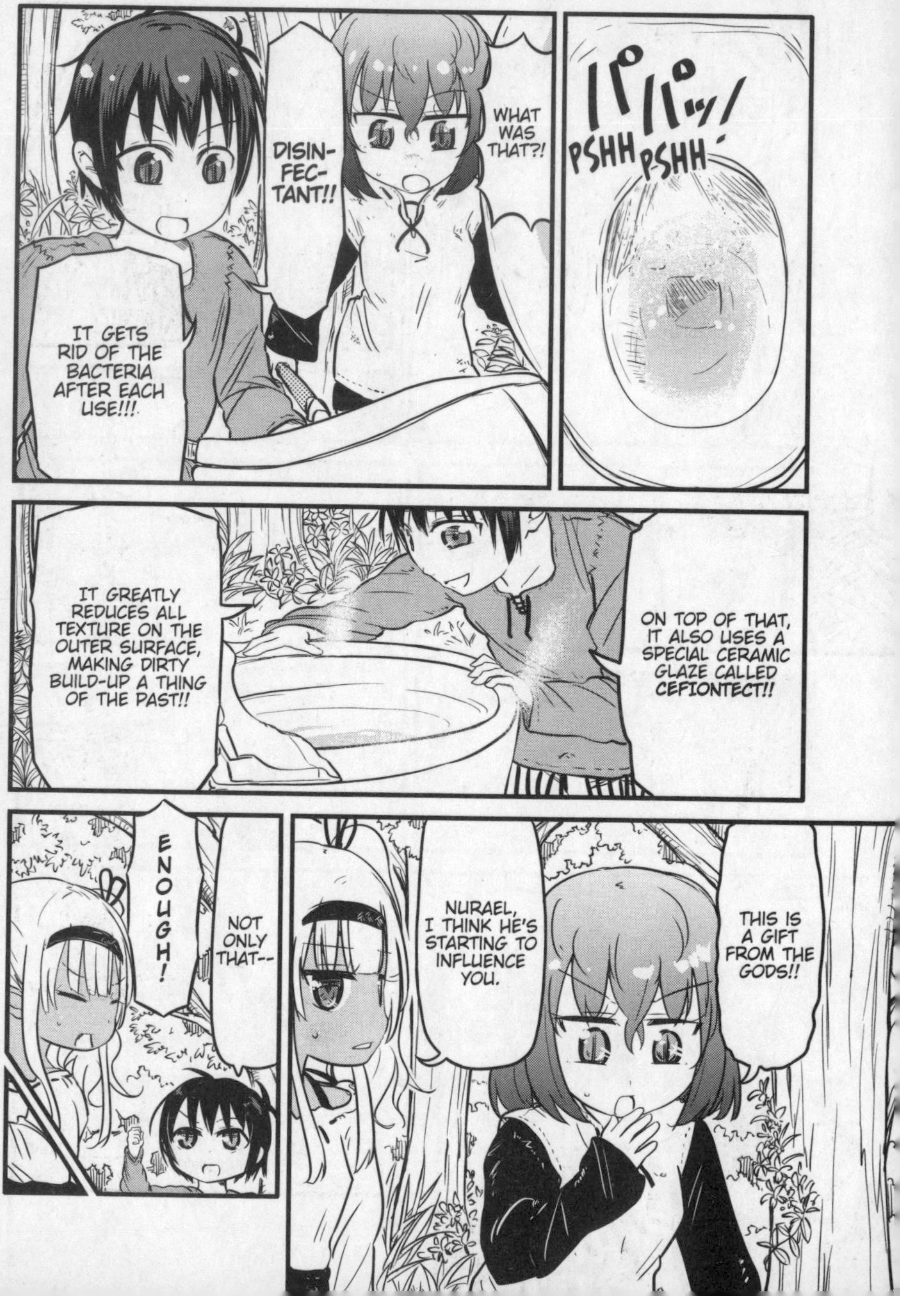
パパッ!
PSHH PSHH
WHAT WAS THAT?!
DISIN-FECT-ANT!!
IT GETS RID OF THE BACTERIA AFTER EACH USE!!!
ON TOP OF THAT, IT ALSO USES A SPECIAL CERAMIC GLAZE CALLED CEFIONTECT!!
IT GREATLY REDUCES ALL TEXTURE ON THE OUTER SURFACE, MAKING DIRTY BUILD-UP A THING OF THE PAST!!
THIS IS A GIFT FROM THE GODS!!
NURAEL, I THINK HE'S STARTING TO INFLUENCE YOU.
NOT ONLY THAT--
ENOUGH!